AUG 1 8 1998

Critical Essays on
KATHERINE ANNE PORTER

CRITICAL ESSAYS
ON
AMERICAN LITERATURE

James Nagel, General Editor
University of Georgia, Athens

Critical Essays on

KATHERINE ANNE PORTER

edited by

DARLENE HARBOUR UNRUE

G. K. Hall & Co.
An Imprint of Simon & Schuster Macmillan
New York

Prentice Hall International
London   Mexico City   New Delhi   Singapore   Sydney   Toronto

G. K. Hall & Co.
An Imprint of Simon & Schuster Macmillan
1633 Broadway
New York, NY 10019

Library of Congress Cataloging-in-Publication Data

Critical essays on Katherine Anne Porter / edited by Darlene Harbour
Unrue.
    p.   cm. — (Critical essays on American literature)
    Includes bibliographical references (p.) and index.
    ISBN 0-7838-0022-3 (alk. paper)
    1. Porter, Katherine Anne, 1890–1980—Criticism and
interpretation.   2. Women and literature—United States—
History—20th century.   I. Unrue, Darlene Harbour.   II. Series.
PS3531.0752Z54   1997
813'.52—dc21   97-4104
                                                CIP

10 9 8 7 6 5 4 3 2

Printed in the United States of America

For Tillie Olsen

Contents

General Editor's Note

◆

This series seeks to anthologize the most important criticism on a wide variety of topics and writers in American literature. Our readers will find in various volumes not only a generous selection of reprinted articles and reviews but original essays, bibliographies, manuscript selections, and other materials brought to public attention for the first time. This volume, *Critical Essays on Katherine Anne Porter,* is the most comprehensive gathering of essays ever published on one of the most important modern writers in the United States. It contains both a sizable gathering of early reviews and a broad selection of more modern scholarship. Among the authors of reprinted articles and reviews are Eudora Welty, Allen Tate, Robert Penn Warren, Cleanth Brooks, Joan Givner, Sarah Youngblood, Janis P. Stout, and Edward Schwartz. In addition to a substantial introduction by Darlene Harbour Unrue, there are also two original essays commissioned specifically for publication in this volume, new studies by Ruth M. Alvarez on pre-Hispanic art and ritual in "María Concepción," and a provocative examination of the influence of Sigmund Freud on Porter's fiction by Professor Unrue. We are confident that this book will make a permanent and significant contribution to the study of American literature.

JAMES NAGEL
University of Georgia, Athens

Publisher's Note

◆

Producing a volume that contains both newly commissioned and reprinted material presents the publisher with the challenge of balancing the desire to achieve stylistic consistency with the need to preserve the integrity of works first published elsewhere. In the Critical Essays series, essays commissioned especially for a particular volume are edited to be consistent with G. K. Hall's house style; reprinted essays appear in the style in which they were first published, with only typographical errors corrected. Consequently, shifts in style from one essay to another are the result of our efforts to be faithful to each text as it was originally published.

Introduction

DARLENE HARBOUR UNRUE

Katherine Anne Porter rose to prominence in American letters after a long and obscure apprenticeship. For nearly 20 years, while contending with severe challenges to her physical and emotional survival, Porter struggled to find her artistic medium and then to refine it. She was 40 years old when she was thrust on the American literary scene with the publication of *Flowering Judas,* her first collection of stories.

Flowering Judas appeared in 1930 to a chorus of praise that widened Porter's reading audience and secured her critical position in modern literature.[1] Margaret Cheney Dawson's review in the *New York Herald Tribune* expressed the critical excitement *Flowering Judas* generated. "It is a dramatic moment in the life of a patient reader," Dawson wrote, "when, after all efforts to be judicial, all carefully balanced yeas and nays, a book presents itself that compels a loud, hearty, unqualified <u>yes</u>. *Flowering Judas* is such a book."[2] Others were nearly as enthusiastic. John McDonald compared Porter's stories to chamber music, and Edward Weeks judged the stories "superb." Yvor Winters, who had been instrumental in convincing Harcourt, Brace to publish the collection, expressed his faith in Porter's talent. "I can think of no living American," he said, "who has written short stories at once so fine in detail, so powerful as units, and so mature and intelligent in outlook, except [William Carlos] Williams." Louise Bogan went even further, declaring that "no other writer has a talent quite like [Porter's]." In a perceptive analysis of these early stories, Allen Tate determined Porter's art "fully matured."[3]

Indeed it was. After writing columns, essays, and reviews for newspapers and magazines, rewriting fairy tales, writing a pamphlet to accompany an exhibit of Mexican art, and ghostwriting a young American woman's account of her marriage to a Chinese student,[4] Porter in 1922 published "María Concepción," her first original piece of fiction.[5] By 1930 Porter had published eight more stories, honed her fictional style, and found her themes. During the next 15 years she would produce almost all the rest of her short fiction, on which the weight of her critical reputation rests.[6]

Reviews of Porter's work between 1930 and 1944 sustained with few exceptions the judgment of the reviewers of *Flowering Judas.* Reviews of Porter's long story *Hacienda,* published separately in a limited edition by Harrison of Paris in 1934, were some of the exceptions. Calling the story "disappointing" and even "diabolic," reviewers described various perceived deficiencies in the story.[7] In spite of *Hacienda*'s initially cool reception, however, when it appeared in 1935 in *Flowering Judas and Other Stories,* an expansion of *Flowering Judas* by four stories,[8] most reviewers considered it in the context of the other stories and acknowledged its artistic merit. Only Eleanor Clark cited it as one of the new collection's "failures." Clark, however, praised the whole book as "one of small patterns written with subdued and exceptional brilliance." In other reviews Porter's maturity and style were again praised.[9]

Flowering Judas and Other Stories received critical attention abroad. Although the anonymous reviewer in the *Times Literary Supplement* faulted the stories for depending "too much on the workings of the characters' minds" and for suffering "from lack of pattern," Graham Greene in the *Spectator* declared that Porter's were "the best stories that have come out of America since the early Hemingways."[10]

Noon Wine was the second of Porter's short novels to appear as a separate book in a limited edition,[11] and it was not much better received than the limited-edition *Hacienda.* Writing in the *Nation,* Ben Belitt conceded Porter's "technical skill" but thought the skill obscured by Porter's "gangling artlessness." Dorothy Brewster in *New Masses* and Edith Walton in the *New York Times Book Review* chided Porter for not presenting her theme clearly or credibly.[12] When "Noon Wine" was included in Porter's 1939 collection of stories, *Pale Horse, Pale Rider: Three Short Novels,* however, it was received with praise at least equal to that for "Pale Horse, Pale Rider" and "Old Mortality." Wallace Stegner in fact thought it the best of the three short novels, illustrating again that Porter's works were most often appreciated in collections that revealed their thematic integration. Other reviewers commended Porter for her "beautiful writing," her ability "to create by suggestion," and her "sense of time."[13] Paul Rosenfeld was the first reviewer to compare Porter to Gustave Flaubert, Nathaniel Hawthorne, and Henry James.[14]

British reviewers also were favorably impressed. *Pale Horse, Pale Rider: Three Short Novels* was recommended in the *TLS* as "first choice" of the novels of the week, although the reviewer found in Porter's work "a strain of poetry . . . [appearing] more bravely than to discreet advantage." Forrest Reid in the *Spectator* thought Porter had discovered in the long short story "the form which exactly suits her particular gifts."[15]

In 1944 the last small collection of Porter's stories appeared as *The Leaning Tower and Other Stories.*[16] Diana Trilling and Irving Kristol were among the most approving, Trilling contending that the collection was the best of Porter's three volumes and Kristol asserting that Porter had redeemed contemporary literature from its tendency toward Steinbeck's social issues and Kafka's myth making.[17] The qualified praise of Gertrude Buckman writing in the *Partisan Review* and of F. O. Matthiessen in *Accent* was more typical of the American reviews. Edmund Wilson contributed an important perception to Porter criticism by identifying Porter's method of making an object "the self-developing organism" in each story.[18]

British reviews were mixed. The *TLS* cited "The Source" as an especially good example of American stories "told simply and unaffectedly and with the lightest, implicit emotion." David Daiches thought the stories had virtues but lacked "the imaginative compulsion which enables the writer to break the bounds of a story and expand its significance almost indefinitely." Charles Morgan in the (London) *Sunday Times* commended the stories but charged Porter with an "unwillingness to commit herself to the full hazard of story-telling."[19]

After 1944 Porter gave her creative attention to writing a long novel. Since the 1930s the imminent appearance of such a novel had been announced by Harcourt, Brace.[20] After 1957 the publication was announced by Atlantic–Little, Brown, which bought out Porter's obligation to Harcourt and assumed the frustration of trying to bring the novel to fruition. By the time the novel was published, on April Fool's Day 1962, as *Ship of Fools*, critical expectations were high. The first reviews suggested that Porter indeed had written a masterpiece worth the wait. Mark Schorer set the initial tone in his influential review in the *New York Times Book Review* by asserting that *Ship of Fools* could be compared only with the greatest novels of the past hundred years. Other reviewers were in near agreement with Schorer. Warren Beck, writing for the *Chicago Sunday Tribune,* called the novel "masterly," and Louis D. Rubin Jr. considered it "a work of genius." Perhaps anticipating other reviewers' assessments, Louis Auchincloss argued that the novel was "not a disappointment" but was "rich enough to be read on many levels."[21]

Many other reviewers agreed on the importance of *Ship of Fools* but qualified their praise. Bernard D. Theall, for example, called the book depressing but said it was nevertheless "immensely readable," and the *McCall's* reviewer said that in spite of the "bitterness," the story was told with "skill and suspense." Victor R. Yanitell granted the novel "superb character portrayals and effective symbolism" but finally decried the length and the excessive number of characters.[22]

Most American reviews fell into two camps on two issues: whether Porter's view of humanity was justified or not and whether the novel's structure was an enhancement or a detriment to Porter's artistic purpose. In an essay in the *Yale Review* in the summer of 1962, Wayne Booth asked a core question directly related to the second issue. Booth compared *Ship of Fools* with new novels by Aldous Huxley, George P. Elliott, Marcel Ayme, and Maureen Howard and measured them all against F. R. Leavis's definition of *novel.* In asking "Yes, but are they really novels?" Booth answered more or less in the negative. Booth was critical of Porter's method of narration, which he described as "sporadic, almost desultory," and of the novel's unity "based on theme and idea rather than coherence of action." Ironically, although Booth was able to see some relationship between Huxley's *Island* and such "non-Leavisonian 'great tradition' works" as *Candide, Gulliver's Travels,* and *Rasselas,* which use "fictional devices to provoke thought," he missed Porter's satiric intention in *Ship of Fools,* which he said lacked "by design, a grand causal, temporal sequence" and "depended for complete success on the radiance of each part."[23]

Theodore Solotaroff's October review in *Commentary* was as significant as either Schorer's or Booth's but for an entirely different reason.[24] If Schorer spared no praise, Solotaroff spared no scorn. Although a few early reviews had been predominantly negative, such as Stanley Kaufman's in the *New Republic* and Robert R. Kirsch's in the *Los Angeles Times,*[25] none approached the scathing attack mounted by Solotaroff as he assailed Schorer and Auchincloss and all other reviewers who had praised *Ship of Fools.* Objecting in particular to Porter's unflattering characterization of Julius Löwenthal, the only Jew aboard Porter's ship, he accused Porter of snideness, failing to understand history, and lacking "consciousness." He said *Ship of Fools* revealed little more than misanthropy and clever technique. Because of his extreme position on the novel, Solotaroff's essay often has been cited in overviews of Porter criticism as a counterpoise to Schorer's, and his indictment of the novel has colored its aggregate assessment. M. M. Liberman's "The Responsibility of the Novelist: The Critical Reception of *Ship of Fools,*" John P. McIntyre's " 'Ship of Fools' and Its Publicity," and Robert Penn Warren's introduction to *Katherine Anne Porter: A Collection of Critical Essays* directly address Solotaroff's as well as Booth's objections.[26]

Solotaroff's review to the contrary, the American reception of *Ship of Fools* was on balance more enthusiastic and praising than it was condemning. Abroad, the critical reception, with a few exceptions, was decidedly different. In England and Germany the novel was received with either dismissive coolness or righteous outrage. Sybille Bedford's long review in the *Spectator* focused on the novel's strengths, but she also detailed what she perceived as its faults. The *TLS* reviewer, in spite of some serious reservations (the novel is a "drastic failure"), conceded that in the novel "there are moments of great power and compassion" but identified such moments as the achievements "of a great short-story writer." Malcolm Bradbury in *Punch* termed *Ship of Fools* "remarkable" but regretted its repetitiousness and mechanical effects; Anne Duchene in the *Manchester Guardian* called *Ship of Fools* "good" but said it lacked "the pulse of nervous communication so often present in Miss Porter's smaller works." Robert Taubman, writing in the *New Statesman,* compared the novel to a fruitcake, "solid and soft at the same time," altogether "not satisfying." The harshest English review appeared in the *London Observer,* in which

Angus Wilson labeled *Ship of Fools* disappointing, formulaic, muddled, and "middlebrow."[27]

German reviews were largely indignant and clearly political. Even before a German translation of *Ship of Fools* appeared, reviews of the novel had been published in German newspapers and journals. The first was Herbert von Borch's review in *Die Welt,* which carried the headline "The Germans Are Still Cruel, Evil, and Fanatic" and a subhead that called *Ship of Fools* a "document of hatred." Sabina Leitzmann, Norbert Muhlen, and an anonymous reviewer in *Der Spiegel* wrote similar reviews. One reviewer, Heinz Praecter, extracted Solotaroff's objection to Porter's treatment of the Jew and applied it to Porter's treatment of Germans. George and Willene Hendrick point out that Praecter quoted Solotaroff as showing that "out of her masochistic pessimism towards civilization, Miss Porter gives up every discrimination, and that this attitude makes her unable to characterize even the real Nazis in their depravity."[28]

Except in the German reviews and in the early, enthusiastic American reviews, a common opinion expressed in both American and English reviews was that Porter was a first-rate writer of short fiction who in her only long novel had not matched her earlier brilliance. That distinction between Porter's short fiction and her long novel was upheld by the response to Porter's collected stories. When the stories from the three volumes *Flowering Judas and Other Stories; Pale Horse, Pale Rider: Three Short Novels;* and *The Leaning Tower and Other Stories* were gathered, expanded by four stories in the American and second British editions, and published as *The Collected Stories of Katherine Anne Porter,*[29] reviews were largely laudatory. Although some reviewers, such as John W. Aldridge and Stephen Donadio, disliked Porter's approach and narrowly circumscribed subjects,[30] the majority of reviewers praised the collection. Granville Hicks wrote in the *Saturday Review,* "One has the feeling, with almost every story, that it is absolutely right." Howard Moss in the *New York Times Book Review* placed Porter in the company of James Joyce, Thomas Mann, Anton Chekhov, Henry James, and Joseph Conrad, and Harry T. Moore favorably compared Porter to Willa Cather, although he thought Porter "more complex." Malcolm Bradbury in the *Manchester Guardian* decreed Porter "a very important writer," and V. S. Pritchett concluded that Porter had solved the basic problem of the short-story writer: "how to satisfy exhaustively in writing briefly."[31]

Several important differences are apparent between the reviews of *The Collected Stories* in 1964 and 1965 and those of the small volumes of 1930, 1935, 1939, and 1944. Critical opinions and literary taste had changed over the course of 35 years, and the later reviews reflect in part those changes. But by 1964 serious critical attention had been directed to Porter, and reviews of her work, including those of *Ship of Fools,* had become more probing. While most reviewers of the 1930, 1935, 1939, and 1944 volumes had failed to grasp Porter's methods and themes, many reviewers in 1965 discerned distinguishing elements in Porter's subjects and techniques. Joseph Featherstone and Denis Donoghue defined Porter's use of the past in her stories, Robert Kiely pointed out Porter's theme of illusion and her distance from 1960s romanticism, and John Hagopian saw a common "Camusian . . . existentialism" in the stories.[32] Acclaim for *The Collected Stories* culminated in its winning both the Pulitzer prize and the National Book Award in 1966 and affirmed the opinion that Porter was a superb writer of short fiction, regardless of the critical assessment of *Ship of Fools.*

GENERAL CRITICISM OF THE FICTION

Lodwick Hartley's "Katherine Anne Porter," appearing in the spring 1940 issue of the *Sewanee Review,* was the first scholarly examination of Porter's work.[33] Although the essay is finally more evaluation than probing criticism, Hartley did attempt to define both Porter's artistic qualities and the distinguishing traits of her short stories and short novels. The importance of the essay is that Hartley presented Porter and her fiction as a proper subject for critical essays in scholarly journals. Two years later, Robert Penn Warren's now-classic essay "Katherine Anne Porter (Irony with a Center)" was published in the *Kenyon Review.* It remains unsurpassed in its accurate delineation of Porter's themes and methods, and the fiction Porter published after 1942 in no way challenges his generalizations. In 1945 Vernon Young, in "The Art of Katherine Anne Porter," attempted to analyze Porter's style and method of characterization, and in 1946 Charles Allen investigated the complex elements of Porter's characterization, which he believed provided the "extraordinary power" for her fictional themes.[34]

The first long critical study on Porter, Harry John Mooney Jr.'s *The Fiction and Criticism of Katherine Anne Porter,* a pamphlet in the University of Pittsburgh Press's Critical Essays in English and American Literature series, appeared in 1957. Mooney properly saw a unity in the Miranda stories and thought all the stories except "The Cracked Looking-Glass" treated the theme of "the terrible predicament of the individual in the modern world."[35] At about the same time, important general critical essays were contributed by Charles Allen, who identified Porter's common theme as "the betrayal of life that develops" when physical and social needs are repeatedly denied fulfillment; by Robert B. Heilman, who placed Porter's fiction in the context of southern literature, with its senses of the concrete, elemental, ornamental, representative, and macroscopic; by Charles Kaplan, who defined Porter's central concept of "truth"; and by William Van O'Connor, who established Porter in the tradition of Henry James.[36]

During the 1960s interest in Porter exploded, owing in part to the publication of *Ship of Fools* and *The Collected Stories* and to Porter's receiving the Pulitzer prize and the National Book Award. The decade began with significant articles on Porter appearing in major scholarly journals. James William Johnson in "Another Look at Katherine Anne Porter" was the first serious scholar to propose a unifying locus for Porter's fiction. Johnson, however, stopped short of defining a canonical theme, and he conceded that not all the stories fit the pattern he constructed.[37] Other important early general articles are George Greene's "Brimstone and Roses: Notes on Katherine Anne Porter," Edward Schwartz's "The Fictions of Memory," and Marjorie Ryan's "*Dubliners* and the Stories of Katherine Anne Porter." Greene argued that all of Porter's stories "constitute a challenge hurled against the uncertainties" of our age; Schwartz analyzed Porter's autobiographical character Miranda's levels of initiation; and Ryan pointed out Joycean echoes in many of Porter's stories. Sister M. Joselyn was the first critic to thoroughly consider Porter's use of animal imagery in her fiction. George Core published "The Best Residuum of Truth," an important essay in which he examined the relationship between Porter's themes and style and traced her debt again to Henry James. Among such critics who were looking for Porter's literary forebears was Patrick Cruttwell, who included Porter in the company of Jonathan Swift.[38]

The first major books on Porter appeared in this decade. In *Katherine Anne Porter and the Art of Rejection,* William F. Nance attempted to establish a canonical motif, a "life-pattern" of rejection, and to categorize all of Porter's characters according to their sources in Porter's personal experience, "alpha" characters being autobiographical, "beta" characters removed from "an autobiographical center." In the first thorough overview, *Katherine Anne Porter,* George Hendrick considered all of Porter's fiction and her nonfiction and placed the fiction in categories according to theme and setting. Another important book was *Katherine Anne Porter: A Critical Symposium,* a compilation by Lodwick Hartley and George Core of reviews, personal and critical essays, and previously published interviews with Porter. In *Katherine Anne Porter,* a pamphlet in the University of Minnesota American Writers Series, Ray B. West Jr. examined Porter's fiction for autobiographical elements and analyzed her use of memory as a creative approach. In *Katherine Anne Porter: The Regional Stories,* a pamphlet in the Southwest Writers Series, Winfred Emmons evaluated Porter's fiction by the success with which her stories convey a sense of place.[39]

In the 1970s books and collections of critical essays on Porter's works continued to appear, notable among them John Edward Hardy's *Katherine Anne Porter* and M. M. Liberman's *Katherine Anne Porter's Fiction.* Hardy found consistency in Porter's treatment of evil and corruption and pointed out the thematic relationship among "Hacienda," "The Leaning Tower," and *Ship of Fools.* He also astutely noted Porter's reliance on caricature as a narrative mode. In chapters that closely address individual subjects and works Liberman considered Porter's use of various rhetorical devices and defined the genres represented in her fiction. Reacting against a plethora of creative symbol hunts in Porter's fiction, he warned against reading her stories too exclusively for their symbolism. *Katherine Anne Porter: A Collection of Critical Essays,* edited by Robert Penn Warren and part of the Twentieth Century Views series, was received with particular interest for Warren's careful examination of the *Ship of Fools* critical controversy and for his introductory essay, in which he established the "inner coherence" of Porter's fiction.[40]

Feminist scholars and critics, emerging early in the decade, began to show an interest in Porter's work, correctly identifying mythic feminism in her fiction. Rosemary Henessy argued that the Miranda cycle is a bildungsroman, with Miranda the model for modern women, and Barbara Harrell Carson examined the Miranda stories to illustrate Miranda's liberation from the invisible bonds of "family, tradition, custom" and from a "reluctance to seize independence."[41] In addition, important general articles were published. Eileen Baldeshwiler identified three "modes" in Porter's fiction, those of syllogism, memory, and a "new, post-Chekhovian form." Edwin W. Gaston Jr. measured Porter's use of southern myth against that of Faulkner, and Colin Partridge found a link between Porter's theme of betrayal and her experience in Mexico. Joan Givner tied Porter's understanding of the art of caricature to her moral philosophy, and Joseph Wiesenfarth examined Porter's stories for their common theme of the struggle for self-knowledge and love.[42]

After Porter's death in September 1980, the publication of such works as Hank Lopez's *Conversations with Katherine Anne Porter: Refugee from Indian Creek* and Joan Givner's *Katherine Anne Porter: A Life* ensured an increased critical interest in Porter and her work.[43] Lopez's biography of Porter is based on interviews he had with her late in her life. Although the book contains numerous errors, some important information remains. Givner's was the first comprehensive biography of Porter to appear, and although a great number of persons who knew Porter objected to the portrait Givner painted, she did correct many errors of fact about Porter's life. In the 1980s appeared Jane DeMouy's *Katherine Anne Porter's Women: The Eye of Her Fiction* (1983) and my *Truth and Vision in Katherine Anne Porter's Fiction* (1985) and *Understanding Katherine Anne Porter* (1988). *Katherine Anne Porter's Women* is a study of Porter's fiction based on principles of feminine psychology. *Truth and Vision in Katherine Anne Porter's Fiction* is a thematic classification that unites all of Porter's works in a canonical theme. *Understanding Katherine Anne Porter,* part of the University of South Carolina's Understanding Contemporary American Literature series, is an overview of Porter's life and works, including her nonfiction. Joan Givner edited *Katherine Anne Porter: Conversations,* a collection of interviews Porter gave over the years, and Harold Bloom edited *Katherine Anne Porter,* another collection of reprinted critical essays.[44]

Since 1990 critical essays on Porter have reflected current trends in American criticism. Of significance is Debra Moddelmog's interdisciplinary study "Concepts of Justice in the Fiction of Katherine Anne Porter," which combines judicial theory with literary criticism.[45] Many essays about Porter written from the perspective of feminist criticism have appeared in collections of essays. Representative of the best of such essays are those by Peggy Whitman Prenshaw and Ruth M. Vande Kieft in *The Female Tradition in Southern Literature,* edited by Carol S. Manning. Prenshaw placed Porter's Miranda in the context of the southern white woman who was a "shaping symbol of the patriarchal Old South," and Vande Kieft compared Porter's mythos of love with that of Eudora Welty and Carson McCullers.[46]

Between 1990 and 1996 additional books about Porter and her fiction were published. Two books focus on Porter's Texas childhood and consider its influence on her fiction. *Katherine Anne Porter and Texas: An Uneasy Relationship,* edited by Clinton Machann and William Bedford Clark, is a collection of biographical, critical, and personal essays and an annotated bibliography of works related to Porter's Texas heritage. James T. F. Tanner's *The Texas Legacy of Katherine Anne Porter* treats in particular "He," "Noon Wine," "Holiday," and stories in the Miranda cycle. In *Katherine Anne Porter and Mexico: The Illusion of Eden* Thomas Walsh brought together his many years' work on Porter's fiction set in Mexico enhanced by his access to primary materials and his knowledge of Mexican social history. Robert Brinkmeyer's *Katherine Anne Porter's Artistic Development: Primitivism, Traditionalism, and Totalitarianism* is an examination of Porter's various religious and political stances and the effect they had on her fiction. Janis Stout's *Katherine Anne Porter: A Sense of the Times* is an intellectual biography that locates Porter in the context of the twentieth century and applies contemporary critical theories to her politics and "the issue of gender."[47]

BIBLIOGRAPHIES

The first specialized Porter bibliography, William A. Sylvester's *Selected and Critical Bibliography of the Uncollected Works of Katherine Anne Porter,* appeared in 1947. The first comprehensive secondary bibliography was Edward Schwartz's *Katherine Anne Porter: A Critical Bibliography,* which appeared five years later with an introduction by Robert Penn Warren. In 1967 such early bibliographies were supplanted by *A Bibliography of the Works of Katherine Anne Porter and A Bibliography of the Criticism of the Works of Katherine Anne Porter,* by Louise Waldrip and Shirley Ann Bauer. Useful to a point, the Waldrip and Bauer bibliography was impaired by some errors and an unhandy organization. More dependable was Robert Kiernan's *Katherine Anne Porter and Carson McCullers: A Reference Guide,* which listed in chronological order, with abstracts, critical studies of Porter through 1974. Published in 1990, the thorough and accurate *Katherine Anne Porter: An Annotated Bibliography,* by Kathryn Hilt and Ruth M. Alvarez, complete through 1988, in turn superseded Kiernan and Waldrip and Bauer.[48]

CRITICISM OF INDIVIDUAL WORKS

Porter's fiction is considered in varying degrees in the critical books and pamphlets published since 1957. But individual fictional works have received attention in separate essays. Among the stories, "Flowering Judas" and "Noon Wine" have received the most individual attention. Ray B. West Jr. was the first critic to closely analyze "Flowering Judas," his "Symbol and Theme in 'Flowering Judas' " setting the standard for symbol hunting in Porter's fiction. Other influential early studies of "Flowering Judas" include "Death's Other Kingdom: Dantesque and Theological Symbolism in 'Flowering Judas,' " by Leon Gottfried, who associated the world of "Flowering Judas" with T. S. Eliot's poems of spiritual death; and "Laura and the Unlit Lamp," by Sister Mary Bride, who contended that Laura in failing to choose good over evil and in rejecting love, effectively repudiates life. David Madden's "The Charged Image in Katherine Anne Porter's 'Flowering Judas' " is a consideration of the story's themes embodied in its visual images. The definitive essay on "Flowering Judas," however, is "The Making of 'Flowering Judas,' " by Thomas Walsh, who examined Porter's experiences and acquaintances in Mexico as sources for the story. It is included with six other critical essays and four background pieces in *Katherine Anne Porter, "Flowering Judas,"* a casebook edited by Virginia Spencer Carr for the Women Writers: Texts and Contexts series at Rutgers University Press.[49]

The variety of critical approaches to "Noon Wine" illustrates the story's richness and power. Porter's own account of the genesis of this story, " 'Noon Wine': the Sources," directed some of the subsequent criticism, but additional important commentary is found in "Porter's 'Noon Wine': A Stifled Tragedy," by J. Oates Smith, and in "Point of View: Katherine Anne Porter's 'Noon Wine,' " by Marvin Pierce. Both Smith and Pierce interpreted the story by the precepts of classic tragedy. M. Wynn Thomas, in "Strangers in a Strange Land: A Reading of 'Noon Wine,' " and Janis Stout, in "Mr. Hatch's Volubility and Miss Porter's Reticence," studied language and style in the story as keys to theme and structure. In "Deep Similarities in 'Noon Wine' " and "The 'Noon Wine' Devils," Thomas Walsh considered the story as a doppelgänger and as a Faust story, comparing it to Stephen Vincent Benet's "The Devil and Daniel Webster" as well as to the Faust myth in Christopher Marlowe's *Doctor Faustus* and in Johann Wolfgang von Goethe's *Faust.*[50]

Other stories have been examined to some small extent in individual essays. Joseph Wiesenfarth's "Illusion and Allusion: Reflections in 'The Cracked Looking-Glass' " has been widely considered the most important analysis of that story. Wiesenfarth defined the story's theme of illusion versus reality and traced specific allusions in the story to Henry James, James Joyce, and the Bible. In *Katherine Anne Porter's Women: The Eye of Her Fiction,* Jane DeMouy builds on Wiesenfarth's explication by interpreting the story from a feminist perspective. Wiesenfarth, on the other hand, is the only critic to successfully treat "The Jilting of Granny Weatherall" in a single essay, identifying order as the central motif of the story.[51]

"He" and "Theft," both written in the 1920s, have generated a small interest. Debra Moddelmog and Bruce Jorgensen published companion pieces on "He" in *Modern Fiction Studies,* Moddelmog taking the position of the postmodern theorist and Jorgensen applying formalist techniques.[52] "Theft" has been successfully analyzed by Joan Givner, who summarized the story's theme as "self-delusion in the face of evil"; by Joseph Wiesenfarth, who traced the stages of the unnamed protagonist's loss of innocence; and by Leonard Prager, who showed how Porter implants the story's meaning in the complex symbolism of the protagonist's purse.[53]

Porter's Miranda cycle includes "Old Mortality," "Pale Horse, Pale Rider," and the seven pieces that constitute "The Old Order"—"The Source," "The Journey," "The Circus," "The Fig Tree," "The Witness," "The Last Leaf," and "The Grave." Approaching the stories collectively was George Cheatham, who saw death as the "obsessive center" throughout the Miranda stories, and Janis Stout, who explained Miranda's "reticence" and the cycle's "positive center."[54] Other Miranda stories have been grouped for analysis. Jane Hafen considered the classical influence on the stories that make up "The Old Order" as illustrated in an allusion to Agamemnon. Mary Titus in " 'Mingled Sweetness and Corruption': Katherine Anne Porter's 'The Fig Tree' and 'The Grave' " regarded those stories as "explorations of . . . sexual terror and guilt."[55] The most important critical exegesis of "The Grave" remains Cleanth Brooks's 1966 essay "On 'The Grave,' " in which Brooks defended his choice of "The Grave" to illustrate Porter's "genius as a writer" by explicating the"physical and social context that gives point to Miranda's discovery of truth." M. M. Liberman compared Porter's early and last drafts of "Old Mortality" to discover the story's "deepest meaning." Other informative examinations of "Old Mortality" are Thomas Walsh's "Miranda's Ghost in 'Old Mortality,' " which focused on the parallels between Miranda and the dead Amy, and Suzanne Jones's stylistic examination of the story from the perspective of feminist criticism.[56] The most enlightening essays on "Pale Horse, Pale Rider" are Thomas Walsh's psychoanalytic examination of the five dream sequences that make up the story and Sarah Youngblood's study of the story's three units of increasing psychological complexity.[57] Some readers and critics consider "Holiday," with its unnamed, Miranda-like protagonist, a part of the group. George Core's " 'Holiday': A Version of Pastoral" was an application of Empson's mythic apparatus, and John Edward Hardy's "Katherine Anne Porter's 'Holiday' " placed the story in a comic mode ordered by the themes of bestiality and human recognition.[58]

The only valuable interpretations of "Rope," "Magic," "A Day's Work," "The Downward Path to Wisdom," and "The Leaning Tower" have appeared in general critical studies of Porter's fiction. Willene and George Hendrick analyzed "The Leaning Tower" by identifying its autobiographical elements and by studying Porter's method of addressing the "German problem." "Virgin Violeta," "The Martyr," "María Concepción," "Hacienda," and "That Tree," all stories set in Mexico, have received only a modest amount of attention outside of critical books. Ruth M. Alvarez's previously unpublished " 'Royalty in Exile': Pre-Hispanic Art and Ritual in 'María Concepción' " is an authoritative comment on the influence of Mexican art and aesthetic theory on Porter's fiction and notably on her first published story, set in Mexico. Robert L. Perry pointed out that the topicality of "Hacienda" should not have obscured the artistry of the story, whose central theme he identified as change.[59]

Criticism of *Ship of Fools* has been limited, much of it included in book-length studies of Porter's fiction. But several essays are important for their close analysis of Porter's methods and themes. Robert Heilman's study of Porter's style in the novel also shed light on the fictional style in general, and Smith Kirkpatrick's study of Porter's appropriation of a classical device directed readers to Porter's artistic purpose. Jon Spence's article on the novel as a satire approached Porter's intention probably more closely than any other single article, although Liberman's identification of its association with the medieval-beast fable was near the mark ("Responsibility of the Novelist").[60] *Ship of Fools* is episodic by design, and Porter's rational construction of the novel, with intentional satiric parallels, aligns it not only with Sebastian Brant's *Das Narrenschiff* but also with Sir Thomas More's *Utopia,* Voltaire's *Candide,* Jonathan Swift's *Gulliver's Travels,* and other satires of the seventeenth and eighteenth centuries, literary periods that, along with the late Middle Ages, Porter credited with having molded her values and having fashioned her sense of literature. An increasing number of critics are pointing out that a complete assessment of *Ship of Fools* must take into consideration Porter's satiric methods and purposes.

The Nonfiction

Porter's first collection of essays, *The Days Before,* was published in 1952.[61] It included book reviews and other essays Porter had published during the preceding 30 years. Reviewers such as Ruth Chapin in the *Christian Science Monitor* treated it generally with respect and praised Porter's style and occasionally her insights. Some critics thought most highly of the collection. Carlos Baker described the work as "magnificent," David Daiches called the book "wholly delightful," Arthur Mizener said the pieces showed Porter's "fine mind" at work, and Robert E. Spiller, identifying Porter as "one of the finer artists of our time," told readers of the *Saturday Review* that every word Porter said was "worth listening to."[62] But other reviewers pointed out what they saw as Porter's thin critical powers. Mark Schorer praised some of the essays but considered two-thirds of the book not worth rereading and called some of the pieces "vulgar" or "dull." Leslie Fiedler spoke of Porter's "absurdities . . . connected with . . . a tradition that has outlived its usefulness," and John Edward Hardy found the essays "more glow than critical cogency." Edward Schwartz reviewed the volume for the *Nation,* and he also wrote a detailed essay, "The Way of Dissent: Katherine Anne Porter's Critical Position," in which he constructed Porter's aesthetic theory based on her essays both in the collection and elsewhere.[63]

Porter's later collection of nonfiction, *The Collected Essays and Occasional Writings of Katherine Anne Porter* (1970), folded in *The Days Before* and added a selection of poetry and other pieces of nonfiction.[64] Following the triumphant appearance of *The Collected Stories* and the critical storm of *Ship of Fools, The Collected Essays* was greeted with outright admiration, lukewarm praise, or vigorous disparagement. The collection was described variously as "a necessary complement" to the stories, an enhancement to Porter's "already exalted reputation," and "some of the best work of one of our finest writers."[65] In the *Hudson Review* William H. Pritchard made critical distinctions among the pieces, saying that in the best ones "a superb intelligence" was evident. But reviewers in the *Washington Post, Kirkus Reviews,* and the *New Republic* thought some of the pieces did not deserve reprinting, and Glendy Culligan wrote in the *Saturday Review* that the collection was weighted down with occasional "fragments of uneven quality and of impermanent interest except to biographers yet unborn."[66]

When Porter's memoir of her participation in the Sacco–Vanzetti affair of the 1920s, *The Never-Ending Wrong,* was published during the 50th anniversary year of the anarchists' execution,[67] reviewers were either charmed by the style and the message or were put off by Porter's blending of fact and fiction. Eudora Welty in an approving review in the *New York Times* summarized Porter's achievement in the work. On the other hand, John Deedy, who had studied the event for 30 years and believed Sacco and Vanzetti innocent, explained his disappointment in Porter's account. He said that passages of the book, such as those "describing the death-watch outside Charlestown State Prison, . . . are gripping in their suspense and almost poetic in their beauty," but he also said that instead of leaving behind "an important historical document," Porter willed "the world a thin and garbled memoir, beautifully expressed and deeply felt, but so much less than we might expect."[68] The most serious critical attention devoted to *The Never-Ending Wrong* was Will Brantley's *Feminine Sense in Southern Memoir,* in which he wove Porter's work into a contextual comparison with memoirs by other twentieth-century southern women.[69]

In the 1990s collections of Porter's nonfiction that had not been previously gathered were published. Isabel Bayley edited *Letters by Katherine Anne Porter,* I edited *"This Strange, Old World" and Other Book Reviews by Katherine Anne Porter,* which included 51 reviews not in *The Collected Essays,* and Ruth

M. Alvarez and Thomas F. Walsh edited *Uncollected Early Prose of Katherine Anne Porter,* which made available early book reviews, journalistic pieces, and essays Porter wrote before 1932. In 1996 the University of South Carolina Press published and I edited *Katherine Anne Porter's Poetry,* which brought together the 9 poems Porter chose for *The Collected Essays,* 6 published poems that had not been previously collected by Porter, all the translations in *Katherine Anne Porter's French Song-Book,* and 19 previously unpublished poems by Porter culled from manuscripts and letters in the Porter Papers at the University of Maryland. In the introduction to the volume I traced Porter's development as a poet and considered the relationship between Porter's fiction and the poetry.[70]

As the end of the century approaches, critical interest in Porter is high. New critical studies are appearing, new biographies are being written, more of Porter's letters are being gathered for publication, more foreign editions of her works are being published, and the Library of America is planning Porter volumes. Porter's childhood home is being opened as a museum, and both a Katherine Anne Porter Society, made up of persons with personal or scholarly interest in Porter, and a Katherine Anne Porter Association, devoted to the preservation of Porter artifacts, have been established.

Notes

1.   *Flowering Judas,* published by Harcourt, Brace in a limited edition of 600 copies, includes in addition to the title story the following five stories: "María Concepción," "Magic," "Rope," "He," and "The Jilting of Granny Weatherall."

2.   Margaret Cheney Dawson, "A Perfect Flowering," *New York Herald Tribune Books,* 14 September 1930, 3–4.

3.   John McDonald, "Chamber Music," *Boulevardier* 6 (December 1930): 22; Edward Weeks, "The Atlantic Bookshelf," *Atlantic Monthly* 147 (May 1931): 32; Yvor Winters, "Major Fiction," *Hound & Horn* 4 (January–March 1931): 303–5; Louise Bogan, [Nothing Is Fortuitous], *New Republic* 64 (22 October 1930): 277–78; Allen Tate, "A New Star," *Nation* 131 (1 October 1930): 352–53.

4.   For a list of Porter's publications see Kathryn Hilt and Ruth M. Alvarez, *Katherine Anne Porter: An Annotated Bibliography* (New York: Garland, 1990).

5.   "María Concepción," *Century* 105 (December 1922): 224–39.

6.   Although "The Fig Tree" (1960), "Holiday" (1960), and "The Spivvelton Mystery" (1971) were published after 1945, they were written in the 1920s and 1930s.

7.   See Elizabeth Hart, "Slight and Short Stories," *New York Herald Tribune Books,* 16 December 1934, 15; and Charles G. Poore, "A New Story by Katherine Anne Porter," *New York Times Book Review,* 23 December 1934, 4.

8.   Besides "Hacienda," the stories added to *Flowering Judas* were "Theft," "That Tree," and "The Cracked Looking-Glass."

9.   Eleanor Clark, "Cameos," *New Republic* 85 (25 December 1935): 209. See also John Chamberlain, "Books of the Times," *New York Times,* 11 October 1935, L-23; and "Complexity and Depth," *Saturday Review of Literature* 13 (14 December 1935): 16.

10. "Mexican Contrasts," *Times Literary Supplement,* 18 April 1936, 333; Graham Greene, "Legend," (London) *Spectator* 154 (24 April 1936): 766.

11. *Noon Wine* was published in 1937 in a limited edition of 250 copies by Schuman's (Detroit).

12. Ben Belitt, "South Texas Primitive," *Nation* 144 (15 May 1937): 571; Dorothy Brewster, "Worth Waiting For," *New Masses* 23 (25 May 1937): 25–26; and Edith H. Walton, "An Ironic Tragedy," *New York Times Book Review,* 11 April 1937, 7.

13. Wallace Stegner, "Conductivity in Fiction," *Virginia Quarterly Review* 15 (Summer 1939): 444–45; [Review of *Pale Horse, Pale Rider*], *Booklist* 35 (15 April 1939): 27; Clifton Fadiman, "Katherine Anne Porter," *New Yorker* 15 (1 April 1939): 77–78; Evelyn Page, "The Novel as Poetry," *Washington Post,* 20 August 1939, section 3, p. 10.

14. Paul Rosenfeld, "An Artist in Fiction," *Saturday Review of Literature* 19 (1 April 1939): 7.

15. "Away from Near-War Consciousness," *Times Literary Supplement,* 27 May 1939, 311; and Forrest Reid, "Fiction," *Spectator* 162 (9 June 1939): 1010.

16. *The Leaning Tower and Other Stories* (New York: Harcourt, Brace, 1944) included, in addition to the title story, "The Source," "The Witness," "The Circus," "The Old Order" (later retitled "The Journey"), "The Last Leaf," "The Grave," "The Downward Path to Wisdom," and "A Day's Work."

17. Diana Trilling, "Fiction in Review," *Nation* 159 (23 September 1944): 359–60; Irving Kristol, "This Majestic and Terrible Failure," *New Leader* 27 (16 December 1944): 11.

18. Gertrude Buckman, "Miss Porter's New Stories," *Partisan Review* 12 (Winter 1945): 134; F. O. Matthiessen, " 'That True and Human World,' " *Accent* 5 (Winter 1945): 121–23; Edmund Wilson, "Books," *New Yorker* 20 (30 September 1944): 72–74.

19. [Review of *The Leaning Tower and Other Stories*], *Times Literary Supplement,* 10 November 1945, 533; David Daiches, [Review of *The Leaning Tower and Other Stories*], *Tomorrow* (November 1944): 79; Charles Morgan, "A Lady of Quality," (London) *Sunday Times,* 2 December 1945, 3.

20. Porter's "novel in progress" had various working titles, among them "Many Redeemers," "Midway This Mortal Life," "Promised Land," and "No Safe Harbor." A long novel planned during the 1920s, "Thieves Market," was set in Mexico, but late in the decade Porter conceived of a three-part novel that was to be heavily autobiographical. There is substantial evidence that it was the third segment of the planned work that became *Ship of Fools.* Porter's 1931 voyage from Veracruz to Bremen provided the surface motif.

21. Mark Schorer, "We're All on the Passenger List," *New York Times Book Review,* 1 April 1962, 1, 5; Warren Beck, "Masterly Novel Crowns Author's Notable Career," *Chicago Sunday Tribune,* Magazine of Books, 1 April 1962, 1–2; Louis D. Rubin Jr., "A Work of Genius," *Baltimore Evening Sun,* 30 April 1962, A-24; Louis Auchincloss, "Bound for Bremerhaven—and Eternity," *New York Herald Tribune,* 1 April 1962, 3, 11.

22. Bernard Theall, " 'Ship of Fools' Portrays Man's Life on Earth," *San Francisco Monitor,* 11 May 1962; "Sight and Sound," *McCall's* 89 (April 1962): 14; Victor R. Yanitell, "Fiction," *Best Sellers* 22 (15 April 1962): 25–26.

23. Wayne C. Booth, "Yes, But Are They Really Novels?" *Yale Review* 51 n.s. (Summer 1962): 632–34.

24. Theodore Solotaroff, " 'Ship of Fools' and the Critics," *Commentary* 34 (October 1962): 277–86. Reprinted in Robert Penn Warren, ed., *Katherine Anne Porter: A Collection of Critical Essays* (Englewood Cliffs, N.J.: Prentice-Hall, 1979).

25. Stanley Kaufman, "Katherine Anne Porter's Crowning Work," *New Republic* 146 (2 April 1962): 23–25; Robert R. Kirsch, "The Long-Awaited 'Ship of Fools' Flounders," *Los Angeles Times-Mirror,* Calendar, 25 March 1962, 22.

26. M. M. Liberman, "Responsibility of the Novelist: The Critical Reception of *Ship of Fools,*" *Criticism* 8 (Fall 1966): 377–88; John P. McIntyre's " 'Ship of Fools' and Its Publicity,"

Thought 38 (Summer 1963): 211–20; Robert Penn Warren, introduction to *Katherine Anne Porter: A Collection of Critical Essays* (Englewood Cliffs, N.J.: Prentice-Hall, 1979).

27.   Sybille Bedford, "Voyage to Everywhere," (London) *Spectator* 209 (16 November 1962): 763–54; "On the Good Ship Vera," *Times Literary Supplement,* 2 November 1962, 837; Malcolm Bradbury, "New Novels," *Punch* 243 (21 November 1962): 763–64; Anne Duchene, "Twenty Years Agrowing," *Manchester Guardian,* 2 November 1962, 12; Robert Taubman, "A First-Class Passenger," *New Statesman* 64 (2 November 1972): 619–20; Angus Wilson, "The Middle-Class Passenger," *London Observer,* 28 October 1962, 27.

28.   Herbert von Borch, "Die Deutschen sind allzumalgrausam, boese und fanatisch/Dokument des Hasses: K. A. Porter's 'Narrenschiff,' " *Die Welt,* 9 June 1962; Sabina Lietzmann, "Eine Allegorie von der deutschen Gefahr/Der neue amerikanische Bestseller 'Narrenschiff' von Katherine Anne Porter," *Frankfurter Allgemeine Zeitung,* 16 July 1962, 16; Norbert Muhlen, "Deutsche wie sie im Buche Stehen," *Der Monat,* December 1962, 38–45; "Das Narrenschiff," *Der Spiegel,* 12 September 1962, 74, 77. See Willene Hendrick and George Hendrick, *Katherine Anne Porter* (revised, Boston: Twayne, 1988), 102–3.

29.   The British edition of 1964 (London: Jonathan Cape) contained only the stories in the collections of 1935, 1939, and 1944. The British edition of 1967 followed the first American edition of 1965 (New York: Harcourt, Brace), which included in addition to the stories of *Flowering Judas and Other Stories; Pale Horse, Pale Rider: Three Short Novels;* and *The Leaning Tower and Other Stories* a preface by Porter ("Go Little Book") and four stories previously uncollected: "The Martyr," "Virgin Violeta," "The Fig Tree," and "Holiday."

30.   John W. Aldridge, "Hors d'oeuvres for an Entree," *New York Herald Tribune,* Book Week, 19 September 1965, 4, 22; Stephen Donadio, "The Collected Miss Porter," *Partisan Review* 33 (Spring 1966): 278–84.

31.   Granville Hicks, "A Tradition of Story Telling," *Saturday Review* 48 (25 September 1965): 35–36; Howard Moss, "A Poet of the Story," *New York Times Book Review,* 12 September 1965, 1, 26; Harry T. Moore, [Review of *The Collected Stories*], *Chicago Tribune Books Today,* 3 October 1965, 3; Malcolm Bradbury, "Perspectives," *Manchester Guardian,* 10 January 1964, 7; V. S. Pritchett, "Stones and Stories," *New Statesman* 67 (10 January 1964): 47–48.

32.   Joseph Featherstone, "Katherine Anne Porter's Harvest," *New Republic* 153 (4 September 1965): 23–26; Denis Donoghue, "Reconsidering Katherine Anne Porter," *New York Review of Books* 5 (11 November 1965): 18–19; Robert Kiely, "Placing Miss Porter," *Christian Science Monitor,* 24 November 1965, 15; John V. Hagopian, "Reviews," *Studies in Short Fiction* 4 (Fall 1966): 86–87.

33.   Lodwick Hartley, "Katherine Anne Porter," *Sewanee Review* 48 (April–June 190): 206–16.

34.   Robert Penn Warren, "Katherine Anne Porter (Irony with a Center)," *Kenyon Review* 4 (Winter 1942): 29–42; Vernon A. Young, "The Art of Katherine Anne Porter," *New Mexico Quarterly Review* 15 (Autumn 1945): 326–41; Charles A. Allen, "Southwestern Chronicle," *Arizona Quarterly* 2 (Summer 1946): 90–95.

35.   Harry John Mooney Jr., *The Fiction and Criticism of Katherine Anne Porter,* Critical Essays in English and American Literature, no. 2 (Pittsburgh: University of Pittsburgh Press, 1957; reprinted in revised and expanded form in 1962).

36.   Charles A. Allen, "Katherine Anne Porter: Psychology as Art," *Southwest Review* 41 (Summer 1956): 223–30; Robert B. Heilman, "The Southern Temper," *Hopkins Review* 6 (Fall 1952): 5–15; Charles Kaplan, "True Witness: Katherine Anne Porter," *Colorado Quarterly* 7 (Winter 1959): 319–27; William Van O'Connor, "The Novel of Experience," *Critique* 1 (Winter 1956): 37–44.

37.   James William Johnson, "Another Look at Katherine Anne Porter," *Virginia Quarterly Review* 36 (Autumn 1960): 598–613.

38.   George Greene, "Brimstone and Roses: Notes on Katherine Anne Porter," *Thought* 36 (Autumn 1961): 421–40; Edward Schwartz, "The Fictions of Memory," *Southwest Review* 45

(Summer 1960): 204–15; Marjorie Ryan, *"Dubliners* and the Stories of Katherine Anne Porter," *American Literature* 31 (January 1960): 464–73; Sister M. Joselyn, "Animal Imagery in Katherine Anne Porter's Fiction," in *Myth and Symbol: Critical Approaches and Applications,* ed. Bernice Slote (Lincoln: University of Nebraska Press, 1963), 101–15; George Core, "The Best Residuum of Truth," *Georgia Review* 20 (Fall 1966): 278–91; Patrick Cruttwell, "Swift, Miss Porter, and 'The Dialect of the Tribe,' " *Shenandoah* 17 (Summer 1966): 27–38.

39. William L. Nance, *Katherine Anne Porter and the Art of Rejection* (Chapel Hill: University of North Carolina Press, 1964); George Hendrick, *Katherine Anne Porter* (New York: Twayne, 1965; revised with Willene Hendrick and reprinted, 1988); Lodwick Hartley and George Core, eds., *Katherine Anne Porter: A Critical Symposium* (Athens: University of Georgia Press, 1969); Ray B. West Jr., *Katherine Anne Porter,* University of Minnesota Pamphlets on American Writers, no. 28 (Minneapolis: University of Minnesota Press, 1963); and Winfred Emmons, *Katherine Anne Porter: The Regional Stories,* Southwest Writers Series, no. 6 (Austin: Steck-Vaughn, 1967).

40. John Edward Hardy, *Katherine Anne Porter* (New York: Frederick Ungar, 1973); M. M. Liberman, *Katherine Anne Porter's Fiction* (Detroit: Wayne State University Press, 1971); Robert Penn Warren, ed., *Katherine Anne Porter: A Collection of Critical Essays* (Englewood Cliffs, N.J.: Prentice-Hall, 1979).

41. Rosemary Hennessy, "Katherine Anne Porter's Model for Heroines," *Colorado Quarterly* 25 (Winter 1977): 301–15; Barbara Harrell Carson, "Winning: Katherine Anne Porter's Women," in *The Authority of Experience: Essays in Feminist Criticism,* ed. Arlyn Diamond and Lee R. Edwards (Amherst: University of Massachusetts, 1977), 239–56.

42. Eileen Baldeshwiler, "Structural Patterns in Katherine Anne Porter's Fiction," *South Dakota Review* 11 (Summer 1973): 45–53; Edwin W. Gaston Jr., "The Mythic South of Katherine Anne Porter," *Southwestern American Literature* 3 (1973): 81–85; Colin Partridge, " 'My Familiar Country': An Image of Mexico in the Work of Katherine Anne Porter," *Studies in Short Fiction* 7 (Fall 1970): 597–614; Joan Givner, "Katherine Anne Porter and the Art of Caricature," *Genre* 5 (March 1972): 51–60; Joseph Wiesenfarth, "Negatives of Hope: A Reading of Katherine Anne Porter," *Renascence* 25 (Winter 1973): 85–94.

43. Enrique Hank Lopez, *Conversations with Katherine Anne Porter: Refugee from Indian Creek* (Boston: Little, Brown, 1981); Joan Givner, *Katherine Anne Porter: A Life* (New York: Simon and Schuster, 1982; revised and reprinted, Athens: University of Georgia Press, 1991).

44. Jane Krause DeMouy, *Katherine Anne Porter's Women: The Eye of Her Fiction* (Austin: University of Texas Press, 1983); Darlene Harbour Unrue, *Truth and Vision in Katherine Anne Porter's Fiction* (Athens: University of Georgia Press, 1985); Darlene Harbour Unrue, *Understanding Katherine Anne Porter* (Columbia: University of South Carolina Press, 1988); Joan Givner, ed., *Katherine Anne Porter: Conversations* (Jackson: University Press of Mississippi, 1987); Harold Bloom, ed., *Katherine Anne Porter* (New York: Chelsea House, 1986).

45. Debra A. Moddelmog, "Concepts of Justice in the Work of Katherine Anne Porter," *Mosaic* 26, no. 4 (Fall 1993): 37–52.

46. Peggy Whitman Prenshaw, "Southern Ladies and the Southern Literary Renaissance," in *The Female Tradition in Southern Literature,* ed. Carol S. Manning (Urbana: University of Illinois Press, 1993): 73–78; Ruth M. Vande Kieft, "The Love Ethos of Porter, Welty, and McCullers," in Manning, ed., *The Female Tradition in Southern Literature,* 235–58.

47. Clinton Machann and William Bedford Clark, eds., *Katherine Anne Porter and Texas: An Uneasy Relationship* (College Station: Texas A&M University Press, 1990); James T. F. Tanner, *The Texas Legacy of Katherine Anne Porter* (Denton: University of North Texas Press, 1991); Thomas F. Walsh, *Katherine Anne Porter and Mexico: The Illusion of Eden* (Austin: University of Texas Press, 1992); Robert H. Brinkmeyer Jr., *Katherine Anne Porter's Artistic Development: Primitivism, Traditionalism, and Totalitarianism* (Baton Rouge: Louisiana State University Press, 1993); Janis Stout, *Katherine Anne Porter: A Sense of the Times* (Charlottesville: University Press of Virginia, 1995).

48. William A. Sylvester, "Selected and Critical Bibliography of the Uncollected Works of Katherine Anne Porter," *Bulletin of Bibliography* 19 (January–April 1947): 36; Edward Schwartz, "Katherine Anne Porter: A Critical Bibliography," *Bulletin of the New York Public Library* 57 (May 1953): 211–47 (published as a separate volume the same year by the New York Public Library); Louise Waldrip and Shirley Ann Bauer, *A Bibliography of the Works of Katherine Anne Porter and a Bibliography of the Criticism of Katherine Anne Porter* (Metuchen, N.J.: Scarecrow, 1979); Robert F. Kiernan, *Katherine Anne Porter and Carson McCullers: A Reference Guide* (Boston: G. K. Hall, 1976); Kathryn Hilt and Ruth M. Alvarez, *Katherine Anne Porter: An Annotated Bibliography* (New York: Garland, 1990).

49. Ray B. West Jr., "Katherine Anne Porter: Symbol and Theme in 'Flowering Judas,' " *Accent* 7 (Spring 1947): 182–88; Leon Gottfried, "Death's Other Kingdom: Dantesque and Theological Symbolism in 'Flowering Judas,' " *PMLA* 84 (January 1969): 112–24; Sister Mary Bride, "Laura and the Unlit Lamp," *Studies in Short Fiction* 1 (Fall 1963): 61–63; David Madden, "The Charged Image in Katherine Anne Porter's 'Flowering Judas,' " *Studies in Short Fiction* 7 (Spring 1970): 277–89; Thomas F. Walsh, "The Making of 'Flowering Judas,' " *Journal of Modern Literature* 12 (March 1985): 107–30; Virginia Spencer Carr, ed., *Katherine Anne Porter: Flowering Judas* (New Brunswick, N.J.: Rutgers University Press, 1993).

50. Katherine Anne Porter, " 'Noon Wine': The Sources," *Yale Review* 46 (September 1956): 22–39; J. Oates Smith, "Porter's *Noon Wine*: A Stifled Tragedy," *Renascence* 17 (Spring 1965): 157–62; Marvin Pierce, "Point of View: Katherine Anne Porter's 'Noon Wine,' " *Ohio University Review* 3 (1961): 95–113; M. Wynn Thomas, "Strangers in a Strange Land: A Reading of 'Noon Wine,' " *American Literature* 47 (May 1975): 230–46; Janis Stout, "Mr. Hatch's Volubility and Miss Porter's Reticence," *Essays in Literature* 12 (Fall 1985): 285–93; Thomas F. Walsh, "Deep Similarities in 'Noon Wine,' " *Mosaic* 9 (Fall 1975): 83–91; Thomas F. Walsh, "The 'Noon Wine' Devils," *Georgia Review* 22 (Spring 1968): 90–96.

51. Joseph Wiesenfarth, "Illusion and Allusion: Reflections in 'The Cracked Looking-Glass,' " *Four Quarters* 12 (November 1961): 30–37; Jane DeMouy, *Katherine Anne Porter's Women: The Eye of Her Fiction* (Austin: University of Texas Press, 1992), 61–72; Joseph Wiesenfarth, "Internal Opposition in Porter's 'Granny Weatherall,' " *Critique* 11, no. 2 (1969): 47–55.

52. Debra Moddelmog, "Narrative Irony and Hidden Motivations in Katherine Anne Porter's 'He,' " *Modern Fiction Studies* 28 (Autumn 1982): 405–13; Bruce Jorgensen, " 'The Other Side of Silence': Katherine Anne Porter's 'He' as Tragedy," *Modern Fiction Studies* 28 (Autumn 1982): 395–404.

53. Joan Givner, "A Re-Reading of Katherine Anne Porter's 'Theft,' " *Studies in Short Fiction* 6 (1969): 463–65; Joseph Wiesenfarth, "The Structure of Katherine Anne Porter's 'Theft,' " *Cithara* 10 (May 1971): 65–71; Leonard Prager, "Getting and Spending: Porter's 'Theft,' " *Perspective* 11 (Winter 1960): 230–34.

54. George Cheatham, "Death and Repetition in Porter's Miranda Stories," *American Literature* 61 (December 1989): 610–24; Janis Stout, "Miranda's Guarded Speech: Porter and the Problem of Truth Telling," *Philological Quarterly* 66 (Spring 1987): 259–78.

55. P. Jane Hafen, "Katherine Anne Porter's 'The Old Order' and Agamemnon," *Studies in Short Fiction* 31 (1994): 491–93; Mary Titus, " 'Mingled Sweetness and Corruption': Katherine Anne Porter's 'The Fig Tree' and 'The Grave,' " *South Atlantic Review* 53 (May 1988): 111–25.

56. M. M. Liberman, *Katherine Anne Porter's Fiction* (Detroit: Wayne State University Press, 1971), 37–51; Thomas F. Walsh, "Miranda's Ghost in 'Old Mortality,' " *College Literature* 6 (Winter 1979): 57–63; Suzanne W. Jones, "Reading the Endings in Katherine Anne Porter's 'Old Mortality,' " *Southern Quarterly* 31, no. 3 (Spring 1993): 29–44.

57. Thomas F. Walsh, "The Dream Self in 'Pale Horse, Pale Rider,' " *Wascana Review* 14 (Fall 1979): 61–79; Sarah Youngblood, "Structure and Imagery in Katherine Anne Porter's 'Pale Horse, Pale Rider,' " *Modern Fiction Studies* 5 (Winter 1959–60): 344–52.

58.   George Core, " 'Holiday': A Version of Pastoral," in Lodwick Hartley and George Core, eds., *Katherine Anne Porter: A Critical Symposium* (Athens: University of Georgia Press, 1969), 149–58; John Edward Hardy, "Katherine Anne Porter's 'Holiday,' " *Southern Literary Messenger* 1 (1975): 1–5.

59.   Willene Hendrick and George Hendrick, *Katherine Anne Porter* (revised; Boston: Twayne, 1988), 90–96; Robert L. Perry, "Porter's 'Hacienda' and the Theme of Change," *Midwest Quarterly* 6 (Summer 1965): 403–15.

60.   Robert B. Heilman, "*Ship of Fools:* Notes on Style," *Four Quarters* 12 (November 1962): 46–55; Smith Kirkpatrick, "*Ship of Fools,*" *Sewanee Review* 71 (Winter 1963): 94–98; Jon Spence, "Looking Glass Reflections: Satirical Elements in *Ship of Fools,*" *Sewanee Review* 82 (Spring 1974): 316–30; M. M. Liberman, "The Responsibility of the Novelist: The Critical Reception of *Ship of Fools,*" *Criticism* 8.4 (1966): 377–88.

61.   Katherine Anne Porter, *The Days Before* (New York: Harcourt, Brace, 1952).

62.   Ruth Chapin, "They Wrote with Differing Purpose," *Christian Science Monitor,* 4 December 1952, 18; Carlos Baker, "Good Reading: Review of Books Recommended by the Princeton Faculty," *Princeton Alumni Weekly* 4 (14 November 1952): 3; David Daiches, "A Master," *Manchester Guardian,* 30 October 1953, 4; Arthur Mizener, "A Literary Self-Portrait," *Partisan Review* 20 (March–April 1953): 244–46; Robert E. Spiller, "Wiles & Words," *Saturday Review* 36 (10 January 1953): 12.

63.   Mark Schorer, "Biographia Literaria," *New Republic* 127 (10 November 1952): 18–19; Leslie A. Fiedler, "Love Is Not Enough," *Yale Review* 42 (Spring 1953): 456, 458–59; John Edward Hardy, "Interesting Essays by a Novelist," *Baltimore Evening Sun,* 20 January 1953, 16; Edward Schwartz, "Miss Porter's Essays," *Nation* 175 (15 November 1952): 452–53; Edward Schwartz, "The Way of Dissent: Katherine Anne Porter's Critical Position," *Western Humanities Review* 8 (Spring 1954): 19–30.

64.   Katherine Anne Porter, *The Collected Essays and Occasional Writings of Katherine Anne Porter* (New York: Delacorte/Seymour Lawrence, 1970).

65.   See Joseph Wiesenfarth, [Review of *The Collected Essays and Occasional Writings*], *Commonweal* 92 (7 August 1970): 396–98; Janet Overmeyer, "Roving Lady Novelist at Large," *Christian Science Monitor,* 7 May 1970, B-9; *New York Times Book Review,* 7 June 1970, 39–40.

66.   William H. Pritchard, "Tones of Criticism," *Hudson Review* 23 (Summer 1970): 365–66; William McPherson, "Porter at 80—In Print," *Washington Post,* 15 May 1970, C1–C2; *Kirkus Reviews,* 15 December 1969, 1360; Charles Thomas Samuels, "Placing Miss Porter," *New Republic* 162 (7 March 1970): 25–26; Glendy Culligan, "Belles-Lettres," *Saturday Review* 53 (28 March 1970): 29–30.

67.   Katherine Anne Porter, *The Never-Ending Wrong* (Boston: Little, Brown, 1977).

68.   Eudora Welty, "Post Mortem," *New York Times Book Review,* 21 August 1977, 9, 19; John Deedy, "Sacco and Vanzetti," *Commonweal* 104 (2 September 1977): 571–72.

69.   Will Brantley, *Feminine Sense in Southern Memoir: Smith, Glasgow, Welty, Hellman, Porter, and Hurston* (Jackson: University Press of Mississippi, 1993).

70.   Isabel Bayley, ed., *Letters of Katherine Anne Porter* (New York: Atlantic Monthly Press, 1990); Darlene Harbour Unrue, ed., *"This Strange, Old World" and Other Book Reviews by Katherine Anne Porter* (Athens: University of Georgia Press, 1991); Ruth M. Alvarez and Thomas F. Walsh, *Uncollected Early Prose of Katherine Anne Porter* (Austin: University of Texas Press, 1993); Darlene Harbour Unrue, ed., *Katherine Anne Porter's Poetry* (Columbia: University of South Carolina Press, 1996).

REVIEWS OF THE FICTION

◆

FLOWERING JUDAS

[Nothing Is Fortuitous]

LOUISE BOGAN

Miss Porter's stories, here collected for the first time, have appeared during a period of some years in *transition, The American Caravan* and in commercial magazines appreciative of distinguished writing. In each of the five stories in the present book, Miss Porter works with that dangerous stuff, unusual material. Two stories have a Mexican locale. Two contain passages which describe lapses into the subconscious and the dream. "Magic" briefly explores the survival of frayed but savage superstition. "Rope" follows the rise and fall of an hysterical mood, and "He" sets against simple human devotion an idiot's non-human power and suffering.

It is to Miss Porter's high credit that, having fixed upon the exceptional background and event, she has not yielded in her treatment of them, to queerness and forced originality of form. With the exception of "Magic" (which I should prefer to think of as an experiment, since its effect is false, for reasons only too easily defined—the use of the fustian maid-to-mistress monologue, for one), the stories do not lean upon the doubtful prop of manner for its own sake. Miss Porter has a range of effects, but each comes through in its place, and only at the demand of her material. She rejects the exclamatory tricks that wind up style to a spurious intensity, and trusts, for the most part, to straightforward writing, to patience in detail and to a thorough imaginative grasp on cause and character. She has "knowledge about reality," and has chosen the most exacting means to carry her knowledge into form.

The fact, and the intuition or logic about the fact, are severe coordinates in fiction. In the short story they must cross with hair-line precision. However far the story may range, the fact and its essence must direct its course and stand as proof to the whole. The truth alone secures form and tone; other means distort the story to no good end and leave within the reader's mind an

Reprinted from the *New Republic* 64 (22 October 1930): 277–78. In the public domain.

impression far worse than that produced by mere banality. Joyce's "Ivy Day in the Committee Room" depends wholly upon the truth of the fact; Chekhov's greatest stories, say "The Duel" and "Lights," have command of reasons in the first place, of emotion, taste and style secondarily. The firm and delicate writing in Miss Porter's "Flowering Judas," a story startling in its complexity, were it not based on recognizable fact, would be to no purpose. As it is, its excellence rises directly from the probity of the conception. It is as impossible to question the characters of the fanatical girl and the self-loving man—the "good revolutionist," who softened to a state beyond principle, is fit only for a career—as it is to find a flaw or lapse in the style that runs clear and subtle, from the story's casual beginning to the specter of life and death at the end. "Rope," after "Flowering Judas," is perhaps the most remarkable story in the book. It makes no claim; its integration becomes apparent only when the reader tries to recount it to himself in any other form than its own. The mood is put together so accurately that its elements cannot be recombined.

"María Concepción" does not entirely come up to Miss Porter's standard. A slight flavor of details brought in for their own sake mars its intensity, and one does not entirely trust María's simplicity of motive. For the most part, however, the stories in *Flowering Judas* can claim kinship with the order of writing wherein nothing is fortuitous, where all details grow from the matter in hand simply and in order. Miss Porter should demand much work of her talent. There is nothing quite like it, and very little that approaches its strength in contemporary writing.

A New Star

Allen Tate

Miss Porter's stories have appeared in some of the more "literary" magazines whose circulation is not large, and her great distinction as a prose stylist has been known only to a few readers. This collection of six stories, which is her first book, is a limited edition of six hundred copies—evidence of the notoriously mysterious character of the publishing mind. It is doubtless better for the author to win six hundred readers of six stories in book form than to continue to be sampled by a thousand or ten thousand in the scattered and scattering medium of the magazines. But there is no reason why she should not win six or sixty thousand readers—unless indeed the formidable integrity of artistic purpose evinced in every one of these stories is, according to superstition, necessarily detrimental to popularity.

This is not to say that Miss Porter is an author for the "few," or an experimenter writing for other craftsmen. I mean rather that she neither overworks a brilliant style capable of every virtuosity nor forces the background of her material into those sensational effects that are the besetting sin of American prose fiction. There is almost no American writer who escapes the one vice or the other. Of the former, the works of Hergesheimer and Cabell are conspicuously guilty types; types of the latter range all the way from the "social thesis" novels of writers like Miss Glasgow and Sinclair Lewis to the borings into Negro life of Mrs. Julia Peterkin and Du Bose Heyward.

The distinction to be drawn here concerning Miss Porter's work is this: while American fiction as a whole is chiefly occupied with the discovery and then the definition of its materials (witness Glenway Wescott's uneasy speculation on the Wisconsin background), Miss Porter already has a scene which is her instinctive, automatic, unconscious possession; a background that she does not need to think out, nor approach intellectually; a given medium which at once liberates the creative impulse from the painful necessity to acquire its material and sets it about the true presentation of it.

This is roughly the character of European fiction as opposed to the more uncertain, more speculative, and thinner American variety. To return to the

Reprinted with permission of the *Nation* magazine from the *Nation* 131 (1 October 1930): 352–53. Copyright by the *Nation* Company, L.P.

two American vices—we have excellent precisians writing about nothing, or we have authors who never achieve a style because they lack that single, unitary mind which comes out of a fixed relation between the author and his material. The results, in the one case, are an excessive subjectivism or plain egomania, and, in the other, a continual blurring of the fictive characters in the constant rationalizing of their social condition. The character does not exist in his own complete and full-bodied right simply because his creator cannot distinguish him from the other rather similar examples of this or that social trend.

Miss Porter's mind is one of those highly civilized instruments of perception that seem to come out of old societies, where the "social trend" is fixed and assumed. The individual character as the product of such a background also has a certain constancy of behavior which permits the writer to ignore the now common practice of relating individual conduct to some abstract social or psychological law; the character is taken as a fixed and inviolable entity, predictable only in so far as familiarity may be said to make him so, and finally unique as the center of inexhaustible depths of feeling and action. In this manner Miss Porter approaches her characters, and it is this that probably underlies many of the very specific virtues of her writing.

For one thing, her style is beyond doubt the most economical and at the same time the richest in American fiction. Only in the first story, "María Concepción," is there any uncertainty of purpose. In the five others there is not a word gone to waste—and there is no under-writing. There is none of that alternation of natural description and character exposition which is the hallmark of formula-made fiction. There is much sensuous detail, but no decoration. For Miss Porter has a direct and powerful grasp of her material as a whole; this makes every sentence, whether of description, narration, or dialogue, create not only an inevitable and beautiful local effect, but contribute directly to the final tone and climax of the story.

For another thing, Miss Porter's stories are never told in the same way. Each character, or set of characters, in the given scene requires a different approach; their own inherent quality, their inviolable isolation as human beings, determines the form; and no two of these six stories have anything like the same form. While the quality of the style is the same in all of them—there is the same freshness of imagery, the same rich personal idiom—the method is always different. And—this is her great distinction—the method is always completely objective. It would be difficult to "place" an art like this, unless we may timidly call on the word *classical*. For here is a combination of those sensuous qualities usually accredited to a dissociative romanticism, with a clear, objective, full-bodied outside world.

Flowering Judas is not a promising book; it promises nothing. It is a fully matured art. We may only hope to have more of it.

FLOWERING JUDAS
AND OTHER STORIES

Cameos

ELEANOR CLARK

Miss Porter is not an easy author. Her scope is limited, and she counteracts this weakness by satire so pointed and compressed and such perfection of style that one is sometimes forced to concentrate more on word patterns than on the substance of a story. It is not absurd to speak of perfection in this context. One dares to use the word for miniatures.

These generalizations apply to Miss Porter's talent as a whole. They have to be qualified when one deals with the stories separately. Besides "Flowering Judas," two of the stories in this book, "Maria Concepcion" and "The Cracked Looking Glass," would be almost perfect by any standard. In these two, and to a lesser extent in "He," the author has superimposed rhythm and melody on the confused feelings of an inarticulate person, not in such a way as to bring pattern into a life that lacks it, but rather to bring into the reader's senses, more often by sound than definition, the emphases inherent in a character's living. When Miss Porter is writing on this level one cannot be suspicious of restraint. The essentials are there, and we know them through an unfaltering series of trivialities. All the reticence, violence and power of Maria Concepcion are in the carriage of her body when she takes her fowls to market.

In the title story a sensitive but inhibited girl is in love with a young Mexican revolutionary and in order to save him is forced to suffer the attentions of Braggioni, a labor organizer whose "gluttonous bulk has become a symbol of her many disillusions." Her lover kills himself in prison, she comes home and listens to Braggioni's singing. "He sighs and his leather belt creaks like a saddle girth." When he leaves her, sleep confuses her feeling with the symbolism of the Judas tree. It is impossible to imagine reverence of emotion conveyed with more precision than in this story, precision that gives a first

Reprinted from the *New Republic* 85 (25 December 1935): 209. In the public domain.

impression of hardness as if its purpose were to clarify feeling into non-existence, but that serves actually to lop off irrelevancies so that the impact of a mood is subtle and complete. The portrait of Braggioni is a triumph of deflation in few words, and this without comment from the author. The elements of his character are exposed, with rare cruelty, to each other, and automatically tear down his own image of himself.

The methods of this style—understatement, rigid selection and sympathetic music in words—are relatively unsuccessful in three of the new stories added to the original edition of *Flowering Judas*. Particularly in "Hacienda," where the author is trying to describe a bustle of contradictory characters, the result is superficial and not pointed enough to give contour to any of the people involved. These few failures can be forgiven in a book that is primarily one of small patterns written with subdued and exceptional brilliance.

Legend

Graham Greene

When Henry James was accused of having falsified the capering, acquisitive type of young American woman in the person of Daisy Miller, he defended himself by saying that Daisy was "pure poetry." Daisy Miller in other words is a legendary figure, as Maupassant's or Mr. Maugham's, Boule de Suif or Ashenden, are not, just as Madame Bovary *is* legend, and in her lesser way María Concepción who in Miss Porter's magnificent story murders the loose village woman and discovers how the other village women rally to protect her from the police. ("They were around her, speaking for her, defending her; the forces of life were ranged invincibly with her against the beaten dead.") Legend, figures which will dramatise the deepest personal fantasy and the deepest moral consciousness of a man's time: this, if one is not to be an anecdotist or a documentary writer, is the only thing worth attempting.

Miss Porter is twice brilliantly successful, though brilliant is a misleading word to use for the magnificent deep sobriety of her style. These seem to me the best short stories that have come out of America since the early Hemingways, and there is more promise of future life in them, the sense of a consciousness open to any wind, a style adaptable to any subject.

Reprinted with permission of the journal from the (London) *Spectator* 156 (24 April 1936): 766.

PALE HORSE, PALE RIDER: THREE SHORT NOVELS

Conductivity in Fiction

WALLACE STEGNER

There is in all these three novelettes [in *Pale Horse, Pale Rider*] an absoluteness of technique and a felicity of language that are seldom encountered even in the best fiction. Both the title story, set in the influenza epidemic of 1918, and "Old Mortality," the indirectly told tragedy of a Southern belle, are as keen and polished as slim steel. Still, "Noon Wine" seems to me the best of the three, though not as perfectly proportioned. It is the story of a Texas dairy farmer whose life falls to pieces after he has inadvertently killed an amateur detective bent on returning to the asylum the Swede farmhand who has brought prosperity and comfortable self-respect to the farmer. It is not the swifter action that makes this story the best of the three; it is the tense transmission of the farmer's feelings as he goes about the neighborhood after being exonerated by the courts, trying to recapture the respect and belief of his neighbors by telling the story over and over, patiently, knowing they don't believe him, but driven to re-establish his former comfortable and easy peace of mind.

That story communicates; it has voltage. The other two, for all their perfection, seem to me to move away from the qualities that made *Flowering Judas* so exciting a book. They show a more and more elaborate attention to form, and although one grants that fiction is an art of indirection, there is a point at which obliquity defeats itself and becomes sterile. I found myself reading all three novelettes with admiration, but only "Noon Wine" with excitement. Somehow the other two do not conduct.

Reprinted with permission of the journal from the *Virginia Quarterly Review* 15 (Summer 1939): 444–45.

Away from Near-War Consciousness

ANONYMOUS

After war consciousness, post-war consciousness and crisis consciousness, there is something like white-war or near-war consciousness. It seems to be the worse of the lot and the most damaging to novelists and novels. No doubt imaginative talent has almost always chosen the wrong time to be born; no doubt, too, there is seldom a crop of masterpieces in the space of a few months. But it is plain that the going has of late become rougher and more difficult for the novelist, plain that by comparison with even a year ago the present standard of performance is appreciably lower. Good novelists turn out inferior stuff or none at all, while the competent commercial product is more visibly in the ascendant. On the whole the most interesting novels this year have come from America, or at any rate from over the sea and far away, where a near-war consciousness has less than the whole field to itself or can be indulged with an air of greater detachment.

In reserving the week's nosegay for *Pale Horse, Pale Rider* something more is intended than making the best of a bad job. The book consists of three long short-stories—they are best described as short stories rather than *contes* or *novellas* or the "short novels" of the title-page—by an American writer with a previous collection of attractive quality to her credit. What gives distinction to Mrs. Porter's [*sic*] work is the strain of poetry in it. The poetry is consistently elegiac and therefore of a vulnerable kind in prose narrative; but it is nevertheless very welcome, and for a good reason. Ordinarily, if as story-teller you are going to get away from the burning topicalities and agitations of the immediate hour, two ways seem open. One is through the humdrum realism of eternal verities such as catching the 9.5, being unhappily married, finding a new love and watching the baby cut its first tooth. The other is through the doubtfully authentic thrill and glamour of the frozen North, the tropic sun or, say, Wellington's Peninsula campaign. Both fashions, it must be said, are a little too much with us at the moment. The thing that comes all too rarely in fiction nowadays, the thing that is most sorely missed and that reconciles so-called escapism with literature, is the poetic vision—the seeing eye, the invocatory

Reprinted with permission of the (London) *Times* from the *Times Literary Supplement*, 27 May 1939, 311. Copyright Times Supplements Limited 1939.

and evocative power of words. Prose is not poetry; but good fiction never lacks a quality that must ultimately be called poetic. It is this that appears, perhaps rather more bravely than to discreet advantage, in each of the three stories in Mrs. Porter's volume.

In the first, "Old Mortality," two small girls learn the history of Aunt Amy, a Texan beauty of the nineties, who had been much loved, who had been unhappy and died young. The past is delicately conjured in family legend, in the flaunting airs and graces of the South, in dove-coloured velvet and eighteen-inch waists; the present materializes in the fat, shabby and lugubriously sentimental person of Uncle Gabriel, whose bride Amy had been for a few weeks. The effect is too deliberate, but all the same something of enchantment hangs over Amy and her capricious duel with death. "Noon Wine" is the story of a Swede who turned up one day at a small Texan dairy farm asking for work and stayed there for nine years. The man was blankly, oppressively silent, shut in on himself. It is the discovery that he had escaped from a madhouse that brings murder and self-destruction into a tale that had seemed to grow to idyllic shape. Again the effect is both suddenly piercing and slightly manufactured. The title-story, in which the child Miranda of "Old Mortality" has become a newspaper reporter, is an elegy-rhapsody of love in the last year of the War. It strikes tender and passionate notes, it captures vivid and arresting images, but it also cultivates beauty too assiduously.

That, indeed, is the failing of the book. The realistic and passionless transcript and the heroic romance are both being overdone just now, and it is a poetic sense such as Mrs. Porter tries to communicate in these stories that might best fortify the novelist not yet paralysed by war fever or enslaved by Miss Literature. But as for beauty, almost the last way of achieving it in a novel is by cultivating it.

THE LEANING TOWER
AND OTHER STORIES

Miss Porter's New Stories

GERTRUDE BUCKMAN

It has for a long time been apparent that Katherine Anne Porter consistently writes a luminous prose, of an exactness of choice and suggestiveness of phrasing, which is altogether extraordinary. Miss Porter's work has probably been subjected to the kind of scrutiny that most writers hardly dare to hope for, rarely achieve, and can almost never withstand. That Miss Porter can bear such careful reading proves her much more than simply an excellent stylist. Even at their slightest, even when as in this, her latest collection, she has written stories which at first glance seem to be little more than self-indulgent puffs of nostalgia, she holds so fast to reality, there is so much heart in her accuracy, that the stories spread out beyond the bare meanings of the words and the incidents related, to become authoritative and substantial images of an entire society.

Though there are no stories in this volume as first-rate as her previous best, and the group has none of the unified impact, the impressiveness of the earlier books, her essential qualities of purity and delicacy are again revealed. It is difficult to trace the literary influences that have shaped her writing; whatever of them she has found useful, she has absorbed; there has been a transmutation of elements; she continues to speak in her own voice, clear, straightforward, serene.

Miss Porter moves freely in a number of realms; her sensibility has not impelled her to breathe only in a rarer atmosphere; she is *of* the world, its objects are her familiars, she recognizes them and enjoys them for what they are, knows their place in our lives. Her imaginative power springs from her alert sense of the actual. Though as "feminine" a writer as Virginia Woolf, she could hardly be more different from her in this. She has avoided neither squalor nor evil in their many aspects. To watch the ways of human beings is

Reprinted with permission of the journal from the *Partisan Review* 12 (Winter 1945): 134.

to witness too many horrors, and Miss Porter has not been afraid to look at anything, nor to tell what she has seen, and a straight categorical account of the betrayals, thefts, murders, hatreds and terrors in her stories would make her out another James Cain. What lifts her every time is love; not love that sentimentalizes corruption, but love that gives her a sad wisdom even as it carries her to joyousness. In the face of ugliness she neither becomes hard nor succumbs to the bald jargon of the amateur analyst. She utilizes her knowledge in the ways of art. Her tone undergoes the subtlest of alterations with her theme; and if she does not shock us it is because she knows how to prepare us. She properly leaves the sensationalism to the lesser artists, herself using a stricter method, which is more admirable even where it does not altogether succeed, and which makes it possible to contemplate a page of her writing, come upon unexpectedly, with a sense of peace.

"That True and Human World"

F. O. MATTHIESSEN

Miss Porter's high reputation among nearly all schools of critics may now have reached the point where it is doing her a disservice. She is bracketed as "a writer's writer," which she certainly is, so far as that phrase implies that almost any other craftsman can learn important things from her about the handling of both language and structure. But the common reader has too frequently been led to believe that "style" is something esoteric, something to be relished apart from what it conveys, and that Miss Porter's relatively slim production must mean that she has not much to say. This misconception has also been nourished unwittingly by her admirers who like her quality so much that they want more and keep urging her to write a novel. But Miss Porter herself, when introducing the work of Eudora Welty, saw that for the master of the short story the novel may simply be the next trap ahead. The assumed superiority of the longer form is a product of our American supposition that bigger must be better, and has blown up many a lyric poet into an abortive epic bard, as well as the content adequate for a decent novel into a limp trilogy.

What we tend to forget is that in such a characteristically French form as the novelette, in the story of twenty to forty thousand words, we have also an American tradition. The kind of intensification that Melville gained in *Benito Cereno* and *Billy Budd,* and that James, working so differently, accomplished in *Pandora, The Coxon Fund, The Bench of Desolation,* and a dozen others, would seem to have much to offer to our period whose syntheses are often so precarious that they may be lost through extension. Miss Porter has set her special signature on this form, as Hemingway has on the contemporary practice of the short story. Not that she hasn't worked brilliantly in short stories as well, but sometimes hers can seem too fragmentary, as, for instance, do the first half dozen pieces in this new volume in comparison with the more integrated structure of *Old Mortality,* which dealt with the same descendants of Kentucky against a Louisiana and Texas background.

Yet these very stories can demonstrate the searching originality of her content. She may seem to be dealing with the stock material of the local colorists,

Reprinted with permission of *Accent* from *Accent* 5 (Winter 1945): 121–23.

with older Southern manners and customs as they persisted down into this century. Yet you quickly realize, in "The Old Order" and "The Last Leaf," that the human relationships are being examined with a new depth and honesty, that the sentimental view of the devoted old slave living on serenely with her former mistress is punctured once for all by such a quiet observation as that Nannie thrived on "a species of kindness not so indulgent, maybe, as that given to the puppies."

Such discoveries of the living intricacy in any relationship are Miss Porter's most recurrent resource. A passage at the end of "The Grave," the last of this group, gives a very explicit clue as to how she comes into possession of her material. This passage records how Miranda, by a chance of seemingly irrelevant association, is suddenly struck with the full violence of an episode long buried in her childhood, by her first knowledge of the mystery of birth as it had come to her through seeing a pregnant rabbit that her brother had shot and was skinning. This passage, too long to quote here, reveals Miss Porter's understanding of how much enters into any mature experience, of how deeply bathed in imaginative richness any event must be if it is to become a fluid and viable symbol.

The frequence with which violence lies at the heart of her discoveries helps to explain a main source of strength in her delicate prose. "The Circus," the best short story here, conveys the naked agony with which Miranda, too young to grasp the conventions, reacts to the dangers and brutalities of the show. What the others can take in the comic spirit presses upon her as a first initiation into the pity and terror of life. Violence in modern fiction has been so often a substitute for understanding that Miss Porter's ability to use it to reveal ethical values is another of her particular distinctions, as she showed especially in *Noon Wine*. In "The Downward Path to Wisdom," one of the three longer stories in this collection, her control seems far less sure, since the brutalities which are poured down upon the helpless child by his elders are not sufficiently motivated to make a coherent pattern. Violence seems to have been manipulated almost for its own sake.

Still another of Miss Porter's distinctions has been her refutation of the local colorists and other narrow regionalists by her extraordinary ability to portray a whole series of different environments. It may only be our anticipation of so much variety from her that causes a story like "A Day's Work" to seem for the first time a repetition of material handled more freshly in "The Cracked Looking-Glass." In comparison with that earlier story, which was a sustained miracle of Irish feeling and rhythm, both the situation and characters here may seem slightly expected. But when we turn to the longest story, to the novelette which gives title to the volume, we have again the rare combination of virtuosity with moral penetration.

Here Miss Porter uses a controlling symbol in the way that James often did, since the leaning tower not only is a souvenir of the Berlin landlady's long past happiness in Italy, but also becomes a compelling image for the tottering balance of the German world in the year before Hitler's rise to power. Many best-selling accounts have now been written of that time, and yet it seems doubtful whether any of them will preserve its form and pressure longer than Miss Porter's presentation of it through the consciousness of a young American painter. The reason for her success may be suggested by a comment James once made when noting that Turgenieff's *Memoirs of a Sportsman,* dealing with the question of serfdom, had appeared in the very same year as *Uncle Tom's Cabin:* "No single episode pleads conclusively against the 'peculiar institution' of Russia; the lesson is the cumulative testimony of a multitude of fine touches—in an after-sense of sadness that sets wise readers thinking . . . It offers a capital example of moral meaning giving a sense to form and form giving relief to moral meaning."

Some of Miss Porter's "fine touches" consist in her recurrent stress on the city's poverty, through Charles Upton's gradual realization of the difference from the depression he had left behind at home, where everybody took it for granted that things would improve, whereas in Berlin "the sufferers seemed to know that they had no cause for hope." No journalist or social historian analyzing the collapse of the republic has come closer to the central cause. And concerning the interpenetration of form and moral meaning, a comparison with Christopher Isherwood's *Good-Bye to Berlin* in instructive. Isherwood looked back to the same kind of student and boarding house life, and he dealt more explicitly with some of the manifestations of social decay. But his characters seem self-consciously worked up from a Freudian hand-book, or they exist to shock like the figures in a cinema thriller. They have none of the deep authenticity that springs from Miss Porter's humility and tenderness before life. She has been able to apprehend many kinds of Germans, ranging from the lumpish solemn mathematician who "loves study and quiet" to the young aristocrat whose new cheek-wound brings out in his expression a mixture of "amazing arrogance, pleasure, inexpressible vanity and self-satisfaction." Miss Porter does not slight the bestial brutalities in this hard city. No more, however, does she indulge in easy propaganda. When Charles Upton remarks lightly that Americans are sentimental and "like just everybody," the young mathematician stares at him earnestly and says: "I do not think you really like anybody, you Americans. You are indifferent to everybody and so it is easy for you to be gay, to be careless, to seem friendly. You are really cold-hearted indifferent people."

As a result of weaving back and forth through contradictions and incongruities, from one flickering center of human conviction to another, Miss Porter has done again what she did in *Pale Horse, Pale Rider.* She has created the atmosphere of a haunting moment of crisis. In that earlier novelette she gave us the end of the last war as it was felt in America through the crazy fever of the flu epidemic. Here, as she brings her group of students close together for a moment of New Year's Eve conviviality, what reverberates through their every speech and gesture is a premonition of disaster. In writing of Miss Welty, Miss Porter warned the artist against political beliefs, but here we can see that her remark was not the reactionary one that such a remark generally is. For she has penetrated into the economic and social sicknesses that brought on Fascism, but she has also held to her knowledge that the realm of the creator of fiction must be broader and more resilient than theories or opinions, that it can be nothing less than "that true and human world of which the artist is a living part."

SHIP OF FOOLS

Bound for Bremerhaven—and Eternity

LOUIS AUCHINCLOSS

Katherine Anne Porter's first novel, which she started in 1941 and completed two decades later, brings none of the disillusionment usually associated with long awaited things.

Miss Porter has selected neither her country nor her countrymen as her principal models. We know precisely the where and when of her characters for they are all passengers or crew of the North American Lloyd S. A. Vera en route from Veracruz to Bremerhaven, August 22–September 17, 1931. As the author states in a foreword, she has taken the "old and durable and dearly familiar" image of the ship of this world on its voyage to eternity. The small, first class contains a motley of nationalities, prevailingly German, and in steerage are 876 Spanish workers, deported from Cuba to Spain because of the failure of the sugar market. Jammed in below deck in a fetid atmosphere of sweating flesh where seven babies are born in the course of the trip, they are presented to the reader as a mass, a device which successfully simulates the pyramid of the human condition of earth: a huge poverty-stricken base and a tiny self-conscious peak. Steerage is never insisted on in the novel; it never becomes a bore, but the reader, like the first-class passengers, even the most hard-boiled of them, is always uneasily aware that it is there.

First class, like first class anywhere, is rampant with offended vanities and frustrations. Nobody is treated in accordance with what he deems to be his dignity. Nobody is satisfied with his cabin, his cabin mates, his table or table companions. The wretched little shipboard romances are all abortive. The stout publisher of the ladies garment trade journal fails with the skinny Fraulein Lizzi, the Texan engineer with the Spanish dancer, the ship's doctor with the Condesa, the young officer with the middle-aged Mr. Treadwell, the sixteen-year-old Swiss girl with the Cuban medical student. And Jenny and David, the American lovers who have been separated for the trip in different cabins, find, in the artificial barrier between them, opportunities for newer and deeper misunderstanding.

Only two major events occur on the whole trip: a German businessman is removed from the Captain's table when it is discovered that his wife (not on board) is a Jewess, and a poor old bulldog, pushed over the rail by a pair of villainous Spanish children, is rescued by a steerage passenger who is drowned in the process. It is no doubt significant that the rescuer is a woodcarver, whose knife has been confiscated, and that three great whales appear, spouting and swimming southward, immediately after his burial at sea. Miss Porter's book is rich enough to be read on different levels and will keep the lovers of symbols happy. To me it is enough that the woodcarver is the one person on board capable of a disinterested act. If he has redeemed the ship's company by his self-sacrifice, it is not long before they need redemption again.

For Miss Porter does not moon like a modern playwright over loneliness and the tragic difficulties of communication. Her characters cannot communicate because they reject communication. They have decided in advance what is due them in the way of honor, friendship and love, and they have predefined their friends and lovers as persons who must supply these needs. They are not looking for human beings but for fantasies. Consequently, they must reject, even hate the persons who seem to offer friendship or love. But their plight is not really pitiable. Selfishness and egotism are not pitiable. They can be funny and parts of the book are uproariously funny. But Miss Porter is never guilty of the sentimentality that masquerades as compassion. When she evokes pity, it is for the sheer horror of what she describes: the beggar at Veracruz, at the beginning of the novel, who has been so intricately maimed in preparation for his calling that he hardly resembles a human being. He does not come aboard, but a hunchback does, and we never lose sight of either.

How then does the author sustain the interest through five hundred pages dominated by a group of Germans, pedantic, sentimental, prejudiced and cruel, who are going to stamp their feet and shout themselves hoarse for Hitler in a year's time? Because this vivid, beautifully written story is bathed in intelligence and humor. Because Miss Porter can make her reader feel how easy it would be for anyone to turn into even the most repellent of these incipient Nazis, how simply the most monstrous things can grow out of fear. None of us is so different; we are all, as her title implies, fools—German, Spanish, Cuban, Swiss, American fools. The Spanish dancers shrug at the anti-Semitism of the Germans, the Germans at the thievery of the Spanish dancers. The American girl observes and ineffectively protests. And out of our foolishness a world may be born that is worse than the world we inherited. But it doesn't have to be. There is no feeling in the book that the fools are doomed to be fools. They can be what they wish—all but the maimed beggar.

There is a magnificent scene at the Captain's table after Herr Freytag has been expelled because of the discovery of his absent wife's Jewish origin. Until then nobody has had a thing against him; immediately afterwards he represents a threat and his elimination an infinitely reassuring factor. The ring is closed again; the faces relax with sensual gratification. They exchange toasts, smack their lips and say "Ja, ja!" "Even little Frau Schmitt, who suffered at the very thought of the miseries of the world; who wished only to love and to be loved by everybody; who shed tears with sick animals and unhappy children now felt herself a part of this soothing yet strengthening fellowship." The gas chambers are ready.

Miss Porter supplies a passenger list to which it is necessary to make frequent references in reading her early chapters. But, as in the case of the big Victorian novels, the effort involved in meeting the characters pays off in the richness of illusion created. The reader feels that he has been on board the Vera for the twenty-six days of her voyage but unlike his fellow passengers, he is reluctant to disembark.

Voyage to Everywhere

Sybille Bedford

Ship of Fools, Das Narrenschiff, Stultifera Navis: I took for my own this simple
almost universal image of the ship of this world on its voyage to eternity. It is
by no means new—it [is] very old and durable and dearly familiar . . . and it
suits my purpose exactly. I am a passenger on that ship. Katherine Anne
Porter has written a tremendous novel. It took twenty years. One might
pause for an instant to imagine this. Twenty years. The courage, the discipline, the fortitude; the cost of every kind, the pressures involved in bearing
what must have been at times an almost intolerable burden. And here it is at
last, the legend become print: the book has been out (in the United States)
for barely half a year and already something of its substance has eaten itself
into the marrow of those who read it. The Great American Novel has
appeared; ironically, it has turned out to be a great universal novel.

The framework is a voyage on a ship of the North German Lloyd from
Veracruz to Bremerhaven in 1931, lasting twenty-seven days. The theme is
not (as might be said) an icy condemnation of the human race, but a condemnation of its condition: a clinical exposition, point counterpoint, of the facts of
the flesh, the quakings of the spirit, the unavailing antics and defences against
the whole unalterable mesh of fear, lust, greed, decay, private demons, random
malice, death and alienation. The passengers embark—*"Quand partons-nous vers
le bonheur?"*—at Veracruz. And here at once in a few opening pages we have
what may well endure as one of the indelible set-pieces of black literature: the
gruesomeness and beauty of Mexico, and its blank indifference, the anguish
of all journeys. The Mexicans of the white-linen class staring behind their iced
limeades into the square, the shapeless, sweaty, pink-faced travellers trudging
from stony-eyed clerk to clerk, from customs shed to office, the cycle of the
fish-scrap (gross Germanic soup-scoops as well as delicious things: Miss
Porter's dichotomous attitude to the food on her ship invites a thesis), we sit
in those musty cabins while the men shave and the women let their hair
down, we hear them and above all, we see. The lamentable shape of many of
the German passengers, the youth and slenderness of the Spanish sluts, the

Reprinted with permission of the journal from the (London) *Spectator* 209 (16 November 1962):
763–64.

huge, mysteriously tormented Swede sleeping with his feet outside the upper bunk, Herr and Frau Professor mopping up after their dog. We see the captain's wattles swell purple in temper and the greasy pores of the unloved Swiss girl. We see them skip and waddle and stride towards one another—on Katherine Anne Porter's ship the people are what they look, and they do as they are. They sleep with each other, or try to (she is a virtuoso of such situations), take virulent dislikes, band together, score off, snub. A man goes overboard: there are some acts of violence (the least expected of them has a disturbing echo in one of the author's early stories). Some ugly things occur. Every scene, every incident, every interchange, is convincing, alive, is happening, has happened before our eyes. When it is over, one stops (if one does stop) and asks, how was it done? How does she do it? With words, evidently. Miss Porter's style is elegant and precise; it is straight without being thin, rich without the slightest trace of cloying. It is neither colloquial nor baroque, and she never permits herself a mannerism or an idiosyncrasy. In fact, it is a very fine style, put to use with the greatest skill, but this style and her words have a way of vanishing from consciousness and the page while flesh and blood take over.

Miss Porter's contrapuntal theme of hopelessness is perhaps most originally sustained by six of her main characters, or rather by three couples. These are: the Spanish twins; the American lovers, Jenny angel and David darling; and two of the Germans, Herr Rieber and Fräulein Lizzi Spöckenkieker. The Spanish twins are six years old. They are dead-end characters (a Katherine Anne Porter specialty), born purely malevolent, without a spark of anything else, and nothing whatsoever will redeem them. (We *are* made to believe this.) This little boy and girl, "as light as if their bones were hollow," hate all grown-ups, other children, animals, and they make the children in *A High Wind in Jamaica* and *The Turn of the Screw* appear rational, amenable human beings. The young American lovers, conscious creatures of good will, enact throughout one irremediable predicament: they cannot love each other in each other's presence. They meet filled with tenderness, remorse; they walk round deck, and once again they melt and hope. And here, too, it is made quite clear that they cannot let each other go, nor ever be at peace together. Herr Rieber is a bouncing, bumptious, genial little German, full of coyness, sentimentality and good cheer, who goes off the deep end on the subject of the master race. There is one notable passage.

> Herr Rieber and Lizzi Spöckenkieker pranced on to the deck, and Lizzi screamed out. . . . "Oh, what do you think of this dreadful fellow? Can you guess what he just said? I was saying 'Oh, these poor people, what can be done for them?' and this monster"—she gave a kind of whinny between hysteria and indignation—"he said, 'I would do this for them: I would put them all in a big oven and turn on the gas.' Oh," she said weakly, doubling over with laughter, "isn't that the most original idea you ever heard?"

Herr Rieber stood by smiling broadly, quite pleased with himself. . . . Lizzi said, "Oh, he did not mean any harm, of course, only to fumigate them, isn't that so?"

"No, I did not mean fumigate," said Herr Rieber stubbornly.

The other Germans on board, who think that Herr Rieber, whom they look down on socially, goes too far, are heftily united in their feelings about German blood, their nationalism, their laments over the lost war, their contempt for America (polluted by The Negro) and their terror of and disgust with the smell of the poor, the Spanish rabble in the steerage. When there is some trouble down there, the captain, a blustering bully, behaves abominably out of sheer acquired inhumanity and funk; and there is one very nasty episode indeed, an act of anti-Semitism, not violent and rather more sinister for being aimed at the absent wife of a Christian passenger, which leaves a mark on the whole voyage.

Ship of Fools will be and has been called anti-German. One might as well say that the book is anti-human. The Spaniards, Americans, Mexicans and Cubans on that ship come out differently, but they do not come out any better. Two out of the limited number—four?—six?—of "decent" characters are German, Dr. Schumann and Frau Otto Schmitt. Miss Porter took some Germans of the early 1930s as she found them, but surely this choice of nationalities is subordinate and incidental to the main theme of her work? If she had chosen, she might have had her ship captained by a chauvinistic French climber or a jingoistic Englishman with the same ultimate effect.

Faults? Miss Porter believes in the repeated blow, the massed detail. The book might have been even more effective, more stunning, for less length. Bulk, whatever the quality, blunts. Also, there is perhaps rather too much insistence (de-verbalized Huxleyan) on armpits, smells and fat. And we would have been *as* horrified if she had gone a little more lightly on the grotesques. Did the only Jew on board have to be such an utter wretch? did he *have* to trade in rosaries? Could we not have done without the actual hunchback on the passenger list? But this comes dangerously near to quarrelling with the artist's vision. (Being not wholly certain about Mrs. Treadwell does not. She is the one main character over whom the author seems to waver. There is something magaziney about that lady and her inner monologues.) There is something else that might be looked at as a flaw: the novel remains static, the characters move on trampolines towards crescendos, not towards development; there is accumulation, straws on camels' backs, but no choice, no crossroads, no turning-points. But this *is* quarrelling with the artist's vision, for the point is that hers is not in terms of classical tragedy or Jamesian decisions: her cards *are* already stacked, the tableau *is* the *donum*.

There are moments of transport, of otherness. When the boy and the Spanish dancer make love for the first time (the boy having about killed his uncle to get some money to pay the girl and her pimp), the key changes and one is utterly carried away, and it is young and sensuous and good. Then there are the Mexican bride and groom, the lovers who do not speak, who float, silent, hand in hand, past the more solid apparitions. But the Mexican lovers have been left on another plane, they are never substantiated and remain, too faintly, a symbol. Perhaps the high moment of the book comes when the whales are seen, three whales flashing white and silver in the sunlight, spouting tall white fountains, and the Spanish twins wave their arms in pure ecstasy, and "not one person could take his eyes from the beautiful spectacle . . . and their minds were cleansed of death and violence."

But the whales recede. There are no windows after all on that voyage, no wider views, no liberation. Only escapes. Wine, food and loving destroy the body. The intellectuals on board are arid pedants. Religion does not get off the ground; art remains extraneous; pity is self-pity; love the *angst*-ridden cry of self-love. There is one single italicized passage in the book, it comes towards the end, and it goes:

> What they were saying to each other was only, "*Love me, love me in spite of all! Whether or not I love you, whether I am fit to love, whether you are able to love, even if there is no such thing as love, love me!*"

They will not. Not for long; not enough. On that ship there is no help, no hope, no light, no change. *There will be no message.* The best one can do is to muster a thin form of modern stoicism, some *tenue,* behave with a little more dignity than the next person. It is better not to cry in public, not to wolf one's food, to keep one's waistline, carry one's liquor, for women to wear clothes accordant with their age; there is something to be said for the masculine passion for physical discipline, the German addiction to duty. . . . It is not the noblest hypothesis about the voyage; it is one that has been held—and denied—by artists and laymen through centuries. *Ship of Fools* is a sustained version. Katherine Anne Porter has given us a Brueghel; we can hope, but cannot be sure, that it is less true than a Piero della Francesca.

THE COLLECTED STORIES

A Poet of the Story

Howard Moss

Praised so often as a "craftsman," a "stylist" and a "master of prose"; Katherine Anne Porter must occasionally long to be admired for what she is—a writer. Through an inability to compromise and sheer endurance, Miss Porter, who is an artist, has come to represent Art, and though the role has never obscured the quality of her work, it has shifted attention away from the content of the work itself. The first concern of these stories is not esthetic. Extraordinarily well-formed, often brilliantly written, they are firmly grounded in life; and the accuracy and precision of their surfaces, so disarmingly easy to read, hold in tension the confused human tangles below. Experience is the reason for their having been written, yet experience does not exist in them for its own sake; it has been formulated, but not simplified.

These stories turn on crises, as stories should, but two special gifts are evident: depth of characterization, which is more usually the province of the novelist, and a style that encompasses the symbolic without sacrificing naturalness. Miss Porter is a "realist," but one who knows the connotations as well as the meaning of words. Understatement and inflation are equally foreign to her; she is never flat and she is never fancy. In the best of her work, the factual and the lyrical are kept in perfect balance.

She values the symbol, but she is not, strictly speaking, a symbolic writer. Observed life is the generating factor, and though it may connect with a larger metaphor it is rooted in the everyday realities of people, situations and places. The names of the three books collected here supply us with a clue to their author's method: though the stories from which they are drawn have, of course, their singular characters and actions, the title of each suggests a wider meaning. Betrayal in "Flowering Judas," death in "Pale Horse, Pale Rider," and precarious balance in "The Leaning Tower" are both specific and general. Their titles do not belie their particular natures. Yet, being them-

Reprinted with permission of the *New York Times* from the *New York Times Book Review*, 12 September 1965, 1, 26.

selves, they are more than themselves. They have subjects, but they also have themes.

The clarity of the prose in which these stories are written allows for subtle undercurrents. The qualities of poems—compression, spontaneity, the ability to make connections, the exploitation of all the resources of language—are present, but nothing could be more inimical to Miss Porter's way of doing things than the self-consciousness of "poetic prose." Incident and character are her means; syntax is her instrument; and revelation is her goal. Cocteau once made a distinction between poetry in the theater and the poetry *of* the theater. Miss Porter is a poet *of* the short story, and she never confuses the issue.

Because the ambiguity of good and evil is the major theme, betrayal is a frequent subject of these stories—betrayal of the self as well as of others. Certain preoccupations reoccur: the hollowness of faith, both religious and political; the mask of charitableness used by the uncommitted and the unloving to disguise their lack of involvement; the eroding effects of dependency; the power of delusion. Many of the characters have something in common: their actions being hopelessly at war with their motives, with the best of intentions, they are lured toward an ironic terror.

Representatives of one of Miss Porter's major notions—since we cannot leave each other alone, it is not always as easy as it looks to tell the victim from the victimizer—they struggle to escape the necessity of confronting themselves. Vaguely hopeful of doing the right thing, they are hurled into a maelstrom of conflict by forces as mercurial and cunning as those used by the Greek gods. Fate is not, however, an abstraction in these stories. It is more the consequence of character—of weakness, dependence, or the inability to let go of illusion—than it is the drawing out of cosmic plots. Only in "Pale Horse, Pale Rider" do forces outside the self, war and disease, become the adversaries.

Evil, to Miss Porter, is a form of moral hypocrisy. In the person of Homer T. Hatch, the malevolent, Lucifer-like catalyst of "Noon Wine," who roams the country collecting rewards on escaped prisoners and mental patients, it operates under the banner of social justice in the cause of profiteering. In Braggioni, the successful revolutionary of "Flowering Judas," it is seen as the degraded daydream of the ideal, which has not only been corrupted by power and sentimentality, but has transformed itself into a complacent form of intimidation. In the two Liberty Bond salesmen who menace Miranda in "Pale Horse, Pale Rider," it takes on the totalitarian cloak of enforced "patriotism."

Moral hypocrisy can disguise itself as anything from a worldwide political movement to self-delusion—but the self-deluded are not necessarily evil. They can evoke our sympathy, perhaps treacherously; they are distinguished from the evil-doer by two important facts. Evil is single-minded—a rough definition of it, in the canon of Miss Porter's fiction, might simply be a view of life that cannot see that everything is at least two-sided. And it lies in a special way, by producing terror in the name of good. By having the power—or worse, by being given it—to impose its vision of the world on other people, it destroys.

The nature of how and why power is given, where the distinction between the victim and the victimizer gets blurred, is the subject of "Theft." More than a purse is stolen; identity and self-respect are lost by a middle-aged woman who allows herself to be victimized. The innocent can be made to feel guilty. But Miss Porter brings up an unpleasant question: By *allowing* themselves to be *made* to feel guilty, are they *not* guilty? The problem becomes more profound as the field widens or deepens. In "The Leaning Tower," the identity and self-respect of a whole nation is at stake. In "Noon Wine," the very nature of guilt, identity and self-respect is brought under scrutiny.

Miss Porter can reverse the binoculars either way; she is after the small despot as well as the large one. No one knows better than she that tyranny begins at home. The egotism, pride and self-pity of the Germans in "The Leaning Tower" have their domestic counterparts in an American family in "The Downward Path to Wisdom." It ends with a little boy singing a song to himself that goes "I hate Papa, I hate Mama, I hate Uncle David, I hate Old Janet, I hate Marjory, I hate Papa, I hate Mama." The little boy, unlike some of the characters in "The Leaning Tower," has not yet learned to hate whole races and nations. But since his song is an early composition, the chances that he will are good.

The closest thing to a spokesman the author allows herself is a woman called Miranda, but the one truly innocent world that emerges from these stories can be found in the eight reminiscences of the South that were originally published in "The Leaning Tower." Officially "fiction," they seem to be creations of pure memory and are filled with the sights and sounds of childhood recollection. Beyond this limited nostalgia, innocent but often painful, only the natural and the primitive remain undamaged by the counter claims of the world.

That may be why Miss Porter's two favorite settings are Texas and Mexico. In both, a primitive view of life does not exclude what is morally decent and necessary. The Indian peasants in the Mexican stories, the farmers and Negroes in the Southern ones, are neither good nor bad in any conventional sense. They may be violent, but they act from an implicit set of values in which instinct and feeling have not yet been corroded. The heroine of "María Concepción" kills her rival but is protected from the police by her friends—and even her enemies—in a pact as ancient as jealousy and murder. Morality is pragmatic and involves the living. The mere fact of being alive is more important than justice for the dead.

A different but analogous situation confronts Miranda in "Old Mortality." Nurtured on a romantic version of the past, she learns others; having come to doubt them all, she believes that in *her* life, at least, she will be able to separate legend from falsehood—"in her hopefulness, her ignorance," Miss Porter adds. But the code of the Indian peasant is centered on the continuation of life; it is less concerned with truth as a specific fact, and least of all with truth as an abstract generalization. María Concepción is separated from Miranda by a wide gulf. María has faith in life, whereas Miranda puts her trust in the truth. Over and over in these stories, they turn out not to be the same thing. María (like Mr. Thompson in "Noon Wine") commits an act of murder that is, paradoxically, an act of faith in life. Miranda (like Laura in "Flowering Judas" and Charles in "The Leaning Tower") has no faith in the name of which an act can be committed.

The author has added to this collection of her three books of stories, a magnificent new long story, "Holiday," three shorter ones and a modest preface. Good as most of these stories are, they are overshadowed by one work. If it is the function of the artist to produce a masterpiece Miss Porter may rest easy. In "Noon Wine" she has written a short novel whose largeness of theme, tragic inevitability, and steadiness of focus put it into that small category of superb short fiction that includes Joyce, Mann, Chekhov, James and Conrad. A study of the effects of evil, it is a story one can turn around in the palm of one's hand forever. So many meanings radiate from it that each reading gives it a new shade and a further dimension. Without once raising its voice, it asks questions that have alarmed the ages, including our own: When a good man kills an evil man, does he become evil himself? If the answer is yes, then how are we to protect ourselves against evil? If the answer is no, then how are we to define what evil is? It is one of the nicer ambiguities of "Noon Wine" that the two "good" men in it commit murder while the one character who is "evil" does not.

In the fateful meeting of the farmer, Mr. Thompson, the deranged Swedish harmonica player, Mr. Helton, and the Devil's salesman, Mr. Hatch, Miss Porter has constructed one of those dramas that seem not so much to have been written as discovered intact, like a form in nature. In the perfection of "Noon Wine," she has achieved what she has worked for—the artist in total command, totally invisible.

CRITICAL ESSAYS
ON THE FICTION
◆

Katherine Anne Porter (Irony with a Center)

ROBERT PENN WARREN

The fiction of Katherine Anne Porter, despite the wide-spread critical adulation, has never found the public which its distinction merits. Many of her stories are unsurpassed in modern fiction, and some are not often equalled. She belongs to the relatively small group of writers—extraordinarily small, when one considers the vast number of stories published every year in English and American magazines—who have done serious, consistent, original, and vital work in the form of short fiction—the group which would include James Joyce, Katherine Mansfield, Sherwood Anderson, Ernest Hemingway, and Kay Boyle, for example. This list does not pretend to be exhaustive, and does not include a considerable number of other writers who, though often finding other forms more congenial, the novel or poetry, have scored occasional triumphs in the field of short fiction—such writers as William Faulkner, Willa Cather, John Steinbeck, John Bishop (I refer to his story, "If Only"), Caroline Gordon, Delmore Schwartz, Conrad Aiken, Yvor Winters. This list could be quite long. Then, of course, there is a very large group of writers who have a great facility, a great mechanical competence, and sometimes moments of real perception, but who work from no fundamental and central conviction. Their work feeds the hungry presses from which drop out the magazines.

It was once fashionable to argue complacently that the popular magazine had created the short-story—had provided the market and had cultivated an appetite for the product. But at the same time, and progressively, the magazine has corrupted the short story. For instance, a story by William Faulkner in *Collier's* is a cruel parody of his serious work. What the magazine encourages is not so much the short story as a conscious or unconscious division of the artistic self of the writer. Now one can still discover (as in an address delivered last year by Mr. Frederick Lewis Allen to the American Philosophical Society) a genial self-congratulation in the face of "mass appreciation." But, writes Mr. R. P. Blackmur in reply:

> In fact, mass appreciation of the kind which Mr. Allen approves represents the constant danger to the artist of any serious sort: the danger of popularization

Reprinted with the permission of the Robert Penn Warren Estate from *Kenyon Review* 4 (Winter 1942): 29–42.

before creation. . . . The difference between great art and popular art is relatively small; but the difference between either and popularized art is radical; and absolute. Popular art is topical and natural, great art is deliberate and thematic. What can be popularized in either is only what can be sold . . . a scheme which requires the constant replacement of the shoddy goods. He [Mr. Allen] does not mean to avow this; he no doubt means the contrary; but there it is. Until American or any other society is educated either up to the level or *back* to the level of art with standards, whether popular or great, it can be sold nothing but art without standards. . . .

This seems to be a good description of the context in which the contemporary writer of fiction must work. Some serious writers—and I mention again William Faulkner—have survived the division of the artistic self; others—William Saroyan, for instance—do not appear to be able to survive it. And this is the context which lends an additional, and not wholly adventitious, distinction to the stories of Miss Porter. She has not attempted to compromise with the situation.

The fact that she has not attempted a compromise may account for the relatively small body of her published fiction. There was the collection of stories published in 1931 under the title *Flowering Judas;* an enlarged collection, under the same title in 1935, which includes two novelettes, *The Cracked Looking Glass* and *Hacienda,* the latter of which had been previously published by Harrison, in Paris; a collection of three novelettes under the title *Pale Horse, Pale Rider,* in 1939; the Modern Library edition of *Flowering Judas;* and a few pieces, not yet in book form, which have appeared in various magazines, for instance, sections of the uncompleted biography of Cotton Mather and the brilliant story which appeared in the anniversary issue of *The Nation.*

Her method of composition does not, in itself, bend readily to the compromise. In many instances, a story or novelette has not been composed straight off. Instead, a section here and a section there has been written—little germinal scenes explored and developed. Or scenes or sketches of character which were never intended to be incorporated in the finished work have been developed in the process of trying to understand the full potentiality of the material. One might guess at an approach something like this: a special, local excitement provoked by the material—character or incident; an attempt to define the nature of that local excitement, as local—to squeeze it and not lose a drop; an attempt to understand the relationships of the local excitements and to define the implications—to arrive at theme; the struggle to reduce theme to pattern. That would seem to be the natural history of the characteristic story. It is a method which reminds one of a little of that of Turgeniev. Certainly, it is a method which requires time, scrupulosity, and contemplation. In other words, we find here an artistic integrity which is to be differentiated, on the one hand, from the "professional" sense which sets itself the half-million words a year of—I believe—Arnold Bennett's first writing year, and on the other hand, from the professional pride in being unprofessional, in the artistic sense—the pride in shutting your eyes and spilling your innards, in pouring out the pure spirit—the way of the writers whom Philip Rahv has called the "redskins" of American literature.

The method itself is an index to the characteristics of Miss Porter's fiction—the rich surface detail scattered with apparently casual profuseness and the close structure which makes such detail meaningful; the great compression and economy which one discovers upon analysis; the precision of psychology and observation, the texture of the style. Most reviewers commenting upon Miss Porter's special distinction, refer to her "style"—struck, no doubt, by an exceptional felicity of phrase, a precision in the use of metaphor and simile, and a rhythmical subtlety. But, no doubt, such comments, in the reviews, have chilled the heart of the potential reader, who—and I believe quite rightly—does not want to be lulled or titillated exquisitely by "beautiful style." He is put off by the reviewer's easy abstracting of style for comment and praise; his innocence repudiates the fallacy of "agreeable style." Style does not come to his attention as style.

But let us linger upon the matter of Miss Porter's style in the hope that it can be used as a point of departure. Take, for example, a paragraph from the title story of *Flowering Judas,* the description of Braggioni, the half-Italian, half-Indian revolutionist in Mexico, "a leader of men, skilled revolutionist, and his skin has been punctured in honorable warfare," and his followers "warm themselves in his reflected glory and say to each other: 'He has a real nobility, a love of humanity raised above mere personal affections.' The excess of this self-love has flowed out, inconveniently for her, over Laura"—the puzzled American girl who has been lured to Mexico by revolutionary enthusiasm and before whom he sits with his guitar and sings sentimental songs, while his wife weeps at home. But here is the passage.

> Braggioni . . . leans forward, balancing his paunch between his spread knees, and sings with tremendous emphasis; weighing his words. He has, the song relates, no father and no mother, not even a friend to console him; lonely as a wave of the sea he comes and goes, lonely as a wave. His mouth opens round and yearns sideways, his balloon cheeks grow oily with the labor of song. He bulges marvelously in his expensive garments. Over his lavender collar, crushed upon a purple necktie, held by a diamond hoop: over his ammunition belt of tooled leather worked in silver, buckled cruelly around his gaping middle: over the tops of his glossy yellow shoes Braggioni swells with ominous ripeness, his mauve silk hose stretched taut, his ankles bound with the stout leather thongs of his shoes.
>
> When he stretches his eyelids at Laura she notes again that his eyes are the true tawny yellow cat's eyes. He is rich, not in money, he tells her, but in power, and this power brings with it the blameless ownership of things, and the right to indulge his love of small luxuries. "I have a taste for elegant refinements," he said once, flourishing a yellow silk handkerchief before her nose.

"Smell that? It is Jockey Club, imported from New York." Nonetheless he is wounded by life. He will say so presently. "It is true everything turns to dust in the hand, to gall on the tongue." He sighs and his leather belt creaks like a saddle girth.

Indeed the passage is sharp and evocative. Its phrasing embodies a mixture, a fusion, of the shock of surprise and the satisfaction of precision—a resolved tension, which may do much to account for the resonance and vibration of the passage. We have in it the statement, "his mouth opens round and yearns sideways"—and we note the two words *yearns* and *sideways;* in the phrase, "labor of song"; in, "he bulges marvelously"; in, "Braggioni swells with ominous ripeness." But upon inspection it may be discovered that the effect of these details is not merely a local effect. The subtle local evocations really involve us in the center of the scene; we are taken to the core of the meaning of the scene, and thence to the central impulse of the story; and thence, possibly, to the germinal idea of all of this author's fiction. All of these filaments cannot be pursued back through the web—the occasion does not permit; but perhaps a few can be traced to the meaning of the scene itself in the story.

What we have here is the revolutionist who loves luxury, who feels that power gives blameless justification to the love of elegant refinements, but whose skin has been punctured in "honorable warfare"; who is a competent leader of men, but who is vain and indolent; who is sentimental and self-pitying, but, at the same time, ruthless; who betrays his wife and yet, upon his return home, will weep with his wife as she washes his feet and weeps; who labors for the good of man, but is filled with self-love. We have here a tissue of contradictions, and the very phraseology takes us to these contradictions. For instance, the word *yearns* involves the sentimental, blurred emotion, but immediately afterward the words *sideways* and *oily* remind us of the grossness, the brutality, the physical appetite. So with the implied paradox in the "labor of song." The ammunition belt, we recall, is buckled *cruelly* about his "gaping middle." The ammunition belt reminds us that this indolent, fat, apparently soft, vain man is capable of violent action, is a man of violent profession, and sets the stage for the word *cruelly,* which involves the paradox of the man who loves mankind and is capable of individual cruelties, and which, further, reminds us that he punishes himself out of physical vanity and punishes himself by defining himself in his calling—the only thing that buckles in his sprawling, meaningless animality. He swells with "ominous ripeness"—and we sense the violent threat in the man as contrasted with his softness, a kind of great over-ripe plum dangerous as a grenade, a feeling of corruption mixed with sentimental sweetness; and specifically we are reminded of the threat to Laura in the situation. We come to the phrase "wounded by life," and we pick up again the motif hinted at in the song and in the lingering rhythms: "He has, the song relates, no father and no mother, nor even a friend to console him; lonely as a wave of the sea he comes and goes, lonely as a wave." In nothing is there to be found a balm—not in revolution, in vanity, in love—for the "vast cureless wound of his self-esteem." Then, after the bit about the wound, we find the sentence: "He sighs and his leather belt creaks like a saddle girth." The defeated, sentimental sigh, the cureless wound, and the bestial creaking of the leather.

If this reading of the passage is acceptable, the passage itself is a rendering of the problem which the character of Braggioni poses to Laura. It is stated, in bare, synoptic form, elsewhere:

> The gluttonous bulk of Braggioni has become a symbol of her many disillusions, for a revolutionist should be lean, animated by heroic faith, a vessel of abstract virtues. This is nonsense, she knows it now and is ashamed of it. Revolution must have leaders, and leadership is a career for energetic men. She is, her comrades tell her, full of romantic error, for what she defines as cynicism is to them merely a developed sense of reality.

What is the moral reality here? That question is, I should say, the theme of the story, which exists in an intricate tissue of paradox, and is only in the dream of Laura at the end, a dream which eludes but does not resolve the question.

But let us take one of the more extended pieces, one of the novelettes, *Old Mortality,* and consider the matter of the patterning of character and incident, and not of stylistic detail.

To begin, *Old Mortality* is relatively short, some 20,000 words, but it gives an impression of the mass of a novel. One contributing factor to this effect is the length of the time-span; the novelette falls into three sections, dated 1885–1902, 1904, and 1912. Another factor is the considerable number of the characters, who, despite the brevity of the story, are sketched in with great precision; we know little about them, but that little means much. Another, and not quite so obvious but perhaps more important, factor is the rich circumstantiality and easy discursiveness, especially in Part I, which sets the tone of the piece. The author lingers on anecdote, apparently just to relish the anecdote, to extract the humor or pathos—but in the end we discover that there has been no casual self-indulgence, or indulgence of the reader; the details of the easy anecdote, which seemed to exist at the moment for itself alone, have been working busily in the cellarage of our minds.

I shall be compelled, for evidence, to summarize the action of the story. Part I, 1885–1902, introduces us to two little girls, Maria and Miranda, aged twelve and eight, through whose eyes we see the family. There is the grandmother, who takes no part in the action of the story, but whose brief characterization, we discover, is important—the old lady who, "twice a year compelled in her blood by the change of seasons, would sit nearly all day beside old trunks and boxes in the lumber room, unfolding layers of garments and small keepsakes . . . unwrapping locks of hair and dried flowers, crying gently and easily as if tears were the only pleasure she had left." (Her piety—stirred by the equinoxes, as unreflecting as tropisms—provides the basic contrast for the end of the story; her piety does not achieve the form of legend—merely a compulsion of the blood, the focus of old affections.) There is the father, "a pleasant everyday sort of man"—who once shot to protect the family "honor" and had to run to Mexico. There is Cousin Eva, chinless and unbeautiful amidst the belles, who, when we first meet her, teaches Latin in a female seminary and tries to interest Maria and Miranda in that study by telling them the story of John Wilkes Booth, "who handsomely garbed in a long black cloak"—so the story is recast by the little girls—"had leaped to the stage after assassinating President Lincoln. 'Sic semper tyrannis,' he had shouted superbly, in spite of his broken leg." There is Amy, dead, already a legend, a beautiful sad family story, the girl who almost had a duel fought over her in New Orleans, who drove her suitor and cousin, Gabriel, almost to distraction before she married him, and who died under mysterious circumstances a few weeks after her marriage. There is Gabriel himself, fond of the races, cut off by his grandfather without a penny, a victim of the bottle in his bereavement; he marries again, Miss Honey, who can never compete with the legend of the dead Amy. In this section, the little girls attempt to make the people they know and the stories they have heard fit together, make sense; and always at the center is the story of Amy.

Part II, in contrast with Part I with its discursiveness, its blurring of time, its anecdotal richness, gives one fully developed scene, dated 1904. The father takes the little girls, on holiday from their convent school, to the races. There, out of family piety, they bet their dollar on Uncle Gabriel's horse—a poor hundred-to-one shot. (Piety and commonsense—they know even at their tender years that a hundred-to-one bet is no bet at all—are in conflict, and piety wins only because of the father's pressure.) But Gabriel's horse comes in, and they see for the first time their romantic Uncle Gabriel—"a shabby fat man with bloodshot blue eyes . . . and a big melancholy laugh like a groan"—now drunk, and after his victory, weeping. But he takes them to meet Miss Honey, Amy's successor, in his shabby apartment, and the little girls know that Miss Honey hates them all.

Part III, 1912, shows us Miranda on a train going to the funeral of Uncle Gabriel, who had died in Lexington, Kentucky, but has been brought home to lie beside Amy—to whom he belongs. On the train she meets Cousin Eva, whom she has not seen for many years, who has, since the days at the seminary, crusaded for woman suffrage and gone to jail for her convictions. The talk goes back to the family story, to Amy, beside whom Gabriel will now rest. "Everybody loved Amy," Miranda remarks, but Cousin Eva replies; "Not everybody by a long shot. . . . She had enemies. If she knew she pretended she didn't. . . . She was sweet as honeycomb to everybody. . . . That was the trouble. She went through life like a spoiled darling, doing as she pleased and letting other people suffer for it." Then: "I never believed for one moment," says Cousin Eva, putting her mouth close to Miranda's ear and breathing peppermint hotly into it, "that Amy was an impure woman. Never! But let me tell you, there were plenty who did believe it." So Cousin Eva begins to re-interpret the past, all the romantic past, the legend of Amy, who, according to Cousin Eva, was not beautiful, just good-looking, whose illness hadn't been romantic, and who had, she says, committed suicide.

Cousin Eva defines the bitter rivalry under the gaiety of the legend, the vicious competition among the belles. And more:

> Cousin Eva wrung her hands. "It was just sex," she said in despair; [The word *despair,* caught in the frustrated and yet victorious old woman's casual gesture, is important—a resonance from her personal story which gives an echo to the theme of the story itself.] "their minds dwelt on nothing else. They didn't call it that, it was all smothered under pretty names, but that's all it was, sex."

So Cousin Eva, who has given her life to learning and a progressive cause, defines all the legend in terms of economics and biology. "They simply festered inside," she says of all the Amy's, "they festered."

But Miranda, catching a Baudelairian vision of "corruption concealed under lace and flowers" thinks quite coldly: "Of course, it was not like that. This is no more true than what I was told before, it's every bit as romantic." And in revulsion from Cousin Eva, she wants to get home, though she is grown and married now, and see her father and sister, who are solid and alive, are not merely "definitions." But when she arrives her father cannot take her in, in the old way. He turns to Cousin Eva. And the two old people, who represent the competing views of the past—love and poetry opposed to biology and economics—sit down together in a world, their world of the past, which excludes Miranda. Miranda thinks: "Where are my own people and my own time?" She thinks, and the thought concludes the story: "Let them go on explaining how things happened. I don't care. At least I can know the truth about what happens to me, she assured herself silently, making a promise to herself, in her hopefulness, her ignorance."

So much for the action of the story. We see immediately that it is a story about legend, and it is an easy extension to the symbol for tradition, the meaning of the past for the present. We gradually become acquainted with the particular legend through the little girls, but the little girls themselves, in their innocence, criticize the legend. Their father, speaking of Amy's slimness, for instance, says: "There were never any fat women in the family, thank God." But the little girls remember Aunt Keziah, in Kentucky, who was famous for her heft. (Such an anecdote is developed richly and humorously, with no obvious pointing to the theme, beyond the logic of the context.) Such details, in Part I, develop the first criticism of the legend. In Part II, the contrast between Gabriel as legend and Gabriel as real extends the same type of criticism, but more dramatically; but here another, a moral criticism, enters in, for we have the effect of Amy on other people's lives, on Gabriel and Miss Honey. This, however, is not specified; it merely charges the scene of the meeting between Miranda and Cousin Eva on the way to Gabriel's funeral. Part III at first gives us, in Cousin Eva's words, the modern critical method applied to the legend; as if invoking Marx and Freud.

Up to this point, the line of the story has been developed fairly directly, though under a complicated texture. The story could end here, a story of repudiation, and some readers have interpreted it as such. But—and here comes the first reversal of the field—Miranda repudiates Cousin Eva's version, as romantic, too, in favor of the "reality" of her father and sisters, whom she is soon to see. But there is another shift. Miranda is cut off from her father, who turns to Cousin Eva, whose "myth" contradicts his "myth," but whose world he can share. Miranda, cut off, determines to leave them to their own sterile pursuit of trying to understand the past. She will understand herself, the truth of what happens to her. This would provide another point of rest for the story—a story about the brave younger generation, hope, courage, and honesty, and some readers have taken it thus. But—withheld cunningly until the end, until the last few words—there is a last reversal of the field. Miranda makes her promise to herself in "her hopefulness, her ignorance." And those two words, *hopefulness, ignorance,* suddenly echo throughout the story.

Miranda will find *a* truth, as it were, but it, too, will be a myth, for it will not be translatable, or, finally, communicable. But it will be the only truth she can win, and for better or worse she will have to live by it. She must live by her own myth. But she must earn her myth in the process of living. Her myth will be a new myth, different from the mutually competing myths of her father and Cousin Eva, but stemming from that antinomy. Those competing myths will simply provide the terms of her own dialectic of living.

We remember that the heroine's name is Miranda, and we may remember Miranda of Shakespeare's *Tempest,* who exclaims, "O brave new world, that has such people in it!" Perhaps the identity of the name is not an accident. Miranda of *Old Mortality* has passed a step beyond that moment of that exclamation, but she, too, has seen the pageant raised by Prospero's wand— the pageant evoked by her father, the pleasant everyday sort of father, who, however, is a Prospero, though lacking the other Prospero's irony. For *Old Mortality,* like the *Tempest,* is about illusion and reality, and comes to rest upon a perilous irony.

In *Old Mortality* Miss Porter has used very conventional materials; the conventional materials, however, are revitalized, by the intellectual scope of the interpretation and the precision and subtlety of structure. But Miss Porter has not committed herself to one type of material. The world of balls and horsemanship and romance is exchanged in *Noon Wine* for a poverty-ridden Texas farm, in *Pale Horse, Pale Rider,* for a newspaper office and a rooming house at the time of the World War I, in *Hacienda, Flowering Judas* and *Maria Concepcion* for Mexico, etc. We may ask, what is the common denominator of these stories, aside from the obvious similarities of style (though the style itself is very flexible)? What is the central "view," the central intuition?

In *Noon Wine* we have the story of a murder and suicide. Mr. Thompson, the farmer, kills the stranger who has come to take back to the lunatic asylum the farmhand who has made the farm pay. He does not know how or why he kills him, to protect the farmhand, into whose stomach he thinks he sees the stranger's knife being thrust, to protect his own interests, in self-defense, out of instinctive hatred for the stranger. He is acquitted in court, but his world is different. He feels a compulsion to explain himself to everyone, and to himself, and that becomes his obsession. At last, when he discovers that his own sons think of him as a murderer, he commits suicide, still fumbling for the definition of his own guilt. The nature of guilt, here, a paradox of motives, not the paradox of fact and myth. But the issue here, as in *Old Mortality,* is not to be decided simply; it is, in a sense, left suspended, the terms defined, but the argument left only at a provisional resolution. Poor Mr. Thompson— innocent and yet guilty—and in his passion for absolute definition unable to live by provisional.

The Cracked Looking Glass, too, is about guilt, the story of a high-spirited, pleasure-loving Irish girl, married to a much older man, faithful to him, yet needing the society of young, fun-provoking men, to whom she takes a motherly or sisterly attitude. She lives a kind of lie—in fact, she can't tell anything without giving it a romantic embroidery. Then she is horrified to discover that her Connecticut neighbors think her a bad woman, suspect her of infidelities. At the end, sitting in her tight kitchen with Old Dennis, "while beyond were far off places full of life and gaiety . . . and beyond everything like a green field with morning sun on it lay youth and Ireland," she leans over and puts her hand on her husband's knee, and asks him, in an ordinary voice: "Why ever did you marry a woman like me?"

Dennis says mind, she doesn't tip the chair over, and adds that he knew he could never do better. Then:

> She sat up and felt his sleeves carefully. "I want you to wrap up warm this bitter weather, Dennis," she told him. "With two pairs of socks and the chest-protector, for if anything happened to you, whatever would become of me in this world?"
>
> "Let's not think of it," said Dennis, shuffling his feet.
>
> "Let's not, then," said Rosaleen. "For I could cry if you crooked a finger at me."

Again the provisional resolution of the forces of the story: not a solution which Rosaleen can live by with surety, but one which she must re-learn and re-earn every day.

In these stories, and, as I believe, in stories like *Theft, Flowering Judas, Pale Horse, Pale Rider,* and other pieces, with the exception of *Hacienda* and *Magic* (which seem to lie outside the general body of Miss Porter's work), there is the same underlying structure of contrast and tension, the same paradoxical problems of definition, the same delicate balancing of rival considerations, the same scrupulous development of competing claims to attention and action, the same inter-play of the humorous and the serious, the same refusal to take the straight line, the formula, through the material at hand. This has implied for some readers that the underlying attitude is one of skepticism, negation, refusal to confront the need for immediate, water-tight, fool-proof solutions. The skeptical and ironical bias is, I think, important in Miss Porter's work, and it is true that her work wears an air of detachment and contemplation. But, I should say, her irony is an irony with a center, never an irony for irony's sake. It simply implies, I think, a refusal to accept the code, the formula, the ready-made solution, the hand-me-down morality, the word for the spirit. It affirms, rather, the constant need for exercising discrimination, the arduous obligation of the intellect in the face of conflicting dogmas, the need for a dialectical approach to matters of definition, the need for exercising as much of the human faculty as possible.

This basic attitude finds its correlation in her work, in the delicacy of phrase, the close structure, the counterpoint of incident and implication: that is, a story must test its thematic line at every point against its total circumstantiality, the thematic considerations must, as it were, be validated in terms of circumstance and experience, and never be resolved in the poverty of statement.

Concepts of Justice in the Work
of Katherine Anne Porter

Debra A. Moddelmog

One of the most promising developments in the interdisciplinary study of literature and law has emerged from the practice of critics who are analyzing literature for the cultural "work" it does. Within this perspective, literary works are seen, according to Jane Tompkins, as "agents of cultural formation" and are read for the way in which they "serve as a means of stating and proposing solutions for social and political predicaments" (xvii). Among the studies that interrelate law and literature in this kind of cultural-historical project are Susan Gillman's *Dark Twins* (1989) and Brook Thomas's *Cross-Examinations of Law and Literature* (1987). Gillman brings together legal writings and other "non-literary" materials in order to contextualize the work of Mark Twain as it refers to issues of identity, while Thomas uses "literary texts to interpret a period's legal history and a period's legal history to interrogate literary texts" (254).

These approaches are related to the one that I will take in this essay in that I, too, will attempt to illustrate the way in which literary and nonliterary texts can be interpreted in terms of the legal ideology they implicitly articulate and advance. I will argue that we can locate within the extended work of an individual author (fiction, letters, reviews, speeches and essays) a line of thinking that aligns that author with the proponents of a specific legal philosophy. Through this kind of investigation we not only increase our understanding of the writings and worldview of an author, but also add another dimension to the view that literary work does cultural work, that literature embodies the social and political debates and solutions of a society.

My specific case in point is Katherine Anne Porter, a 20th-century American writer known primarily for her finely crafted short stories about Mexico and the southern United States and her novel, *Ship of Fools* (1962), which became a best-seller, a Book-of-the-Month-Club selection and a Hollywood movie. Also an outspoken political activist who disdained belonging to

Reprinted with permission of the journal from *Mosaic:* A Journal for the Interdisciplinary Study of Literature 26, no. 4 (Fall 1993): 37–52.

political parties, Porter was concerned throughout her life with the question of and quest for justice. From her first published short story, "María Concepción" (1922), to her last publication, *The Never-Ending Wrong* (1977), from her participation in the protest against Sacco's and Vanzetti's executions to her refusal to sign an oath of allegiance to the United States during the Communist witch hunts of the McCarthy years, Porter was interested in justice and how to achieve it—and, more frequently, with injustice and how to stop it. Her interest was extensive and covered all areas of human relations. Many of her best stories are, in fact, about the efforts of individuals to maintain, attain or regain justice in their dealings with others. One thinks of individuals seeking fair treatment within the family, such as Miranda of the "Old Order" stories and Stephen of "The Downward Path to Wisdom." Or one recalls women like Sophia Jane and Nannie Gay who discover the inequities of their patriarchal and racist world, and who are able to rectify some of the imbalance in their own lives. Of course, the desire to right personal wrongs sometimes drives Porter's characters to extremes. For example, the see-sawing power struggles of couples such as the Hallorans of "A Day's Work," the unnamed partners of "Rope" and David and Jenny of *Ship of Fools* often turn into verbal, mental and even physical attempts at revenge.

Porter's concern for justice thus ranged far and wide, encompassing all spheres of human life (including the spiritual, as we see in "The Jilting of Granny Weatherall") and lasting at least 70 years. Obviously, it would be foolish to claim that she worked out a specific political platform for correcting the ills of the world, or even a 12-step program for attaining justice. As she said, "Literature isn't social criticism, except by inference" (qtd. in Givner, *Porter* 293). Indeed, the guidance Porter did offer was quite vague: "our political and social evils are remediable," she asserted again and again, "if only all of us who want a change for the better just get up and work for it. . . . Half the wrongs of human life exist because of the inertia of people who simply will not use their energies in fighting for what they believe in" (*Letters* 291).

Literature, however, as Porter also pointed out, "isn't altogether decoration either, or something to play with" (qtd. in Givner, *Porter* 293). Although we cannot expect from Porter the precision, the consistency or the comprehensiveness of a legal theorist—especially given her fervent opposition to political dogma of any kind—her work suggests that our failures at achieving justice in this century have resulted, *in part,* from particular principles that we have accepted as the cornerstones of our criminal justice system. To be specific, I will argue that Porter finds serious problems with utilitarianism, which, according to Graeme Newman, has "always been the most dominant guiding principle of punishment in Western civilization" (202) and with the more recently introduced social defense system. A more ethical and constructive system, she implies, would be that proposed by the exponents of retributive justice, for it seeks its authority in principles that respect the autonomy and free will of individuals, principles that Porter also believes must inform our dealings with each other in our personal lives.

Before making my case, I need to set forth a few qualifications. First, in the preceding paragraph I have stressed the phrase "in part" for several reasons, but mainly because, as I shall discuss later. I think that Porter would have agreed with many legal theorists who insist that the present social and economic circumstances of the Western world render "true" justice impossible, even under a retributive system which maintains the autonomy and equal rights of all. As Jeffrie G. Murphy states, in most societies "retributivism functions merely to provide a 'transcendental sanction' for the status quo" (95). What I am concerned with, however, is the ideal that Porter presents in her fiction, even as I hope to recognize fully her awareness that under our current political conditions this ideal typically fails. Second, I cannot begin to do justice in this essay to the complex histories of retributivism and utilitarianism. Not only have legal theorists defined several versions of these two systems, with the systems actually overlapping in some versions, but our present criminal justice system is an ideological hybrid, drawing upon diverse utilitarian and retributive principles and practices. By concentrating on certain fundamental ideas shared by all versions of utilitarianism and retributivism, I am obviously simplifying a complicated situation.

Finally, it is important to acknowledge that Porter occasionally expressed opinions that contradicted her belief in individual rights and equal treatment under the law. For example, as Joan Givner relates, Porter responded angrily in the 1950s to school desegregation (*Porter* 451); in 1958, the *Richmond News Leader* quoted her as saying that the "down-trodden minorities are organized into tight little cabals to run the country so that we will become the down-trodden vast majority, if we don't look out" ("Desegregation" 40). For a writer who composed sympathetic portraits of blacks living in the South during Reconstruction and who championed the rights of oppressed people in many parts of the world, these are strange and disturbing words. Indeed, in the 1960s, we find Porter expressing the opposite position, declaring her horror at circumstances in America that forced blacks to resort to rioting "to gain something they should have had all along" (qtd. in Givner, *Porter* 453).

Darlene Unrue notes that Porter's "private opinions, uttered impulsively and subject to change, sometimes were at odds with her public voice" (Introduction xvi), and Givner raises the possibility that Porter altered her views based on her audience. But Givner also suggests that Porter was often truly ambivalent: "Her own inner conflicts cause her contradictions" (Introduction xvii). As an example of Porter's ambivalence, Givner points out that in *Ship of Fools* Porter could not depict a likable Jewish character, yet the book consciously shows "the irrational, mindless, dangerous nature of such prejudice and, by implication, its devastating course toward the Holocaust" (*Porter*

453). Although Porter's expressions of racism and anti-Semitism should not be taken lightly. I hope to show that Porter's fiction, and much of her non-fiction, not only criticizes utilitarian principles but also portrays a view of justice that is fundamentally aligned with retributivism.

Following a position formulated by Thomas Hobbes and formalized in its most elaborate detail by Jeremy Bentham, utilitarians argue that punishment should be administered not for a past evil, but for a future good. Their major emphasis is thus on the general prevention of crime. All persons are seen as crime-prone, but they are deterred from committing a crime by the threat of punishment issued by the state. Because the utilitarians view punishment as evil, they must justify it, which they do by claiming that it maintains order and hence is a lesser evil than anarchy (Newman 157). According to Jeffrie Murphy, utilitarians justify punishment in terms of its social results—e.g., deterrence, incapacitation and rehabilitation—and hence even a guilty man, sentenced in accordance with this theory, is being punished "because of the instrumental value the action of punishment will have in the future" (94). Thus an important consequence of the utilitarian approach to punishment is, as Newman observes, that it not only deters citizens but teaches them morals by communicating, through punishment, standards of "right" and "wrong" (205).

In the 20th century, the "social defense" school of punitive theory introduced a basic feature that was adopted by many utilitarians: society must be protected not only by the repression of crime but also by the treatment of offenders (Newman 213). This feature turned the emphasis significantly away from the offense to the offender. The major criteria for determining the severity of a crime became the measure of the harm done to the society and the offender's dangerousness. Furthermore, according to this theory, with each relapse, the criminal should face increased punishment (Newman 212–16).

Because utilitarians have worked hard and have spoken vociferously for both social and punitive reform from the 18th to the 20th century, most people (including academics) have viewed them as "progressive" and "humanitarian" (Newman 202). Yet despite utilitarianism's identification with liberal morals. Porter implicitly criticizes it in some of her fiction, especially *Ship of Fools,* a work whose allegorical and historical dimensions enlarge the meaning of each character's actions. In this novel set in the late summer of 1931, Porter portrays the 27-day voyage on a freighter-passenger ship of a group of passengers whose diversity establishes them as a microcosm of the Western world and especially of the Western world about to engage in World War II. These passengers hail from many nations (Germany, Switzerland, Spain, Mexico, Sweden and the United States), belong to various socio-economic classes and hold different religious beliefs. In charge of their affairs is the German Captain Thiele, a legal agent whose attempts to enforce law and order not only depict the utilitarian system at work but also disclose the dangers that Porter sees in living under it.

From the moment he picks up the deported sugar workers at Havana, Captain Thiele devotes much effort and thought to controlling the "rabble" in the steerage. When two of these workers fight and draw blood, the Captain first warns that he will "lay the troublemakers in irons for the rest of the voyage" should a second outbreak occur (159) and later orders the confiscation of all weapons, however insignificant, from everyone in the steerage (173). By utilitarian standards, the Captain's measures are necessary and justified; he has promised punishment for any future misbehavior, and he has taken precautions to protect society from that threat. He tells Frau Schmitt and the other women who voice concern over the seizure of innocent persons' property: "In the end I alone am answerable not only for your safety but for the very life of this ship; therefore, please do allow me to advise you that I act from the gravest motives of responsibility" (176).

Captain Thiele justifies his decree on the assumption that it considers the best interests of the entire ship. Even so, Frau Schmitt's complaint has a point, for his order also punishes at least one individual, the woodcarver Echegaray, for whom a knife is an artistic tool, not a weapon. Without his knife, Echegaray is demoralized and tormented; when he dies trying to save the Huttens' bulldog, we are left wondering whether he committed suicide, if not intentionally then at least willingly, in the sense that upon finding himself in the ocean, he apparently found no reason to save himself from drowning. Captain Thiele could not, of course, have predicted the depths to which Echegaray's despair would carry him, so there is no reason for the ship's passengers to hold him accountable for the woodcarver's death. In fact, when a fight breaks out at Echegaray's funeral, the Captain is highly praised: "No knives, thank God," Karl Baumgartner says, "due to the firmness and foresight of our Captain" (330). Echegaray's death becomes only an unfortunate incident, a small price that society must pay to maintain order.

Two objections might be raised about this analysis of Porter's presentation of the logic and effects of utilitarian justice. First, one might argue that Captain Thiele is not a fair agent of the utilitarian system. After all, he typically acts rashly, from personal motives, not from a reasoned consideration of how to obtain the greatest good for the greatest number. For example, his decision to confiscate all weapons comes hastily, after a violent daydream in which he imagines himself in the midst of a catastrophic battle, standing on the bridge, "somehow in full command of the situation, and completely calm" (173). By the time he is called to account publicly for his orders, however, he has transformed his overworked imagination into a utilitarian mode, and his action seems justified and just.

This example actually illustrates an extreme peril of living continually under a utilitarian system. Newman points out that although the state depends for its existence on the approval of the people, "the more it punishes, the less precarious is its existence, since, according to twentieth-century theorists, the people will believe that the state is 'right' and will learn to 'obey' " (206). As Michel Foucault states, "ultimately, what one is trying to restore in this technique of correction is not so much the juridical subject, who is caught up in the fundamental interests of the social pact, but the obedient subject, the individual subjected to habits, rules, orders, an authority that is exercised continually around him and upon him, and which he must allow to function automatically in him" (128–29). Under these circumstances, even when the state issues unjust laws, the people lack the moral resources or energy to identify or criticize them as such. To stress Foucault's point: when living under this regime of perpetual discipline, the people *become* the state by internalizing its laws. After the Captain chastises Frau Schmitt for questioning his command, she bows her head, submitting quietly, and later calls his rebuke "well merited" (247).

One might answer with a second objection, as many modern utilitarians do, that besides the state, society contains other institutions, such as the family, the church, the school and the workplace, that teach moral behavior (Newman 206). The *Vera,* in fact, carries a few passengers who protest the Captain's threats and actions more strongly than Frau Schmitt. Yet Arne Hansen's socialist criticism blusters into political generalities and is not taken seriously by the others, and Jenny Brown's history of activism-as-entertainment makes readers suspect the sincerity of her desire to picket the Captain, especially when she does not even know what happened. Besides, as Wilhelm Freytag tells her, picketing would not do any good (164). Thus Porter shows how apathy, ignorance and misdirected or mawkish liberalism allow the state's authority to go unchecked and consequently to grow even stronger.

The historical associations to pre-Nazi Germany that Porter sets up in her novel add special emphasis to her position that a utilitarian-based political and social system fosters disaster and tragedy. As many critics have pointed out. Porter attempts in *Ship of Fools* to portray historical conditions that led to the rise of Nazi Germany and of fascism. Willene and George Hendrick assert that Porter makes "her meaning clear by using as a focal point the rise of fascism in the 1930s, and the worldwide calamity that resulted from the mass movements led by Hitler, Mussolini, and Franco" (111). Some critics, however, have proposed that Porter's historical portrait fails in one way or another. For instance, Lodwick Hartley states that Porter's zeal for revealing the germ of the disease that led to the Holocaust precludes her attention "to those who neglected to apply the clyster" (222). Similarly, Theodore Solotaroff, in perhaps the most famous negative review of Porter's book and its critics, claims that Porter's insistence upon a "general failure" of humanity "creates not only a feeble portent of Hitler's Germany but . . . a brutally indiscriminate one" given that no one on board the *Vera* is more repulsive than the Jew Julius Löwenthal (143).

As I noted earlier, Porter's treatment of Löwenthal can be seen as contradicting her understanding of the racism that fueled the Holocaust; nevertheless, some of the criticisms of Porter's portrayal of the *Vera*'s passengers might be answered by recognizing that part of her purpose in *Ship of Fools* is to depict the consequences of living under utilitarian rule. Bruno Bettelheim argues that, when confronted with the phenomenon of National Socialism during the 1930s, the uneducated middle classes in Germany had "no consistent philosophy which would protect their integrity as human beings. . . . They had obeyed the law handed down by the ruling classes, without ever questioning its wisdom. They could not question the wisdom of the law and of the police, so they accepted the behavior of the Gestapo as just. What was wrong was that *they* were made objects of persecution which in itself *must* be right, since it was carried out by the authorities" (qtd. in Hawkins 559).

According to Gordon Hawkins, Bettelheim's characterization of Nazi Germany reveals not only the way in which "respect for legal authority may help to secure social control but also why it is important not to confuse acceptance of, and submission to, authority with morality" (559). In her portrayal of many of the German passengers who submit wholly, as does Frau Schmitt, to the Captain's authority, Porter, too, suggests that learning to obey the state leads to mass inertia and limits the ability of a person to determine when and what to resist. Granted, Porter does not imply that utilitarian law is the sole cause of fascism, but she indicates that it plays a crucial role. In Porter's worldview, utilitarianism paves the way for authoritarianism.

Retributivists differ from utilitarians in many ways, most fundamentally in the way they construct the relationships between the individual and the state and between the legal and the moral orders. Retributivism developed in its modern form out of the philosophical writings of Kant and Hegel. It has, however, suffered some bad press because many people associate it with the knee-jerk reflex for revenge or with a strictly interpreted *lex talionis,* whereby one exchanges an eye for an eye, a tooth for a tooth, and so on. Actually, retributivists do believe that the criminal deserves to be punished, but they are careful to distinguish authorized punishment from personal revenge. This is not to say that retributivists totally dismiss feelings of revenge from the institution of punishment, for many assume that one of the goals of punishment is to allow society a vicarious release of vengeful desires toward the offender. One of the ways that retributivists separate personal revenge from societally sanctioned punishment is to acknowledge the impossibility—and potential immorality—of punishing the criminal in exactly the same way that the criminal harmed the victim. Rather, they argue, after Kant, that "punishment can never be used merely as a means to promote some other good for the criminal himself or for civil society, but instead it must in all cases be imposed on him only on the ground that he has committed a crime; for a human being can never be manipulated merely as a means to the purposes of someone else and can never be confused with the objects of the Law of things"

(100). Further, punishment must be imposed in proportion to the severity of the criminal's wrongdoing.

The precise moral and social imperatives that sanction punishment and the proportionality between a crime and its penalty are worked out by retributivists in a number of ways, but most agree on certain fundamental precepts. First, they insist that the individual who committed the crime is solely responsible and should be punished only for the act he/she committed. The main aim in punishing is not to reform the offender or to deter others, as it is with utilitarians, but simply to correct a wrong done to society. Second, this approach to punishment is founded on the principle of respect for individuals—as M. Margaret Falls puts it, on "our obligation to respect persons as ends in themselves, as choosing beings capable of autonomous moral decision-making" (25–26). Punishment lets offenders know that society condemns their acts and holds them morally accountable, but it does not attempt to coerce or torture them into changing. Retributive justice thus affirms a moral order that transcends the social and political orders, and allows individuals to retain their right to deviate.

Porter's fiction does not present a legal system that functions exclusively according to retributive principles, probably for the very good reason that such systems are virtually non-existent. Instead, her work presents several situations that allow the reader to align Porter's views with this philosophy. A number of her stories indicate, for example, that the moral and legal orders must be separated and that the people are the final arbiters of both orders. The clearest indication of this belief emerges in "María Concepción," Porter's story about an Indian woman who murders her husband's lover. When the police question María's husband and her neighbors, everyone comes to her defense: "They were around her, speaking for her, defending her. . . . Their eyes gave back reassurance, understanding, a secret and mighty sympathy" (*Stories* 20). A smiling young mother, Anita, baby at breast, delivers the crowning blow to the police investigation: "If no one thinks so, how can you accuse her?" (19). So the police must leave without a shred of evidence, even though they feel certain that María Concepción committed the murder.

The justice administered by the community in Porter's story is often explained as a kind of primitivism. For instance, Darlene Unrue proposes that the villagers protect María Concepción in "an ancient ritual and code of justice that defies the laws of the civilized government" (*Understanding* 26) and states that the story depicts the difficulty of "civilizing" the Indian (Introduction xiv). Similarly, Anna Camati refers to the primitive code that operates in the story and the "primitive consciousness" of the Indians (45). Although I do not wish to suggest that Porter condones murder—indeed, in commenting on the actual incident upon which her story was based, Porter stated that the Indian villagers possessed "deep layers of crossed emotions that are chilling to contemplate" (Lopez 72)—her point seems more complex than Unrue and Camati would have it. At the heart of her story is the question of who has the author-ity to punish, a question that has been problematic for both retributivists and utilitarians. Kant agrees that "[t]he legislative authority can be attributed only to the united Will of the people" (78), but he also claims that the people can-not legitimately resist the legislative chief of the state, "for resistance to the supreme legislation can itself only be unlawful" (86). Kant's position has been interrogated by many critics, as can be seen by his reply, included in later edi-tions of *The Metaphysical Elements of Justice,* to a contemporary reviewer who wondered about this "most paradoxical of all paradoxes" (138).

The climax of "María Concepción" turns upon this paradox. In the actions of María's neighbors, Porter suggests that the people must have—and must act on—the right to resist a legal system that they find unjust, espe-cially, perhaps, when they did not establish that system themselves. In essence, this is what María Concepción's society does. They intercept the offi-cial agents of the law, a law that has been imposed on them by a conquering country, and try her themselves as a jury of her peers. They do not find her innocent, for everyone knows that she killed Maria Rosa, but they do not believe she should be punished for her act. In addition, they approve María Concepción's declaration that Maria Rosa and Juan's baby now belongs to her. The ending of Porter's story affirms this community's judgment that jus-tice has been served and the moral order restored. The final view is of María Concepción and the child breathing in harmony with the rhythms of nature (21). Porter's story thus shows a primary principle of the retributivist scheme: criminals are punished on behalf of the people, not on behalf of the state.

The situation in "Noon Wine" might be described as a photographic negative to that of "María Concepción"; its ultimate view of the relationship between the morality of a community and the letter of the law is, however, an exact reproduction. In "Noon Wine," Mr. Thompson murders the bounty hunter, Homer T. Hatch, believing that Hatch has just stabbed Mr. Helton, the hired hand on Mr. Thompson's farm. When his vision clears, Mr. Thomp-son discovers that Helton is unharmed, and he cannot make sense out of the circumstances that led him to bring his ax down upon Hatch's head and of the fact that he is now a murderer.

After a brief trial, the law declares Mr. Thompson not guilty of Mr. Hatch's murder on the grounds that he acted in self defense. But Mr. Thomp-son finds no satisfaction in this verdict that is based on an incomplete version of the case and that, more important, does not coincide with the verdict of his neighbors, wife, sons and—despite his inability to admit it—even himself. Although Mr. Thompson attempts to untangle in his mind the confused strands of what "really" happened in his struggle with Mr. Hatch, he can never work out the knots in a way that justifies his act: "It still seemed to him that he had done, maybe not the right thing, but the only thing he could do, that day, but had he? *Did he have to kill Mr. Hatch?*" (265). Unlike María Concepción, Mr.

Thompson cannot exonerate himself, even though he tries until the very end to pin the blame on Mr. Hatch: "[Mr. Hatch] caused all this trouble and he deserved to die but I am sorry it was me who had to kill him" (268).

Equally important, Mr. Thompson's community—the more important jury of his peers—refuses to absolve him. One or two of them may claim to have "about come to the point where [they] believe in such a thing as killing in self-defense," but in actuality they view Mr. Thompson as a murderer, and the air around Mr. Thompson becomes "so thick with their blame he fought and pushed with his fists." Further, despite defending him to their neighbors, Mrs. Thompson "never said anything to comfort him" (262); his wild dream in which he reenacts the murder finally forces her to accuse him not with words but with her violent, frightened estrangement. Mr. Thompson claims that he commits suicide as a last attempt to justify his behavior to his neighbors and himself, but his act is, in reality, the execution of a guilty man. And although such an ending stands in stark contrast to the peaceful union of mother and child that ends "María Concepción," Mr. Thompson's story provides another example of a law of the moral sphere conflicting with and finally taking precedence over a law of the state.

I hope that no one assumes from these analyses that I think Porter, or proponents of retributive justice, would urge us all to take the law into our own hands whenever we become frustrated with the police, the lawyers and the judges—or to commit suicide when we, or our community, believe we have done wrong. The situations in "María Concepción" and "Noon Wine" cannot be readily duplicated in our complex, heterogeneous world where the people's will is usually neither so verifiable nor so unified. Nevertheless, in "María Concepción," at least, we do find the antithesis to the situation on the *Vera* where people allow the will of the state, no matter how unjust or unapproved, to stand in for their own will. In her own participation in the movement seeking a fair trial for Sacco and Vanzetti, Porter herself demonstrated how people living in the complex societies of the Western world might counter the official arm of justice. Of that experience, she wrote:

we do know now, all of us, that the most appalling cruelties are committed by apparently virtuous governments in expectation of a great good to come, never learning that the evil done now is the sure destroyer of the expected good. Yet no matter what, it was a terrible miscarriage of justice; it was a most reprehensible abuse of legal power, in their attempt to prove that the law is something to be inflicted—not enforced—and that it is above the judgment of the people. (*The Never Ending Wrong* 57)

Here, as in "María Concepción," Porter presumes that the law and its agents are granted their authority by the people; they must continually justify themselves to those people, rather than vice versa.

Another way to establish the affinities of Porter's beliefs with retributive theory is to examine how her characters deal with moral offenses in the social sphere. As many legal theorists observe, a society's treatment of criminal offenders is intricately connected to its treatment of moral wrong-doers. In other words, a society's, or a person's, views about the activities of criticism and blame inform their views about the criminal process. As S. I. Benn puts it, "Morality and law are alike rule systems for controlling behaviour, and what blame is to one, punishment is to the other. Since they are closely analogous as techniques for controlling undesirable conduct, by making its consequences in different ways disagreeable, the principles of awarding them largely coincide" (qtd. in Duff 39).

Although Porter's stories are replete with characters who criticize and blame, rarely do they go about these activities in a way that Porter suggests we should admire. Most blame the wrong people for the wrong reasons, as Mrs. Whipple ("He") does her husband for their troubles ("it was terrible to have a man you couldn't depend on not to get cheated" [54]); or as Mr. Thompson blames Mr. Hatch ("It was Mr. Homer T. Hatch who . . . caused all this trouble" [268]). Or they exceed the bounds of fair criticism and lust after revenge, as does Braggioni, the revolutionary leader of "Flowering Judas," who brags that a thousand women have paid for his first heartbreak (99). Tadeusz Mey, the Polish pianist of "The Leaning Tower," might be expressing the sentiments of a number of Porter characters when he tells Charles Upton, "If someone steps on your foot, you should not rest until you have raised an army to avenge you" (484).

Another typical Porter character is the individual whose criticism never reaches its deserving target. This kind of character has already shown up in my analysis of *Ship of Fools;* there I noted that some of the passengers condemn the Captain's policies among themselves but never confront him with their views. Equally serious is the widespread refusal of the passengers to oppose the behavior of Ric and Rac, the Cuban students and the zarzuela dancers, even though the behavior of all these groups includes slander, intimidation and theft. Certainly, a few of the passengers promise a confrontation. Professor Hutten, for instance, tells his wife that they will ignore the Cuban students' existence unless "they persist in their savagery to a point where this is no longer possible or commensurate with our own dignity, then—retaliation, swift, painful, and certain." He guarantees that, when the time comes, he will find a way to let them feel the sharpness of his rebuke (343). Yet when the students' pranks escalate, the Professor fails to make good his promise.

The only passenger to resist these three groups with any kind of force is Dr. Schumann. He saves the ship's cat from the clutches of Ric and Rac; he admonishes the Cuban students for their lack of consideration for La Condesa, insisting that they stop visiting her in the evening (237); and he advises the Spanish dancers to change their methods and their manners, at least for the rest of the voyage (348). None of his criticisms has much effect, probably because these groups have developed their pernicious behavior unchecked by anyone, including official authorities. Still, that should not prevent readers from seeing Dr. Schumann's actions as desirable and necessary.

By condemning the past conduct of these offenders, by treating them as moral agents responsible for their acts, by requesting that they change their ways to accord with the rules of society, and simply by expressing his regard for those rules despite the fact that he knows his blame will not initiate any great change, Dr. Schumann reveals himself to be one of Porter's most admirable characters—and an advocate of retributive justice. Moreover, Porter implies that the refusal of the other passengers to act likewise is a major cause of the spread of evil throughout all levels of society. In fact, Dr. Schumann's behavior closely approximates that of Porter herself who stressed again and again in her personal life that we should not allow others to commit immoral acts with impunity. For instance, after hearing rumors "of the foulest and most irresponsible slanders and nasty stories about me," she wrote: "I have lost patience, and decided not to keep silent any longer . . . I think we are all guilty of criminal collusion in any case, to allow, as we do, such tongues to run on so foully, unrebuked . . ." (*Letters* 281; Porter's ellipses).

Finally, a clear indication of Porter's position regarding both criminal and moral offenders comes from the unlikely source of Frau Hutten, who, after years of submission to her authoritarian husband, bursts out at last with this truth:

> I do know well there are many evil people in this world, many more evil than good ones, even the lazy good ones; evil by nature, by choice, by deepest inclination, evil all through; we encourage these monsters by being charitable to them, by making excuses for them, or just by being slack. . . . And we do not punish them as they deserve, because we have lost our sense of justice, and we say. "If we put a thief in jail, or a murderer to death, we are as criminal as they!" Oh what injustice to innocent people and what sentimental dishonesty and we should be ashamed of it. . . . yes, we do evil in letting them do evil without punishment. They think we are cowards and they are right. At least we are dupes and we deserve what we get from them. (294–95)

Frau Hutten's moment as the voice of Katherine Anne Porter is short-lived, for almost immediately she regrets her betrayal of her husband and denies her position. Her retraction, however, cannot stop these words from reverberating as one of the major themes of Porter's novel and also of Porter's life.

Indeed, twelve years after the publication of *Ship of Fools,* in an article published in *The Atlantic,* Porter was still expressing these views, and this time there is no doubt that she is speaking her own thoughts, in her own words. In this piece, Porter claims that she must work to resist "all the softheaded western Christian sentiments" she was brought up with, for she has seen how we can "persuade ourselves that the victim, not the killer, was really in the deepest sense the guilty one." Porter derides such "misguided sympathies" and declares that she is "still able to draw that fine hairline between justice and revenge. They are two quite opposite procedures that may sometimes have a surface resemblance; they are both real, and they mean what they say, and both serve their ends perfectly" ("Notes on Texas" 106). In this response, Porter recites the basic tenets of retributivism.

According to some legal scholars, retributivism is making a comeback. Many people—from legal theorists to legal authorities to the general public—are recognizing that utilitarian theory has failed, sometimes miserably, in practice (most studies show that punishment rarely deters crime and criminals are rarely rehabilitated). Further, these proponents are actually preferring the values and morality of retributivism itself. As J. S. Bainbridge, Jr., puts it: "Paradoxically . . . retributive principles favor fairness and free will. . . . What retribution [means] is that if people make choices about what they do, they must face the consequences" (63). This return to retributivism is one that I believe Porter would have welcomed, but is also one that others, especially feminist legal theorists, view with suspicion. In the first place, these critics argue that retributivism can never be fairly practiced so long as social and economic disparities prevent citizens from being treated as equal and autonomous agents under the law. To quote Diana Majury, "in the absence of an 'equal' world, the dominant groups in a society will inevitably set the standards for 'equality' " (323).

As I noted previously, retributive theorists have been the first to admit that fair and equal treatment under the law will never be possible so long as society itself fosters and enables inequities among its citizens. Even such a vocal proponent of retributive theory as Jeffrie Murphy concedes, "social conditions as they obtain in most societies make . . . retributivism largely inapplicable within those societies. . . . If this is so, then the only morally defensible theory of punishment [retributivism] is largely inapplicable in modern societies. The consequence: modern societies largely lack the moral right to punish" (95).

Porter, too, recognized that the inability to provide legal justice was tied to the many social inequities of Western society, be they found on the hacienda in Mexico, in the Berlin boarding house, or on the microcosmic passenger ship traveling across the Atlantic ocean. Indeed, Porter's reaction to reviewers' disapproval of Mary Treadwell's beating of William Denny stands as yet another illustration of her awareness that the law does not provide equal treatment and protection to all members of society. According to Joan Givner, Porter was shocked when reviewers of *Ship of Fools* condemned Mary Treadwell for beating Denny with the heel of her slipper after he attacked her, although no one spoke against Denny for his attempted rape. Porter claimed that if she had found herself in the same position, she would have done the same, and she hoped she would have had a more effective weapon (Givner, *Porter* 467–68).

Porter would have been less likely to agree with a second attack on retributivism mounted by feminist legal theorists along with others, an attack that is potentially more damaging in that it questions whether concepts such as "equality" and "autonomy," the linchpins of retributive theory, can function at all within our patriarchal society and legal system, or even whether they are desirable objectives. At the heart of this attack lies a critique of liberal individualism. Such a critique insists that because people come into being through social discourse, a discourse that is given to us (or developed in us) through our interactions with others, there can be no such thing as the self-made person or the essential self. From this perspective, the idea that people are capable of autonomous moral decision-making loses credence as does the idea that we can locate responsibility for wrong-doing with a single individual.

The view that the individual lacks autonomy or free will is one that Porter, a self-identified "liberal idealist" (*Never-Ending Wrong* 13), typically rejected. Again and again, she argued that "a man may choose between the good and the evil in his own soul" (*Letters* 258) and stressed that a man has only to choose to be good or evil and to "take upon *himself* the responsibility for his own acts" (*Letters* 342). These attitudes might seem overly optimistic and limited to some legal theorists, yet as Jennifer Nedelsky observes, the contemporary critique of individualism is not without problems of its own, especially since "No one among the feminists or communitarians is prepared to abandon freedom as a value, nor, therefore, can any of us completely abandon the notion of a human capacity for making one's own life and self" (8).

As a result of this desire to retain the possibility of freedom, some feminist legal theorists have argued that we need not totally cast out the ideas of "autonomy" and "equality" but must redefine them. For example, Majury submits that instead of seeking a single meaning for "equality," we should place this concept in perpetual motion. "We need," she writes, "to retain a flexible approach to equality in order to be able to respond to multiple inequalities" (332). Similarly, throughout her article on autonomy, Nedelsky analyzes and revises the idea of autonomy from a feminist legal perspective, arguing that autonomy never arises in isolation but is always produced within the social context in which individuality comes into being. She concludes that autonomy must be reconceived in connection to the collective.

Whether Porter would have agreed with the need for redefinition is anybody's guess. What is undeniable is that she believed in individualism—even though she sometimes expressed views that conflicted with this belief. For the most part, Porter's fiction presents her devotion to individual rights, and this presentation is supported by her statements in essays, letters, and reviews. To cite one such statement: in "Act of Faith: 4 July 1942," Porter writes that our liberties "were not accidental by any means; they are implicit in our theory of government, which was in turn based on humanistic concepts of the importance of the individual man and his rights in society. . . . They are not inalienable: the house was built with great labor and it is made with human hands; human hands can tear it down again, and will, if it is not well loved and defended" (*Essays* 196). With such ideals underlying her political philosophy, Porter could hardly fail to create works in which retributivism is rendered as justified and just.

In a 1982 article reviewing the interdisciplinary relations of literature and law, Richard Weisberg and Jean-Pierre Barricelli cite Porter's "Noon Wine" as an example of law-related fiction that depicts a full legal procedure (a trial) and advances as a central theme the relation of law, justice and the individual (151). Such an observation, while accurate, not only limits our vision of Porter's interest in legal matters to the visible surface of a single story but also defines the interdisciplinary project itself as a kind of theme-hunting. Giles B. Gunn notes that interdisciplinary studies have been transformed by "developments in literary and critical theory" as well as by "the emergence of new notions of textuality and intertextuality, particularly as they apply to the concept of culture itself" (245). By adopting the lessons of cultural studies, which collapses boundaries between literary and nonliterary works and assumes that literature is always organized in relation to a particular ideology, I have been able to suggest that Porter's writings embody one of the central intellectual debates of the modern Western world (what legal system is the most ethical, equitable and effective?) and offer retributivism as an answer. Analyzing an artist's work for the cultural work that it does provides one way in which we might enlarge our understanding of what it means to read the law in literature or to view literature as a source of law.*

Works Cited

Bambridge, J. S., Jr. "The Return of Retribution." *ABA Journal* 71 (1985): 60–63.

Camati, Anna Stegh. "Violence and Death: Their Interpretation by K. A. Porter and Eudora Welty." *Revista Letras* 32 (1983): 39–59.

"Desegregation Ruling Criticized by Author." *Richmond News Leader* 20 November 1958. Rpt. in *Katherine Anne Porter: Conversations.* Ed. Joan Givner. Jackson: UP of Mississippi, 1987, 39–41.

*I want to thank my friends and colleagues, Ruth Ann Hendrickson, Rosaria Champagne, Pat Mullen, Mary Wehrle, Reta Roberts and Patrick Morrow for their help in shaping my ideas and presentation of this article.

Duff, R. A. *Trials and Punishments*. Cambridge: Cambridge UP, 1986.

Falls, M. Margaret. "Retribution, Reciprocity, and Respect for Persons." *Law and Philosophy* 6.1 (1987): 25–51.

Foucault, Michel. *Discipline and Punish: The Birth of the Prison*. Trans. Alan Sheridan. 1977. New York: Vintage, 1979.

Gillman, Susan. *Dark Twins: Imposture and Identity in Mark Twain's America*. Chicago: U of Chicago P, 1989.

Givner, Joan. Introduction. *Katherine Anne Porter Conversations*. Ed. Joan Givner. Jackson: UP of Mississippi, 1987, ix–xix.

———. *Katherine Anne Porter: A Life*. New York: Simon, 1982.

Gunn, Giles. "Interdisciplinary Studies." *Introduction to Scholarship in Modern Languages and Literatures*. Ed. Joseph Gibaldi. 2nd ed. New York: MLA, 1992, 239–61.

Hartley, Lodwick. "Dark Voyagers." *Katherine Anne Porter: A Critical Symposium*. Ed. Lodwick Hartley and George Core. Athens: U of Georgia P, 1969, 211–26.

Hawkins, Gordon. "Punishment and Deterrence: The Educative, Moralizing, and Habituative Effects." *Wisconsin Law Review* 2 (1969): 550–65.

Hendrick, Willene, and George Hendrick. *Katherine Anne Porter*. Rev. ed. Boston: Twayne, 1988.

Kant, Immanuel. *The Metaphysical Elements of Justice*. Part 1 of *The Metaphysics of Morals*. Trans. John Ladd. Indianapolis: Bobbs, 1965.

Lopez, Enrique Hank. *Conversations with Katherine Anne Porter: Refugee from Indian Creek*. Boston: Little, 1981.

Majury, Diana. "Strategizing in Equality." *At the Boundaries of Law: Feminism and Legal Theory*. Ed. Martha Albertson Fineman and Nancy Sweet Thomadsen. New York: Routledge, 1991, 320–37.

Murphy, Jeffrie G. *Retribution, Justice, and Therapy: Essays in the Philosophy of Law*. Boston: Reidel, 1979.

Nedelsky, Jennifer. "Reconceiving Autonomy: Sources, Thoughts, and Possibilities." *Yale Journal of Law and Feminism* 1.1 (1989): 7–36.

Newman, Graeme. *The Punishment Response*. Philadelphia: Lippincott, 1978.

Porter, Katherine Anne. *The Collected Essays and Occasional Writings of Katherine Anne Porter*. New York: Dell, 1973.

———. *The Collected Stories of Katherine Anne Porter*. New York: New American Library, 1970.

———. *Letters of Katherine Anne Porter*. Ed. Isabel Bayley. New York: Atlantic Monthly P, 1990.

———. *The Never-Ending Wrong*. Boston: Atlantic Monthly P, 1977.

———. "Notes on the Texas I Remember." *The Atlantic* 235.3 (1975): 102–6.

———. *Ship of Fools*. Boston: Little, 1962.

Solotaroff, Theodore. "*Ship of Fools* and the Critics." *Commentary* 34 (1962): 277–86. Rpt. in *Katherine Anne Porter: A Collection of Critical Essays*. Ed. Robert Penn Warren. Englewood Cliffs: Prentice, 1979, 134–49.

Tompkins, Jane. *Sensational Designs: The Cultural Work of American Fiction, 1790–1860*. New York: Oxford UP, 1985.

Thomas, Brook. *Cross-Examinations of Law and Literature: Cooper, Hawthorne, Stowe, and Melville*. Cambridge: Cambridge UP, 1987.

Unrue, Darlene Harbour. Introduction. *"This Strange, Old World" and Other Book Reviews by Katherine Anne Porter.* Ed. Darlene Harbour Unrue. Athens: U of Georgia P, 1991. xi–xxxvi.

————. *Understanding Katherine Anne Porter.* Columbia: U of South Carolina P, 1988.

Weisberg, Richard, and Jean-Pierre Barricelli. "Literature and Law." *Interrelations of Literature.* Ed. Jean-Pierre Barricelli and Joseph Gibaldi. New York: MLA, 1982, 150–75.

Katherine Anne Porter and Sigmund Freud

DARLENE HARBOUR UNRUE

Katherine Anne Porter's attitude toward Sigmund Freud was ambivalent, to say the least. Her comments about him ranged from defending him against misinterpretation of his theories[1] to attacking him as one of the "trinity of Evil" in modern civilization.[2] Between the two extremes is abundant proof of Porter's careful consideration of Freud's ideas and her artistic use of them. Moreover, Porter's disagreements with Freud, acknowledged in letters and marginalia, illuminate some of the canonical themes of her fiction.

Many modern writers knew Freudian theory (or corrupted versions of it) secondhand, but Porter read Freud, according to her own account, soon after 28 of his lectures were published in English in 1920 as *A General Introduction to Psycho-Analysis*.[3] In 1947 Porter acquired what she identified as her second copy of Freud's *General Introduction*. As she reread it, she underlined or set off passages significant to her and wrote in the margins, agreeing or disagreeing with Freud and confirming in many instances her artistic interests and her fictional themes. Porter's textual marking proves that she read *General Introduction* from beginning to end at least once, but in all probability she read it through several times, as she said.

Porter was interested in Freudian theory for many reasons, some of which were personal and some of which were artistic. Self-educated as she was, though not academically scholarly, she was an avid reader, a voracious absorber of literary, artistic, and intellectual experience. Early on, she probably read Freud out of curiosity and perhaps, like many people, in search of relevant comment about her personal problems. But given her reliance on dreams as fictional technique, the prominence of child characters in her fiction, and her thematic concern with the nature of evil, she would have been drawn to Freud's seminal work on the interpretation of dreams and to his theories about the psychological development of children, about the roles of mothers, fathers, and society in that development, and about the source of evil.[4] Much of what Freud had to say about dreams, in fact, applied to the other subjects as well.

This essay was written especially for this volume and is published here for the first time with permission of the author.

80

Porter paid close attention to her own dreams, much as Freud used his dreams to test his theories. She occasionally described in letters to friends and relatives strange dreams she had, often adding a tag such as "Don't let Dr. Freud hear of this."[5] From the very beginning Porter's fictional works included dreams and reveries laden with psychological symbols. Written in the 1920s, "María Concepción," "Virgin Violeta," and "The Jilting of Granny Weatherall" depend on dreams for their crucial meanings. "Flowering Judas," published in 1930, culminates in a truth-telling dream, and Porter continues to use the technique throughout the stories in the Miranda cycle (all but one were published during the 1930s) and in such stories as "The Cracked Looking-Glass" (1932), "Noon Wine" (1937), "Pale Horse, Pale Rider" (1938), and "The Leaning Tower" (1941). "Pale Horse, Pale Rider," the third novella in the Miranda cycle, turns on the five dreams of Miranda,[6] and dreams are among the primary subjects of "The Cracked Looking-Glass."[7] In the early 1940s, when Porter was carefully rereading Freud, she also was writing the first pages of the novel that would finally be titled *Ship of Fools*. That novel contains the broadest evidence of Freudian influence, much of it illustrated in the significant dreams that are vehicles for the novel's most universal themes.

According to her marginalia and comments in letters, Porter apparently agreed with Freud's general theories about dreams and about the relation between childhood and dreams. Taking his text from Aristotle, Freud defined the dream in *General Introduction* as the "life of the mind during sleep" and sleep as "a necessary recuperation," an "intermission in our engagement with the outer world."[8] Sleep was ideally a periodic withdrawal into a condition Freud saw as similar to an intrauterine existence: warm, dark, and relatively absent of stimuli. Hypothetically, if a sleeper had no unresolved conflicts, unfulfilled wishes, or physical stimuli, sleep would continue unremarkably. But during sleep the unconscious took over from the reasoning and censoring conscious, or ego, and allowed what Freud called the dream work, the attempt by the psyche to translate unconscious "thoughts" into images or to resolve conflicts, fulfill wishes, and satisfy physical stimuli, that is, to restore sufficient mental equilibrium so that sleep could continue without tension.

Freud made a distinction between the latent and manifest contents of dreams, the latent content being the hidden meaning and the manifest content being the dream as related through images. Because during dreaming the latent, or unconscious, content rises to a preconscious area of the mind, the censor may be activated, distorting any objectionable latent material and transforming it into disguised and acceptable representation. Freud also pointed out that even when the censor is absent, that is, when the latent content is unobjectionable, the dream work still uses symbolism to translate the latent thought into manifest images. Distortion, the primary production of the dream work, makes dreams seem strange and incomprehensible by composite, indefiniteness, condensation, omission, modification, regrouping, displacement, substitution, ambiguity, metonymy, puns, and allusion (*General*

Introduction, 122, 134). Aside from Freud's common use of literature to illustrate or explain his hypotheses, it is easy to see why literary artists (Porter obviously was no exception) were drawn to dream symbolism and why some critics, especially in the 1920s and 1930s, undertook literary interpretation with the approach of the psychoanalyst. The relation between literary artist and text or between critic and text was nearly identical to that between psychoanalyst and couch-reclining subject. Language was the medium, with artist, critic, and analyst all examining expressed language for its symbolic link to latent or subtextual meanings.

Freud regarded the great majority of dreams as attempts at wish fulfillment, but he pointed out that the wish might be that of the punishing, censorious facet of the personality and the resulting dream might be troubling or anxiety filled. The dream work also might not be wholly successful in alleviating tension or pain, and part of the painful feeling in the latent thoughts might be carried over into the manifest dream (pp. 191–92). Simple and complex dreams, wish fulfilling or anxiety ridden, appear throughout Porter's fiction. At the end of her first published story, "María Concepción," María Concepción, who recently has murdered her husband's mistress and has taken the dead woman's child for her own, falls asleep feeling at one with the earth, her thwarted maternalism now satisfied, her deepest wish fulfilled, in a state of "strange, wakeful happiness."[9] In "Flowering Judas," however, Laura's complex dream following the death of Eugenio is so terrifying she awakes trembling and afraid to go to sleep again. Freud maintained that such anxiety dreams generally wake us, breaking off our sleep before the repressed wish behind the dream overcomes the censorship and reaches complete fulfillment (*General Introduction,* 194). Laura's wish is that of the censor in her psyche, directing her to the truth of her involvement in a revolution that practices death rather than life, violating her essentially female role and threatening her instinct for self-preservation.

Several dreams in *Ship of Fools* are clear examples of wish fulfillments and unresolved tension. The first dream described in the novel is a simple one of Nicolasa, the Indian maid to Señora Esperon y Chavez de Ortega, new mother and wife of the attaché to the Mexican legation in Paris. A voice Nicolasa does not recognize but believes to be her dead mother's often calls her name in a warning tone as she sleeps, the warning to remind Nicolasa of her nighttime duty to her upper-class employer. Porter's appended comment that Nicolasa weeps in her sleep "because she has lived her whole life among strangers who care nothing for her" raises ambiguous Freudian possibilities of Nicolasa's wishing for the return of the dead mother (who does love her) and the paradoxical identifying of parental authority with the very society that has placed Nicolasa in a subservient position.[10]

More complex dreams in the novel are those by Jenny Brown and Dr. Schumann. In her sleep Jenny lives through something she saw once in broad daylight traveling by bus from Mexico City to Taxco.[11] Passing through an

Indian village, Jenny saw half a dozen Indian men and women watching a man and woman locked in a death battle:

> They swayed and staggered together in a strange embrace, as if they supported each other; but in the man's raised hand was a long knife, and the woman's breast and stomach were pierced. The blood ran down her body and over her thighs, her skirts were sticking to her legs with her own blood. She was beating him on the head with a jagged stone, and his features were veiled in rivulets of blood. They were silent, and their faces had taken on a saintlike patience in suffering, abstract, purified of rage and hatred in their one holy dedicated purpose to kill each other. Their flesh swayed together and clung, their left arms were wound about each other's bodies as if in love. Their weapons were raised again, but their heads lowered little by little, until the woman's head rested upon his breast and his head was on her shoulder, and holding thus, they both struck again. (*Ship,* 144)

When the scene repeats itself horrifyingly in Jenny's dreams, it always has a grotesque variation she does not understand. In the most recent version the faces of the Indian pair have become hers and David's. Before the drama is completed or the wish fulfilled, Jenny wakes in relief and melancholy, having been led closer to the truth of the universal relationship between love and hate, a subject both Porter and Freud discussed, and of the death in her emotional and sexual relationship with David.

Jenny's recurring dream seems to be an adult dream created in the tension of a romantic and sexual alliance. But Freud contended, in passages Porter set off with marginal lines, that there was a direct line of development between the adults' dreams and their childhoods, as there was considerable similarity between the dreams of adults and the dreams of children, most of the latter dreams being wish fulfillments in which the latent and manifest contents are the same. Thus the wish-fulfillment component of the adult dream was infantile, and the era to which the dream work took the dreamer was primitive in a twofold sense: the early days of the individual, that is, the dreamer, and the early stage of the human race. Thus the dream was both personal and phylogenetic, insofar, Freud said, as "each individual repeats in some abbreviated fashion during childhood the whole course of the development of the human race" (*General Introduction,* 177, 184).

Although the most obvious interpretation of Jenny's dream is that she identifies David and herself with the fighting-to-the-death Indian couple, Freud would go much further, and based on other scenes in the novel, one might readily conclude that Porter was reaching in the same direction.[12] The primitive violence, the piercing of the woman's breast and stomach by the phallic dagger, and the blood on the woman's thighs represent equally in Freudian symbolism sexual union and the process of giving birth, both acts the objects of childish curiosity that Freud discussed and Porter noted (with comments and marginal lines), in the 14th and 20th lectures, respectively

"Wish Fulfillment" and "The Sexual Life of Man."[13] Freud might have suggested that Jenny Brown feared both sex and birthing, but he would see the dream as containing also, and especially, a wish fulfillment of the unsatisfied childhood desires to gaze on the sexual activities of the parents and to witness a birth (p. 322). Freud said that the thoughts represented in a dream might be anything—for example, a warning, a resolve, or a preparation—but besides this, it was always the fulfillment of an unconscious wish. To reach the core of the meaning in a recurring dream, Freud said that the analyst (or the reader/critic) must look for the *tertium comparationis,* the common factor (p. 167). In Jenny's recurring dream what does not change is the violence, the blood, and the presence of the knife, which strongly represents the childish wish that underlies all the other meanings in the dream.

The manifest content of Dr. Schumann's dream, which occurs near the end of the novel, is more absurdly distorted and enigmatic than Jenny's dream. Fearing his own death from progressive heart disease, Dr. Schumann suffers also from the belief that in his love for La Condesa and in his providing drugs for her, he has violated all he has valued and held dear—his marriage vows, his commitment to Roman Catholicism, the Hippocratic oath. Thus his conflict is both the ancient one between awareness of mortality and the desire to preserve life, and the social conflict between his ideal self and knowledge of his moral failings. He has told La Condesa, "I have not loved you innocently . . . but guiltily and I have done you great wrong, and I have ruined my life . . ." (*Ship,* 369). Afterward he falls into a troubled, bitter sleep:

> La Condesa's face floated bodiless above him, now very near, peering into his eyes; then retreating and staring and coming again in ghostly silence. The head rushed away into the distance, shrunken to the size of an apple, then bounded back, swollen and white like a toy balloon tossed upward by a hand, a deathlike head dancing in air, smiling. Dr. Schumann in his sleep rose and reached up and out before him and captured the dancing head, still smiling but shedding tears. "Oh, what have you done?" the head asked him. "Oh, why, why?" not in complaint, only in wonder. He held the head tenderly between his spread palms and kissed its lips and silenced it; and went back to bed with it, where it lay lightly on his breast without smiles or tears, in silence, and he slept on so deeply he did not know it was a dream. (pp. 469–70)

In conformity with Freud's theories about dream symbolism, which Porter applies here, the disembodied head of La Condesa represents not only death but also metonymically the woman herself. The head's transformation into apple and balloon defines more graphically La Condesa's sexuality, her life-giving, nourishing femaleness; Freud explained that balloons, with their expanding property, might symbolize the phallus, but in general, spheres of any kind almost always symbolize, in addition to their other values, the female breast (*General Introduction,* 138). The apple, however, associates La

Condesa with Eve, the archetypal mother and female temptress, the allusion drawn from racial memory. The toy balloon, although a symbol of death in its swollen and bloodless whiteness, also paradoxically associates La Condesa with an innocent and milk-white childhood, when Dr. Schumann's images of woman as mother, female, and sexual object were initially formed. According to Freud, floating, swelling, and dancing, like flying, represent sexual desire, here perceived in such images by Dr. Schumann and centered on the symbol of La Condesa. In the dream the libidinous Dr. Schumann is allowed by his censoring self to kiss the head tenderly, an acknowledgment of his illicit love and an acceptable representation of sexual fulfillment, which he denies himself in his waking life. That he sleeps deeply without disturbance after the dream indicates the success of the dream work.

In consciously regarding the "wickedness" of his relationship with La Condesa and also in observing the "evil" twins Ric and Rac, Dr. Schumann has occasion to muse on the source and nature of evil. He has a conversation on the subject with Herr Professor and Frau Hutten, and Porter places among Dr. Schumann's words and thoughts her own views of evil, which rest partly on Freud's theories, as the marginalia in her copy of *General Introduction* confirm. In the 13th lecture, "Archaic and Infantile Features in Dreams," Freud describes the material of the adult's forgotten childish experience, in which persists, in the unconscious, the child's mental life, which is often identified as "evil" in adults. Porter set off with left and right marginal lines Freud's amplification of this theory:

> [O]ur dreams take us back every night to this infantile stage. This corroborates the belief that the Unconscious is the infantile mental life, and, with this, the objectionable impression that so much evil lurks in human nature grows somewhat less. For this terrible evil is simply what is original, primitive, and infantile in mental life. . . . By regressing to this infantile stage our dreams appear to have brought the evil in us to light, but the appearance is deceptive . . . ; we are not so evil as the interpretation of our dreams would lead us to suppose. (p. 184)

Porter's depiction of Ric and Rac, namesakes of rascally comic-strip terriers, illustrates this point well. Viewed through other passengers' eyes, the twins are described as "little demons one expected to blow up with a smell of brimstone and disappear before one's eyes" (*Ship*, 268). The other passengers silently think Ric and Rac are "outside the human race" and that "overboard, the deeper the better, would have been a most suitable location" for them. When Dr. Schumann looks in the eyes of Ric and Rac, he sees something primitive and evil that he identifies as common human racial heritage, his own and that of the other passengers as well as that of the twins. His view is validated when Porter traces the source of the twins' evil to their parents' failure to love them. When Ric and Rac steal La Condesa's pearls and throw them overboard, the parents, Lola and Tito, are horrified, not at the twins' thieving but at the possibility that the troupe's own dishonest machinations have been exposed. The parents torture the children by pressing their finger-nails down and turning their eyelids back and by threatening to stick pins under their nails and pull their teeth out, universal methods of torture drawn from a common racial source. When the parents leave, Ric and Rac crawl "into the upper berth looking for safety; they lay there half naked, entangled like some afflicted, misbegotten little monster in a cave, exhausted, mindless, soon asleep" (p. 348). "Mindless" and "cave" are reminders of the precon-scious, prenatal, and elemental source of the Children's "evil" behavior, and the parents' responsibility is emphasized in Dr. Schumann's confrontation with the dance troupe. As they stare him down, he gets the impression "that he was gazing into eyes that had got misplaced: they belonged to some species of fierce beast peering out of a cave or ready to leap in a jungle, prowl-ing and sniffing for blood; the same expression, only older, more intensely aware and ready, that had dismayed him in the eyes of Ric and Rac" (p. 348).

Freud described a contemporary manifestation of such evil. In the ninth lecture, "The Dream Censorship," Freud asked rhetorically, "Are you ignorant of the fact that all the excesses and aberrations of which we dream at night are crimes actually committed every day by many who are wide awake? What does psycho-analysis do in this connection but confirm the old saying of Plato that the good are those who content themselves with dreaming of what others, the wicked, actually do." Porter set off with marginal lines that passage and its continuation as Freud applied the theory to World War I, much of which she saw as relevant to World War II, anticipated in the 1931 setting of *Ship of Fools:*

And now look away from individuals to the great war still devastating Europe: think of the colossal brutality, cruelty and mendacity which is now allowed to spread itself over the civilized world. Do you really believe that a handful of unprincipled place-hunters and corrupters of men would have succeeded in let-ting loose all this latent evil, if the millions of their followers were not also *guilty?* [Porter's italics.] Will you venture, even in these circumstances, to break a lance for the exclusion of evil from the mental constitution of human-ity?

You will accuse me of taking a one-sided view of war, and telling me that it has also called out all that is finest and most noble in mankind, heroism, self-sacrifice, and public spirit. That is true; but do not now commit the injustice, from which psycho-analysis has so often suffered, of reproaching it that it denies one thing because it affirms another. It is no part of our intention to deny the nobility in human nature, nor have we ever done anything to dispar-age its value. On the contrary, I showed you not only the evil wishes which are censored but also the censorship which suppresses them and makes them unrecognizable. We dwell upon the evil in human beings with the greater emphasis only because others deny it, thereby making the mental life of mankind not indeed better, but incomprehensible. If we give up the one-sided ethical valuation then, we are sure to find the true formula for the relation of evil to good in human nature. (*General Introduction,* 130)

In 1947 Porter wrote in the margin at the conclusion of Freud's passage:

I said in the last war that the reason the world loves the oppressors so and promises them everything and helps them again to rise is because they actually do all the monstrous things the other "civilized" people dream of doing. . . . Even the sentimental refusal to believe that the Germans actually did such things is only a refusal to face their own evil impulses.

In Dr. Schumann's and the Huttens' discussion of evil in *Ship of Fools,* Porter posits Schumann's (and Freud's) theories against those of the dry academic's, Hutten's, and his ill-informed wife's. Herr Dr. Hutten declares the problem of good and evil "insoluble." He asks whether good and evil really exist, except as concepts in the human mind. Dr. Schumann responds with his conventional theory that it is a theological question and that "our collusion with evil is only negative, consent by default." His further explanation, however, is more Freudian than theological, and in fact part of it is Porter's paraphrase of Freud's text. Dr. Schumann says, "I suppose in our hearts our sympathies are with the criminal because he really commits the deeds we only dream of doing! Imagine if the human race were really divided into embattled angels and invading devils—no, it is bad enough as it is, . . . with nine-tenths of us half asleep and refusing to be waked up" (*Ship,* 294).

Throughout Porter's marked copy of Freud's *General Introduction* there is ample evidence that Porter drew on Freud's ideas and symbols for *Ship of Fools* as well as for much of her other fiction. In addition to already cited examples of Freudian influence on *Ship of Fools,* Freud's explanation of insanity (*General Introduction,* 228–29), which Porter set off with marginal lines, may have helped her develop the character of La Condesa, just as she noted and possibly used Freud's discussion of primitivism and neuroticism in children (pp. 184, 319) as a guide in developing the characters Ric and Rac. And it is Freud's discussion of cruelty and sadism that may explain the complex motivation of the dying Herr Wilibald Graf. In Porter's other fictional pieces, symbols and images seem to have particular significance in light of Freud's explanations. For example, children symbolized in dreams as animals (p. 137) directs us to a new understanding of Porter's use of animal imagery, particularly in "The Grave," "The Downward Path to Wisdom," and "Holiday."[14] The symbolism of hats and furnace in "Theft" and the imagery of machinery in "Flowering Judas" have Freudian overtones (pp. 136, 139), and Freud on "knowing" and "knowledge" relates directly to experiences of the child Miranda in "The Circus" and "The Grave."[15] Freud's description of "the spirit of death" that "extinguishes the torch of life" (*General Introduction,* 174) seems to be evoked in "The Jilting of Granny Weatherall"; Granny at the moment of her death "stretched herself with a deep breath and blew out the light" (*Collected Stones,* 89).

As strong as the evidence is, however, of Porter's conscious use of Freud's symbols and ideas, there were areas of strong disagreement. Early on, anticipating dissenting psychoanalysts and later feminists, Porter took issue with Freud's view of art and the artist and with his phallocentricity. As Freud explained his theory of art as neurosis and the artist as a would-be neurotic, Porter chided Freud with sadness rather than anger: "Poor dear doctor," she wrote in a marginal note in *General Introduction,* "it is just not so simple!" (p. 328). But elsewhere in *General Introduction,* whenever Freud remarked on penis envy or on the castration complex in little girls or on females' wish to become males, Porter took umbrage, once countering Freud in a marginal note:

> I never had the faintest envy of a boy, or remember having curiosity about them; but they looked closed up, and I thought they must be very uncomfortable! I have never had and have not now any sense of inferiority as a woman. My sexual pride is very natural and easy. I belong to the sex that has the values. (p. 277)

Porter amplified this point in 1958 in a long letter to Edward Schwartz, who had sent her the manuscript draft of his essay "The Fictions of Memory":[16]

> And that brings me to Freud, and your use of his theories in one passage on "Pale Horse, Pale Rider" . . . about illness as escape, "[Miranda's] opportunity to assume the active role of the male," and the note about the sailing away into the jungle (Freudian point of view) "a wish for the male role." To me this is so wrong it is shocking, and yet it is almost impossible for any woman to convince any man that this is false.

Analyzing this misconception, Porter continued:

> In the first place, there are so many women, and we have all heard them, who wish loudly they had been born men, simply because they have been taught that men have more freedom, in every direction. What they really want, I think, is not a change of sex, but a change of the limited conditions of their lives which have been imposed because of their sexual functions. They do not seem to realize that men are not free either, and exactly on the grounds of their sexual functions. The uneasy sexual vanity . . . makes a man resent a woman who is his equal mentally or in any other way.[17]

Porter addressed a personal pique here, one that she commented on many other times; her feeling of being regarded in a lesser light than male writers. But in spite of her avant-garde feminism, now clearly traced by a number of critics,[18] Porter rejected the label of "feminist" for herself, preferring "modern" instead and identifying *feminist* with *political activist,* a role she considered incompatible with the purpose of the artist.

Porter's differences with Freud increased over the years even while she was mining his theories to construct dreams or symbols in her fiction or paraphrasing his comments for use in *Ship of Fools.* Finally, in 1975, as she approached the end of her life, she ignored what she once had clearly regarded as the usefulness of Freud's ideas, which had seemed so sound and revolutionary in the 1920s, and she summarized Freud's contribution to civilization as an "evil" one. Placing him in the company of Darwin and Marx, she objected to what she perceived as their mechanistic determinism that lifted moral responsibility from humankind. While she no doubt subscribed to the natural human proclivity toward cruelty and violence, she believed passionately in the redemptive power of love. Like her modernist contemporaries, she believed that men and women must continually search for moral order in a seemingly chaotic universe. For all of Freud's brilliant charting of the unseen dimension of the human personality and his certain valid insights into human motivation, he finally violated Porter's deeply rooted mythic feminism and her dominating moral standard, which she paradoxically had used him to help define in *Ship of Fools:* the collusion with evil by passive acceptance of it.

Notes

    1.   In unpublished autobiographical notes in her papers at the University of Maryland at College Park, under the title "The Land That Is Nowhere," Porter wrote, "Freud was so far misunderstood all the young clever people thought he meant you must sleep with anybody you chose or you would be crippled for life." Quoted with permission of the University of Maryland at College Park Libraries and Barbara Thompson Davis, trustee, Katherine Anne Porter Literary Estate.

    2.   Marginalia, "Twentieth-Century Southern Literature," in *Southern Literary Study: Problems and Possibilities,* Louis D. Rubin Jr. and Hugh Holman, eds. (Chapel Hill: University of North Carolina Press, 1975), 135; Porter's marked copy is preserved in the Katherine Anne Porter Room at the University of Maryland at College Park. This and all other quotations from Porter's marginalia used with permission of the University of Maryland at College Park and Barbara Thompson Davis, trustee, Katherine Anne Porter Literary Estate.

    3.   Freud's lectures were published for the first time in English in 1920 (when Porter was 30 years old) by Horace Liveright. Porter wrote in the margin of "Twentieth-Century Literature" (see note 2) that she read Freud from her 18th year until her 25th. Although Porter had an imperfect sense of historical chronology and a faulty memory of dates, she no doubt knew of Freud's theories at that time (1908–1915) but actually read his lectures sometime during the 1920s. She noted in her 1947 copy of Freud's *General Introduction to Psychoanalysis,* trans. Joan Riviere (Garden City, NY: Garden City Publishing, 1920), that she had not read Freud at the time of World War I. Porter's marked copy, which she identified as her second copy, is preserved at the University of Maryland at College Park.

4.   All of these subjects are treated in *A General Introduction to Psycho-Analysis,* but Freud's theories of dream symbolism were generally well known before 1920. "The Interpretation of Dreams" was published in 1900.

5.   See, for example, Katherine Anne Porter to Paul Porter (nephew), 21 May 1943, and Katherine Anne Porter to Allen Tate, 27 January 1931, in *Letters of Katherine Anne Porter,* ed. Isabel Bayley (New York: Atlantic Monthly Press, 1990), 262, 30.

6.   For detailed discussions, see Thomas F. Walsh, "The Dream Self in 'Pale Horse, Pale Rider,' " *Wascana Review* 45 (Summer 1960): 204–15; and Sarah Youngblood, "Structure and Imagery in Katherine Anne Porter's 'Pale Horse, Pale Rider,' " *Modern Fiction Studies* 5 (Winter 1959–1960): 344–52.

7.   For a good analysis of the story, see Jane Krause DeMouy, *Katherine Anne Porter's Women: The Eye of Her Fiction* (Austin: University of Texas Press, 1983), 61–72.

8.   Sigmund Freud, *A General Introduction to Psycho-Analysis,* 79. All subsequent references to Porter's copy of this work are cited in the text with parenthetical page numbers.

9.   Katherine Anne Porter, "María Concepción," *The Collected Stories of Katherine Anne Porter* (New York: HarcourtBrace, 1965), 21. All subsequent quotations from Porter's stories are taken from this edition and are cited with parenthetical page numbers.

10.   Katherine Anne Porter, *Ship of Fools* (Boston: Atlantic, Little-Brown, 1962), 131. All subsequent quotations from *Ship of Fools* are taken from this edition and are cited with parenthetical page numbers.

11.   Jenny's dream is a version of an experience Porter described to Caroline Gordon as having had the year before she took the voyage that provided the surface realism for *Ship of Fools:* "On that terrible and beautiful road, something like a Coney Island scenic railway magnified beyond all human reason, I saw an Indian man and woman beside the dusty way, engaged in killing each other with knives and stones . . . his shaven head was gashed round and the blood streamed down his face which looked like the Indian Christ's in the country churches; he was done for, his face showed it, but she was still screaming and wild and furious . . . we rattled and bounded by in a whirl of dust and gasoline fumes." Unpublished letter, Katherine Anne Porter to Caroline Gordon, 13 August 1931, Katherine Anne Porter Papers, University of Maryland at College Park Libraries; quoted by permission of the University of Maryland at College Park and Barbara Thompson Davis, trustee, Katherine Anne Porter Literary Estate.

12.   See, in particular, the scenes in *Ship of Fools* between the child Hans and his parents.

13.   In marginal notes Porter comments that her "earliest remembered belief" was that "babies came from the navel" (p. 279).

14.   See Sister J. Joselyn, O.S.B., "Animal Imagery in Katherine Anne Porter's Fiction," in *Myth and Symbol: Critical Approaches and Applications,* ed. Bernice Slote (Lincoln: University of Nebraska Press, 1963), 105–115.

15.   I address these points in "Katherine Anne Porter, Politics, and Another Meaning of 'Theft,' " *Studies in Short Fiction* 30 (1993): 119–126; *Truth and Vision in Katherine Anne Porter's Fiction* (Athens: University of Georgia Press, 1985), 57, 59; and *Understanding Katherine Anne Porter* (Columbia: University of South Carolina Press, 1988), 37–38.

16.   Edward G. Schwartz, "The Fictions of Memory," *Southwest Review* 45 (Summer 1960): 204–15.

17.   Katherine Anne Porter, *Letters,* 548.

18.   See, for example, Jane Flanders, "Katherine Anne Porter's Feminist Criticism: Book Reviews from the 1920s," *Frontiers* 4 (Summer 1979): 44–48; and DeMouy, *Katherine Anne Porter's Women.*

"Royalty in Exile": Pre-Hispanic Art and Ritual in "María Concepción"

RUTH M. ALVAREZ

"María Concepción," the earliest work Katherine Anne Porter claimed as part of her canon, was written as a direct result of her first two visits to Mexico (November 1920 to autumn 1921 and April to June 1922). Intrigued by accounts of the country, its culture, and its history recounted by Mexican acquaintances and friends she encountered in New York City after moving there in late 1919, Porter found in Mexico both aesthetic theories and subjects for her literary and journalistic work. The work that grew out of her Mexican visits brought Porter recognition and respect in New York literary circles and enabled her to indulge her compulsion to write, her only lifelong "preoccupation."[1]

Published in *Century* in December 1922, "María Concepción" is Porter's first mature work of fiction. Like all her other work written after her first visit to Mexico, it is markedly different from her previous work. What came before is either apprentice work or journalism, none of it rising much above competent professionalism. Part of this difference can be attributed to her contact with Mexican art.

Much of the power of Porter's best work comes from her ability to use the resources of the writer's art to draw images that are essentially visual. Porter's first two visits to Mexico were of utmost importance to her as a writer. Contact with Mexican popular and fine art stimulated Porter and brought about a direct change in her writing. Beginning with "The Fiesta of Guadalupe," Porter began to employ a technique of delineating, or "painting," a series of verbal pictures similar in content and focus to some of the Mexican art she began to observe in Mexico: landscapes and genre scenes featuring the native Indians, including depictions of fiestas and daily life and of famous sites and buildings.[2] It is also significant that in "The Fiesta of Guadalupe" she describes or alludes to Mexican art: a Mexican codex of pre-Hispanic times, the sixteenth-century image of the Virgin of Guadalupe, and

This essay was written specifically for this volume and is published here for the first time by permission of the author.

a later painting of the Virgin of Guadalupe. It was her exposure to the pre-Hispanic and colonial art as well as to the contemporary art of her Mexican friends and acquaintances both in and out of Mexico that allowed her to begin to develop as an artist. Porter needed the visual image, be it a person, place, or thing she observed in life, a painting, a piece of folk art, a pre-Hispanic object, or a photograph, in order to ground her work. In her fiction, she observes and records what she has seen, a technique essentially more characteristic of visual art than of written art. But as with a painter or a photographer, it is the choice of the subject, the point of view, the elements for emphasis or deletion, that reveal the author's bias.

"María Concepción" draws on Porter's knowledge of Mexican art: the pre-Hispanic art she helped excavate in Azcapotzalco with American archaeologist William Niven, the folk art she observed and admired in researching and writing *Outline of Mexican Popular Arts and Crafts* (completed in May 1922), as well as the religious art and contemporary art she observed in her first two trips to Mexico. Porter also sophisticatedly used the customs and festivals of the Indians of the Anahuac valley that she had seen or studied. What is remarkable is how skillfully she weaves all these elements together in her story. Porter's previously published fiction had given no clue that she could produce fiction this powerful, although the evocative pieces "The Fiesta of Guadalupe" and "In a Mexican Patio" would seem to point toward what was to be expected in her real art.[3]

In "María Concepción," Porter makes use of the pictorial method she exploited effectively in "The Fiesta of Guadalupe," "Xochimilco,"[4] and "In a Mexican Patio" for the first time in her published fiction. The story opens with a series of completely realized portraits of the indigenous peasant woman María Concepción Manriquez depicted against the backdrop of an authentic Mexican landscape. These are followed by verbal portraits of two additional native characters: María Rosa, the local beekeeper, who is being chased by María Concepción's husband, Juan de Dios Villegas. We have learned from the narrator that María Concepción, as her name with its reference to the Virgin of the immaculate conception implies, is a "good Christian" and an "energetic, religious woman,"[5] unique among the native women of her village for having actually been married by a priest in the church. But Porter's pictures are at odds with that knowledge. This is a landscape that appears as it might have before the Conquest, the locale, the vegetation, and the native structures remaining unchanged. Only part of María Concepción's clothing and part of the clothing of María Rosa and Juan indicate that the time of the story is post-Conquest. The force of these verbal pictures is to emphasize the continuity of Indian life and traditions into contemporary times. In contrast to these native traditions, the practice of Roman Catholicism and the elements of Spanish colonial culture are a mere veneer on the real life of contemporary Mexican Indians.

The next sequence of descriptions portrays the activities and person of the American archaeologist, Givens. Givens employs nearly all the men of this small community outside Mexico City in uncovering the lost city of their ancestors. Givens first appears emerging from the newest of the "long deep crevasses, in which a man might stand without being seen," which "criss-crossed like orderly gashes of a giant scalpel" the field of excavation (p. 6). What is being uncovered are pre-Hispanic artifacts: "small clay heads and bits of pottery and fragments of painted walls" (p. 6).

These particular scenes are interesting because they are drawn from Porter's own observations and, perhaps, from photographs. Porter had met William Niven, the model for this character, in November 1920 in Mexico City.[6] Soon after, she visited the site he was then excavating and herself dug pre-Hispanic artifacts from the earth. The story mentions photographs of Givens: "He would fairly roar for joy at times, waving a shattered pot or a human skull above his head, shouting for his photographer to come to make a picture of this!" (p. 7). Such photographs of William Niven were taken, some in Porter's sight. In Ramon Mena's *Great Archaeological Discovery: The Ancient Tecpanecs in the Valley of Mexico,* which may have been one of Porter's sources for *Outline,* there are five photographs of Niven digging in the trenches of a site.[7] This monograph describes discoveries made at Pec-panecan sites northwest of Mexico City from 1918 to 1919. It seems likely that Porter saw this monograph because in *Outline* she refers to the five civilizations represented by the five layers of archaeological strata delineated by Mena in the work. Also there seems to be a direct allusion to one or more of the clay figures unearthed in these excavations later in "María Concepción." It is significant that María Concepción's "grand manner" reminds Givens of "royalty in exile." This subtle allusion to pre-Hispanic nobility and rites provides an important submerged message that emerges as the story unfolds.

The chronological time of the story is also approximately fixed with the aid of this monograph and another by Mena published in 1921.[8] Although Niven had been working on archaeological excavations in Mexico since 1891, the general location of the story near Mexico City suggests that the events must be taking place during the period of roughly 1918 to 1920, when Niven was completing the work in the area described in the monographs. María Rosa and Juan Villegas participate in a war for a period of approximately one year from the time of their departure. The war may be the one that ensued after General Alvaro Obregón's pronouncement against President Carranza in late April 1920. The resulting struggle for succession to power continued long after Carranza's assassination in May. Although Obregón was elected president in September 1920 and inaugurated on November 30, turmoil continued during the entirety of Porter's first visit to the country. Individuals plotted and engineered assassinations; there were clashes of Roman Catholics and socialists. There is little doubt that the events of the story take place during this period.

Porter further hints at the survival of pre-Hispanic ritual in her portrayal of María Concepción during the year she is abandoned by Juan for María Rosa and the battlefield. María Concepción's face is changed and "blind-looking" as she kneels in the church "with her arms spread in the form of a cross for hours at a time" before the saints (p. 9). She becomes a gaunt figure with sunken eyes, her chicken-butchering knife in her hands. The pagan form of Roman Catholicism she practices is suggested in the painful, almost inhuman rites of penance she performs both in the period of Juan's absence and as part of her observance of the church year. Later in the story, her regular practice of crawling on her knees toward the shrine at Guadalupe Villa is mentioned (p. 14). María Concepción's practice of these rituals, however, does not prevent the death of her baby, nor does it bring her husband's prompt return. The portrait with butchering knife calls to mind not only the ritual sacrifices of the Christian Bible but also the sacrificial rites of the ancient indigenous religions of Mexico, in some of which priests removed the still-beating hearts of victims with obsidian knives. The portrait here foreshadows and suggests María Concepción's murder of María Rosa, which takes place in the last chronological sequence of the story. The practice of this pagan rite of sacrifice, unlike the Christian ritual, is effectual: it returns Juan to the marital home and bed and replaces María Concepción's dead baby.

Two-thirds of the story is devoted to the events that take place when Juan and María Rosa return to the village after deserting from the army. These events take place during one day, one calendar year after the couple departed, that is, approximately two years after María Concepción wed Juan Villegas (on the Monday after Holy Week). This subtle placing of the events of the story in the spring suggests both pagan and Christian rites of sacrifice to appease deities and assure fruitful harvests.

In pre-Hispanic times, there were native Mexican rituals in which a surrogate for a god or goddess acted the role of that deity for a period of up to a year before being sacrificed to that very deity. It seems highly likely that Porter read Hubert H. Bancroft's *Native Races* in preparing *Outline* and incorporated elements gleaned from Bancroft into "María Concepción."[9] There seem to be too many allusions to *Civilized Nations,* volume 2, of this work to be merely coincidental. In chapter 9, "Public Festivals," there are descriptions, drawn from Spanish colonial accounts, of the practices of the Aztec religion. The accounts include that of the sacrifice of a man who acted as the mortal representative of the god Tezcatlipoca for a year. Twenty days before his death during the festival in May, the victim was married to four damsels representing four goddesses: Xochiquetzal, Xilonen, Atatonan, and Huixtocioatl. Finally, he was sacrificed by having his heart cut out. Bancroft also records the other festivals of the Aztec religious year, which included the sacrifice of women who were dressed to represent goddesses. Sacrifices honored such goddesses as Huixtocihuatl, the goddess of salt; Xilonen, a corn goddess; Centeotl, the mother-goddess; and Ilamatecutli, an aged goddess.[10]

Other details drawn from Aztec festivals as described by Bancroft seem to be alluded to in "María Concepción." At the outset of the festival of Tezcatlipoca, "young men and women devoted to the service of the temple . . . strewed the ground with maguey-thorns, that the devout might step upon them and draw blood in honor of the god."[11] Porter's opening portrait of María Concepción shows her walking on a road covered with "maguey thorns and the treacherous curved spines of organ cactus" (p. 3). On one day during the celebration of the feast of the war god Huitzilopochtli, the king appeared as the "sacerdotal character," took four quails, wrenched their heads off one after the other, and threw "the quivering bodies before the idol; the priests did the same, and then the people," after which the birds were prepared and eaten.[12] Porter may be hinting at this practice in her depiction of María Concepción's twisting off the head of a chicken for Givens (p. 7).

Details in the story establish María Rosa's yearlong enactment of the role of María Concepción. Like María Concepción before her, she puts up only token resistance to Juan's sexual advances outside marriage; she becomes lean, as does María Concepción, during the year at the war; she bears Juan's child. The Christian Easter holiday provides the foregrounding for the submerged allusions to pagan rites in the story. María Concepción's practice of Roman Catholicism and the references to her marriage immediately after Holy Week roughly place the events of the story from Easter to Easter of one calendar year.

Allusions to elements of Christ's Passion in the story illuminate the shallow Roman Catholicism of the Mexican Indians. Some of the events of the last part of the story resemble some events of the last week of Christ's life: his entry into Jerusalem, the Last Supper, his being taken prisoner, his trial and execution, the lamentation or pietà, and the Resurrection. Porter does not connect all of these to one character; she merely uses them as a context to imply that although Christianity is visible in the daily life of the Mexican peon, the pagan spirit and religion have remained ascendant. Although it is Juan who returns and is imprisoned and tried and María Rosa who is killed and lamented, it is María Concepción's resurrection that takes place. When she repudiates her Christian religion, does not turn the other cheek, and in revenge kills María Rosa, she reverts to her pagan indigenous religious roots and is reborn as an avatar of a fertility goddess. It is not an inconsequential detail that the *pulque* shop in the village is named "Death and Resurrection"; the death and eternal resurrection of the pagan spirit of Mexico is an underlying theme.

Porter subtly connects María Concepción and her surrogate María Rosa in descriptions connecting them with pre-Hispanic objects.

[María Concepción] sat down quietly under a sheltering thorny bush and gave herself over to her long devouring sorrow. . . . Drawing her rebozo over her head, she bowed her forehead on her updrawn knees, and sat there in deadly silence and immobility. From time to time she lifted her head where the sweat formed steadily and poured down her face, drenching the front of her chemise, and her mouth had the shape of crying, but there were no tears and no sound. (p. 13)

This depiction of the character very much resembles a clay or stone prehistoric figure, particularly in its masklike, almost stylized face. It calls to mind the faces of sculptures of the "jaguar type" with their grotesque downturned mouths.[13] After María Concepción's face is formed in this ancient cast, she rises, throws her rebozo off her face, and sets out walking on her way to murder or, perhaps more appropriate in this context, to perform the ritual sacrifice of María Rosa, a scene that is not described in the story.

Porter's later description of María Rosa's facial expression when she is laid out in her coffin is startling: "The mouth drooped sharply at the corners in a grimace of weeping arrested half-way. The brows were distressed; the dead flesh could not cast off the shape of its last terror" (p. 17). Her face, significantly, mirrors the earlier expression on María Concepción's, the downturned mouth of the jaguar type. It is the face of the surrogate who has acted the role of the goddess and who has been sacrificed in her stead.

The final sequence of scenes in the story shows the return to "the right inevitable proportions" once the gods are appeased. It begins with two images drawn from religious art. In one, María Concepción, with the baby in her arms, follows Juan out of the clearing around María Rosa's lighted jacal, which suggests the flight of the Virgin and Joseph into Egypt. In the second, Juan lies on his back, "his arms flung up and outward," (p. 21) which suggests a crucifixion. Porter then establishes the return to ancient customs and practices with the scenes of María Concepción with the mother goat and its kid, first allowing the kid to suckle and then milking the mother into a small clay jar. This signifies a return to the pre-Hispanic culture's ancient customs of agriculture and husbandry and to the consequent harmony with nature that implies.

María Concepción takes on the pose of an ancient goddess in the closing scene as she observes the landscape of the Anahuac Valley. Her pose here is significant: "She sat against the wall of her house, near the doorway. The child, fed and asleep, was cradled in the hollow of her crossed legs" (p. 21). Ramon Mena's *A Great Archaeological Discovery,* which contains the previously mentioned pictures of William Niven, also reproduces photographs of some rather unusual clay figures that bear strong resemblance to this depiction of María Concepción in the closing image of the story. Figure 6 of this monograph contains photographs of three different small clay figures of mothers with their babies. Two of the figures cradle their babies in the hollow of their

legs made as they are seated with their feet touching. The second of these figures, which most closely resembles María Concepción because the first has a
second baby strapped to her back, is said to represent a goddess who cradles
"not a live child, but a household god."[14] It seems inconceivable that Porter is
not alluding to this image in this closing portrait of María Concepción. The
resurrection of the ancient indigenous religion and spirit of Mexico is implied
in this allusion. It is Porter's way of announcing her sympathy with the aims
of the idealists among the Mexican government who felt that the salvation of
Mexico lay in turning to art and culture of the indigenous population for values and models.

Porter uses María Concepción to represent the indigenous population of
Mexico. The "perilous adventure" (p. 20) she undertakes inscribes a circle.
Her initial state of complete contentment is disturbed, and she experiences
pain, anger, grief, isolation from the community, sorrow, and suffering that
led her to an act of ritual murder and sacrifice. This act brings repentance, a
dream, and fear that, in turn, allow the relinquishing of her residual rancor
toward her now-dead enemy. Freed from her enmity, María Concepción is
reintegrated into the community, now "guarded, surrounded, upborne by her
faithful friends" with "reassurance, understanding, a secret and mighty sympathy" (p. 20). Once again an integral part of the indigenous community,
María Concepción returns to a state of contentment characterized by softness
and warmth, delicious rest, repose, ease, and happiness (p. 21). Through her
dramatic act of ritual sacrifice, María Concepción restores the order to her
community that had been disrupted by forces alien to it.

Once again, Porter condemns, as she does in "The Mexican Trinity,"[15]
the foreigners, the church, and the Mexican government or political figures
who exploited the autochthonous Mexicans, the Indians. The American
archaeologist Givens is the representative foreigner who patronizes and infan-
tilizes the indigenous men of the community while divesting them of their
history and art. The church, here represented by María Concepción's devout
Roman Catholicism, seems to serve only to isolate and alienate the individual
from his or her community. Mexican government and politics have generated
the war that separated Juan and many others like him from the communal
agricultural activities that successfully sustained their ancestors physically
and spiritually for centuries.

Porter's skillful appropriation of pre-Hispanic ritual and art in "María
Concepción" conveys one of its submerged messages, an idea that was articulated in her essay "Where Presidents Have No Friends," published only five
months before the story. That message is "redemption":

> They are all convinced, quite simply, that twelve millions of their fifteen
> millions of peoples cannot live in poverty, illiteracy, a most complete spiritual
> and mental darkness, without constituting a disgraceful menace to the state.
> They have a civilized conviction that the laborer is worthy of his hire, practical

perception of the waste entailed in millions of acres of untilled lands while the working people go hungry. And with this belief goes an aesthetic appreciation of the necessity of beauty in the national life, the cultivation of racial forms of art, and the creation of substantial and lasting unity in national politics.[16]

Notes

1.   In a letter dated 21 July 1924 to her sister Gay, Porter wrote: "But I do not want to stop in one place, for long at a time. Nothing is life for me, dear sister, except my preoccupation with writing. And that I did not choose. It merely remains, and I must suffer it" (Papers of Katherine Anne Porter; quoted with permission of Barbara Thompson Davis, trustee of the Katherine Anne Porter Literary Estate, and the University of Maryland at College Park Libraries).

2.   Katherine Anne Porter, "The Fiesta of Guadalupe," *El Heraldo de México* (13 December 1920): 10; reprinted in Ruth M. Alvarez and Thomas F. Walsh, eds., *Uncollected Early Prose of Katherine Anne Porter* (Austin: University of Texas Press, 1993).

3.   Porter, "In a Mexican Patio," *Magazine of Mexico* (April 1921); reprinted in Alvarez and Walsh.

4.   Porter, "Xochimilco," *Christian Science Monitor,* 31 May 1921, p. 10; reprinted in Alvarez and Walsh.

5.   *The Collected Stories of Katherine Anne Porter* (1965; rpt. San Diego: Harcourt Brace Jovanovich, 1979), 4. All parenthetical page references for quotations from "María Concepción" refer to page numbers in this edition.

6.   Porter's notes on a letter she received from Margaret Signer of Harcourt, Brace & World of 18 June 1965 state that "María Concepción" was "based on the story of Mr. Niven's real digger and his wife at Azcapotzalco" (Papers of Katherine Anne Porter).

7.   Ramon Mena, *A Great Archaeological Discovery: The Ancient Tecpanecs in the Valley of Mexico* (Mexico City: Imprenta Nacional, 1920); Katherine Anne Porter, *Outline of Mexican Popular Arts and Crafts* (Mexico City: S.I.C. y T./Los Angeles: Young and McCallister, 192; reprinted in Alvarez and Walsh).

8.   Ramon Mena, *Archaeological Novelties. The Cihuapipiltin (Spirit Goddesses), The Tzitzimime (Monsters), Teotihuacan Vases* (Mexico City: n.p., 1921).

9.   Bancroft is one of the historians Porter reports having read in preparing *Outline*. See Hubert Howe Bancroft, *The Native Races of the Pacific States of North America,* 5 vols. (New York: D. Appleton, 1874–76).

10.   Bancroft, 319–21, 325–27; 331–32; and 337–38.

11.   Bancroft, 322.

12.   Typically, villages such as the one in the story held fiestas reenacting the events of Christ's Passion during Holy Week. Indeed, the 1911 edition of *Terry's Mexico* notes that a "crude sort of Passion Play" was performed in the village of Azcapotzalco on Good Friday." See T. Philip Terry, *Terry's Mexico: Handbook for Travelers* (London: Gay and Handcock, 1911), 421.

13.   Justino Fernández in *A Guide to Mexican Art from Its Beginnings to the Present* (Chicago: University of Chicago Press, 1969) mentions and reproduces pictures of examples of such sculptures (11–12, 14, 15, 206, 209, 212).

14.   See Ramon Mena, *A Great Archaeological Discovery,* 21, 33.

15.   Katherine Anne Porter, "The Mexican Trinity," *Freeman* 3 (3 August 1921): 493–95; reprinted in Katherine Anne Porter, *The Collected Essays and Occasional Writings of Katherine Anne Porter* (New York: Seymour Lawrence/Delacorte, 1970).

16.   Katherine Anne Porter, "Where Presidents Have No Friends," *Century* 104 (July 1922): 273–84; reprinted in *Collected Essays.*

A Re-Reading of Katherine Anne Porter's "Theft"

Joan Givner

"Theft" has been interpreted with ingenuity by several critics. Many more have commented on its qualities while evading the crucial issue of its interpretation. I believe that the meaning of the story is unambiguous. The theme, which it shares with many other of Katherine Anne Porter's stories, is self-delusion in the face of evil and is most clearly developed in *Ship of Fools*. The purpose of this paper is to expound the theme and show how certain passages in the novel emphasize its close relationship with the story.

"Theft," like *Ship of Fools*, describes a journey during which the protagonist meets with evil in various but unmistakable forms. Camilo, Bill, and the defeminized janitress are important only as representatives of moral laxity, and they are particularized only by details that reveal the degree and the kind of their wickedness. The evil in each of them is indicated by profanity, insobriety, and thieving.

Camilo is merely beginning to gravitate towards evil. He is almost sober, almost honest, and only slightly profane. (The common New Testament expression that he uses frivolously suggests to Mr. William Bysshe Stein a reference in Peter.[1] Surely much more appropriate to the story are the words of Christ to the buyers and sellers in the temple, "It is written my house shall be called a house of prayer; but ye have made it a den of thieves").

Bill is deeply entrenched in his evil ways. He is drunk, profane, and dishonest. He does not even trouble, as Camilo does, to hide his dishonesty. He has moved from overt, conscious deceit to self-deception. When others refuse to permit his abuse, he sobs with self-pity. When the girl asks for her money, he feels like the martyred Caesar.

The janitress represents evil in its most extreme and undisguised form. She is not drunk but "crazy"—a detail that is possibly illuminated by Dr. Schumann's belief, in *Ship of Fools*, that madness is "the temporary triumph of Evil in the human soul."[2] Her stealing is the outright theft of a precious

Reprinted with permission of the journal from *Studies in Short Fiction* 6 (1969): 463–65. Copyright 1969 by Newberry College.

object, and here, as in *Ship of Fools,* theft is the unequivocal symbol of wickedness. Her appearance, sketched in crude strokes, is evocative of the devil in a medieval play—a suggestion entirely appropriate to Porter's concept of evil as a recognizable, physical entity.

The girl's dilemma in the face of the three evil people is that which the Lutzes and the Baumgartners discuss before their departure from Tenerife. Frau Lutz speaks with sarcasm against the failure of the company to concern itself with such "pecadilloes" as the twins' theft of the pearls and their parents' robbery of the merchants. She is rebuked by her husband for whom it is an article of faith to ignore "petty pilfering." Herr Glocken alone of the group recognizes his own cowardice.

The girl in "Theft" closely resembles the voyagers in her failure to oppose the evil-doers, but her reasons are her own. She does not share Herr Glocken's physical fear nor Herr Lutz's indifference, but instead takes pride in "some principle of rejection in her that made her uncomfortable in the ownership of things." It is interesting to compare with her explanation Frau Hutten's statement on the subject:

> . . . I do know well there are many evil people in this world, many more evil than good ones, even the lazy good ones; evil by nature, by choice, by deepest inclination, evil all through; we encourage these monsters by being charitable to them, by making excuses for them, or just by being slack, as Dr. Schumann says. Too indifferent to be bothered so long as they do not harm *us.* And sometimes even if they *do* harm us. They don't in the least care that we are being scrupulous to treat them fairly and honestly—no, they laugh up their sleeves at us, and call us fools, and go on cheating us even more, because they think we are too stupid to know what they are doing to us! And we do not punish them as they deserve, because we have lost our sense of justice, and we say, 'If we put a thief in jail, or a murderer to death, we are as criminal as they!' Oh what injustice to innocent people and what sentimental dishonesty and we should be ashamed of it. Or we go on blindly saying, 'If we behave well to them, they will end by behaving well to us!' That is one of the great lies of life. I have found that this makes them bolder, because they despise us instead of fearing us as they should—and it is all our own weakness, and yes, we do evil in letting them do evil without punishment. They think we are cowards and they are right. At least we are dupes and we deserve what we get from them. . . .[3]

Frau Hutten's words are crucial in the novel because they express and explain the author's strong indictment of the negative collusion of evil. They are no less relevant to the short story. In particular, they confirm what I have always felt to be the point of the cumulative effect of the girl's encounters. Miss Porter places these in increasing order of seriousness not merely to show that the girl's inclination to let herself be wronged is habitual and persistent even in the case of an outright theft. The author's purpose, I believe, is to show that the girl is directly responsible for the increasing boldness of the evil-doers because she encourages them. Furthermore, she is responsible for their ill-treatment of other people. For this reason the author has carefully mentioned the other personal involvements of Roger, Bill, and the janitress.

Equally important to both works is the following description of the crisis in Dr. Schumann's life. The narrator makes it directly.

> At this moment his own suffering in his own guilt drew him slowly into a vast teeming shapeless wallow of compassion for every suffering thing, a confusion so dark he could no longer tell the difference between the invader and the invaded, the violator and the violated, the betrayer and the betrayed, the one who loved and the one who hated or who jeered or was indifferent. The whole great structure built upon the twin pillars of justice and love, which reached from earth into eternity, by which the human soul rose step by step from the most rudimentary concepts of good and evil, of simple daily conduct between fellow men, to the most exquisite hairline discriminations and choices between one or another shade of faith and feeling, of doctrinal and mystical perceptions—this tower was now crumbling and falling around him.[4]

This provides an interesting commentary on the girl, who accepts the guilt of those who deceive her. When she sees Camilo hiding his hat, she feels that she is the betrayer. Bill's refusal to pay his debts takes the form of the accusation, "you, too." Finally, the janitress accuses her victim of theft.

The passage has the additional interest of illuminating the key incident in the story. Here the girl meets Roger, with whom she has shared "a long amiable association." They are associated in terms of the theme of the story because they are both incapable of positive action. They allow themselves to be used and swayed by stronger, usually evil, people. Their precarious taxi ride between the pillars of the Elevated is a symbolic indication of the dangerous course they hold. Together they share three encounters that are miniature versions of the three main episodes of the story. Although the characters they meet together are suggested by the merest detail, they are clearly marked as dangerous, selfish, and materialistic people. (Bird imagery in her portraits is almost invariably a mark of Miss Porter's distaste). Roger, who understands fully the "difficulty of holding out" against dangerous people, shrugs off the meetings with such remarks as "homicidal maniac" and "nuts, pure nuts," and he longs for a drink to steady himself. As they ride, the "outlines and shapes of things" are blurred by the rain. When they part, it is made clear that Roger's values have become confused, and he aligns himself with the evil characters. Like them, he treats the girl with empty solicitude and shirks his responsibility towards her. He postpones her moment of awareness until the end of the story.

One of the difficulties for readers of "Theft" is in finding the main emphasis of the story. The girl is evidently being criticized because she allows others to take advantage of her. But this is not very unusual, interesting, or even very bad. Consequently, critics have tended to inject more spectacular elements into their commentaries. William B. Stein, in the account mentioned above, reads the story as "the betrayal of the holistic ideal of Christian love." Leonard Prager sees it as "the problem of an 'emancipated' career woman who is starving emotionally in the Wasteland of urban anonymity and alienation."[5] I think that a reading of *Ship of Fools* corrects the perspective of such interpretations, for it makes clear the writer's attitude to the girl's kind of casualness. It may not ordinarily be regarded as a criminal kind of carelessness, but to Katherine Anne Porter it is monumentally disastrous in its consequences. The whole of *Ship of Fools* expresses this point of view, and the passages I have quoted conveniently epitomize it.

Notes

1.   " 'Theft': Porter's Politics of Modern Love," *Perspective* 11 (Winter 1960): 223–28.
2.   Katherine Anne Porter, *Ship of Fools* (Boston: Atlantic, Little-Brown, 1962), 115.
3.   Porter, 295.
4.   *Ibid.,* 372.
5.   Leonard Prager, "Getting and Spending: Porter's 'Theft,' " *Perspective* 11 (Winter 1960): 230–34.

Internal Opposition in Porter's "Granny Weatherall"

Joseph Wiesenfarth

> We learn from a study of the whole that mankind can never definitively attain
> a thoroughly purposive life-order, inasmuch as this order itself is rent in sunder
> by internal oppositions.
>
> Karl Jaspers

Katherine Anne Porter's story "The Source"[1] is an anecdote about order and
disorder. In the spring of each year Grandmother goes to the country to put
things in order. The primitive life of the Negroes on the farm and the ineffec-
tiveness of her widower son Harry both there and in town represent disorder
to Grandmother. She and such authors as Dante, Pope, Shakespeare, and
Johnson, whose works she carefully preserves on the bookshelves of the country house, stand for order. Where she is, order is; where she is not, order is
absent. When things are relatively in order in the town house, she goes to the
country. When things are in order there, she returns home to start all over
again. The story is, then, about a woman's need for order, the good that order
effects and the inconveniences it causes. But "The Source" is something more
than this too.

Grandmother leaves the town house when things still need to be done.
She finds she must return to the farm each spring, a return which is for her a
source of something. Of what, it is unclear. Perhaps of life, perhaps of self-
assurance, perhaps even of self-deception about the waste and disorder that
time is working in her. For instance, Grandmother sees her horse aging and
slowing down, but not herself. "This yearly gallop with Fiddler was important to her; it proved her strength, her unabated energy."

The sense of yearly recurrence, the repetition of a seasonal activity of
cleaning and restoring, and Grandmother's seasonal assurance of vitality that
comes with riding Fiddler suggest ritual. Furthermore, "The Source" is written in the past tense and gives the impressions of a pattern of life repeated
again and again. Irony sounds in the story, though, with the sense one has of

Reprinted with permission of the Helen Dwight Reed Educational Foundation from *Critique* 11, no.
2 (1969): 47–55. Copyright 1969.

Grandmother's lineal decline in the face of this circular pattern of renewal. Gently the story suggests that she is unable to accept the changes time brings, unable to accept and understand that the inevitable order of timeless laws must be accepted if any personal order is to be significant. As a story of this kind—in which surface order keeps from awareness the demands of a more radical personal need—"The Source" suggests the pattern of its more brilliant counterpart, "The Jilting of Granny Weatherall."[2]

On her deathbed Granny Weatherall's emotional and spiritual well-being is threatened by the revival of her memory of the fiancé who jilted her. George left her at the altar when she was twenty years old, and in her eightieth year Granny is threatened by his appearance:

> What does a woman do when she has put on the white veil and set out the white cake for a man and he doesn't come. She tried to remember. No I swear he never harmed me but in that. He never harmed me but in that . . . and what if he did? There was the day, the day, but a whirl of dark smoke rose and covered it, crept up and over into the bright field where everything was planted so orderly in rows. That was hell, she knew hell when she saw it. For sixty years she had prayed against remembering him and against losing her soul in the deep pit of hell, and now the two things were mingled in one and the thought of him was a smoky cloud from hell that moved and crept in her head. . . .

The smoky cloud from hell, the thought of George, threatens to obscure "the bright field where everything was planted so orderly in rows." This image is a miniature of the conflict in "The Jilting of Granny Weatherall." Which will prevail, the cloud or the orderly bright field—the memory of George or the order that has made life's day bright enough to render one cloud unimportant?

Granny gave order to her life after her jilting. Now in retrospect she praises it: it is good to "spread out a plan of life and tuck in the edges orderly." "She had fenced in a hundred acres once, digging the post holes herself and clamping the wires with just a negro boy to help." Even now Granny feels like jumping out of bed, "rolling up her sleeves and putting the whole place to rights again." Granny sees her life as orderly and complete: "Everything came in good time. Nothing left out, left over." She even feels that she has death under control: "She had spent so much time preparing for death there was no need for bringing it up again." Ellen Weatherall is convinced, therefore, even though the "whole bottom dropped out of the world" when she was jilted, that she has "found another [life] a whole world better."

But when one world is taken apart and another world is put together, there are bound to be similar things in both worlds. If Ellen Weatherall lost a husband in George, she gained one in John. If she had no children by one, she had Jimmy, Lydia, Hapsy, and Cornelia by the other. If she did not make a home for George and the children she could have had by him, she did make one for John and his children. The orderly life Granny remembers having had continuously calls to mind the life of love she might have had save for the jilting. This process of association threatens to bring the memory of George, which for Granny Weatherall is hell.[3]

For instance, Granny's passionate concern for the order of the world she made through marriage gives the reader his first indication of the two men in her life. As she thinks that "It was good to have everything clean and folded away," she remembers something she has not yet taken care of: "The box in the attic with all those letters—George's letters and John's letters and her letters to them both—lying around for the children to find afterwards made her uneasy. Yes, that would be tomorrow's business. No use to let them know how silly she had been once." To put her letters in order is to put her life in order. Granny seems to think that a symbolic gesture can undo an actual event.

When Granny thinks of her children now, she remembers how they were years ago. Lydia comes to her mother to ask her advice when one of the children jumps the track. Jimmy asks her advice on finances, Cornelia cannot change the furniture around without Granny's direction. "Little things, little things! They had been so sweet when they were little." Little things become little children, and Granny remembers how she directed the children when they were little: "I want you to pick all the fruit this year and see that nothing is wasted. There's always someone who can use it. Don't let good things rot for want of using. You waste life when you waste food. Don't let things get lost. It's bitter to lose things. Now, don't let me get to thinking, not when I am tired and taking a little nap before supper. . . ." But Granny cannot stop the train of associations once it is underway. A few seconds later she remembers that she once "set out the white cake for a man" and he did not come. It was wasted, and so too was part of her life. Later she again remembers "the day the wedding cake was not cut, but thrown out and wasted" and that with the wasted cake she lost one world. The things of the world which Granny made inevitably return her to the world she lost: the tidy house to the untidy love letters, the children and the orchard to waste, and waste to the uneaten wedding cake. Granny's orderly world returns inevitably to its source—the wedding day that never was.

Granny's poignant sensuous recollections are symbolic and distract her attention from the present to remind her of her husband, her children, and her religion, points of order in her past; they also remind her of George, the source of disorder in her life. The light by her bed reminds Granny of the ritual of lighting the lamp for the children: "Lighting the lamps had been beautiful. The children huddled up to her and breathed like little calves waiting at the bars in twilight. Their eyes followed the match and watched the flame rise and settle in a blue curve, then they moved away from her. The lamp was lit, they didn't have to be scared and hang on to the mother any more." The nearby light not only reminds Granny of the ceremony of lighting the lamp for her children, but also of the day of her jilting:

> Granny lay curled down within herself, amazed and watchful, staring at the point of light that was herself; her body was now only a deeper mass of shadow in an endless darkness and this darkness would curl around the light and swallow it up. God, give a sign!
> For a second time there was no sign. Again no bridegroom and priest in the house.

The pressure beneath Granny's breast from shortness of breath becomes for her the pangs of childbirth: "Her breath crowded down under her ribs grew into a monstrous frightening shape with cutting edges; it bored up into her head, and the agony was unbelievable: Yes, John, get the Doctor now, no more talk, my time has come." But this pain does not only remind Granny of the birth of her children, who were her consolation, but it also recalls the abortive wedding day: "His hand caught her under the breast, she had not fallen, there was the freshly polished floor with the green rug on it, just as before. He had cursed like a sailor's parrot and said, 'I'll kill him for you.'"

Granny made her new life out of things that compose the worlds of most women: "I had my husband . . . and my children and my house like any other woman." Besides this Granny had her religion: "She had her secret comfortable understanding with a few favorite saints who cleared a straight road to God for her." It is only fitting that Father Connolly should come to her deathbed to minister to her: "the table by the bed had a linen cover and a candle and a crucifix." This reminds Granny of an altar and of the day that she was left at it by George: "What if he did run away and leave me to face the priest by myself?"

Her daughter Cornelia reminds Granny of Hapsy, a daughter whom she seems to love most but who also seems to have caused her most pain. Hapsy also recalls George. Hapsy seems to have been Granny's last child, the "one she had truly wanted." Hapsy becomes confused with Granny's very self: "She had to go a long way back through a great many rooms to find Hapsy standing with a baby on her arm. She seemed to herself to be Hapsy also, and the baby on Hapsy's arm was Hapsy and himself and herself, all at once, and there was no surprise in the meeting." Granny keeps asking for Hapsy. At one time she thinks that Lydia is Hapsy, at another she mistakes Cornelia for Hapsy; altogether she asks for Hapsy on five occasions. But Hapsy never comes. As Granny is dying, presumably in pain, watching the light within her, aware of the priest nearby, Hapsy does not come, just as George did not come under similar circumstances sixty years ago.[4] Disorder breaks through the order of Granny's life; no sign comes to give meaning to the delay of the heavenly bridegroom, who merges with Hapsy (who does not come) and with

George (who did not come), and Granny is overwhelmed: "She could not remember any other sorrow because this grief wiped them all away. Oh, no, there's nothing more cruel than this—I'll never forgive it. She stretched herself with a deep breath and blew out the light."

The disorder of Granny's past—inevitably associated with the order of her having been wife, mother, and Catholic—forces itself through the surface order that has been covering it, and Granny's fear of George's return to memory materializes. With the memory of him comes a darkness that prevents her from seeing the order of her life just as previously in her memory the "whirl of dark smoke" covered "the bright field where everything was planted so carefully in orderly rows." Granny, who had so carefully controlled life, cannot control death: "Oh, my dear Lord, do wait a minute. I meant to do something about the Forty Acres, Jimmy doesn't need it and Lydia will later on. . . ." But death will not wait for Granny to put the last shreds of her life in order. She is once again left to face the priest alone. Granny is forced to a final decision: she blows out the light of her life.

One must avoid being simplistically moral and declaring that Granny tried to love God without forgiving the man who jilted her, that she did not heed the command to leave her gift at the altar and make peace with her fellow man before trying to offer it, and that therefore Granny came to the end of her days like one of the foolish virgins without sufficient oil in her lamp to attend the bridegroom's coming.[5] Each of these statements may be partly true, and the imagery of the story may even support such a reading. But one must not read the story so simply, for Granny tried to do what she thought right. Her success was limited because she thought that in being orderly she could be human. She forgot that the order of her life was compelled into being the day she was jilted; she forgot that the jilting was as much a part of her personal existence as the married life and the religion that made up for it; she forgot that the jilting was the source of disorder as well as order; and that the elements of that order—as the structure of the story shows—lead ineluctably to their disorderly source.

In this connection the most telling sentence in "Granny Weatherall" is "Beads wouldn't do, it must be something alive." As Granny dies she drops her rosary and grasps the hand of her son. The central fact of Granny's life has been her jilting at age twenty; the remaining sixty years of her life constituted her attempt to reorder life through marriage, rearing a family, and devotion to her religion. But each of these implies for Granny something other than "alive." Like the beads she drops, they constitute a conventional order; but they are really meaningless since they are without a vitalizing human principle. Thus, as her life ends, the fact of her jilting shows itself as her life-source and challenges the conventional order of her existence. Granny finds that all the order she has put into her life has not enabled her to cope with the tragedy of her jilting sixty years before. Here, at the moment of death, she learns that neither marriage, nor children, nor religion suffices to bring her a peace of soul and human wholeness that can reconcile her to the once unfaithful George. At this moment of death a question earlier posed is answered for Granny: "Oh, no, oh, God, there was something else besides the house and the man and the children. Oh surely they were not all? What was it?"

Love was denied Granny the day she was jilted and she herself never again dared to love. But without love Granny's radically human hurt was never healed: "To a woman all reformation, all salvation from any sort of ruin," writes Dostoyevski, "and all moral renewal is included in love and can only show itself in that form."[6] Granny required a love more human than any order she had created to heal the rankling wound left in her soul by George's infidelity. This need to love could have no approximation in her life. In spite of all that she did and all that she overcame to give her life meaning, Granny was unsuccessful because, in the end, she never again dared seek a love as vital as the one she was once cruelly denied. Rather she settled for the safer and seemingly less dangerous way of order. But Granny's life of order, as we have seen, "is rent in sunder by internal oppositions."[7]

"The Jilting of Granny Weatherall," then, is not a moral tale about forgiveness, a gospel parable in modern dress. We are not asked in this story to face with a shudder the damnation of an octogenarian. The next world enters the story to give meaning to this world. The boundary situation is here for the sake of the land of the living, not of the dead. We are directed to look at Granny Weatherall and to realize what she—trapped by the inability to understand the paradox of order—cannot: that in spite of showing great courage, that in spite of pushing against the stone of her jilting, that in spite of doing more than many another person might have done in similar circumstances, she has lived a less than truly satisfying life. We are asked to see that the problem of existence has been vexing and difficult for Granny and that she has not satisfactorily solved it. In short, we are asked to see in "The Jilting of Granny Weatherall" that to weather all is not necessarily to live—to see that beads alone will never do, that there "must [always] be something alive."

Notes

1. *The Leaning Tower and Other Stories* (New York: Harcourt, Brace, 1944), 3–10.
2. *Flowering Judas and Other Stories* (New York: Harcourt, Brace, 1935), 121–36.
3. I find it impossible to agree with William L. Nance's description of Ellen Weatherall's relation to George as "an evanescent love affair," because it stays with her till death; or with his description of it as "simply a romantic dream, never in danger of becoming real," because it takes her all the way to the altar and the moment of marriage. Nance's interpretation is guided by his thesis of a *rejection* pattern in Katherine Anne Porter's stories: "the puritanical fear of sex instilled into her by her religious and moral tradition" makes Ellen Weatherall "essentially true to this pattern." In interpreting Granny's relation to George, Nance is the

victim of his thesis. See *Katherine Anne Porter and the Art of Rejection* (Chapel Hill: University of North Carolina Press, 1964), 42–46.

4.   George Hendrick suggests that the baby on Hapsy's arm—"himself" in the passage quoted above—"was undoubtedly George, whom she couldn't call by name," *Katherine Anne Porter* (New York: Twayne, 1965), 92. This is probably not the case. More probably George is recalled by Granny's association of Hapsy with frustrated love and with expectation because, in the end, she is unfulfilled.

5.   Ray B. West, Jr., *Katherine Anne Porter* (Minneapolis: University of Minnesota Press, 1963), 9, has pointed out the parallel between the earthly and heavenly bridegroom. So too has Robert G. Cowser in "Porter's 'Jilting of Granny Weatherall,' " *Explicator* 21 (December 1962): 4.

6.   *Notes from the Underground,* trans. Constance Garnett, revised by Avrahm Yamolinsky (New York, 196), 293. Katherine Anne Porter details her own view of reformation by love when she commends E. M. Forster's "unalterable belief in the first importance of the individual relationships between human beings founded on the reality of love—not in the mass, not between nations, nonsense!—but between one person and another. This is of course much more difficult than loving just everybody and everything, for each must really do something about it, and show faith in works," *The Days Before* (New York, 1952), 219.

7.   Karl Jaspers, *Men in the Modern World,* trans. Eden and Cedar Paul (New York, n.d.), 75.

"The Other Side of Silence": Katherine Anne Porter's "He" as Tragedy

BRUCE W. JORGENSEN

"He" ends as Mrs. Whipple is taking her feeble-minded, unnamed son to the County Home where she has finally admitted He may receive better care and no longer physically burden his family for whom "Life was very hard."[1] On the way He begins to cry, "rubbing His nose with His knuckles, and then with the end of the blanket" and "scrubbing away big tears that rolled out of the corners of His eyes" (p. 58). Neither we nor Mrs. Whipple can know for certain the motive of His weeping, but it drives in upon His mother the awareness she has warded off all of His life—that, however hindered by His condition from showing love or gratitude, He is far more a human being, a person, than she has allowed herself to think. The knowledge is terrible; whatever the reason for His weeping.

> Mrs. Whipple couldn't bear to think of it. She began to cry, frightfully, and wrapped her arms right around Him. His head rolled on her shoulder: she had loved Him as much as she possibly could, there were Adna and Ernly who had to be thought of too, there was nothing she could do to make up to Him for His life. Oh, what a mortal pity He was ever born.
>
> They came in sight of the hospital, with the neighbor driving very fast, not daring to look behind him. (p. 58)

Miss Porter once remarked that "Any true work of art has got to give you the feeling of reconciliation—what the Greeks would call catharsis, the purification of your mind and imagination—through an ending that is endurable because it is right and true. . . . Sometimes the ending is very tragic, because it needs to be."[2] The ending of "He," I believed when I first tried to discuss the story with beginning literature students, intends just such a catharsis, "endurable because it is right and true" and "tragic because it needs to be." Surely the last two sentences intend to focus for our minds and imaginations the classic emotions that Aristotle said tragedy purifies—pity

Reprinted with the permission of The Johns Hopkins University Press from *Modern Fiction Studies* 28 (Autumn 1982): 395–404.

and terror; and surely those emotions are proper to the situation and action of "He."

My students had a hard time seeing it: either they excessively, sentimentally pitied Mrs. Whipple, or they excessively, moralistically condemned her. I have since learned that recent critics of Miss Porter's story have fared little better: most of them lean either toward excessive pathos or toward excessive, even contemptuous irony. Thus James W. Johnson in 1960, though mentioning "the unavoidable tragedy of the abnormal child, the victim of a biological accident" (thus seeming to use the word in its loose, non-literary sense of "deep misfortune"), moralistically implied that Mrs. Whipple might have suffered less had she not "refus[ed] to accept the facts."[3] Harry John Mooney came a little closer in 1962, speaking of the "pathetic ending" as a "final" and "grim tragedy in a mother's life" and of the story itself as "a small tragedy"; but he did not point to the pity and terror of the ending as evidence, nor did he explain what he meant, and he sentimentalized Mrs. Whipple in seeing her as "altogether committed to Him."[4] In 1963 Paul F. Deasy, though seeing that in the last scene Mrs. Whipple realizes "He is as real as anybody," read the story moralistically as showing how Mrs. Whipple's "failure to face reality leads to frustration"; he saw her love for her child as "unreal" and argued, without explaining how, that "Peace would lie in accepting Him as He is."[5]

William L. Nance in 1964 viewed the story as "a masterpiece of finely balanced satire and pathos" with an "all-judging ironic narrator"; he found no one in the story "with whom the author or reader is inclined to identify sympathetically," and like Deasy he condemned Mrs. Whipple's "totally inadequate response to reality," her "folly of self-delusion" or "willful blindness"; he rightly called attention to "the failure of the boy's parents to recognize his personality" as "the root of their error and suffering" but also, without evidence, blamed their poverty on "their own laziness and ineptitude"; though finally allowing that the last scene "leaves the reader suspended between condemnation and sympathy for this weak woman in her hard fate," he seemed to miss the way the last sentence about the driver brings into focus the tragic emotion of terror.[6]

In 1965, George Hendrick saw the story as "stressing the irony of the situation but ending with compassion for both mother and child," yet he did not allow that the reader could have compassion for Mrs. Whipple before the end; he felt, rightly I think, that the boy is "beyond human help," able to "receive but . . . not [to] return love"; yet far too simplistically he saw Mrs. Whipple's "professed love" as merely "a cover for hatred" thinly masked "with Christian piety"; for him, finally, the story was "completely pessimistic."[7] Winfred S. Emmons in 1967 allowed the Whipples "a certain dignity, though small," and admitted the boy was "a problem that nobody could solve"; but he also saw Mrs. Whipple as "very possibly hat[ing] Him," as certainly "wish[ing] He had never been born" (though that is not precisely what she says), and as practicing "the eleventh commandment, which is to put up the appearance of a virtue if you cannot manage the real thing"; for him, the story's tone was "unrelievedly pathetic."[8]

In 1971, in the fullest discussion so far, Myron M. Liberman called "He" one of the most "harrowing" stories in English, "a little gem of enormous thematic magnitude" in which "a universe of human suffering is worked out . . . in a way that involves the reader most painfully, without resorting to sentimentality or preachment," and in which the author "succeeds as always in maintaining that 'delicate balance of rival considerations' " that Robert Penn Warren long ago cited as a primary quality of her work; like Hendrick, Liberman saw the ironic narrative voice as allowing the reader to feel compassion for Mrs. Whipple only at the end; reading more cautiously than Hendrick or Emmons, he noted that "no matter how His mother feels about Him, that feeling is bound to be something less than unalloyed love," yet he did not clearly define her feeling; he did see what I would call the "choral" function of the last sentence about the neighbor, and thus came close to defining the story's catharsis; most importantly, he pointed out that "the burden of the story is the terrible question of how many of us could have succeeded in giving love where Mrs. Whipple failed."[9]

That remark, of course, is the perfect answer to those critics who find it too easy to condemn Mrs. Whipple, and after Liberman's care and clarity it is a letdown to come to John Edward Hardy's comment in 1973 (which acknowledged a debt to Liberman's discussion of the neighbor's final reaction), for Hardy saw Mrs. Whipple as having an "obsession" with her retarded son which she is "pleased to call . . . love"; he regarded her as "severely punished" in the end for the "cruel folly" of her pride; thus he found it "easy justice on the reader's part to refuse [Mrs. Whipple the pity] she so despises."[10]

The main irony of the critical history of "He" is that its earliest commentators, those of the Thirties and Forties, read the story most clearly, whereas those of the Sixties and Seventies, supposedly better trained, have so persistently misconstrued it or seen it partially rather than as a whole. Thus Mary Orvis in 1948 saw Mrs. Whipple as "caught in a moral trap" from which "there is in all reality no possible escape" and in which her final action "is at best a compromise that must confront her all the rest of her life," leaving her "only the agony of guilt."[11] Mrs. Orvis did not use the word "tragedy" in her comment, yet she defined the story clearly in a way that would accord with Karl Jaspers' dictum, "Absolute and radical tragedy means that there is no way out whatsoever."[12] Claude M. Simpson and Allan Nevins in 1941 also viewed the ending of the story as "an incident of genuine tragedy," though without explaining why.[13] But surely the most accurate comment on the story was the earliest, Howard Baker's single paragraph published in 1938, which used "He" to represent Miss Porter's "remarkable attainment" in *Flowering Judas,* her "perfection of a highly selective realistic method": viewing the retarded boy as "a kindly, helpful, and beloved creature, whom his parents cannot avoid taking advantage of, and who exceeds little by little their capacity for caring for him," Baker saw how the author was able "to indicate fully the thousand-fold aspects of the parents' predicament—the love, the misgivings, the rationalizings, the blind hope, the impotence, the awareness of need for help, the shame at having the neighbors know"—in such a way that "the story becomes genuinely tragic."[14]

The problem "He" poses for its audience, critics and common readers alike, is moral as much as literary: how to avoid easy pity or easy contempt for Mrs. Whipple; how to arrive at the justice of a clear, balanced estimate of her situation, character, and actions. Baker's summary displays the kind of critical negative capability that the problem demands—the capacity to see Mrs. Whipple in terms of both/and rather than either/or, to see that she can and does love her retarded son even at the same time she compulsively exposes Him to danger and harm, and to see that intolerable moral paradox as defining her tragic predicament. Baker took a long step forward in understanding the story, which unfortunately most recent critics failed to follow. Those who saw Mrs. Whipple's love as a mere mask for her "real" hatred and thus found it easy to condemn her would have done well to take the advice Blake once addressed in a couplet "To God":

> If you have form'd a Circle to go into,
> Go into it yourself & see how you would do.[15]

Liberman at least brought the discussion back to this point.

The audience's problem with Mrs. Whipple, I suspect, was also the author's problem, and I further suspect that she began to solve it by going into the circle she had formed, sympathetically trying to see Mrs. Whipple's situation from inside, though with greater clarity of intelligence than Mrs. Whipple could possibly bring to bear on it. We might formulate the moral problem Mrs. Whipple faces in this way: because her son is retarded (and after a head injury forgets the few words He has learned), so that He cannot respond to His family or express His feelings with anything approaching the fullness of even relatively inarticulate people like the Whipples, He is in some sense hindered from being fully a person, but He is not a dumb animal either. Mrs. Whipple must in the beginning have loved Him as instinctively as most parents love the infants who must utterly depend on them; but as His body grew, He remained in that infantile dependence, and Mrs. Whipple already had one child older than He, and later another younger, both of whom were normal and who thus not only outgrew their total dependence but also were capable of returning their parents' affection and of responsibly caring for some of their own needs. In the family's "hard" life (which, significantly, Miss Porter defines for us before introducing their second son), Mrs. Whipple cannot possibly care adequately for all three, so she compromises, giving Him a larger share of privation and risk because "He don't really mind" (p. 51); in this, of course, her judgment is already distorted by unconscious resentment of His disability and by guilt for that resentment. And so the fabric of Mrs. Whipple's self-deceptions and rationalizations weaves around her to the point where she cannot, until the end, realize or admit the degree to which He is a person. How *would* we do in that circle?

The great risk to our justice as we enter the circle is the temptation of sentimental identification with Mrs. Whipple, of excessive pity for her as the victim of impossible circumstances. The audience, and I suspect the author as well, needed some check on compassion, and the ironic narrative voice provides that check. Contra Hendrick and Liberman, I do not hear Miss Porter's irony as consistent throughout the story up to its last scene; to my ear its effects are intermittent, local rather than pervasive, and qualified by context so as not entirely to undercut Mrs. Whipple's view of herself.

Thus in the story's exposition we first see how Mrs. Whipple's stubborn, petty pride motivates the duplicity she practices "when the neighbors were in earshot" (p. 49); but with a retarded child and *those* neighbors, how would we do? For they talk "plainly among themselves" of how the child's defect is "the sins of the fathers," the result of "bad blood and bad doings somewhere, you can bet on that" (pp. 49–50). We can hardly blame Mrs. Whipple for not wanting to be looked down on by such neighbors, even if she doesn't know exactly what they say behind her back.

Similarly, that Mrs. Whipple is "forever saying" that she loves "her second son . . . better . . . than the other two children put together" and occasionally "even throw[ing] in her husband and her mother for good measure" (p. 49) does not necessarily mean that she simply hates her son. Mr. Whipple, bitter and cynical as he is, implicitly accepts that she does have "feelings about Him" (p. 49). As she says, "It's natural for a mother" (p. 49), and we need not deny her natural affection, even as we see that because it is also "expected," she exaggerates its quantity and purity and thus makes it increasingly difficult for herself to know her own true feelings.

Again, it seems quite true that, at one level, Mrs. Whipple "wouldn't have anything happen to Him for all the world" (p. 50), though this masks her unadmitted guilt over His defect and her suppressed resentment at His passive dependence. She does patently overstate His invulnerability ("He can do anything and not get a scratch"), and she takes a desperate though quite real and deep solace in the preacher's saying that "The innocent walk with God" (p. 50). In the incident of the plank striking His head, the irony is heavy and lucid: clearly He was injured, for "He had learned a few words, and after this He forgot them"; but it may also be simply true that "He never seemed to know it" (p. 50). We arrive at the same sort of judgment when "in bad weather" the Whipples give Emly "the extra blanket off His cot," rationalizing that "He never seemed to mind the cold" (p. 50): obviously it cannot be good for Him, yet He may indeed not "mind" it. It must be simply true that, however much she deceives herself about such compromises, "Just the same, Mrs. Whipple's life was a torment for fear something might happen to Him" (p. 50); but the torment must be compounded almost unimaginably by her fear of the neighbors' judgment, by her unacknowledged hostility and by her guilt over it.

In the exposition of "He," then, an ironic narrative voice, always qualified by context so as to preclude easy, simplistic condemnation, requires us to make such complex judgments, allowing the validity of Mrs. Whipple's natural motherly feelings but also insisting on the reality of her unadmitted guilt and hostility. Miss Porter was not the kind of writer who, in Arthur Mizener's words, "encourage[s] people to enjoy the insidious pleasures of righteousness unearned by understanding" by pretending she and her reader "are Christ harrowing a hell full of all the people who disagree with them"[16]; the hell she imagines in "He" is not for other people, but for herself and her readers, too. And Miss Porter's irony—certainly in this story—is not a headsman's axe but a weight in the scale of justice to keep mercy from overtipping the balance. It serves to maintain a clear vision of Mrs. Whipple's flaws and errors and also to prevent the excess of pity that could blind a reader to her very real self-deceptions and to her internal conflicts, including the complicated guilt that corrodes her love for her son.

Throughout "He," except in the last paragraphs where it is no longer needful, that kind of irony operates from time to time, counterpoising Mrs. Whipple's professed feelings by clarifying her unacknowledged ones, as the story's action unfolds in a well-knit plot comprising three main episodes: the pig slaughtered to feast Mrs. Whipple's brother and his family; He leading a neighbor's bull to pasture at the Whipples' as payment for the bull's breeding their cow; His final removal to the County Home. In the first, Mrs. Whipple's pride brings her to endanger her son to serve its turn, and it also leads her toward a possible recognition of His personality and of her guilt: "When He saw the blood" as she slit the pig's throat, "He gave a great jolting breath and ran away" (p. 52); but Mrs. Whipple only thinks "He'll forget and eat plenty" and—probably correctly, though it is another rationalization—"He'd eat it all if I didn't stop Him" (p. 52). (At the meal, He won't enter the dining room where the pig lies in the center of the table, but presumably He does eat the "big plate" that Mrs. Whipple serves Him in the kitchen.) When on Sunday morning she boxes His ears for getting dirty, "His face hurt[s her] feelings," and her suppression of this incipient realization makes her physically weak (p. 53). The episode ends in despair for Mrs. Whipple ("—oh, honest, sometimes I wish I was dead!") but with no clarification because she is so full of self-pity (p. 54).

The Whipples' hardship the following winter comes partly from the improvident slaughter of the pig, which would have meant "three hundred pounds of pork" to use or to sell; with poor crops, they have barely enough money for food and thus too little for clothes. Most of that goes to Adna and Emly; because "He sets around the fire a lot, He won't need so much" (p. 54).

He almost gets pneumonia, and, although He seems well next spring, "He walked as if His feet hurt Him" (p. 55)—probably a sign of some residual infection. The bull episode that summer develops from Mr. Whipple's effort to save "paying out money when [he hasn't] got it" (p. 55), and it once again reveals the intensity of Mrs. Whipple's moral and emotional conflicts. At first she feels "easy in her mind about sending Him for the bull," but then she starts thinking, "and after a while she could hardly bear it any longer" (p. 55). He returns, "leading the big bulk of an animal by a ring in his nose, . . . never looking back or sideways, but coming on like a sleepwalker with His eyes half shut" (p. 55) in what could be either near-paralyzing fear or just simple-minded insouciance. Mrs. Whipple possibly exaggerates the danger, for the bull lumbers "along behind Him as gently as a calf" (p. 56), but she recalls "awful stories about how [bulls] followed on quietly enough, and then suddenly pitched on with a bellow and pawed and gored a body to pieces," and she thinks how "Any second now that black monster would come down on Him" (p. 55). She imagines this so vividly that, when the bull harmlessly "horn[s] the air at a fly," she involuntarily shrieks, almost precipitating the violence that she fears and perhaps at the same time unconsciously desires. For her this episode ends in a frantic, self-serving prayer and nervous prostration, yet again without any recognition because her fear is so self-centered: "Lord, you *know* people will say we oughtn't to have sent Him. You *know* they'll say we didn't take care of Him. Oh, get Him home, safe home, safe home, and I'll look out for Him better! Amen" (p. 56).

The recognition does come in the final episode—a *peripeteia* and *anagnorisis* as close to the classical tragic pattern as anyone has ever come in a realistic short story. Mrs. Whipple is hardly a classical tragic heroine. Perhaps she hardly reaches the stature of Arthur Miller's "common man" who becomes tragic in being "ready to lay down his life, if need be, to secure one thing—his sense of personal dignity"[17]: one might say she destroys her integrity to maintain a partly specious sense of dignity. Yet her final tragic recognition, like that of Oedipus, does fall on her because of her most important traits of character, which have conflicted throughout the story—her quite genuine feeling for her son and her pride (she refuses the ambulance because she "couldn't stand to see Him going away looking so sick as all that," and when she rides with Him, she wears her most dignified "black shirt waist" because "She couldn't stand to go looking like charity" [p. 58]). In sending Him to the hospital, the Whipples simply intend His good, though his going will relieve them of practical burdens they can no longer bear (they can neither care well enough for Him themselves nor pay for the doctor's care; to keep Him would simply mean worsening poverty and privation, which could do Him no good). Yet, in a powerful situational irony, He weeps at what is happening, and there is no way Mrs. Whipple can ignore it or attribute it to anything except her present or past actions. The story's closing tableau is a devastating Pietà as the mother holds and weeps over her son, whose well-being and whose humanity she has continually sacrificed piecemeal to her confused feelings, and whose well-intentioned sacrificial expulsion now brings illumination but no release from guilt.

The cathartic ending of "He," "tragic because it needs to be" and "endurable because it is right and true," calls to mind a passage from Chapter Twenty of *Middlemarch,* in which George Eliot says,

> That element of tragedy which lies in the very fact of frequency, has not yet wrought itself into the coarse emotion of mankind; and perhaps our frames could hardly bear much of it. If we had a keen vision and feeling of all ordinary human life, it would be like hearing the grass grow and the squirrel's heart beat, and we should die of that roar which lies on the other side of silence. As it is, the quickest of us walk about well wadded with stupidity.

Miss Porter's subject in "He," tightly circumscribed by the Whipples' hard life and the ineludible moral dilemma of their feeble-minded son, is simply the tragic nature of ordinary familial love, of which, as she wrote twenty years after the story, "hatred is part . . . the necessary enemy and ally."[18] With a keen vision and feeling of that ordinary love in her ordinary characters, the last scene of Miss Porter's story shows Mrs. Whipple finally hearing the roar on the other side of her son's inarticulate silence and of her own self-deceiving silence as well; it shows the terrified neighbor hearing both those roars; and it has the reader hearing all three in full fidelity. No one in our century has put the short story to nobler use—or to stricter discipline—than Katherine Anne Porter, and "He," a compact tragedy in the low mimetic mode of realistic fiction,[19] is simply one of the finer instances of that fact: a classic story written "with all the truth and tenderness and severity"[20] that Miss Porter intended as the hallmark of all her work.

Notes

1. *The Collected Stories of Katherine Anne Porter* (New York: Harcourt Brace Jovanovich, 1965), p. 49. Subsequent references will be documented parenthetically by page number.

2. "An Interview," in *Katherine Anne Porter: A Critical Symposium,* ed. Lodwick Hartley and George Core (Athens: University of Georgia Press, 1969), p. 14.

3. "Another Look at Katherine Anne Porter," *Virginia Quarterly Review,* 36 (Autumn 1960), 11; reprinted in Hartley and Core, p. 89.

4. *The Fiction and Criticism of Katherine Anne Porter* (Pittsburgh, PA: University of Pittsburgh Press, 1962), pp. 47–50. Mooney elsewhere noted that society, which is "narrowly domestic" in "He," is "never foolproof against the dire threats of the half-grasped and unadmitted human motive" (p. 53)—an acute comment if applied to Mrs. Whipple.

5. "Reality and Escape," *Four Quarters,* 12 (January 1963), 28, 31.

6. *Katherine Anne Porter and the Art of Rejection* (Chapel Hill: University of North Carolina Press, 1964), pp. 18, 19, 20, 21. Nance did point out how the story's impact widens to a "sense of the tedious oppressiveness of hypocrisy, of family life, of existence itself" (pp. 21–22)—a view that, except for its stress on dreary pessimism, might move toward tragedy.

7. *Katherine Anne Porter* (New York: Twayne, 1966), pp. 84, 85, 86. Oddly, Hendrick warned "the unwary . . . not to fall into the trap of identifying Him with Jesus" (p. 85). Given the capitalized pronoun, the neighbors' remark, "A Lord's pure mercy if He should die" (p. 49), His imagistic link with the slaughtered pig (pp. 50, 52), and the Madonna-and-Child of Pietà configuration of the final tableau (p. 58), it seems reasonable to see Him as a pathetically and ironically unredemptive sacrificial victim.

8. *Katherine Anne Porter: The Regional Stories* (Austin, TX: Steck-Vaughn, 1967), pp. 26–27, 28.

9. *Katherine Anne Porter's Fiction* (Detroit, MI: Wayne State University Press, 1971), pp. 87–88, 90. Liberman's sensitive discussion of the judgments the narrative voice demands of us unfortunately does not attend closely enough to the qualifying contexts of the obvious ironies, and it elides the body of the story. His comment on the implications of what the driver would see "behind him"—"a career of human error, human imperception, human deficiency in the face of human demands on us for generosity, even when, having received little, we have little to give" (p. 90)—makes sharply clear the neighbor's choral function, though without calling it that. The phrase from Warren occurs in his "Irony with a Center: Katherine Anne Porter" in *Selected Essays* (New York: Vintage, 1966), p. 154.

10. *Katherine Anne Porter* (New York: Ungar, 1973), pp. 36, 37. Hardy's attempt to trace the story's action in terms of Mrs. Whipple's pride is useful, and he perhaps goes further than Liberman toward perceiving the tragic implications of the neighbor's fear: "If . . . we dare not look behind us, it is the essential, universal, and eternal misery of the human condition that we cannot countenance" (p. 38).

11. *The Art of Writing Fiction* (New York: Prentice-Hall, 1948), p. 66.

12. 'The Tragic Awareness; Basic Characteristics; Fundamental Interpretations,' *Tragedy: Modern Essays in Criticism*, ed. Laurence Michel and Richarad H. Sewall (Englewood Cliffs, NJ: Prentice-Hall, 1963), p. 8.

13. *The American Reader* (Boston, MA: Heath, 1941), p. 864.

14. "The Contemporary Short Story," *Southern Review*, OS 3 (Winter 1938), 595.

15. *The Complete Writings*, ed. Geoffrey Keynes (London: Oxford University Press, 1966), p. 557.

16. "What Makes Great Books Great" in *Highlights of Modern Literature*, ed. Francis Brown (New York: New American Library, 1954), p. 19.

17. "Tragedy and the Common Man," in *Tragedy: Vision and Form*, ed. Robert W. Corrigan (San Francisco, CA: Chandler, 1965), p. 148.

18. "The Necessary Enemy," in *Collected Essays and Occasional Writings* (New York: Dell, 1973), p. 186.

19. See Northrop Frye, *Anatomy of Criticism* (Princeton, NJ: Princeton University Press, 1957), pp. 34, 38, 39. In Frye's "low mimetic mode," which includes realistic fiction, the hero is "superior neither to other men nor to his environment." "Pathos" (Frye's word for "low mometic or domestic tragedy") "presents its hero as isolated by a weakness which appeals to our sympathy because it is on our own level of experience"; further, "the central figure of pathos is often a woman or a child"; it is "increased by the inarticulateness of the victim"; its "root idea . . . is the exclusion of an individual on our own level from a social group to which he is trying to belong"; "the central tradition of sophisticated pathos is the study of the isolated mind, the story of how someone . . . is broken by a conflict between the inner and outer world"; and its usual type of character is the *alazon* or "imposter, someone who pretends or tries to be something more than he is." In all these respects, "He" seems to fit Frye's category perfectly. I do not understand what Frye means by the "sensational" communication of pity

and fear in low mimetic tragedy, and it seems to me that in "He" those emotions are "purged" or "purified" much as they are in high mimetic tragedy. Although Miss Porter used the term "purification," her whole comment on the matter (see p. 396 and note 2), together with the effect of "He" itself, leads me to feel she might have inclined toward the view of catharsis as "clarification" of the pitiable and terrible incidents that has most recently been argued by Gerald F. Else and Leon Golden. See Leon Golden and O. R. Hardison, eds., *Artistotle's Poetics* (Englewood Cliffs, NJ: Prentice-Hall, 1968), pp. 114–120, 133–137.

20. "No Plot, My Dear, No Story," in *Collected Essays and Occasional Writings,* p. 462.

The Making of "Flowering Judas"

Thomas F. Walsh

Over the years Katherine Porter furnished many autobiographical details about her most celebrated story, "Flowering Judas" (1930), stating that "all the characters and episodes are based on real persons and events, but naturally, as my memory worked upon them and time passed, all assumed different shapes and colors, formed gradually around a central idea, that of self-delusion, the order and meaning of the episodes changed, and became in a word fiction."[1] This essay, drawing from Porter's published comments on the story, her unpublished letters, notes, and fiction,[2] and my conversations with her and with her friend, Mary Louis Doherty, attempts to distinguish between the "real persons and events" and the "different shapes and colors" they assumed. Despite the thin record of Porter's Mexican period, the questionable accuracy of her recollections of it many years later, and her reputation for fictionalizing her life, we can discover many experiences she transformed into "Flowering Judas" and the reasons those transformations took the shapes they did.[3] Thereby we gain a clearer picture of Porter's first year in Mexico and a better understanding of her creative process.

I

Porter's earliest comment on "Flowering Judas" appeared in 1942:

> The idea came to me one evening when going to visit the girl I call Laura in the story. I passed the open window of her living room on my way to the door, through the small patio which is one of the scenes in the story. I had a brief glimpse of her sitting with an open book in her lap, but not reading, with a fixed look of pained melancholy and confusion in her face. The fat man I call Braggioni was playing the guitar and singing to her.

Reprinted with permission of the journal from the *Journal of Modern Literature* 12 (March 1985): 107–30.

Porter "thought" she understood "the desperate complications" of the girl's mind and feelings, but if she did not know "her true story," she did know a story "that seemed symbolic truth." In subsequent interviews Porter gave the expanded versions of the "small seed" from which her story grew. In 1963 she added the Judas tree and identified the girl as her friend "Mary" who was teaching in an Indian school and "was not able to take care of herself, because she was not able to face her own nature and was afraid of everything."[4] In 1965 Porter added the fountain and insisted that the small apartment where "Mary Doherty" lived alone was exactly as it appears in the story. Doherty, whom a young *Zapatista* captain attempted to help from her horse, was a "virtuous, intact, straitlaced Irish Catholic . . . born with the fear of sex," who had asked Porter to sit with her because she was not sure of the man coming to sing to her. This Porter did, outwaiting him until he left in frustration. She refused to identify the man, stating that she rolled "four or five objectionable characters into one" to create Braggioni. She also claimed she was like the girl in the story, taking "messages to people living in dark alleys."[5] A few years later she added that she visited political prisoners in their cells, two of whom she named.[6] In a lecture taped at the University of Maryland in 1972, Porter gave the fullest and least reliable account of her story's genesis, stating that both she and Doherty brought food and sleeping pills to political prisoners, one of whom persuaded Doherty to give him fifty pills with which he killed himself. When Doherty reported the man's death to "Braggioni," he told her they were well rid of him. Later she dreamed that when she refused the attempt of "Eugenio" to lead her to death, "he gave her the flowering Judas buds." "This is her dream," Porter claimed, adding, "You see, my fiction is reportage, only I do something to it; I arrange it and it is fiction, but it happened." In a film made at the University of Maryland in 1976, she stated that Doherty should have known better than to give pills to the prisoner and, for the first time, gave Yúdico as Braggioni's model. As Porter added details about "Flowering Judas" over the years, reality more and more resembled what grew out of it, the story becoming "reportage," mainly of the actions and motives of Mary Doherty, about whom Porter could only speculate in 1942. Porter did indeed "arrange" reality to make it fiction, both in the creation of her story and in her versions of that creation. Her story is "based on real persons and events," but not as in her versions.

II

Porter met most of the "real persons" soon after her arrival in Mexico on November 6, 1920. She found an apartment on 20 Calle de Eliseo, next door to the home of Roberto and Thorberg Haberman. Although Porter never mentioned him publicly, Roberto Haberman, a member of the labor party instrumental in bringing President Alvaro Obregón to power introduced her to the exciting world of Mexican politics. Porter wrote to her family that she was flattered to be accepted into an exclusive group close to or actually "the holders of the government reins." This group was to change Mexico and she expected "to be connected by a small thread to the affair." She also informed her family that she planned to write for *El Heraldo,* where Thorberg Haberman worked, and to collaborate with the Habermans on a revolutionary textbook. She participated in Obregón's inaugural celebration of November 30, drinking tea and champagne with him in his official residence in Chapultepec Castle, and also attended the lottery ticket sellers' ball in company with "the greatest labor leader in Mexico," Luis N. Morones, where she danced with "marvelous carbon colored Indians in scarlet blankets" until two o'clock in the morning. On Christmas day at the Habermans she met other labor leaders, among them her "beloved" J. H. Retinger.

Retinger, like Haberman, was advisor to Luis Morones. Working for CROM [Confederatión Regional Obrera Mexicana], he made valuable connections with international trade unionists in Europe and organized and directed Mexico's Press Agency. A participant in the League of Nations, an acquaintance of Gide, Mauriac, and Arnold Bennett, and a close friend of fellow countryman Joseph Conrad, he represented to Porter "Europe" in all its Jamesian connotations. In her notes she credits him with thoroughly educating her in international politics, but she never mentioned him publicly. They quickly fell in love, but the bickering that fills their letters is evidence enough that their relation would not survive their strong wills.

Mary Doherty, like Porter, was introduced to the labor group by Roberto Haberman.[7] At the Rand School of Economics she met Agnes Smedley, Thorberg Haberman's sister-in-law and later apologist for Red China, who encouraged her to visit Mexico. Doherty arrived in early 1921 and lived with the Habermans through July, briefly losing her bed to the legendary labor agitator, Mother Jones.[8] It was to the Haberman home that Samuel O. Yúdico came to entertain her with his guitar.[9] Doherty was soon assisting Retinger in his publicity work for CROM and teaching twice a week in Xochimilco, a few miles south of Mexico City. She traveled there with Yúdico or, occasionally, Porter and Retinger. Less self-centered and ambitious than Porter, more committed to Mexico's social progress, and, above all, more willing to serve in whatever capacity, Doherty became Porter's confidante and, in a correspondence that spanned fifty years, a continual source of information about Mexico. From the first, Doherty deferred to her more glamorous and talented friend, even rescuing pieces of writing Porter had crumpled up and tossed into the wastepaper basket. More tolerant than Porter of Mexico's shortcomings, Doherty still remembers incidents of her early days in Mexico with pleasure, especially the Sundays she and Porter spent in Chapultepec Park with their friends. She described the happy routine in a letter to her sister in 1921:

We pasear in Chapultepec Park in a coche—those nice old family coaches with either one nice, sleek fat horse or two smaller ones with their clank clank on the pavement. Today being Sunday everyone passears from 12 to 2, the cars barely moving along—up one line and down another—much bowing, etc. You see everyone from Obregon down and since most of the people we know are gov't officials, they all come out in their cars—it is great fun.

(Porter also remembered those Sundays, for in "Flowering Judas" Braggioni "hires an automobile and drives in the Paseo on Sunday morning.")

On her first Sunday in Mexico, Doherty met Felipe Carrillo Puerto, then delegate from Yucatán and its next governor. She remembers him earnestly haranguing from a park bench curious passers-by on the glories of socialism. Porter first met him a few weeks before at the Habermans. They became close friends, often dining and dancing in Mexico City's nightclubs. Among Porter's papers are a description of the sinking of their rowboat in the shallow Chapultepec lagoon, his photograph inscribed to his "dear friend from Felipe," and a story he told her about a woman driven mad by the Revolution. Porter planned to visit him after he became governor in 1922, but Retinger discouraged her from making the arduous trip to Yucatán.

In January 1921, Porter and Doherty attended the convention of the Pan-American Federation of Labor. They both appear in a photograph of a large group of labor leaders, including Samuel Gompers, head of the AF of L, Luis Morones, Carrillo Puerto, and the Habermans. Porter describes in her notes a gathering of these labor people at the Habermans' house, where she fell asleep at the feet of William Green, Gompers's successor in 1925. According to Doherty, she and Porter were among those who saw Gompers off on his return to the United States, Porter contributing a farewell kiss. This was during the brief happy period of Porter's stay in Mexico.

III

The bright prospects Porter anticipated in December 1920 had evaporated by May 1921. She reveals her disillusion in "The Mexican Trinity" (August 1921) and "Where Presidents Have No Friends" (July 1922), the first essay beginning.

Uneasiness grows here daily. We are having sudden deportations of foreign agitators, street riots and parades of workers carrying red flags. Plots thicken, thin, disintegrate in the space of thirty-six hours. A general was executed today for counterrevolutionary activities. . . . Battles occur almost daily between Catholics and Socialists in many parts of the Republic: Morelia, Yucatán, Campeche, Jalisco.[10]

What follows in both essays is highly informative political analysis, written from the point of view of one who firmly supports the goals of the Revolution, but hiding the fact that Porter herself deeply felt the growing "uneasiness." Her situation evolved into Laura's in "Flowering Judas."

"Uneasiness" may understate the politically unstable conditions of 1921. A clash between Catholics and Socialists on May 12 resulted in the death of J. Isaac Arriaga, head of the *Commisión Local Agraria*, which Porter lamented in her journal, connecting it to the centuries-old history of unjust seizures of Indian lands. His death provoked agrarian reformers to storm the Chamber of Deputies which became so unruly that Obregón ordered the fire department to turn on its hoses. Porter witnessed the hosing and reported it in "Where Presidents Have No Friends." About the same time, Obregón, complying with one of the conditions the United States stipulated for its recognition of Mexico, deported about thirty foreign radicals, among them several of Porter's acquaintances.[11] Roberto Haberman was also on the list and went into hiding. This incident frightened Porter, who recorded it many times in her journal and letters, writing to friend Paul Hanna that newspapers were clamoring for Haberman's head. She visited him in hiding and described him sitting on a tumbled bed, pale and drawn, and going over a long piece he had composed about how Americans "crack the whip" over Mexico. Later she began to turn this incident into fiction: "a certain Roumanian Jew agitator" recites "romantic yarns of personal treason" and composes a thesis against giving one man absolute power. He resembles the "prisoners of [Laura's] own political faith in their cells . . . composing their memoirs, writing out manifestoes."

Even more frightening, Porter herself was on the deportation list. She wrote of rehearsing a speech she would make to the police in order to gain time to pack. George T. Summerlin, U.S. chargé d'affaires in Mexico, assured her that her name had been removed, but another informant told her later that it was not. In the meantime, her checks had been held up, and for the first time in her life she experienced hunger. She walked past secret service men sitting on the curb in front of the Haberman house, not caring whether they seized her because at least in jail she would be fed. Not finding Thorberg Haberman inside, she stole a dozen tortillas and a bowl of turkey mole. In another note she writes of crying a great deal and feeling sorry for herself: "Starvation is very hard on the flesh, and the idea of death is very hard on the nerves; I should like to deny that I am terrified but I am."

In a letter to her sister in June 1921, Doherty responds quite differently to the deportation crisis, giving in the process a rare, if brief, contemporary glimpse of Porter in Mexico.

> Of course all our crowd is on the list. . . . Bob [Roberto Haberman] is hiding with the papers yammering for his head. . . . Secret service people guard the house—all want us deported—Obregon would change his mind and cancel

the order, but Americans keep up the rumpus and won't stop until they get Bob. It has been over two weeks now. . . . Strangely enough—no doubt due to the nervous tension and suspense—we who are still around loose are having a very good time—we go forth gayly with the leaders of the very government that has us on the list for deportation. Katherine, Thorberg and I have hilarious times. Of course we are really quite safe, for they won't take us until they get the more important ones and as yet we have done nothing because we can't speak Spanish—only in disrepute because of our beliefs and our associations and Katherine especially because she has refused to associate with the American colony. She is very pretty and very clever and they would like to have her and she is not very radical. . . . It will be very funny to laugh at a year from now—just now a little nervewracking.

This letter is not from somebody "afraid of everything," as Porter claimed Doherty was. Rather, the evidence shows that Porter herself was "terrified." In a note entitled "A month of uncertainties," she begins with the death of five followers of rebel General Lucio Blanco, adding "How on earth does this concern me? Yet it does." She then mentions the trouble stirring Catholics and Socialists in Morelia with "Yúdico and Bob polishing their pistols," the deportation of foreign radicals, Haberman in hiding, Summerlin's information, the hosing in the Chamber of Deputies, and finally her expectations of a summons any minute. At this time her friend Retinger was in the Laredo jail where she wrote him of all her troubles. In her recital Porter intertwines her own fear of deportation with deaths and threatened violence to others. The "uneasiness" in "The Mexican Trinity" is her uneasiness, tempting one to substitute her name for Carranza's in "Where Presidents Have No Friends."

Just as Porter mingles violence and death with her personal fears, so in "Flowering Judas" "the sight and sound of Braggioni singing threaten to identify themselves with all Laura's remembered afflictions and add their weight to her uneasy premonition of the future." Like Porter, Laura feels engulfed by the presence of death: "Laura feels a slow chill, a purely physical sense of danger, a warning in her blood that violence, mutilation, a shocking death, wait for her with lessening patience." And just as Yúdico and Haberman polish their pistols for "a row between the Catholics and Socialists . . . scheduled in Morelia for May 1st," so Braggioni asks Laura to "oil and load his pistols" because of "the May-day disturbances in Morelia." Out of her own remembered fears of 1921 Porter created the deathly atmosphere of "Flowering Judas."

With Laura's "warning in her blood" of "a shocking death" awaiting her, Porter gave full expression to her all-consuming theme. In this story, earlier fictional fragments, and later stories, culminating in "Pale Horse, Pale Rider," death is felt as a terrifying physical presence. In one fragment a character named Natalie complains, "There is something altogether horrible here . . . I am frightened of all sorts of things. I have terrible dreams," to which her friend Paul replies that he is "influenced by some indefinite thing in the air, a hovering and sinister presence." In "Hacienda" the narrator speaks of "the almost ecstatic death-expectancy which is in the air of Mexico. . . . strangers feel the acid of death in their bones whether or not any real danger is near them." Here Mexico is explicitly a place of death, symbolized by the "sour" odor of pulque, "like rotting milk and blood." In "Pale Horse, Pale Rider," the air is contaminated with influenza, infecting Miranda, who smells "the stench of corruption" in her own wasted body. This story was based on Porter's near-death struggle with influenza in 1918, but, she noted in her journal, she felt "the terror of death" stronger in 1921 than in 1918. When she wrote "Pale Horse, Pale Rider" in 1938, the terror she expressed had been magnified by her Mexican experience. Death is the firm link between Porter's Mexican and Miranda stories. She began the outline of the novel she was writing in Mexico with "Book I: Introduction to Death," which was to include Miranda's childhood. "The Grave" (1935) gives that introduction and tellingly ends with odors in Mexico triggering Miranda's childhood memories: "It was a very hot day and the smell in the market, with its piles of raw flesh and wilting flowers, was like the mingled sweetness and corruption she had smelled that other day in the cemetery at home."

IV

Porter's journal and letters give evidence that she viewed Mexico as a continual source for her creative writing. Seemingly nothing occurred that she did not weigh for its literary potential. She wrote local color sketches like "In a Mexican Patio" and "Teotihuacan" and recorded stories told to her by others.[12] But, as we have already seen from the deportation crisis of 1921, her main interests were the political and the personal.

Among Porter's papers is an outline of all the political parties in Mexico along with a thumbnail sketch of the leaders of each party. Her thorough knowledge served her well in such objective reporting as "The Mexican Trinity," but her ultimate goal was fiction. In May 1921, she wrote Paul Hannah of her "strangely assorted contacts" with diplomats, revolutionists, government officials, and unrestrained internationalists, adding, "I am making a story of these opposed forces." Elsewhere she recorded her intention of doing sketches of her revolutionary acquaintances, but what might have begun as reportage soon became "making a story." Thus Yúdico and Morones became Braggioni; Thorburg Haberman, Silberman; Carrillo Puerto, Vicente; and President Elias Calles, Velarde, the name Porter gives him in "Hacienda." The link between fact and fiction was her interest in the revolutionary personality, her estimate of which grew more cynical as time wore on.

Porter's personal experiences appear in her journal, often in the form of probing, guilt-ridden self-analysis, and in fictional fragments in which her alter ego Miranda makes her debut in scenes with her lover Jerome, who is based on J. H. Retinger. Porter intended to write "our story" about herself and Retinger, who was both political mentor and lover. Although she never completed the story, its fragments contributed, as we shall see, to the formation of Laura's personality.

Retinger himself influenced the composition of "Flowering Judas" in two different ways. While in a Laredo jail because of passport problems in May 1921, he wrote Porter to make sure that Luis Morones approved chapters of *Morones of Mexico* which she was editing. It is ironic that she, having read Retinger's adulation of Morones and Yúdico in this book, would eventually use both men as models for her negative portrait of Braggioni. Retinger wrote that "Yúdico, a tall, fair man, is a regular jack of all trades. . . . he knows every corner of the Republic, and understands the sufferings of the workers. Frank and outspoken, his equanimity is appreciated by his companions and his good heartedness makes him a friend of everybody."[13] Apparently Porter reserved Retinger's hollow rhetoric for Braggioni's followers who "say to each other: 'He has real nobility, a love of humanity raised above more personal affections.'"

Although Porter raised the thousand-dollar bail money for Retinger with an offer of five hundred dollars more and traveled to Laredo at the request of Morones to attempt his release, their love affair was fast disintegrating. In her journal she wrote that he would be pained to know how little she cared about his predicament. In later journal entries she described him as "an Austrian Pole much given to international intrigue" and "a complex and fascinating liar." In 1943, she still held a grudge against him, calling him, in a letter to Doherty, her "old enemy and parasite." No wonder her unflattering portrait of him in "Flowering Judas": "The Polish agitator talks love to [Laura] over café tables, hoping to exploit what he believes is her sentimental preference for him, and he gives her misinformation which he begs her to repeat as the solemn truth to certain persons." Behind this scene we can see Retinger professing his love for Porter in 1921 in the Café Colón on the Paseo, according to Doherty, one of their favorite meeting places. In the story, Laura is not deceived by the Pole's tactics as Porter felt she had been deceived by Retinger's. Reading the story, he would know that his former beloved had taken her revenge.

Porter also turned against Roberto Haberman, describing him in her notes as an unprincipled conniver who would practice any deception to advance his radical cause. In "Flowering Judas" he appears as the "Roumanian agitator": "He is generous with his money in all good causes, and lies to Laura with an air of ingenuous candor, as if he were her good friend and confidant."

As early as 1921 Porter planned to combine the political and personal in a novel called *Thieves' Market*. Through the twenties she added to it such events as Carrillo Puerto's death and Morones's fall from power. Later she conceived a three-book structure entitled *Many Redeemers* or *Midway of This Mortal Life,* which was to center on Miranda's whole life, beginning with "the history of the rise and break-up of an American family" and ending in the present with "the record of a rich and crumbling society." Mexico formed only a part of this grand scheme and was to appear as "the Mexican interval which is a tangent for Miranda, the complete negation of all she had known, a derailment up to 1928 or 30." The project would have challenged a Balzac. Begun in disconnected fragments, it ended as fragments of a much larger plan in the form of several short stories, "Old Mortality" coming closest to Porter's idea about the break-up of an American family. In the early thirties Porter visited Germany, which she apparently decided was more important than Mexico for the political statements she wished to make. The result was "The Leaning Tower" and *Ship of Fools,* according to most critics her least successful works, possibly because she was less acquainted with Germans than with Mexicans. But before turning away from Mexico, she did manage "Flowering Judas" to unite the political and personal. She quickly knew what she had accomplished, writing to a friend in April 1930, "It's by far the best thing I ever did and is in the mood and style of the novel." Although she continued to mention a Mexican novel in the forties, there was no need to write it, for her short story was the perfect distillation of everything the novel could have been.

V

The political dimension of "Flowering Judas," ignored by some of Porter's critics, is concentrated in the character of Braggioni. Since Porter did indeed roll "four or five objectionable characters" into one to create him, it is important to see how the revolutionaries she knew contributed to what was, in her jaundiced view, a portrait of *the* revolutionary.

A journal note dated 1921 begins, "Yúdico came in tonight bringing his guitar, and spent the evening singing for Mary." This early record of Porter's inspiration for "Flowering Judas" is devoted, as we shall see, to Mary Doherty with no other reference to Yúdico, but clearly he was the physical and moral prototype of Braggioni. The Yúdico who entertained Doherty was a tall, rather stout man with a fair complexion, light brown hair, and deep green eyes, sedately dressed with no pistols in evidence. His father, like Braggioni's, was Italian. Braggioni's "tight little mouth that turns down at the corners," giving him a "surly" expression, is an accurate, if unkind, description of

Yúdico. Porter lightened Yúdico's hair, but turned his green eyes into "yellow cat's eyes" and his stoutness into "gluttonous bulk" which has become "a symbol of [Laura's] many disillusions" about how revolutionists should look and act. Porter's Yúdico was not the man Mary Doherty described as a friend to her family or the one Retinger idealized in his biography of Morones. If Doherty overlooked Yúdico's defects, Porter, as other journal notes suggest, saw nothing else.

Porter was apparently fascinated with Yúdico from the start. On September 8, 1921, she wrote of doing four portraits of revolutionaries, with his portrait almost complete. Also in 1921 she wrote that she heard Retinger talking with Yúdico, "a completely savage and uneducated Indian revolutionist, a man with the eyes of a cat and paunch of a pig and they both agreed that a woman was good for one thing." In a later note she advised herself, "Get into the scene . . . something of Braggioni's really sinister personality, the soft-spoken, hard-eyed monster." The shift here from Yúdico to Braggioni is imperceptible because Porter always saw Braggioni in Yúdico. Yúdico as sexual menace must have provoked her instinctive hatred. Another note begins, "Yúdico and his wife—went home to wash feet, wife came home sobbing . . ." and then continues, "Third Wife, fiftieth concubine—not faithful to anything. Study of Mexican revolutionary. . . . Given charge of blowing up and destroying Mexico City" if it falls into the hands of the enemy. Here and in "Flowering Judas" the sexual and political intermesh. Braggioni revenges himself on a thousand women for the humiliation one woman caused him in his youth just as he would brutally revenge himself against his political enemies if the need arose. His behavior is pointedly typical of the revolutionary who violates at every step the principles he pretends to uphold. In another note Porter wrote that the "spirit of revolutionaries is to escape from bondage to themselves. Their desire to rule, their will to power, is sort of revenge" to compensate for "their own insignificance, their sufferings." Porter, who attended a feminist meeting with Thorberg Haberman where she became the "79th member of the woman's party in Mexico," certainly viewed the attitudes of Yúdico/Braggioni toward women as a betrayal of the Revolution and a personal affront to herself and Laura.

In 1928 Porter shifted her attention from Yúdico, who died that year, to Luis Morones, explicitly identifying him with Braggioni in her notes. In 1922 she had praised Morones for paying munitions factory workers the highest wages in Mexico. With a thirty-million peso budget and a command of a large reserve of men, he enjoyed the prominence and power Porter attributes to Braggioni, with Retinger and Haberman, like the Polish and Rumanian agitators, contending for his favor. But Morones's reputation as a ruthless, corrupt politician became widespread. Porter's acquaintance, Carleton Beals, ridiculed him as "a big pig-like man . . . always meticulously dressed and perfumed, his hands glittering with diamonds."[14] In the same vein Porter described him in her journal as a "swollen labor leader . . . who removes inordinate silk scarf, and flashes his diamond like spotlights." He has "no higher idea that simple comforts and cheap elegance and direct forthright grabbing of whatever he can get." This description fits Braggioni with his diamond hoop and "elegant refinements" of silk handkerchief and Jockey Club perfume. When Morones's presidential ambitions made him suspect in the plot to assassinate Obregón in 1928, forcing him to resign his ministry, Porter wrote that he had done badly and used his fall from power to prophesy the fall of Braggioni, who "will live to see himself kicked out from his feeding trough by other hungry world saviors." In 1922 she had written in her journal, "if Morones is next president, salvation of Mexico is assured." In "Flowering Judas" words like "salvation" became bitterly ironic.

Angel Gomez and Felipe Carrillo Puerto, whose portraits Porter planned along with Yúdico's, also contributed to Braggioni's character. Gomez pops up in fiction fragments and plays a major role in "The Dove of Chapacalco," always as "the bomb thrower" or "the dynamiter"—for instance, "Gomez spent his time on knees as devotee, looking for chance to plan a dynamiting of the holy statue which is chief fame and revenue to church." A Cuban anarchist and member of the Federation of Workers, Angel Gomez was implicated in the bombing of a jewelry factory and in the invasion of the Chamber of Deputies on May 13. Porter probably met him at this time. She invests Braggioni, who pins his "faith to good dynamite," with Gomez's destructiveness. Braggioni envisions everything "hurled skyward" so that "nothing the poor has made for the rich shall remain." He would be more dangerous if he really believed his apocalyptic rhetoric which reveals his arrogance and hypocrisy since he enjoys the luxuries of the rich whom he would exterminate. To Porter he is the typical revolutionary, one of a "welter of small chattering monkeys busily making over a world to their own desires."

Carrillo Puerto did not live long enough to disillusion Porter, but her notes and financial fragments reveal her ambivalence toward him. He is the "beautiful bandit from Yucatan," "a dreamer of violent and gorgeous dreams," and "a complete dictator." His rhetoric, like Braggioni's, was radical, as were the changes he effected in Yucatán. He claimed direct descent from pre-colonial Mayan nobility, reminding us that Braggioni's Mayan mother was "a woman of race, an aristocrat." Porter's fictional name for Carrillo is Vicente, Braggioni's first name.

More importantly, Carrillo and others are the source of the ironic Christological imagery that unifies Braggioni's portrait. Critics are probably correct in assuming that the image of "Flowering Judas" derives from Eliot's "Gerontion," but the large pattern derives from revolutionary rhetoric. The photograph Carrillo dedicated to Porter had appeared in *Redención* (Redemption), a publication of the Feminist League of Merida, Yucatán, the first issue of which (May 28, 1921) is among Porter's papers. Undoubtedly, socialists, opposed to a Catholic Church that, in their opinion, promised redemption to the poor in another life while collaborating with their oppressors in this one, reinterpreted Christian language imbibed in childhood and offered political and economic redemption here and now. Porter comments on the word in "Where Presidents Have No Friends": Best Maugard's "belief is that a renascence of older Aztec arts and handicrafts among these people will aid immeasurably in their redemption. Redemption—it is a hopeful, responsible word one often hears among these men" (Collected Essays, 414–415). But Porter's own hope vanished, and so Braggioni emerges as a perverse savior who, like Morones, only talks of "sacrificing himself for the worker." He is typical of *Many Redeemers,* which "is all about how men go on saving the world by starving, robbing, and killing each other—lying, meanwhile, to themselves and each other about their motives." Porter's description of her never-completed novel applies to "Flowering Judas."

It took nine years for Porter's views of several revolutionaries to blend and unify in her imagination. The result is the richly complex Braggioni, who is completely individualized in his brutal corpulence and perfectly typical of the revolutionary personality she came to despise. The process of Laura's creation is similar to Braggioni's, but complicated by the involvement of Porter's own personality in ways she may never have completely understood then or was willing to admit later.

VI

In her journal note of June 1921, Porter recorded her impression of Mary Doherty seated at a table, "a little preoccupied, infallibly and kindly attentive" to Yúdico as he entertained her with his guitar. She is "a modern secular nun," "a virgin but faintly interested in love," who "wears a rigid little uniform of dark blue cloth, with immaculate collars and cuffs of narrow lace made by hand." She thinks there is something "dishonest" in lace "contrived by machinery," but "pays a handsome price" for her "one extravagance." Born an Irish Catholic, "her romantic sense of adventure has guided her to the lower strata of revolution" where she "keeps her head cool in the midst of opera bouffe plots" and "submerged international intrigue." She intended to organize working women into labor unions, but does not realize that those who thwart her efforts are not as "clear and straight minded" as she. Although she has developed "a little pucker of trouble between her wide set grey eyes," she still "has the look of one who expects shortly to find a simple and honest solution of a very complicated problem. She is never to find it."

In her portrait of Doherty, Porter's selection and interpretation of details ·
anticipates the creation of Laura. Porter saw Doherty, as she did Yúdico, pictorially, associating her "rigid little uniform" with her nunlike virginity (a uniform Doherty was still wearing in 1926, as Edward Weston's photographs

show). That uniform will eventually symbolize Laura's fearful rejection of love in contrast to Doherty's dawning interest. Doherty's lace, like Laura's, is her one extravagance, but what she "thinks" about the dishonesty of machine-made lace is already a fiction in 1921, for she bought her lace at Altman's in New York, unaware whether it was handmade or not. In "Flowering Judas," Laura feels guilty about wearing the handmade lace when the machine is "sacred" to the revolutionist. From the start Doherty's dress had a meaning, but that meaning changed in the writing of "Flowering Judas."

Porter appropriated other details from Doherty's life to create Laura. Doherty's Irish Catholic background reinforced the image of "secular nun," although, unlike Laura, she was not a churchgoer. Like Laura, Doherty taught Indian children in Xochimilco, but never tried to organize women into labor unions. Her horse once ran away from a former *Zapatista,* Genaro Amezcua, who was head of the agrarian bureau in Cuernavaca where she first met him. Porter also knew him, describing him as "the only intelligent pro-feminist in Mexico," an ironic footnote to Laura's rejection of him and all other men in the story. However, such details do not account for Laura's personality. Doherty's honesty and genuine devotion to revolutionary reform, however naïve they seemed to Porter in her note of 1921, bear little resemblance to Laura's alienation and mechanical performance of duties in "Flowering Judas."

Porter's claim of coming over to Doherty's apartment at her request to protect her from Yúdico is a fiction. Her 1921 journal entry gives no hint of such circumstances. At that time Doherty was not living alone, but with the Habermans. Also, she categorically denies that she was ever afraid of Yúdico, whom she described in a postcard in 1925 as "one of my good friends." Why then Porter's fabrication? Apparently she placed herself outside and inside the scene with Doherty and Yúdico. Outside, she imagined herself coming to the rescue of Doherty, who should have been afraid instead of sitting "infallibly and kindly attentive." Porter's account of outwaiting and frustrating Yúdico is a kind of posthumous revenge on him. Inside the scene, Porter identified with Doherty/Laura's "notorious virginity," expressing her own fear of violation in a world in which men were used to having their way with women. Porter treated endangered virginity in two other works of the period. The "dove" of "The Dove of Chapacalco" is a young servant girl who becomes the prey of a corrupt bishop. "Virgin Violeta" is based on Salomón de la Selva's account of seducing a friend's young daughter. Porter noted, "Salomón is uneasy because I told a friend of his I detested his attitude toward love and women—'If Salomón met the Virgin Mary, he would introduce himself as the Holy Ghost,' I said." And so she detested what she interpreted as Yúdico's advances on the Virgin Mary Doherty, in whom she saw herself, and fictionalized her detestation in "Flowering Judas." In this light Laura's notorious virginity is a positive virtue, other evidence to the contrary. Although it attracts

Braggioni to her in the first place, thereby placing her in danger, it is a power she has over him. He can have his way with others but not with Laura.

Laura's virginity also has its negative side and partly explains why Porter chose not to name her heroine Miranda. Although the two characters resemble each other, there is a difference. Miranda is a woman victimized from childhood by circumstances beyond her control, from a family who does not understand her to influenza that almost kills her. If she has a fault, it is expecting too much from a world that always disappoints her, thereby justifying her reaction against it. Porter's criticism of Laura is much harsher. By insisting on Doherty as the original of Laura, she makes her friend the scapegoat for qualities she found difficult to admit as her own.

Negatively Laura's virginity represents total moral disengagement. She does not, understandably, love Braggioni, but she does not love anybody. Thus she is a traitor to the Revolution and to her own religious principles. Braggioni questions Laura's coldness: "You think you are so cold, *gringita!*", but his hope that she is not is vain, for she suffers from her author's own emotional problems.[15] In her journal Porter recorded Retinger's complaint that her "detachment from people and groups is a mark of her selfishness, is a sin against human solidarity." Another time he told her, "What you need is love. Your body will wither without it." Porter seemed torn between love and its smothering demands. After examining her attraction to Retinger, she concluded, "For I might as well acknowledge . . . love is not for me. . . . Love affects me as a great sickness of the heart, a crushing nostalgia that withers me up, that makes me fruitless and without help." In a fragment from *Thieves' Market,* Miranda "set herself perversely" against Jerome when he was "passionate," refusing to "respond" and feeling "happy in having spoiled his plan for him." Other times she was "really cold, as inaccessible as a virgin." Jerome would then call her "a Russian nun," telling her that she expected "to be taken as if [she] were the Holy Wafer." This fragment best explains Porter's ambivalent attitude toward Laura's virginity which is both revenge against Braggioni and symbol of her sexual and spiritual frigidity.[16]

Laura's spiritual malaise results in her guilt over the death of Eugenio. The facts behind this incident and Porter's visits to prisoners in jail are impossible to verify. Porter accused Doherty of supplying pills to a prisoner and of dreaming about his death, but Doherty firmly denies ever setting foot in prison until she visited photographer Tina Modotti in 1930, whereas Porter, in tears, told me that she herself had given sleeping pills to a prisoner who saved them until he had enough with which to kill himself, adding that only the death of the man who caught influenza from her had affected her as much. Porter's memory of her friend's death in 1918 probably contributed to Laura's guilt, but no corroborating evidence of visits to prison exists.

However, Porter did write of carrying messages that would result in the death of five men against whom she holds no grudge. She wonders if she is participating in "an act of opera bouffe treachery" out of boredom when she finally blames "the enemy within" her that "lives upon sensation" and "loves the sense of power implied in the possession of these letters" so "potent" that "five men will die at dawn" upon their delivery. This fragment may be Porter's fictional attempt to involve herself in the execution of five followers of Pablo Gonzales mentioned in "A Month of Uncertainties." Employing the present tense, it describes what she is about to do, not what she has done, and its language is melodramatic and calculated, "opera bouffe" repeating the expression she used in her portrait of Mary Doherty. On the other hand, it is in the first-person, like other autobiographical entries in her journal, whereas all the clearly fictional pieces of this period are in the third-person. If it is a true account of Porter's activities, then it explains the guilt she assigns to Laura, who also engaged in deadly intrigue she is not committed to.

Whatever the facts behind Laura's relation to Eugenio, her inability to love, deeply rooted in Porter's own personality, is directly linked to her fear of death, just as Braggioni's sexual aggression is linked to his deadly power. Such power Porter feared, writing in her journal, "Now I seem unable to believe in anything, and certainly my doubts of human beings and their motives are founded in a fear of their power over me." But fear of another's power makes love as dangerous as overt aggression and explains Laura's defense system. "Her knees cling together" as she closes herself to the "spread knees" of Braggioni, who fills her with a "purely physical sense of danger." This resistance is also seen in her escape from the romantic advances of the "gentle" *Zapatista* captain and the young typographer. But Laura's protective withdrawal into self only results in a death-like stasis of noncommitment. Her desire to escape perilous human involvement paradoxically leads her to the ultimate escape, suicide. We are told, "Sometimes she wishes to run away, but she stays. Now she longs to fly out of this room, down the narrow stairs, and into the street where the houses lean together like conspirators under a single mottled lamp, and leave Braggioni singing to himself." Here the urge to escape life ends in futile circularity, the conspiratorial houses a nightmarish substitution for Braggioni. This passage Porter developed from a journal entry in which she complains that she would "like exceedingly to die," not having "that sense of urgency" she had when she nearly died of influenza. Then she writes, "The streets are bowl shaped, and the houses lean inward . . . I have continually the sensation of stepping into space, and the side walk seems to curve down from the outer edges." In the next paragraph she predicts, "In a week I shall be dead." The leaning houses here are more explicitly related to suicidal impulse than they are in "Flowering Judas." It is as if Porter were viewing the world through a fish-eye lens, a world of unreal dimension she fears entering. In 1931 she wrote her father that she had struggled a long time "against the very strong temptation just to . . . quit the whole devilish nuisance of life," but now she was "in a healthy mood of resistance and energy." Only resistance applies to Laura. Throughout the story her

"No" is a rejection of life, but her "No" to Eugenio's invitation expresses her rejection of suicide. She at least reaffirms her will to live despite her continuing state of irresolution.

Like Laura's personality, many of the story's details evolved out of Porter's own experience. For instance, the patio of "In a Mexican Patio," an unpublished sketch based on her experiences at 20 Calle del Eliseo, with its fountain and "purple" bougainvillaea, is the source of Laura's patio, with its fountain and Judas tree whose scarlet blossoms turn "a dull purple" in the moonlight. As evening falls, a young man appears as a shadowy presence, like Laura's young typographer, to communicate his love to a servant girl. Like "Flowering Judas," the sketch is narrated in the present tense and ends ominously at night: "In the sunlight one may laugh, and sniff the winds, but the night is crowded with thoughts darker than the sunless world." Journal entries supply other details. Porter's servant Maria was once "the prettiest girl in Guanajuato," the hometown of Laura's servant Lupe. Porter went to union meetings to hear the spell-binding Morones speak, while Laura goes to union meetings to listen to "busy important voices." In a fragment of *Thieves' Market,* Laura in church finds nothing to pray for: "Let me set my heart on something, I don't care how poor it is . . . the legless woman in the Alameda has a perfectly faithful lover—oh God, out of your charity send me something." Porter, who told me that she often saw the legless woman on a park bench sharing money with her lover, assigned Laura's lines about the woman to Braggioni and gave a mechanical "Hail Mary" to Laura, who is soon distracted by the "battered doll-shape of some male saint whose white, lace-trimmed drawers hang limply around his ankles below the hieratic dignity of his velvet robe." The saint originally appeared in "Teotihuacan" as "St. Ignatious Loyola with chaste lace-trimmed trousers showing beneath his black cassock." He is effectively denigrated by the transformation of "trousers" into "drawers." Clearly, "Flowering Judas" is based on Porter's own experiences, great and small.

VII

In 1943 Porter wrote Mary Doherty, "Mexico was new to us, and beautiful, the very place to be at that moment. We believed a great deal—though I remember well that my childhood faith in the Revolution was well over in about six months." By May 1921, the time of the deportation crisis, the prototypes of Braggioni among others had sufficiently convinced her that Mexico as potential paradise was and could be nothing but a dream. But out of the dreamer's failure came the artist's success. If Mexico could not assuage her troubled psyche, it compelled her to contemplate the entwined betrayals of Revolution and of self, and to transform her disillusion and spiritual isolation into Laura's. By donning, as it were, Mary Doherty's nun-like uniform, Porter was able to give voice to all her conflicting emotions and view them with dispassionate objectivity as if they were not her own. In later comments about the creation of her story, she persisted in her disguise, claiming that her friend was the model for Laura. "Flowering Judas" was not the "reportage" she claimed it was in 1972, but it did contain "symbolic truth" of her Mexican experience. Her transformation of purple bougainvillaea of her Mexican patio into flowering Judas is sign of the process that brought art out of life.

Notes

1. *This Is My Best,* ed. Whit Burnett (New York: The Dial Press, 1942), 539.
2. I am grateful to the McKeldin Library of the University of Maryland for permission to examine Porter's papers and to Paul Porter for permission to quote from them.
3. For instance, Joan Givner, in *Katherine Anne Porter: A Life* (New York: Simon and Schuster, 1982), shows that the setting of "Old Mortality" did not derive from Porter's childhood, as Porter claimed, but from her stay in Bermuda in 1929 (211–213).
4. Barbara Thompson, "An Interview," *Writers at Work* (New York: Viking Press, 1963), 15–16.
5. Hank Lopez, "A Country and Some People I Love," *Harper's* 231 (1965), 59–60.
6. Enrique Hank Lopez, *Conversations with Katherine Anne Porter: Refugee from Indian Creek* (Boston: Little Brown, 1981), 119–120. Lopez first tape-recorded Porter's conversations in 1966.
7. Born in Iowa in 1898 and with a degree in Economics from the University of Wisconsin, Doherty served over the years in Mexico as secretary, translator, and researcher for various government officials. I am indebted to her for sharing her memories of Porter and for making her papers available to me.
8. Among Mother Jones's papers is Haberman's letter of April 1921, inviting her to Mexico where she traveled from mid-May until early July. See Dale Fethering, *Mother Jones, The Miner's Angel: A Portrait* (Carbondale: Southern Illinois University Press, 1974) p. 176–77, 247. This information helps verify Doherty's statements about her living arrangements in 1921, which contradict Porter's claim that Doherty was living alone when Yúdico visited her.
9. From 1914 to 1916 Yúdico was one of the ablest leaders and last Secretary General of *Casa Obrero Mundial,* which successfully organized labor syndicates.
10. The *Collected Essays and Occasional Writings of Katherine Anne Porter* (New York: Delacorte Press, 1970), 399. Subsequent references to Porter's essays from this edition appear in my text.
11. John M. Hart, *Anarchism & the Mexican Working Class 1860–1931* (Austin: University of Texas Press, 1978), 160.
12. In a note Porter listed Carrillo Puerto's and photographer Roberto Turnbull's stories of their experiences in the Revolution, both of which exist in rough draft, and Salomón de la Selva's "adventure with Palma's sister," which she transformed into "Virgin Violeta." De le Selva was a Nicaraguan poet, whom Porter, in her unpublished "An Encounter with Herman Goering," accuses of exploiting women, although he was "ingenuously charming and . . . could disarm even most wary persons." She inscribed in her copy of Emily Dickinson's poetry "Salomón de la Selva gave me this book in Mexico City in 1922, after reading every poem in it to me."

13. J. H. Retinger, *The Rise of the Mexican Labor Movement* (Documentary Publications, 1976), 91; originally published in 1926 as *Morones of Mexico*.

14. Carleton Beals, *Glass Houses* (Philadelphia: Lippincott, 1938) 58.

15. Porter reported to Lopez that in Mexico she received "unwanted" attention from men "obviously disconcerted by her coolness. One of her . . . friends once told her that certain comrades considered her a very cold *gringita*. Selectivity was so often equated with frigidity" (*Conversations,* 121). Givner's account of Porter's frigidity indicates that the comrades were right (92–93).

16. Dorothy S. Redden, in " 'Flowering Judas': Two Voices," *Studies in Short Fiction* 6 (1969), argues that one of Porter's voices "concurs in Laura's self-condemnation," while the other approves her "spiritual refusal to yield" (201).

[Maidenhood vs. Matriarchy in "The Cracked Looking-Glass"]

JANE KRAUSE DeMOUY

In ["The Cracked Looking-Glass"], [Katherine Anne] Porter reveals a woman who has not been able to choose between maidenhood and matriarchy. She zeroes in, with horrifying accuracy, on the psychic ossification of a woman who has been denied the one natural transition open to her—the movement from erotic object to mother. If Granny Weatherall [in "The Jilting of Granny Weatherall"] achieves satisfaction in matriarchy and the protagonist of "Theft" is clear-eyed about choosing to be a virgin artist, Rosaleen O'Toole, the protagonist of "The Cracked Looking-Glass," can only be seen as a thwarted mother. In opposition to Mrs. Whipple in "He," Rosaleen has natural maternal instincts but no outlet for them. Consequently, her unsatisfied erotic energy merges falsely with the motherly instincts she is denied using, resulting in a shallow epiphany that produces no real self-knowledge for her in the end.

The conflict in "The Cracked Looking-Glass," that between maiden and mother, is one of the oldest in history, as Aztec and other mythologies demonstrate. Certainly one of the most essential statements of this struggle for vitality and potency is found in the tale "Snow White," which provides several motifs for Rosaleen O'Toole's story, as the title suggests.[1] Porter modernizes the myth by embodying the conflict in one woman and by making it a psychological struggle rather than a physical one, but the characteristics are all the same, and the final issue is still who will have love, sex, and life or death.

Focusing on an Irish farm couple, "The Cracked Looking-Glass" has all the earmarks of a Porter story: an insightful view of the woman's repressed sexuality, a utilization of dreams to provide that insight, and the overriding presence of death. Rosaleen's psychology illustrates the typical dichotomy between the figure of the romantic belle she was in her youth and the matron she ought to become. Her looking-glass symbolizes her narcissisms; with "a crack across the middle" (p. 109),[2] it is divided, as is her perception of herself. Like the wicked queen in "Snow White," Rosaleen has been accustomed to look into her mirror and confirm that she is "the fairest one of all." Now

Reprinted with permission of the author from *Katherine Anne Porter's Women: The Eye of Her Fiction* (Austin: University of Texas Press, 1992), 61–72.

fortyish, in mid-life, with a seventy-five-year-old husband who no longer makes love to her, she must accept the rebellious message of her mirror just as the queen mother of the folktale must. The fair young maiden is no longer reflected in it, and thus at times she can't see "herself" in it. When she does see an image, her face is, significantly, "like a monster's" (p. 122). Thus, it seems there are two Rosaleens in the looking-glass: the high-stepping maiden who was a sought-after belle and the middle-aged matron who must content herself with mothering her elderly husband, Dennis, with whom she is celebrating a twenty-fifth wedding anniversary as the story opens. The missing link in Rosaleen's adult female development is motherhood. Unlike Granny Weatherall, she has had no "fine children out of" her husband, and she has no substitute activity to satisfy her need to generate and create. With language, she spins yarns and tells tall tales—folklore that is the rudimentary stuff of the primitive artist, talk that is fueled by her barely controlled, rampant libidinal energy.

Her attempt to control that sexual energy is the thrust of the story. How difficult that might be is symbolized in the frenetic activity of the several cats which keep Rosaleen company in the kitchen and which scatter "in all directions" when she raises her voice to them. Her favorite, the Billy-cat, is lost to her except for two visions she has of her old pet—a painting of him, "the Billy-cat to the life" (p. 104), and a dream she had in which the cat came to her to tell her of his death. Her dreams and her tales are the offspring of Rosaleen's twenty-five years of marriage, and she feeds her husband, and anyone else who will listen, full of both. A fascinating belle in her youth, she still hungers for male attention and sexual fulfillment although she hasn't the temerity to seek it outside her marriage. When Guy Richards, her neighbor, pays attention to her, his overt sexual appeal is completely unsettling to her. Finally, in the midst of a bitter winter, she dreams that her sister is calling her from her deathbed; consequently, Rosaleen travels to New York and then to Boston to see her. Not finding her sister, she decides that for the first time a dream has "gone back" on her. Meeting a young Irish boy in the streets of Boston, in a maternal gesture she feeds him and then offers him a home in her house. When he calls this a sexual offer, she is outraged and runs him off, but finally admits to herself that she has loved Kevin, a young house painter she sheltered five years earlier. Returning home, aware that both dreams and love are lost, she refuses to tell any stories. But in rejecting tales and dreams, she does not turn toward truth, but toward another kind of fantasy—maybe Kevin will return to her after all. That she remains fixed psychologically, despite her change in attitude, is caught in the final reference to the looking-glass. She has forgotten to replace the cracked one with a clear piece. Her trip has not yielded a new clear vision of herself; the distorted image remains.

Far from being a character with arrested sexuality, like Laura in "Flowering Judas," Rosaleen O'Toole is a spirited woman whose husband remembers her in her youth as "a great tall rosy girl, a prize dancer," who had the boys "fairly fighting over her" when she met him (p. 107). But, like Laura, she is suspended between two images of herself. The passage of time prevents her from returning to her youth, but without becoming a mother she cannot accept age gracefully. It is true enough that, in her own mind, at least, she is still the pretty belle of her youth, with nothing to concern her except dressing and dancing and teasing the boys:

> We used to be the whole day getting ready for the dances, washing our hair and curling it and trying on our dresses and trimming them, laughing fit to kill about the boys and making up things to say to them. When my sister Honora was married they took me for the bride. . . . With my white dress ruffled to the heels and my hair with a wreath. Everybody drank my health for the belle of the ball. . . . (p. 111)

While Rosaleen insists that she is "a settled woman over her nonsense" (p. 116), her husband thinks that she doesn't look "a year older," which heightens their age differences now that he is visibly aging. From the beginning, though, there have been differences in their needs. After he marries her, Dennis finds her a lusty young wife and almost begins to "wish sometimes he had let one of those strong-armed boys have her." Later, "after she cooled down a little, he knew he could have never done better. The only thing was, he wished it had been Rosaleen he had married that first time in Bristol, and now they'd be settled together, nearer an age. Thirty years was too much difference altogether" (p. 107).

The truth is that Rosaleen is not ready to put on age, especially since the joy in her life lies in her maidenhood. She still behaves like a young girl who leads the boys a merry chase. She still loves parties and feast days, still wears bright-colored ginghams and worries about the curl in her red hair; but it is the courtship game that she enjoys most. Teasing the boys and playing hard to get is what she relishes. It satisfies her ego as nothing else can.

In fact, her triumphant girlhood—which she has re-created for Dennis so many times that he knows her youth better than his own—is highlighted by stories of dances and young men kept dangling in hopes of a favor from the heartbreaker Rosaleen:

> I remember a boy in Ireland was a great step-dancer, the best, and he was wild about me and I was a devil to him. . . . He said to me a thousand times, "Rosaleen, why won't ye dance with me just one?" And I'd say, "Ye've plenty to dance with ye without my wasting my time." And so it went for the summer long. . . . till in the end I danced with him. (p. 111)

Afterward she walks home with her patient suitor and a crowd of people under "a heaven full of stars." Before God and everybody, Rosaleen has demonstrated her worth and even increased her value by holding out. After agreeing to "keep steady" with the boy, she "was sorry for it the minute [she] promised." Once the chase is ended, the climax is gone, there is no more pleasure in it. Rosaleen repeats the pattern of tempting, withholding, and finally acquiescing when she meets Dennis.

Having decided after the death of his first wife "never to marry again," Dennis, a man of nearly fifty, succumbs to Rosaleen's charms; characteristically, "she led him a dance then for two years before she would have him" (p. 106). It is not surprising that on the night of their twenty-fifth anniversary Rosaleen confides, "I could feel like dancing itself this night, Dennis" (p. 110), for her dancing was in her youth a sublimation of her sexual energy, an expression of her personal freedom, and the act by which she made men notice her. It is a display of energy, however, that is controlled and made acceptable by the pattern of the dance. Consequently, dancing expressed for Rosaleen youth, freedom, and desirability, while simultaneously controlling her spirit and allowing her the pleasure of feverish anticipation. One ought to be able to trade all that for something better, but Rosaleen has found that marriage does not assuage her narcissistic need for attention.[3]

Being the bride is the prize for those who play the game well, but even on one's wedding day one begins to sink into the obscurity of housewifery. At her sister's wedding, the focus is not on the bride but on Rosaleen, who will "surely be the next bride" (p. 111). While the present bride is eclipsed, her single sister is "the belle of the ball." But Rosaleen learns only through her own experience that being the belle is better than being the bride.

In addition to having traded away the attentions that courtship provides, Rosaleen's marriage bargain leaves her physically unsustained. Instead of her lusty dancing, she now has the quiet chores of the farm, most of which involve the motherly activities of feeding and comforting. Milking links her to the female symbol of the cow. Her sympathy for the animal, which will soon go into heat, contrasts with Dennis's inability to appreciate the animal's [and Rosaleen's] physical needs:

> The cow now—the creature! Pretty soon she'll be jumping the stone walls after the apples, and running wild through the fields roaring, and it's all for another calf only, the poor deceived thing! Dennis said, "I don't see what deceit there is in that." "Oh, don't you now?" said Rosaleen, and gathered up her milk pails. (p. 107)

Milking the cow to relieve its physical burden for the moment, Rosaleen speaks to her as a fellow creature. She says to the cow: "It's no life, no life at all. A man of his years is no comfort to a woman!" (p. 107). When she assures Dennis that the anniversary cake she had made for their dinner "wouldn't upset the stomach of a nursing child," we are reminded again that she is more valuable to him as a mother than as a lover. Dennis himself muses over this difficulty, wondering

> what she thought of him now he was no human good to her. Here he was, all gone, and he had been so for years, and he felt guilt sometimes before Rosaleen, who couldn't always understand how there comes a time when a man is finished, and there is no more to be done that way. (p. 110)

Rosaleen dances no longer, but is still capable of wishing for it.

She understands well enough that "once you've given your word there's nothing to think about. . . ." Marriage is irrevocable, and it is a dead end into which a girl may come dancing, never to escape: "when a young girl marries an old man, even if he has money she's bound to be disappointed . . ." (p. 113). And disappointed Rosaleen has been. Her sexual frustration is unabated, and there has been no chance to sublimate that energy into motherhood.

Her life seems in the twenty-fifth year of her marriage unfulfilled and attended by losses, most unfortunately the loss of the child that could have transformed her from maiden to mother. When Rosaleen thinks of her "half-forgotten child," dead in two days' time (the only child she has had of the aging Dennis), she weeps in fresh agony for the lost son who might have been by now "a fine grown man and the dear love of her heart" (p. 114). Undefined as a mother, Rosaleen is essentially a maiden caught on the other side of mid-life with only the dry laurels of her successful girlhood to drape about her head. Real motherhood has eluded her, and babying animals and an aging husband have proved a frustration rather than a satisfaction. The result is a double, confused identity, reflected in Rosaleen's responses to the men in the story.

With Dennis, the man with whom she can be appropriately sexual, she must not be a wife but a mother. Kevin, the young house painter, and, later, the young Irish boy she meets in Boston represent both suitors and sons to her. She offers them mothering—food and shelter—to hide her sexual attraction to their youthful masculinity. But Richards, her neighbor, is partly attracted to her because of her strong maternal personality. She appeals to him by telling him stories, a double gesture that is both maternal and sexual. Kevin, who is the most significant of them, is Prince Charming to Rosaleen's chaste princess. Part of the delight of their relationship is in its nonphysical nature. There is high attraction between them and the pleasure of sexual tension, but that attraction is never named or acted upon, just as the implicit sexual meanings in fairy tales are never spelled out.

As both substitute lover and son, Kevin materializes at two important junctures in Rosaleen's thoughts. When she thinks of the "fine man" Dennis was when she first knew him, before his "getting old . . . took the heart out of her" (p. 108), his image swiftly becomes Kevin's; when she thinks of her lost son who might have grown into a becoming man, the image again becomes Kevin's. As both Prince Charming and son, he admits both sides of Rosaleen's personality—maiden and mother. He is so much the object of her affection that when he shows Rosaleen a picture of his girlfriend, she cries out and tears come to her eyes. She can neither admit to herself her jealousy nor tolerate this sexual rival, and after he leaves her house, Rosaleen muses that he will come back apologizing for taking up with "somebody not fit to look" at Rosaleen. Like a mother whose Oedipal conflicts remain unresolved, she still waits another five years. Her only alternative is to mother Dennis, but "it wasn't being a wife at all to wrap a man in flannels like a baby and put hot water bottles to him" (p. 109). On the contrary, it is easy to disguise her pining for Kevin as motherly longing: "the darling, the darling lad like her own son" (p. 114).

Well he might be her son, for he, like Rosaleen, is an Irish immigrant isolated from kin and the city by the loneliness of the Connecticut farm country among "heathen Rooshans and Polacks and Wops with their liquor stills and outlandish lingo" (p. 114). A native of County Sligo like her, Kevin understands immediately the conventions which will dominate their relationship and the repartee which will sublimate their attraction to each other. He agrees readily with Rosaleen that he ought to live in her "good Irish house," an oasis among dour natives and heathen foreigners.

> They stood there smiling at each other, feeling they had agreed enough, it was time to think how to get the best of each other in the talk from now on. For more than a year they had tried to get the best of each other in the talk, and sometimes it was one and sometimes another, but a gay easy time and such a bubble of joy like a kettle singling. (p. 115)

Thus Kevin not only reinforces Rosaleen's ego; he also projects the familiarity and comfort of home that her Bristol Irish husband, who "might as well be English," cannot give.

In addition, he tacitly understands that they make love verbally. When he tells Rosaleen about his girlfriend in New York, he commits a double infidelity: first by having a girlfriend at all, and second by speaking of her, thus allowing an interloper to intrude upon the special solace of their conversation. He doesn't realize how much irony there is in his statement "I was greatly wrong to tell ye!" (p. 108). Later, after he is gone from her house, Rosaleen is saddened by the fact that the only "word" she gets from him is a postcard picturing a tall building in New York, which suggests his phallic significance to Rosaleen. It states only: "This is my hotel. Kevin." But it is appropriate that since the relationship is ended he should no longer converse with her. After his departure, Rosaleen can do nothing but drape his picture of her Billy-cat with a strip of crocheted lace and prop it up, shrine-like, in her kitchen, as an excuse to say his name. Significantly, the mention of Kevin angers Dennis.

Presumably, Rosaleen loses her lover/son about the same time her husband loses his sexual potency. She is doubly isolated, then, a city girl in the winter countryside of Connecticut, with no native comforts except an old husband who must be bundled like a baby. She is surrounded by sly, mean neighbors, some of whom she fears for their wildness. Not the least of these is Guy Richards, a man totally unlike the other she has known; he is a man of her own age whom she can neither baby nor tease; thus she cannot control him. Consequently, he is "a great offense" to Rosaleen. She finds his appearance and bold brawling behavior alluringly dangerous. A man with "shaggy mustaches and his shirt in rags till the brawny skin showed through" (p. 115), he clearly attracts her, and she fantasizes about having to "shoot him dead" if he "lays a finger on her." He of course offers to do no such thing; he doesn't need to, for his masculine presence and his bold eyes are enough to unnerve Rosaleen.

As he becomes an occasional visitor in their house, he displays characteristics Rosaleen liked in Kevin, but, being a native of the countryside, he is only a caricature of the Irishman she could love. When he visits her he is loquacious, telling rousing stories of his life and idealizing the memory of his mother. His leisure is spent drinking and dancing, and his bold speech stops Rosaleen cold. "It was enough to make a woman wild not to find a word in her mouth for such boldness," and she spends his visits "racking her mind for some saying that would put him in his place . . ." (p. 117).

Again, the "word" metaphorically suggests sexual connotations: Richards is a bold speaker as he would be a bold lover, and Rosaleen's inability to "put him in his place" verbally underscores the fact that she could never dominate him sexually, or even control the relationship, as she has been able to do with every other lover. Both she and Richards are verbally quick and prone to storytelling, and each is engaged by the other's tales, suggesting that they are sexually quite compatible. When Richards sits "with his ears lengthened" (p. 121) while Rosaleen tells again the story of the Billy-cat, we see that, whoever might dominate, she is as sexually appealing to him as he is to her. It is almost as if she has finally met her match in him: he reveres the memory of a mother while she reveres the memory of a son; both frequently distort reality, he by his drinking and she by her fantasizing.

As the cracked looking-glass suggests, distortion of reality is the most pervasive element in the story, from the first scene in which Rosaleen beguiles the traveling salesman with the story of her Billy-cat while her husband listens at the keyhole, muttering against the "tall tales" she tells as truth, to the scene mentioned above, when Rosaleen, like some rural Scheherezade, spins the tale again for Guy Richards while Dennis himself is enough seduced to wonder if it might be true.

Through several sequences, beginning with the first, the reader has a chance to question the nature of reality in all its duplicity. The Billy-cat, for instance, is real and present by virtue of a painted picture and Rosaleen's memory of him. The picture is said to be the cat's "spittin' image" and "the Billy-cat to life," but his legs look too stuffed "for a living cat," and he wasn't actually sitting on the table pictured, but in Rosaleen's lap, while the picture was being painted. Thus the picture is not an accurate presentation, and Rosaleen's conjuration of him seems less so, since she so frequently merges reality and fantasy in the same breath, playing, like all good raconteurs, to her audience. "He wanted a story, so I gave him a good one. It's the Irish in me" (p. 105). Of course, whether the story parallels actuality or not, it takes on substance and a nature of its own when Rosaleen tells it.

Like María Concepción, Rosaleen has a primitive mind. She thinks animistically, talking to her animals and assuming that her favorite cat is living some kind of life after death. She believes in the physical embodiment of spirits and abstractions, like "the Evil" she has seen as a girl in Ireland. She believes in the power of the word, whether it be calling on the Holy Name to disperse ghosts or uttering imaginative curses against an enemy. Finally, she regards dreams as an important means of communication, not from her unconscious mind, but usually from the world of the dead. Thus her dreams, like her tales, although untrue, have reality because, through her telling, they achieve shape, substance, and actuality.

Through language, Rosaleen is the creator she cannot be through her body. When she invokes youth and Ireland, it is like an incantation which causes events to materialize from the foggy past. The reality of the past, the present, and the imagination become equivalent in her mouth; one begins to wonder if the eighth part of what she says is true. What is more important, however, is the power she wields. Believing what she says, she acts on that belief; she convinces the gullible who like a good story, and she even brings her cynical husband to the point where he longs for tales. When she insists on traveling to Boston to see her sister on the strength of a dream that may or may not be true, Dennis is annoyed and disgusted. But when she returns, he wants the story of that trip to Boston—whether or not it is true. Ultimately, her blarney has a right to exist for its own sake, as a demonstration of the creative power of a woman too confined to realize her potential. Finally, it is another metaphor for Rosaleen's strong sexuality. While the years have put "a quietus" on Dennis, she has become garrulous. There is surely double entendre in Dennis's bitter thought that someday when he is dead "she'll find a man can keep her quiet" (p. 113).

Aside from the creative function of keeping alive loved ones who are gone from her, Rosaleen's dreams are her way of burying her dead. She eases herself of her guilt for her great-grandfather's passing by the double ritual of dreaming of him as a soul in purgatory who can speak to her and by having an extra Mass said for him. In the case of her Billy-cat, the story of his woeful end allows her to bury him psychically and experience the grief that will lead her to accept his death. Likewise, she injures and buries the dancing swain of her youth and, in his turn, Kevin. The final dream, about Honora calling from her deathbed, suggests the demise of her youth, which was so intimately shared with this sister. "My dreams never renege on me," she tells Guy Richards. "They're all I have to go by" (pp. 121–122). It is certainly significant that at the age of forty-five, living with a husband who has one foot in the grave, Rosaleen's dreams are closing chapters in her experience. Of course, it is all too true in a literal sense that the people with whom she has shared love are dead to her, just as surely as she has watched Kevin disappear from her life.

In the final segment, a present experience which neatly balances the twenty-fifth wedding anniversary in all its memories, Rosaleen boards a train to New York and feels content that she is "once more on a train going somewhere" (p. 123). She thinks that having left the frozen waste of the farm and her barren, aged husband, she can pick up the threads of her youth and move forward again, but actually the trip is a journey backward in time, a nostalgic grasping for the past.

Arriving in New York, she wishes for an "hour to visit her old flat in 164th Street" (p. 123); she eyes the delicate and youthful lingerie in shop windows; wallowing in sentiment and sweets, she cries through two movies whose titles reveal the real nature of the restlessness which has motivated her trip. Both *The Prince of Love* and *The Lover King* allow her to weep copiously over the plight of dashing heroes who must overcome tremendous obstacles to marry the unnaturally beautiful girls who are their heart's desire. The love songs go "to her heart like a dagger" (p. 124), while she munches on chocolates; after the movies, she indulges in ice cream topped with strawberry preserves, just like a child on holiday. She goes to pray for Honora in a church richly dressed in candles and flowers and the fragrance of incense. Steeped in girlish romance and emotionalism, with "that lost heathen place," Connecticut, behind her, she boards a boat which will carry her overnight to Boston.

This night sea journey, undertaken to visit the sister of her youth, has several implications. Part of the funeral rites of many cultures, such a voyage ended in the land of the dead; the possible demise of Rosaleen's sister causes her to begin this journey, but she cannot find Honora any more than she can retrieve the happy days of her maidenhood when she had many men to admire her. Rosaleen's poisoned apple is age, and, unlike Snow White, she cannot cough it up. On this voyage, Rosaleen commits her youth to the land of the dead. It might also be read as a psychic journey by which she reverts to memories of past happiness, long buried in her subconscious. Moreover, if we read this journey as a paradigm of Rosaleen's sexual experience, it becomes clear that her readiness to be fructified by a man has always come to a dead end. Significantly, like a child in the womb, she falls asleep that night to the "grand steady beat" (p. 124) of the boat's engine and sleeps a dreamless sleep.

The next morning she finds herself in "dreary, ugly" Boston, and she is unable to "remember any good times there" (p. 125). This ominous note hangs over her attempt to establish a tangible link with her vanished girlhood. She searches for Honora's flat to no avail. No one knows her sister, and even the phone book doesn't list her. Rosaleen's last tie to youth and Ireland, Honora has vanished as surely as Kevin and the Irish step-dancer, confronting Rosaleen with a sharp reality difficult to face: her dream has "gone back on her," both literally—the dream of Honora's illness—and symbolically—the dream of her maidenhood for happiness "ever after" for herself and a dashing prince. She will have to bear other harsh realities in the wake of that loss, especially a recognition of her ambivalent motherhood/seduction.

Meeting a down-and-out Irish boy on the windy street, she feels heartened and feeds him mounds of food before offering him a ten-dollar bill in the name of Kevin and her lost son. Finally, she offers him a home on the farm, but the streetwise boy ignores her motherly intention and calls her invitation as he sees it: "I was caught at it once in Dublin. . . . A fine woman like yourself she was, and her husband peeking through a crack in the wall . . ." (p. 128). Insulted, Rosaleen sends him packing, but in a flash of recognition she sees that "Kevin had loved her and she had loved Kevin, and Oh, she hadn't known it in time! . . . and now he was gone and lost and dead." In other words, her potential lover is as dead to her as the son she never raised. With all her youthful hopes gone, she retreats to the isolation of Connecticut and resolves "never [to] speak to a soul again" (p. 129). She forswears creation, like the menopausal woman she is.

On her return, she cannot forbear telling Dennis that she has "left [Honora] in health," but she tells no tales despite his eagerness to hear them, and she tells him she no longer believes in dreams. Having resolved now that the city is a "wild, heartless place" (p. 130) where she could never live, Rosaleen must still bear the rejection of her heartless neighbors. The haggard mother of the boy who does Rosaleen's chores accuses her of whoring, and Richards, half-drunk, momentarily thinks of stopping that evening but then carelessly drives on, leaving Rosaleen more hopeless than ever. Even if she gives in to the "ruined life [she would have] with such a man," she thinks she would still have to bear his indifference, one more "terrible disappointment." She is left to fantasize about New York and Boston and "places full of life and gayety she'd never seen nor even heard of, and beyond everything like a green field with morning sun on it lay youth and Ireland . . ." (p. 134). Her green field is reminiscent of Granny Weatherall's bright field, where her life is perfectly ordered through marriage to the right lover. Rosaleen has had her choice and has not lived happily ever after, either. So remote is the image that she thinks of it as a dream, as unattainable in her life as it was for Ellen Weatherall.

She has, after all, forgotten to replace the cracked looking-glass, which Dennis has always described as "good enough." A new glass would have removed the "monster" from her vision, but would also reveal an image of herself she is not able to accept, the one seen by the lad in Boston. It is the image of an aging Rosaleen who can no longer attract men through her youth and spirited dancing. If she eschews tale-telling, she will no longer attract Richards, either, as his failure to stop suggests.

Her final stance is both childish and mothering. She sits with Dennis, her head on his knee, and begs him to protect himself against the cold, for without him, she will herself be forced to face the bitter cold of loneliness.[4]

Notes

1.   For a fascinating discussion of female doubling in "Snow White," particularly as it reflects fragmentation and division in literary women, see Sandra M. Gilbert and Susan Gubar, *The Madwoman in the Attic: The Woman Writer and the Nineteenth-Century Literary Imagination* (New Haven and London: Yale University Press, 1979), 3–91.

2.   Parenthetical numbers refer to pages in Katherine Anne Porter, *The Collected Stories* (New York: Harcourt, Brace, 1965). [Ed.]

3.   Karen Horney, "The Problem of Feminine Masochism," in *Psychoanalysis and Women,* ed. Jean Baker Miller (New York: Penguin, 1973), 32, appears to be describing Rosaleen O'Toole when she writes about the way masochistic persons "find reassurance against deep fears": such a person needs to be loved but requires "constant signs of attention, and as he never believes in these signs except momentarily, he has an excessive need for attention and affection." He is easily attached to people, emotional in relationships, and easily disappointed because he can't get what he wants.

4.   The best essay on the story is Joseph Wiesenfarth, "Illusion and Allusion: Reflections in 'The Cracked Looking-Glass,' " *Four Quarters* 12 (1962): 30–37. Wiesenfarth argues that in the conclusion, Rosaleen breaks with the pattern of her life and frees reality from her dreams and illusions, finally accepting her life with Dennis. In this view, then, the failure to replace the cracked glass is perhaps an acceptance of the imperfect that is most prevalent in life. Reprinted in *Katherine Anne Porter: A Critical Symposium,* ed. Lodwick Hartley and George Core (Athens: University of Georgia Press, 1969).

Porter's "Hacienda" and the Theme of Change

ROBERT L. PERRY

Katherine Anne Porter's "Hacienda" is one of those stories whose meaning is blurred by topicality. This story, as many of its readers know, had its genesis in a series of impressions Miss Porter gathered during an extended visit to the Tetlapayac Hacienda, one of the settings for *Que Viva Mexico*. This ill-fated masterpiece, directed by the famous Sergei Eisenstein, aroused great controversy in the States when Upton Sinclair, the film's financial backer, suddenly curtailed production of the film and refused Eisenstein the right to edit it. What followed was an extended legal struggle over the rights to the film in which Sinclair was ultimately the victor. The film was thereupon sold to Sol Lesser and released in 1933 under the title of *Thunder Over Mexico*. Readers wishing to learn more about the story of *Que Viva Mexico* and the people involved in it may consult Marie Seton's excellent biography of Eisenstein published by Grove Press in 1960.

This immense topical interest in the story makes one guess that the failure of critics to discover its unifying theme stems from their unwillingness to read the story as "art," and from their eagerness to read it as a factual, reportorial account of Miss Porter's experiences. Glenway Wescott, for instance, recently wrote in *The Atlantic* (April, 1962) that the story was "mainly a portrait of the great Russian film maker, Eisenstein," although anyone even tolerably familiar with the story knows this simply is not true. And knowing what we do of Miss Porter's profound respect for the craft of fiction, we should find it odd that she would submit for publication a story that was little more than mere journalism.

Since J. W. Johnson writing in *The Virginia Quarterly Review* (Autumn, 1960) has suggested that "Hacienda" is an "amalgam" of Porter's major themes, perhaps we should appraise the story in these terms. Johnson sees five specific themes operating in Porter's works, each represented by a novella prototype and a flock of short stories. The first is "the individual within his heritage" ("Old Mortality"), the second is "cultural displacement" ("The Leaning Tower"), the third is "unhappy marriage" ("The Cracked Looking-Glass"), the

Reprinted with permission of the journal from the *Midwest Quarterly* 6 (Summer 1965): 403–15.

fourth is "the death of love" ("Pale Horse, Pale Rider"), and the fifth is "man's slavery to his own nature and subjugation to a human fate which dooms him to suffering and disappointment" ("Noon Wine"). We can easily find all of these themes operating in "Hacienda." Don Genaro, for instance, clearly represents the theme of "the individual within his heritage," just as Uspensky, Stepanov, Kennerly, and especially Andreyev represent the theme of "cultural displacement." Moreover, we have an "unhappy marriage" between don Genaro and doña Julia, and both the "death of love" theme and the "fate" theme are present in the tragedy of Rosalita, Justino, and Vicente. It seems futile, however, to examine the story in these terms, for to do so would mean focusing on its several parts rather than attempting to see it as a coherent whole. Instead of discovering a series of themes, we must discover a single, all-embracing theme.

At least one of Mr. Johnson's five major themes, the theme of "man's slavery to his own nature and subjugation to a human fate," is worth discussing at length, since it does in fact come near to being the story's controlling idea. This theme appears principally through a series of chase-images which serve to remind us that each character is, to one degree or another, hounded by a personal fate that is inescapable. Such is the case with the unfortunate Justino, who, after murdering his unfaithful sister, "struck through the maguey fields towards the mountains" chased by his friend Vicente, who rode horseback "waving a gun and yelling: 'stop or I'll shoot!'" (Modern Library edition of *Flowering Judas,* New York, 1935, 247.) At times the chase-motif becomes a parody of fate, as when one of don Genaro's "polite, expensive dogs" chases "a little fat-bottomed soldier" back to his barracks (271), or when, to the great delight of Carlos, "three dogs chase a long-legged pig from wallow to barn" (274). The most compelling statement of the drama of fate occurs during the journey by mule-cart to the hacienda, when the narrator sees a valiant rabbit running full speed chased by "lean hungry dogs":

> It was cracking the strings of its heart in flight; its eyes started from its head like crystal bubbles. "Run, rabbit run!" I cried. "Run, dogs!" shouted the big Indian with the red cords on his hat, his love of a contest instantly aroused. He turned to me with his eyes blazing: "What will you bet, senorita?" (250–251)

What are the odds, we might ask, that don Genaro will some day escape the fact that he hates his wife? What are the odds that Kennerly will finally escape the anxieties that hound his perilous career? Although Miss Porter's sympathies, like the narrator's, are with the rabbit, she knows full well he is doomed.

Another theme that is woven into the story's texture is the theme of death, one which serves as a constant reminder of what awaits the quarry at the end of the chase. The ominousness of death is present everywhere in the story, in the "looming mountains" in the distance, the "deepening sky" overhead, and the angular patterns of the spiked maguey plants in the fields (249–250). It is also present in the eyes of the peons, which glitter with "rich enjoyable feelings" when they discuss the funeral preparations made for Rosalita. But most of all the reader feels it in the atmosphere of the hacienda itself, which is scented with the odor of fermenting pulque-juice, "sour, stale, like rotting milk and blood" (269). Pulque is an admirable symbol for death, because it is a sleep-inducing liquor, a Lethe-like beverage that supplies the bondaged peons with their only means besides Christian communion of escaping the wretchedness of their daily existence. Thus the drinking of pulque becomes for the Indian an expression of a profound death-wish. But by drinking pulque, the Indian satisfies not only his own wish but the government's wish that he remain wrapped in his ancient slumber, unheedful of the Agrarian call to revolt. As long as the peons have their pulque, they will never change.

This last brings us to a consideration of the central unifying theme of the story. The most important word in "Hacienda" is change. Throughout the story it is applied manifoldly to the setting, the events, and the characters. The peons on don Genaro's estate are said to live in an "unchanged world." The hacienda "hasn't changed at all" in fifty years, according to an old Spanish gentleman (236), nor has the process of making pulque changed since its discovery. Of Betancourt, art adviser to Uspensky, it is said that "he resisted the idea of change in himself," although he thinks that Carlos, the ballad-writer, is "much changed" (261) after ten years. And on the first page of the story we are told: "Now that the true revolution of blessed memory has come and gone in Mexico, the names of many things are changed, nearly always with a view to an appearance of heightened well-being for all creatures" (223). The irony here, of course, is that although the names are changed, the conditions are not; and, as we learn elsewhere, although the wealth of the country is no longer visibly controlled by the nobility, it is nonetheless in the hands of a "successful revolutionist" (259) named Verlarde who strongly allies himself with the landed gentry. The same irony exists in the fact that the Russians are making a film which will show how the revolution has "swept away" (241) the feudal class structure of old Mexico, and yet they are filming it out of real life on don Genaro's estate. Such ironies occur throughout the story and illustrate its most basic theme, which might be called the illusion of change. It is helpful to think of "Hacienda" as a dramatic rebuttal of Marx's theory of history and indeed of all theories which predicate revolutions and radical social change.

But thus far we have spoken only of historical change. As Miss Porter uses it, the word also applies to individuals, and here also the possibility for change is illusory. For she believes that people are what they are and cannot become something different, at least not overnight. Man is enslaved by his own nature, which is, in turn, the inevitable product of his heritage, and although he may try, he cannot escape its influence. When the young actor-pugilist strides down the aisle of the coach to tell Kennerly's party of the shooting, he possesses "a brilliant air of self-confidence." But when he begins to speak, "the pose would not hold" (244) and his face breaks out into a naive country grin. An Indian cannot become a boxer or a movie actor overnight, for his provincial background has conditioned him otherwise. The extent to which the average Indian is trapped by his heritage is almost unbelievable. When the narrator wakes up in the morning after her arrival and looks out her window at the Indians in the field below, she sees an amazing sight: "A three-year-old man-child ran beside his father; he drove a weanling donkey carrying two miniature casks on its furry back. The two small creatures imitated each in his own kind perfectly the gestures of their elder" (271–272). These are, as Miss Porter says, "figures under a doom imposed by the landscape" (236). Their only knowledge is suffering; their only wisdom is death. Only a cataclysm could shock them out of their pulque-stupor.

Most of the characters in "Hacienda" are people like the young pugilist, people who have tried to throw off their heritage and become "modern" by assuming some superficially modern pose. The one exception to this rule is the elder Genaro. Of him we read that "He had been silenced but in no wise changed in his conviction by the sudden, astonishing marriage of his grandson" (254). This man, the owner of one of the most venerable estates in Mexico, is the last of a vanishing species, the orthodox Spanish aristocrat. As such he is a man of firm, unalterable principle. Thus don Genaro's betrothal to a woman of common blood is to him more than a mere breach of propriety; it is a cataclysm signaling the imminent extinction of his way of life. For him there is only one alternative: to resist change, to stand fast like a stubborn mule while the world passes by. Like the professor in Willa Cather's *The Professor's House,* who in the face of a similar shock retreats to a solitary room in his attic, Grandfather Genaro moves to "the very farthest patio in the old garden," where he lives out his days in "bleak dignity and loneliness" (255).

At first glance, don Genaro seems to be completely different from his grandfather. For the grandson is modern in that he is "always going at top speed, seventy kilometers an hour at least, and never on time anywhere." At one point we learn that "nothing could move too fast for don Genaro," "whether a horse, dog, a woman, or something with metal machinery in it" (257). It is important to notice that unlike Betancourt, Genaro is not punctual: for speed to him is not a means but an end in itself. He is a man virtually obsessed by speed; he is thinking of buying an airplane because he needs "something really fast" (262). But despite his craving for speed, Genaro is actually quite as reactionary as his grandfather. He is, we must remember, "acting as head of the house, accountable to no one" (254) and also is "old-fashioned" in his "taste for ladies of the theatre" (238). In the earliest published version of "Hacienda," in *The Virginia Quarterly Review* of October, 1932, Miss Porter remarks of him that "If you opened his skull you would find there neatly ticketed and labeled, a set of ideas unchanged in essentials since 1650." And despite what his grandfather thinks, he did not mean to flaunt tradition by marrying the theatrical doña Julia; in fact, he meant to fulfill it.

For there is something of don Quixote in don Genaro, some great longing to live in the style of a bygone age. He is forever sallying forth, amid a glory of chickens, accompanied by his mounted man, to joust with some small-time country judge who might as well be a windmill for all that is accomplished. Genaro is a dreamer trying to live up to some impossible romantic conception of himself, and speed is a part of that conception. More likely than not he married doña Julia because he was infatuated with her style: somehow she fit into his dream; but his great mistake was his failure to see that she was a product of a modern urban culture alien to his own. When he returns from the Capital and finds his wife strolling arm-and-arm with his mistress, he is "thunderstruck by the suddenness of this change" (239). The act is so preposterous to his mind that he is completely baffled and does not know how to react. He is not modern enough to cope with the problem; his scruples, for instance, would never permit divorce. In other words, he cannot change. And so he turns to speed as his only escape, and in the time-honored American fashion, forever races into the future in order to forget the past. But in his case the future has been stripped of all meaning except change itself, or rather, the *illusion* of change produced by high speeds. His is an attempt to lose himself in the exhilaration of the moment, speed being for him a drug no less effective than the pulque of his peons. But no matter how fast he travels, he will never escape the mistakes of his youth, especially the awful realization that he hates his wife.

Another character who is closely related to the theme is Betancourt, who by one way of thinking can be considered the epitome of change. Born and raised a Spanish aristocrat, Betancourt changed his politics after the revolution in order to survive (252). In this respect he is directly opposite Grandfather Genaro, who refused to change at the price of surrendering his principles. For Betancourt has no principles worthy of the name: he is, in fact, a changeling. We can easily imagine Betancourt, an aesthete, pandering for the favor of Verlarde, who is doubtless a vulgar demagogue similar to Braggioni of "Flowering Judas." And even though he enjoys Verlarde's favor, Betancourt is forever sniffing the winds of change. He is foresighted enough, for instance, to pay homage to the Communists, who may, he feels, rise to power some day:

> "I am sorry for everything," he said, lifting a narrow, pontifical hand, waving away vulgar human pity which always threatened, buzzing like a fly at the

edges of his mind. "But when you consider"—he made an almost imperceptible inclination of his entire person in the general direction of the social point of
view supposed to be represented by the Russians—"what her life would have
been like in this place, it is much better that she is dead." (253)

This fellow is everything that his name implies: he bets on the favorites and
then courts their favor. To him political change is mere change of fashion;
when governments change, one simply exchanges one set of platitudes for
another. He has no qualms about dismissing the problems of the masses with
one hand and praising Communist ideology with the other. His concern is to
be punctual, to keep up with the times, no matter what the times might
bring.

Besides politics, Betancourt is up-to-date in many other respects. He has
abandoned the conservative attire of the Spanish aristocrat for the flashy dress
of Hollywood, sporting riding trousers and a cork helmet (256). Like Genaro,
he prides himself on his speed, which he considers "modern," and finds "a
great deal of pleasurable stimulation in the control of machinery" (257). In
matters of religion, he is conversant with a wide variety of dubious creeds,
extending from Yoga to Nietzsche, including "the latest American theories of
personality development," and from these has professedly fashioned a "Way
of Life" which will bring him happiness and success (264). But despite his
superficial modernity, Betancourt still remains the effete aristocrat he was
raised to be. In essentials, he has not changed. He still maintains his elegant
manners; he is still contemptuous of the lower classes; and despite his religious pretensions he is capable of stooping to the meanest kind of pettiness:
he spends a good deal of his time, for instance, deriding Carlos for being a
"failure" simply so he can forget that he is hugely indebted to him. For in his
eagerness to keep up with worldly changes, Betancourt has neglected to
superintend a more primary change: the growth of his own soul.

Kennerly is another figure who can be profitably related to the illusion-
of-change theme. Of all the characters, with the possible exception of
Stepanov, he is the most perfect expression of modern technological culture.
At the beginning of the story we find him striding boldly down the aisle of
the coach, with Andreyev and the narrator following "in the wake of his
gigantic progress" (223). He expresses machine culture because he is a symbol of activity without purpose. On the train he is forever motioning wildly,
arranging papers, searching his pockets, hurling bags at the racks, jerking
seatbacks about rudely, and worrying, forever worrying, until finally he falls
asleep in utter exhaustion. He also is immensely involved in time, and
believes that "making good involves all sorts of mysterious interlocking
schedules" (234). Unlike Genaro's obsession with speed, which springs
from some deep psychological need, Kennerly's is almost purely pathologi-
cal, like a nervous tic. At one point we learn that "the muscles of his jaw

jerked in continual helpless rage" (230). Kennerly, in fact, has been conditioned by the frantic tempo of technological civilization just as surely as the drowsy peon has been conditioned by the lethargic tempo of his. In Kennerly's opinion, the peons "don't know the meaning of time" (231), but there is no mistaking that the phrase might equally as well apply to Kennerly himself.

Kennerly's mistake is that he has confused change with motion. He is caught up in a whirligig of change, but it is a false kind of change having nothing whatsoever to do with the inward kind. He thinks that by perpetually rushing about he is changing into a better person, but although he considers himself a member of "the ruling race at large" (225), a person vastly more civilized than the peons he distastefully avoids, he actually is far behind them on the road to spiritual beatitude. In his manners and habits, for instance, Kennerly is quite vulgar; he speaks in "an overwhelming unmodulated voice," takes "ponderous, gargling swigs" from his beer bottle, and "rips open" oranges like a ravenous beast (233, 228, 229). Furthermore, he is incapable of feeling compassion, and takes sadistic glee in the prospect of refilming a murder scene in which Justino will act the part he has already performed in reality (273). But most revealing, and also most amusing, is Kennerly's provincialism. Although he is supposedly sophisticated, he is haunted by absurd small-town fears that his brother-in-law, a militant prohibitionist, will discover that he is a beer-drinker (233). Also, he is blue-nosed enough to be shocked by a hint of lesbianism between Lolita and doña Julia (248). Despite all the outward signs of his modernity, he still bears the marks of a strict Puritan upbringing.

The idealistic Andreyev is also related to the theme. He is a doctrinaire Marxist who sincerely believes that the revolution has wrought great changes in Mexico, even though the facts deny this (241). He is blind to the facts because he induces in himself a "voluntary forgetfulness of his surroundings" (267) by which he continually turns inward in homesick yearning for Russia. For all his ideals, he is essentially unchanged, essentially a young peasant boy torn from his homeland. But he is not a self-deceiver in the manner of Betancourt; his ballad-singing endears him to Miss Porter, for this shows that he is concerned with the truth of emotion and thus is not beyond redemption. His problem, like Laura's in "Flowering Judas," is really one of immaturity. With him, as with her, there is the danger that an emotional reservoir may slowly evaporate in the desert of an alien culture. He must grow up by understanding his Russian past; like the mule that hauls visitors to the hacienda, he must get "a tolerable purchase" on the "tie" (248) before moving, for only by accepting what he is will he be able to change into what he wants to be.

This brings us to the character most closely associated with the theme, Carlos. He is a ballad-writer and a good one, because in his *corridös* he sings the truths of the human heart as he finds them in his own experience. Of the Mexican street ballad, Miss Porter has written:

> The corrido is . . . a ballad. Mexico is one of the few countries where a genuine folk poetry still exists, a word-of-mouth tradition which renews itself daily in the heroic, sensational or comic episodes of the moment, an instantaneous record of events, a moment caught in the quick of life.—*Survey*, X (May, 1924).

This fits Carlos perfectly, for he composes, spur-of-the moment, his ballad to "poor Rosalita" on the same day as the murder itself. And this impromptu act is significant in another way. Betancourt believes that Carlos is a failure, simply because he has not increased his income or been recognized for his ballads. But despite the continual bustling about of "successful" people like Betancourt, Kennerly, and Genaro, Carlos is the only person in the course of the story who gets anything done: he composes a ballad, and a good one at that.

Carlos is a true artist, and like Sophocles, has the power to see life and see it whole. He sees through appearance to reality, and is able to perceive that Justino's shooting of his sister was not accidental but rather the inevitable fruit of incest. Incidentally, it is interesting to note how Miss Porter reveals the true nature of "poetic license." When Carlos makes his ballad of the shooting, he absent-mindedly changes a small detail, making Rosalita die of two bullets in her heart instead of one. When Betancourt points this out, Carlos laughs and says, "Very well, one bullet! Such a precisionist!" (267) The upshot is, of course, that the artist can lie about the little things but must tell the truth about the big things, and that a peevish concern for the accuracy of trivia is the mark of the second-rate mind.

Carlos is the only character in the story who is aware of the true nature of change. Thus far we have spoken of change as being wholly illusory, but this of course is only one side of the paradox. Although people and cultures do not change overnight, they do change gradually, in the process of organic growth. When Betancourt shows the narrator the frescos in the pulque vathouse, he remarks that similar frescos were found by the Spaniards in pre-Conquest pulquerias:

> ". . . Nothing ever ends," he waved his long beautiful hand, "it goes on being and becomes little by little something else."
> "I'd call that an end, of a kind," said Carlos.
> "Oh, well, *you*," said Betancourt, smiling with immense indulgence upon his old friend, who was becoming gradually something else. (276)

For, as a style of painting gradually changes, so does one's soul, for better or worse. Carlos, an artist, is a representative of all those who are interested in soul-change. At the end of her preface to *Selected Stories of Eudora Welty*, Miss Porter quotes this passage from Rilke's *The Journal of My Other Self:*

But now that so much is being changed, is it not time that we should change? Could we not try to develop ourselves a little, slowly and gradually take upon ourselves our share in the labor of love? We have been spared all its hardship . . . we have been spoiled by easy enjoyment. . . . But what if we despised our success, what if we began from the beginning to learn the work of love which has always been done for us? What if we were to go and become neophytes, now that so much is changing?

Death and Repetition
in Porter's Miranda Stories

GEORGE CHEATHAM

Early in "Pale Horse, Pale Rider," in one of Miranda Gay's dreams, Katherine Anne Porter introduces the obsessive center of her final Miranda story, indeed of the whole Miranda series: death, specifically Miranda's perception of her own death. ("The Grave," "Old Mortality," "Pale Horse, Pale Rider"—the major titles alone reveal as much.) "And the stranger [death]? Where is that lank greenish stranger I remember hanging about the place, welcomed by my grandfather, my great-aunt, my five times removed cousin, my decrepit hound and my silver kitten? Why did they take to him, I wonder? And where are they now? Yet I saw him pass the window in the evening. What else besides them did I have in the world? Nothing. Nothing is mine, I have only nothing but it is enough, it is beautiful and it is all mine."[1] Should Miranda take to this stranger, as her grandfather and the others have done, or flee him? Are the others (and would she be, once dead) anywhere now? And what is this beautifully sufficient "nothing" allowed by death? Such questions and their possible answers center on the idea of repetition. In "The Grave," the climatic story in *The Old Order,* the first of two groups of Miranda stories, Miranda initially rejects the perceived bondage of repeated meaning (the symbolic silver dove's interpretation of death) to embrace the freedom of unconnected existence, of modernity—the freedom of the grave. Repeating that earlier day, however, the story's coda allows the adult Miranda a chance to revise her youthful choice, to reaccept repeated meaning as something other than mere bondage. Moreover, "Old Mortality" and "Pale Horse, Pale Rider," the second group of stories, together repeat *The Old Order.* That is, they cover roughly the same chronological years of Miranda's life as *The Old Order* and record the same general movement of her consciousness.[2] The repetitious second set of stories, though, calls into question, rather than exactly reconstituting or forwarding, that revisionary final scene from "The Grave," recovering the possible meaninglessness of Miranda's experiences only latent in that perhaps too pat earlier conclusion.

Reprinted with permission of Duke University Press from *American Literature* 61.4 (December 1989): 610–24.

I

In both archaic and Judeo-Christian traditions, repetition grounds all meaning, knowing, and identity, making possible the mythic and the sacred. As Mircea Eliade in particular has described it, the archaic mind discovered reality as the profane object or event (the single, the unconnected, naked of past and paradigm) repeating itself as the sacred (the double, the connected, informed by past and paradigm, a present repetition of an earlier act). The digging and planting of a field, for example, reproduces the divine act of cosmic fructification; the building of a house reproduces the divine act of cosmic creation. Both human actions "reactualize" something that took place "in the beginning."[3] Such repetition, of course, requires a kind of double perception, so that digging his field, the archaic man must know his tool simultaneously as both an archetypal phallus and a simple spade. Thus life, according to Eliade, "is lived on a twofold plane," taking "its course as human existence and, at the same time, shar[ing] in a transhuman life, that of the cosmos or the gods."[4] In this way the past informs and verifies the present, providing "the doubling context that rescues it from that singleness which, knowing only itself, knows nothing."[5]

The move from this archaic perception of repetition to the Judeo-Christian tradition requires, among other things, a complex shift from a concept of cyclical time to one of linear time, from a theory of eternal return, which valorizes events for their reproduction of prior events, to a theory of progressive history, which instead valorizes events for their position in a foretold cosmic pattern with a beginning, middle, and end.[6] Even so, the archaic and the Judeo-Christian perceptions share a sense of doubleness, a sense of repetition as a solid ground of knowing and identity. Each moment in the life of the individual and in time may be a new moment, according to the linear Judeo-Christian perception, never to come again. Yet each is nonetheless firmly contextualized *in* history—the whole patterned history to be completed in the future but intelligibly predicated in the past. Each new moment thus receives its highest meaning only as a fulfillment, as a repetition in real, actual time of that which has been foretold.[7]

The modern consciousness, however, seeks to undo this notion of grounded repetition, of repetition as the re-enactment of a given ground. The modern consciousness seeks to deny the past's impingement on the present, to deny all confirming priorities. Such denial, according to Paul de Man, is, in fact, the essence of modernity: "a desire to wipe out whatever came earlier, in the hope of reaching at last a point that could be called a true present, a point of origin that makes a new departure."[8] Thus to the modernist, grounded repetition becomes a way of knowing only that dimension of one's self and moment that is similar to what has already been, only that which continues (bondage to the dead past). The modernist quest is to unground repetition, to replace mythic memory with personal memory, thereby establishing the identity of a single solitary self, unlike all others that have ever been or will be (freedom of the unconnected present).[9]

II

In "The Grave" the modern consciousness that has been developing in Miranda throughout the earlier stories in *The Old Order* emerges as she serenely accepts the fact of her own inevitable death without interpretation. That is, Miranda rejects all inherited structures of meaning—the past, the mythic, and the sacred (all suggested by the silver dove)—for the freedom of existence unmediated by structure—for the present, the personal, and the profane (all suggested by the rabbit).

Almost Miranda's whole life (even though she's only nine) has been a sort of modernist quest balancing her desire to escape the tyranny of inherited patterns—represented by her family, especially her grandmother—and her fear of death unmediated by those patterns. She's haunted particularly by the death of her mother. Increasingly, however, the inherited patterns fail to assure her. As an incident in "The Circus" illustrates, they fail to contain or even to lessen Miranda's inescapably real horror of death:

> A creature in a blousy white overall with ruffles at the neck and ankles, with bone-white skull and chalk-white face . . . pranced along a wire stretched down the center of the ring, balancing a long thin pole with little wheels at either end. Miranda thought at first he was walking on air, or flying, and this did not surprise her; but when she saw the wire, she was terrified. . . . He paused, slipped, the flapping white leg waved in space; he staggered, wobbled, slipped sidewise, plunged, and caught the wire with frantic knee, hanging there upside down, the other leg waving like a feeler above his head; slipped once more, caught by one frenzied heel, and swung back and forth like a scarf. . . . The crowd roared with savage delight, shrieks of dreadful laughter. . . . Miranda shrieked too with real pain, clutching at her stomach with her knees drawn up. (Pp. 344–45)

So frightened she has to be taken home immediately, Miranda later that night tries to imagine the beautiful circus acts she missed by leaving early. But her imaginings cannot dispel her terrifying memories of the death's-head clown: "She fell asleep, and her invented memories gave way before her real ones, the bitter terrified face of the man in blousy [*sic*] white falling to his death—ah, the cruel joke! . . . She screamed in her sleep and sat up crying for deliverance from her torments."

Elsewhere religious platitudes such as her sister Maria's in "The Witness" over a dead rabbit—"Safe in Heaven" (p. 342)—fail to satisfy the questions of a "quick flighty little girl of six" who always wants "to know the worst." With Maria's profession of inherited meaning can be compared Miranda's experience in "The Fig Tree." In that story Miranda buries a dead baby chicken under a fig tree, then hears it call to her, she thinks, from the grave. Immediately forced away by her departing family, who threaten to leave her unless she comes at once, Miranda has no time to exhume the chicken and so can only agonize over the horror of its apparently premature burial:

> Miranda felt she couldn't bear to be left. She ran all shaking with fright. Her father gave her the annoyed look he always gave her when he said something to upset her and then saw that she was upset. His words were kind but his voice scolded: "Stop getting so excited, Baby, you know we wouldn't leave you for anything." Miranda wanted to talk back: "Then why did you say so?" but she was still listening for that tiny sound: "Weep, weep." She lagged and pulled backward, looking over her shoulder, but her father hurried her towards the carry-all. But things didn't make sounds if they were dead. They couldn't. That was one of the signs. Oh, but she had heard it. . . . Miranda's ears buzzed and she had a dull round pain in her just under her front ribs. She had to go back and let him out. He'd never get out by himself, all tangled up in tissue paper and that shoebox. He'd never get out without her. (Pp. 356–57)

And even though Great-Aunt Eliza later explains the "weep, weep" as tree frogs calling from the fig tree, Miranda's terror here, like that at the circus, is real and affecting. To her the afterlife, and thus this life too, seems less certain than someone like Maria supposes. To her, the inherited order of family and religion seems increasingly to provide the tyranny but not the security.

Miranda's modernist quest ends, apparently, in "The Grave." There she and Paul are literally questers, hunters, as they often have been before, of rabbits and doves. This day, however, their hunt is special, yielding richly symbolic game, for each of the story's two central episodes, the finding of a silver dove in her grandfather's grave and the skinning of a pregnant rabbit, portentously underscores Miranda's inevitable death. Only the first event, however, the finding of the dove, contextualizes that death; the other merely presents it. Apparently unconsciously, Miranda initially chooses the later, natural event.

Compared to that day's other vision of death, the profanity of the rabbit's death—its singleness, to use Eliade's term—is apparent. Unlike the flesh and blood rabbit, the silver dove—a work of art, an inherited form—provides the doubling context Eliade considers necessary for meaning. The dove promises the fulfillment of a pattern foretold, the resurrection of man's immortal soul through the power of the Holy Spirit, a human repetition of the earlier divine resurrection.[10] The silver dove thus locates Miranda's own death firmly within the whole transhuman history of the world, indeed of the cosmos. The rabbit, on the other hand, without such a paradigmatic structure, is simply dead. Yet in its death inheres a sort of innocence, a freedom beyond the dove's interpretation, a present force apparently uncontained by the dove's fixed form.

Skinning the rabbit, Paul cuts it open to reveal the foetuses:

> Miranda said, "Oh, I want to *see,*" under her breath. She looked and looked . . . filled with pity and astonishment and a kind of shocked delight in the wonderful little creatures for their own sakes, they were so pretty. She touched one of them ever so carefully, "Ah, there's blood running over them," she said and began to tremble without knowing why. Yet she wanted most deeply to see and to know. Having seen, she felt at once as if she had known all along. The very memory of her former ignorance faded, she had always known just this. (P. 366)

Here Miranda tremblingly intuits the raw vitality of unmediated experience in its quintessence. She intuits the mysteriously intertwining chaos of birth and death and intuits also something of her own inevitable participation in that chaos, with an emphasis on her developing woman's body and its reproductive potential: "She understood a little of the secret, formless intuitions in her own mind and body, which had been clearing up, taking form, so gradually and so steadily she had not realized that she was learning what she had to know." Forgotten in this moment is Miranda's earlier fear of death. Forgotten, too, in her implicit choice of the rabbit, are the silver dove and all it suggests. And the moment—the nothingness, to borrow from Miranda's dream, of the uninhibited, uninherited, unconnected present moment—is serenely beautiful. It is enough.

So why, then, the coda? Why not end the story here at the moment Miranda escapes the bondage of the dead past to enter the freedom of the unconnected present? Perhaps because the coda illustrates the consequence of her choice: bleakness, the price Miranda must pay for such freedom as she gains by looking into the ungrounded abyss of nature. For in the freedom of the grave (the modernist freeplay of meaning) inheres that freedom's obverse, the possibility of absolutely blank oblivion (meaninglessness).

The cycle of birth and death in "The Grave" is, as the title suggests, ironically truncated. No birth occurs there, as both the rabbit and her foetuses die, belying Miranda's excitement over her developing reproductive potential and foreshadowing the bleakness of the story's concluding scene. On Miranda, age nine, such irony is lost. But for Miranda twenty years later it is inescapable. The initial gaiety occasioned by the modernist enterprise having given way to its implicit despair, Miranda in the coda is a stranger in a strange country, surrounded by death.

Significantly, the coda's market scene repeats that earlier day from Miranda's childhood, presenting again Miranda, Paul, graves, baby rabbits, and the silver dove. The repetition, however, is not simply a reconstitution of the past event. Rather it's an example of what Kierkegaard calls repetition forward, a synthesis of grounded and ungrounded repetitions,[11] the reflective reinterpretation of the past's impingement on the present.[12] That is, neither wholly grounded and thus able only to imitate its origin, nor wholly ungrounded and thus completely uprooted, able to know only itself, repetition forward recovers new possibilities in repetition while avoiding the utter abandonment of meaning:

> One day [twenty years later] she was picking her path among the puddles and crushed refuse of a market street in a strange city of a strange country, when without warning, plain and clear in its true colors as if she looked through a frame upon a scene that had not stirred nor changed since the moment it happened, the episode of that far-off day leaped from its burial place before her mind's eye. . . . An Indian vendor had held up before her a tray of dyed sugar sweets, in the shapes of all kinds of small creatures: birds, baby chicks, baby rabbits, lambs, baby pigs. . . . It was a very hot day and the smell in the market, with its piles of raw flesh and wilting flowers, was like the mingled sweetness and corruption she had smelled that other day in the empty cemetery at home: the day she had remembered always until now vaguely as the time she and her brother had found treasure in the opened graves. Instantly upon this thought the dreadful vision faded, and she saw clearly her brother, whose childhood face she had forgotten, standing again in the blazing sunshine, again twelve years old, a pleased sober smile in his eyes, turning the silver dove over and over in his hands. (Pp. 367–68)

Given the portentousness of that childhood day, the dove might easily be merely a personal icon for Miranda inevitably associated with her brother, her youth, and the day she lost a bit of her conventional innocence. But Porter's words themselves reinforce the idea of resurrection. The memory "leaps from its burial place." And the initial vision of death, the dead rabbit which she had long ago chosen, she sees now in its "true colors." That "dreadful" vision of death now gives way to that long ago day's other vision of death, her unchanged brother holding the silver dove. The rabbit, the screw head, her brother, the day, the memory—all for her are transfigured in an unexpected re-vision of her youthful choice.

After the bleakness of unmediated existence, Miranda's vision here seemingly reconciles chaos and order, process and design, freedom and bondage, revealing each *living* moment to reflect, mysteriously, the beginning and the end, the pattern of all history, of all meaning. Thus by fusing the mythic and the personal, the past and the present, in a structure of interaction and exchange, "The Grave" first empties the ground of its original power (in this case, the Judeo-Christian interpretation of death), then restores it, re-empowering it according to the desires of the new present. The result is "neither old meaning nor meaninglessness but new meaning, meaning renewed, created now for the millionth time and the first."[13]

III

Chronologically "Old Mortality" and "Pale Horse, Pale Rider" generally over-lap—and thus repeat—the stories in *The Old Order.* Part I of "Old Mortality" covers the years 1885–1902, leaving off when Miranda is eight. Part 2, 1904, picks her up at age ten; Part 3, 1912, at age eighteen. "Pale Horse, Pale Rider," meanwhile, presents Miranda at age twenty-four. During the ten years covered by "Old Mortality" Miranda's escape from the Judeo-Christian perception into the modern is clear, while in "Pale Horse, Pale Rider," as in the coda to "The Grave," she seeks to reconcile the two perceptions. Unlike in the earlier story, however, this second attempt at repetition forward either fails or, at best, remains problematic.

As Robert Penn Warren noted some years ago, Miranda in "Old Mortal-ity" is a quester unsatisfied by any inherited truth. At the end of the story, she has found "*a* truth that will not be translatable, or, finally, communicable. But it will be the only truth she can win, and for better or worse she will have to live by it. She must live by her own myth. But she must earn her myth in the process of living."[14] To find her own truth, however, to replace mythic memory with personal memory (her own myth), Miranda must first, to use de Man's words, "wipe out whatever came earlier." She must first demystify, demythologize, and generally deconstruct the Judeo-Christian tradition, the perceived confirming priorities of the old order, all of which "Old Mortality" encapsulates in the family myth of Aunt Amy and Uncle Gabriel.

Aunt Amy's and Uncle Gabriel's story, and thus the Gay family's sense of truth, involves the whole patterned realm of art and religion. We are told, for example, that Amy belongs to the world of poetry, that she is the heroine of a novel, and that the "romance" of Gabriel's long unrewarded love is like a story in an old book. Amy is "real" to the young Miranda as pictures in books are real. Similarly Amy is called angelic four times, a term suggested also by Gabriel's name. The family's sense of truth is, in short, romantically transcen-dent: "Their stories were almost always love stories against a bright blank heavenly blue sky" (p. 175).

And such is the basic sense of truth the eight-year-old Miranda has absorbed: "There was then a life beyond life in this world, as well as in the next; such episodes [as the discussion after Paderewski's concert] confirmed for [Maria and Miranda] the nobility of human feeling, the divinity of man's vision of the unseen, the importance of life and death, the depths of the human heart, the romantic value of tragedy" (p. 179). In short, despite some doubts (about the size of the family's women, say, or the absolute beauty of Amy) Miranda at the end of Part I accepts meaning as something transcen-dent, as something solidly grounded in a transhuman "life beyond life."

The extent to which she lives on such a two-fold plane is nicely illus-trated at the beginning of Part 2. There the ten-year-old Miranda, before meeting Uncle Gabriel, distinguishes between "life, which was real and earnest, and the grave was not its goal; poetry, which was true but not real; and stories, or forbidden reading matter, in which things happened as nowhere else" (p. 194). So ingrained is young Miranda's double perception that she misses the irony of paraphrasing Longfellow's sentimental verse to distinguish "life" from "poetry."

Later in Part 2, however, and especially in Part 3, a series of disillusioning experiences centered on Amy and Gabriel alters Miranda's sense of truth. After having heard all her young life *the* story, Miranda finally meets one of its characters, the supposedly romantic Uncle Gabriel, now "a vast bulging man with a red face and immense tan ragged mustaches fading into gray" (p. 197). He is also drunk: "Maria and Miranda stared, first at him, then at each other. 'Can that be our Uncle Gabriel?' their eyes asked. 'Is that Aunt Amy's handsome romantic beau? Is that the man who wrote the poem about our Aunt Amy?' Oh, what did grown-up people *mean* when they talked, anyway?"

Years later, when Miranda is eighteen and returning home for the first time after her elopement, Aunt Eva continues the disillusionment, asserting that Amy was not so beautiful as the family said; that Amy was wild, indiscreet, and heartless; that Amy killed herself to escape scandal; and that all the elaborate rituals of romantic love were "just sex" (p. 216). Eva's "truth" about Amy, however, Miranda believes to be every bit as distorted as her father's idealizations. The real truth, she decides, resides somewhere outside the family and its romanticizing stories. Even before encountering Eva, in fact, Miranda has taken a large step toward rejecting the transcendent answers offered by both family and religion. Eloping—to freedom, she thinks—from the Convent of the Child Jesus, where she has been "immured" (p. 193), she has denied both inherited answers at once, both the love stories and their bright blank heavenly blue background.

Her complete rejection of the old order, though, her rejection of all ties actually, occurs as, returning home for Uncle Gabriel's funeral, she hears her father and Aunt Eva tell their stories. Listening, she realizes not just that their stories, that their truth, cannot be hers but that *nothing* inherited, *nothing* from outside her immediate, uninterpreted experience, can be true, at least not true for her:

> Miranda could not hear the stories above the noisy motor, but she felt she knew them well, or stories like them. She knew too many stories like them, she wanted something new of her own. The language was familiar to them, but not to her, not any more. . . . She did not want any more ties with this house, she was going to leave it, and she was not going back to her husband's family either. She would have no more bonds that smothered her in love and hatred. She now knew why she had run away to marriage, and she knew that she was going to run away from marriage, and she was not going to stay in any place, with anyone, that threatened to forbid her making her own discoveries, that said "No" to her. . . . I hate love, she thought, as if this were the answer, I have

loving and being loved, I hate it. And her disturbed and seething mind received a shock of comfort from this sudden collapse of an old painful structure of distorted images and misconceptions. (Pp. 220–21)

Gone for Miranda is the old order, the old painful structure; gone are the Judeo-Christian conceptions of life, death, and afterlife contained, for example, in Uncle Gabriel's poem for Amy's tombstone:

> She lives again who suffered life,
> Then suffered death, and now set free
> A singing angel, she forgets
> The griefs of old mortality. (P. 181)

What remains for Miranda, what she chooses to retain, is only the griefs of old mortality—that is, the freedom of the unconnected present, the here and now of her own experience, of herself and her own world, apparently including death:

Ah, but there is my own life to come yet, she thought, my own life now and beyond. I don't want any promises, I won't have any false hopes, I won't be romantic about myself. I can't live in their world any longer, she told herself, listening to the voices [of her father and Aunt Eva]. Let them tell their stories to each other. Let them go on explaining how things happened. I don't care. At least I can know the truth about what happens to me, she assured herself silently, making a promise to herself, in her hopefulness, her ignorance. (P. 221)

Here in "Old Mortality," Miranda's choice, in this promise to herself, of the personal over the mythic parallels her earlier choice in the first part of "The Grave." The consequence of this choice as well generally repeats "The Grave." For in "Pale Horse, Pale Rider" as earlier, the initial gaiety of her choice turns, ultimately, to despair, as the implicit "ignorance" of that choice becomes manifest. Miranda may dream of a beautiful, sufficient "nothing," but she must awaken each day to face modernity's inescapably nightmarish aspects.

Detached from the past, the mythic, and the sacred, and void also of any future, modern existence is suggested in "Pale Horse, Pale Rider" by a small dance-hall Miranda and Adam frequent, a sort of present hell tightly circumscribed by the suffering and death momently threatened by the story's pervasive background of war and epidemic:

It was a tawdry little place, crowded and hot and full of smoke, but there was nothing better. . . . This is what we have, Adam and I, this is all we're going to get, this is the way it is with us. She wanted to say, "Adam, come out of your dream and listen to me. I have pains in my chest and my head and my heart and they're real. I am in pain all over, and you are in such danger as I can't bear to think about, and why can we not save each other?" (P. 296)

Such salvation as Miranda desires, however, requires some reconciliation, as in *The Old Order*, of the personal and the mythic—there represented by the natural rabbit and by the patterned dove, here by the promise made to herself and the promise (of an apparently Christian life beyond life) made to her long ago. In "Pale Horse, Pale Rider" both promises depend on Adam and the question of his final absence or final presence. And both promises are reflected in comments by Eudora Welty and Caroline Gordon.

IV

Why, after all, can they not save each other? Is it, as Welty says, that "there is no time . . . because tomorrow has turned into oblivion, the ultimate betrayer is death itself"? Or do they, in fact, save each other? Does Adam, at least, save Miranda? Does the story end, in other words, in "the soul's ultimate union with God" (Adam symbolizing God), as Gordon says?[15] Numerous Christian references—a seeming superabundance of them, actually—do float through the story: the work's allusive title, Adam's suggestive name, references to sacrificial lambs and healthy apples, to Hail Marys and confessions, to prayer and Sunday School, to Lazarus and resurrection. The question, though, is whether Miranda (Porter too?) can convincingly reconstruct the Judeo-Christian framework of inherited meaning within which such allusions make sense after having so convincingly vexed it in "Old Mortality." Do the references coalesce around Adam's ultimate presence or disperse at his ultimate absence? That is, does Adam's final ghostly presence—symbolizing the resurrected savior—fulfill a Christian promise made long ago, affirming her near-death vision of an afterlife (grounded repetition): "Why, of course, of course, said Miranda, without surprise but with serene rapture as if some promise made to her had been kept long after she had ceased to hope for it" (p. 311)? Or does his final absence underscore the hollow factitiousness of all supposed meaning (ungrounded repetition)?

In the story's final two paragraphs, the interpretive crux, Miranda must choose to believe or not; she must choose between the transhuman promise made to her long ago and the personal promise made to herself. Sensing an "invisible but urgently present" ghost, "more alive than she," she nevertheless remains unsatisfied. She still clings to the self-promise made in "Old Mortality." She resists the transcendent and clings to the temporal, knowing even as she does so the "unpardonable lie" of such a "bitter desire":

At once [Adam] was there beside her, invisible but urgently present, a ghost but more alive than she was, the last intolerable cheat of her heart; for knowing it was false she still clung to the lie, the unpardonable lie of her bitter desire. She said, "I love you," and stood up trembling, trying by the mere act of her will to bring him up to sight before her. If I could call you up from the grave I would, she said, if I could see your ghost I would say, I believe . . . "I believe," she said aloud. "Oh, let me see you once more." The room was silent, empty, the shade was gone from it, struck away by the sudden violence of her rising and speaking aloud. She came to herself as if out of sleep. Oh, no, that is not the way, I must never do that, she warned herself. (P. 317)

Miranda believes, she says, but is that belief answered? Possibly. For one might interpret this passage as a coalescing of the story's pervasive religious images, generally recalling, as it does, especially the unusual phrase "I believe," the biblical postresurrection narratives, and the difficulty of believing in a risen Christ. Desiring Adam's visible presence, Miranda quickly realizes, is not the way. Such a desire, she understands, is "false," an "unpardonable lie." She should not, as it were, seek the living among the dead. The way is rather for her to accept the transcendent meaning Adam represents. Miranda's situation seems specifically to recall Jesus' words to his doubting disciple: "Thomas, because thou hast seen me, thou hast believed: blessed are they that have not seen, and yet have believed" (John 20:29). The allusions thus suggest that Miranda's final state is one of peaceful acceptance, even blessedness, and not of despair. Miranda now has time to rebuild and to complete her life artfully, basing it on the sure knowledge both of Adam's sacrificial love and of a future paradise, a promise fulfilled "long after she had ceased to hope for it." Interpreted this way, the story's conclusion opens not into oblivion, as Welty says, but into eternity. For Miranda the otherwise single and meaningless present moment is redeemed, as in the coda to "The Grave," by its subsumption into the eternal pattern of Christian history.

Or is it? All the pieces for such a positive interpretation are, of course, present in "Pale Horse, Pale Rider"—the references to Adam, to sacrificial death, to resurrection, and so on—but they never seem quite to come together as do the pieces in "The Grave," even though the story, the text, seems to want such a positively ordered conclusion.[16] For in something of an obverted repetition forward, "Old Mortality" and "Pale Horse, Pale Rider" repeat The Old Order to recover not a new possibility of meaning from Miranda's experiences but the possibility of their meaninglessness. Her thoroughgoing skepticism having upset the delicate balance of force and form, Miranda finally must face the possibility that chaos, once freed, might not be recontainable. Having once ungrounded meaning, in other words, the modern consciousness can never fully escape the doubt that any regrounding is merely a convenient fiction in the face of oblivion. And this unexorcisable doubt haunts the ending of "Pale Horse, Pale Rider" as surely as does the other ghost, threatening momently to dispel Adam's possible presence. Thus the final coalescence of religious references around Adam, their regrounding, remains problematic.

Notes

1. *The Collected Stories of Katherine Anne Porter* (New York: Harcourt, Brace, & World, 1965), pp. 269–70. Subsequent references to this and the other stories are from this edition and are cited parenthetically in the text.

2. Although "Old Mortality" and "Pale Horse, Pale Rider" appeared in print earlier (1939, *The Old Order* in 1944), the stories in *The Old Order* were written first (finished by 1934, "Pale Horse, Pale Rider" and "Old Mortality" by 1936). See Joan Givner, *Katherine Anne Porter: A Life* (New York: Simon and Schuster, 1982).

3. *The Sacred and the Profane: the Nature of Religion,* trans. Willard R. Trask (New York: Harcourt, Brace, & World, 1959), pp. 30–31, 68–69.

4. *The Sacred and the Profane,* p. 167.

5. Donald Kartiganer, "Faulkner's Art of Repetition," Faulkner and Yoknapatawpha Conference, Oxford, Mississippi, 4 Aug. 1987, p. 5—forthcoming.

6. Eliade, *The Myth of the Eternal Return or, Cosmos and History,* trans. Willard R. Trask (Princeton: Princeton Univ. Press, 1971), p. 104.

7. *The Myth of the Eternal Return,* p. 90; *The Sacred and the Profane,* p. 112.

8. *Blindness and Insight: Essays in the Rhetoric of Contemporary Criticism* (New York: Oxford Univ. Press, 1971), p. 148.

9. I've borrowed this discussion of repetition from Kartiganer.

10. For a fuller discussion of the dove as a Christian symbol, see my "Literary Criticism, Katherine Anne Porter's Consciousness, and the Silver Dove," *Studies in Short Fiction,* 25 (1988), 109–15.

11. *Fear and Trembling/Repetition,* ed. and trans. Howard V. Hong and Edna H. Hong (Princeton: Princeton Univ. Press, 1983), p. 131.

12. Louis Mackey, *Kirkegaard: A Kind of Poet* (Philadelphia: Univ. of Pennsylvania Press, 1971), p. 17.

13. Kartiganer, p. 13.

14. *Selected Essays* (New York: Random House, 1958), pp. 153–54.

15. Welty, "The Eye of the Story," in *Katherine Anne Porter: A Collection of Critical Essays,* ed. R. P. Warren (Englewood Cliffs, N.J.: Prentice-Hall, 1979), p. 78; Gordon, "Katherine Anne Porter and the ICM," *Harper's,* Nov. 1964, p. 148.

16. I now see as somewhat oversimplified my argument elsewhere for such a positive interpretation—"Fall and Redemption in 'Pale Horse, Pale Rider,' " *Renascence,* 39 (1987), 396–405.

Katherine Anne Porter's
"The Old Order" and *Agamemnon*

P. JANE HAFEN

Katherine Anne Porter's collection "The Old Order" tells of transition, a rite of passage from an old world to a new. Using life and death imagery, the stories in "The Old Order" detail the changes from slavery to freedom, aristocracy to bourgeoisie, birth to death. The multigenerational narrative elevates the story into mythic time of recollective past, present, and projective future. Ritualized gestures, images, and language enhance the mythic elements of the work. As Leslie K. Hankins observes: "Porter uses the ordered structure of the ritual elements in 'The Old Order' to highlight and intensify the reversal of tradition . . ." (23). The formalized high rhetoric of language is both biblical (Hankins 22) and classically "precise" (Unrue 219). Additionally, Darlene H. Unrue cites allusions to both Whitman and Homer in the section "The Grave," with "the uncropped sweet-smelling wild grass" of the cemetery and its representation of new life (151).

Another powerful image in the section "The Grave" is "discovery of the dead and bleeding rabbits with the concomitant discovery of [Miranda's] own mortality and femaleness" (Unrue 150). The paradoxical dead, yet fertile, rabbit imagery is also a classical allusion to Aeschylus' Greek tragedy *Agamemnon*. In Porter's story Miranda observes:

> Brother lifted the oddly bloated belly. "Look," he said, in a low amazed voice. "It was going to have young ones."
> Very carefully he slit the thin flesh from the center ribs to the flanks, and a scarlet bag appeared. He slit again and pulled the bag open, and there lay a bundle of tiny rabbits, each wrapped in a thin scarlet veil. (366)

In *Agamemnon* the chorus recites a similar image of the unborn rabbits:

> Kings of birds to the kings of the ships,
> one black, one blazed with silver,

Reprinted with permission of the journal from *Studies in Short Fiction* 31 (1994): 491–93. Copyright 1994 by Newberry College.

> clear seen by the royal house
> on the right, the spear hand,
> they lighted, watched by all
> tore a hare, ripe, bursting with young unborn yet,
> stayed from her last fleet running. (42)

Aeschylus is referring to an omen that occurred at the beginning of the Trojan War. The two eagles were symbols of Agamemnon and Menelaus, the Greek rulers who would not only kill the living Trojans but all future generations of Troy, symbolized by the pregnant hare with her offspring forever unborn.

Future generations of Porter's characters, descendants of Sophia Jane and Nannie will not be obliterated, but, like Miranda, forever transformed. The characters of both the play and the short stories bear the responsibility of the past. Agamemnon loses his life, in part, for the heinous deeds of his father. Miranda does not lose her life but bears a historical psychological burden of her family and the South. She tries to shed this guilt through symbolic burials of small creatures.

Nannie's changing place in the family indicates the problems of reconciling an unjust past: "[The children] were growing up, times were changing, the old world was sliding from under their feet, they had not yet laid hold of the new one." They take care of Nannie, as their own fortunes change, recognizing her significant role in their lives.

Perhaps acknowledging a corrupt history is sufficient to stay the justice of the gods. Agamemnon's pride (*hubris*) prevents his awareness of his misdeeds and justifies his murder. Miranda, years later, recalls the rabbit incident with a sense of reconciliation, her evocative, violent vision absolved by the youthful and sober image of her brother.

> An Indian vendor had held up before her a tray of dyed sugar sweets, in the shapes of all kinds of small creatures: birds, baby chicks, baby rabbits, lambs, baby pigs. . . . It was a very hot day and the smell in the market . . . [was like] the day she had remembered always until now vaguely as the time she and her brother had found treasure in the opened graves. Instantly upon this thought the dreadful vision faded and she saw clearly her brother, whose childhood face she had forgotten, standing again in the blazing sunshine, again twelve years old, a pleased sober smile in his eyes, turning the silver dove over and over in his hands. (367–68)

This concluding reflection of all the short stories in "The Old Order" is cathartic in eliciting compassion and hope by harmonizing the violent past to the eternal present through Miranda's mature vision. The classical allusion to the unborn generations, symbolized by the pregnant hare, unifies ancient literature with modern, past to present with a vision to the future.

Works Cited

Aeschylus. *Oresteia: Agamemnon*. Trans. Richard Lattimore. New York: Washington Square, 1973.

Hankins, Leslie K. "Ritual: Representation and Reversal in Katherine Anne Porter's 'The Old Order.' " In *Ritual in America: Acts and Representations,* 20–23. Ed. Don Harkness. Tampa, FL: American Studies, 1985.

Porter, Katherine Anne. "The Old Order." *The Collected Stories of Katherine Anne Porter.* New York: Harcourt, 1979.

Unrue, Darlene H. *Truth and Vision in Katherine Anne Porter's Fiction.* Athens: U of Georgia P, 1985.

On "The Grave"

Cleanth Brooks

If I had to choose a particular short story of Katherine Anne Porter's to illustrate her genius as a writer—the choice is not an easy one—I think that I should choose "The Grave." I did choose it some months ago for a lecture in Athens, where the special nature of the audience, whose English ranged from excellent to moderately competent, provided a severe test. The ability of such an audience to understand and appreciate this story underlines some of Miss Porter's special virtues as a writer. Hers is an art of apparent simplicity, with nothing forced or mannered, and yet the simplicity is rich, not thin, full of subtleties and sensitive insights. Her work is compact and almost unbelievably economical.

The story has to do with a young brother and sister on a Texas farm in the year 1903. Their grandmother, who in some sense had dominated the family, had survived her husband for many years. He had died in the neighboring state of Louisiana, but she had removed his body to Texas. Later, when her Texas farm was sold and with it the small family cemetery, she had once more moved her husband's body, and those of the other members of the family, to a plot in the big new public cemetery. One day the two grandchildren, out rabbit hunting with their small rifles, find themselves in the old abandoned family cemetery.

> Miranda leaped into the pit that had held her grandfather's bones. Scratching round aimlessly and pleasurably as any young animal, she scooped up a lump of earth and weighed it in her palm. It had a pleasantly sweet, corrupt smell, being mixed with cedar needles and small leaves, and as the crumbs fell apart, she saw a silver dove no larger than a hazel nut, with spread wings and a neat fan-shaped tail.

Miranda's brother recognizes what the curious little ornament is—the screwhead for a coffin. Paul has found something too—a small gold ring—and the children soon make an exchange of their treasures, Miranda fitting the gold ring onto her thumb.

Reprinted with permission of Blackwell Publishers from the *Yale Review* 55 (Winter 1966): 275–79.

Paul soon becomes interested in hunting again, and looks about for rabbits, but the ring,

> shining with the serene purity of fine gold on [the little girl's] rather grubby thumb, turned her feelings against her overalls and sockless feet. . . . She wanted to go back to the farm house, take a good cold bath, dust herself with plenty of Maria's violet talcum powder . . . put on the thinnest, most becoming dress she ever owned, with a big sash, and sit in the wicker chair under the trees.

The little girl is thoroughly feminine, and though she has enjoyed knocking about with her brother, wearing her summer roughing outfit, the world of boys and sports and hunting and all that goes with it is beginning to pall.

Then something happens. Paul starts up a rabbit, kills it with one shot, and skins it expertly as Miranda watches admiringly. "Brother lifted the oddly bloated belly. 'Look,' he said, in a low amazed voice. 'It was going to have young ones.' " Seeing the baby rabbits in all their perfection, "their sleek wet down lying in minute even ripples like a baby's head just washed, their unbelievably small delicate ears folded close," Miranda is "excited but not frightened." Then she touches one of them, and exclaims, "Ah, there's blood running over them!" and begins to tremble. "She had wanted most deeply to see and to know. Having seen, she felt at once as if she had known all along."

The meaning of life and fertility and of her own body begin to take shape in the little girl's mind as she sees the tiny creatures just taken from their mother's womb. The little boy says to her "cautiously, as if he were talking about something forbidden: 'They were just about ready to be born.' 'I know,' said Miranda, 'like kittens. I know, like babies.' She was quietly and terribly agitated, standing again with her rifle under her arm, looking down at the bloody heap." Paul buries the rabbits and cautions his sister "with an eager friendliness, a confidential tone quite unusual in him, as if he were taking her into an important secret on equal terms: Listen now. . . . Don't tell a soul."

The story ends with one more paragraph, and because the ending is told with such beautiful economy and such care for the disposition of incidents and even the choice of words, one dares not paraphrase it.

> Miranda never told, she did not even wish to tell anybody. She thought about the whole worrisome affair with confused unhappiness for a few days. Then it sank quietly into her mind and was heaped over by accumulated thousands of impressions, for nearly twenty years. One day she was picking her path among the puddles and crushed refuse of a market street in a strange city of a strange country, when without warning, plain and clear in its true colors as if she looked through a frame upon a scene that had not stirred nor changed since the moment it happened, the episode of that far-off day leaped from its burial place before her mind's eye. She was so reasonlessly horrified she halted suddenly staring, the scene before her eyes dimmed by the vision back of them. An

Indian vendor had held up before her a tray of dyed sugar sweets, in the shapes of all kinds of small creatures: birds, baby chicks, baby rabbits, lambs, baby pigs. They were in gay colors and smelled of vanilla, maybe. . . . It was a very hot day and the smell in the market, with its piles of raw flesh and wilting flowers, was like the mingled sweetness and corruption she had smelled that other day in the empty cemetery at home: the day she had remembered always until now vaguely as the time she and her brother had found treasure in the opened graves. Instantly upon this thought the dreadful vision faded, and she saw clearly her brother, whose childhood face she had forgotten, standing again in the blazing sunshine, again twelve years old, a pleased sober smile in his eyes, turning the silver dove over and over in his hands.

The story is so rich, it has so many meanings that bear close and subtle relations to each other, that a brief summary of what the story means will oversimplify it and fail to do justice to its depth, but I shall venture a few comments.

Obviously the story is about growing up and going through a kind of initiation into the mysteries of adult life. It is thus the story of the discovery of truth. Miranda learns about birth and her own destiny as a woman; she learns these things suddenly, unexpectedly, in circumstances that connect birth with death. Extending this comment a little further, one might say that the story is about the paradoxical nature of truth: truth wears a double face—it is not simple but complex. The secret of birth is revealed in the place of death and through a kind of bloody sacrifice. If there is beauty in the discovery, there is also awe and even terror.

These meanings are dramatized by their presentation through a particular action, which takes place in a particular setting. Something more than illustration of a statement is involved—something more than mere vividness or the presentation of a generalization in a form to catch the reader's eye. One notices, for example, how important is the fact of the grandmother's anxiety to keep the family together, even the bodies of the family dead. And the grandmother's solicitude is not mentioned merely to account for the physical fact of the abandoned cemetery in which Miranda makes her discovery about life and death. Throughout this story, birth and death are seen through a family perspective.

Miranda is, for example, thoroughly conscious of how her family is regarded in the community. We are told that her father had been criticized for letting his girls dress like boys and career "around astride barebacked horses." Miranda herself had encountered such criticism from old women whom she met on the road—women who smoked corncob pipes. They had always "treated her grandmother with most sincere respect," but they ask her "What yo Pappy thinkin about?" This matter of clothes, and the social sense, and the role of women in the society are brought into the story unobtrusively, but they powerfully influence its meaning. For if the story is about a rite of initiation, an initiation into the meaning of sex, the subject is not treated in a doctrinaire polemical way. In this story sex is considered in a much larger context, in a social and even a philosophical context.

How important the special context is will become apparent if we ask ourselves why the story ends as it does. Years later, in the hot tropical sunlight of a Mexican city, Miranda sees a tray of dyed sugar sweets, moulded in the form of baby pigs and baby rabbits. They smell of vanilla, but this smell mingles with the other odors of the marketplace, including that of raw flesh, and Miranda is suddenly reminded of the "sweetness and corruption" that she had smelled long before as she stood in the empty grave in the family burial plot. What is it that makes the experience not finally horrifying or nauseating? What steadies Miranda and redeems the experience for her? I quote again the concluding sentence:

> Instantly upon this thought the dreadful vision faded, and she saw clearly her brother, whose childhood face she had forgotten, standing again in the blazing sunshine, again twelve years old, a pleased sober smile in his eyes, turning the silver dove over and over in his hands.

I mentioned earlier the richness and subtlety of this beautiful story. It needs no further illustration; yet one can hardly forbear reminding oneself how skillfully, and apparently almost effortlessly, the author has rendered the physical and social context that gives point to Miranda's discovery of truth and has effected the modulation of her shifting attitudes—toward the grave, the buried ring, her hunting clothes, the dead rabbit—reconciling these various and conflicting attitudes and, in the closing sentences, bringing into precise focus the underlying theme.

Reading the Endings in Katherine Anne Porter's "Old Mortality"

Suzanne W. Jones

I won't have false hopes, I won't be romantic about myself. I can't live in their world any longer, she told herself, listening to the voices back of her. Let them tell their stories to each other. Let them go on explaining how things happened. I don't care. At least I can know the truth about what happens to me, she assured herself silently, making a promise to herself, in her hopefulness, her ignorance.

With these final sentences of "Old Mortality" (1937), Katherine Anne Porter qualifies the progress eighteen-year-old Miranda has made toward self-knowledge and sophisticated reading strategies. This long story is a bildungsroman of sorts, tracing Miranda's development from childhood to young adulthood, but focusing particularly on her apprenticeship as a reader. Porter links Miranda's quest for self-discovery with her attempts to determine fact from fiction in the stories her family tells about the love affairs, brief marriage, and early death of her beautiful Aunt Amy. By dismissing both her father's romantic legend and her Cousin Eva's feminist critique as untrue—by focusing on narrative as representing reality rather than producing reality—Miranda misses not only the "truths" that both versions of the story contain but also the nature of the ideologies that shape these "truths." By failing to comprehend the complexity of the reading experience, Miranda undermines her own ability to see how she has unconsciously used the romance narrative to script her elopement and the feminist critique to write the erotic plot out of her life. In the end, Porter herself shies away from the feminist politics of the reading experience, by concluding "Old Mortality" with a typical modernist ambiguous ending that runs counter to the plot's interest in creating feminist readers.

By and large the critical commentary on "Old Mortality" has concentrated on Porter's modernist concerns about the difficulty of representing reality and of determining truth rather than on her strong feminist concerns about

Reprinted with permission of the journal from the *Southern Quarterly* 31.3 (Spring 1993): 29–44.

the role of storytelling in the production of the gendered self and the struggle of defining oneself against stereotyped images.[1] In her 1948 notes on "Old Mortality" Katherine Anne Porter wrote that "This book is based on my own experience." It is evident from these notes that she was concerned with the politics of storytelling, not simply the difficulty of representing reality.

> I was given the kind of education and the kind of up-bringing that in no way whatever prepared me for the world I was to face. When I was ready to step out in the world supposedly grown up, I was as ignorant of the world as it is possible to be.
>
> You begin to question, you try to understand, and you try to discover for yourself ways of meeting the world. And you feel you cannot rely on anything that you were told or anything you were taught because everything that you met in your experience was simply, apparently another thing.[2]

One subject that Porter felt she was misinformed about was romantic love and marriage, a topic she returned to over and over in both her fiction and her essays. In "The Necessary Enemy" (1948), she cautions Americans about their naive definition of love.

> Romantic Love crept into the marriage bed, very stealthily, by centuries, bringing its absurd notions about love as eternal springtime and marriage as a personal adventure meant to provide personal happiness. To a Western romantic such as I, though my views have been much modified by painful experience, it still seems to me a charming work of the human imagination, and it is a pity its central notion has been taken too literally and has hardened into a convention as cramping and enslaving as the older one.[3]

In "Old Mortality" Katherine Anne Porter is especially interested in the legends of romantic love that young Southern women, like herself, were brought up with at the turn of the century—the legends that taught them how to entice men, how to be Southern belles. The three-part structure of "Old Mortality" emphasizes Miranda's changing interpretations of family stories as she grows older, and the effects her "readings" of these stories have on her development as a woman. Porter's interest in a reader's cognitive and psychological development as well as the effects his or her gender, personality, family history, cultural experience, and social positions have on reading make for a complex politics of reading indeed.[4] Porter challenges the reader of "Old Mortality" to be alert to the stories that make the reader/self, especially those that constrict options for women, but she ends her long story skeptical about achieving the control over a text the feminist reader hopes for. Porter's skepticism reflects her modernist epistemological doubt and her vexed relation to feminism as well as her frustration with the available plots for women, which fulfill erotic desires or ambitious wishes but never both. While early twentieth-century feminists, such as Dora Russell, were fighting popular opinion that forced women to choose,[5] fictional plots for women continued to set the two desires at odds with each other. In "Old Mortality" Porter rejects the traditional marriage plot and the traditional quest plot, viewing both as narrow options for women.

While Porter's Miranda does not become as sophisticated a reader of her family's stories as she thinks she is, the reader Porter creates with her text is close to Patrocinio Schweickart's "feminist reader," as defined in *Gender and Reading:* this reader "realizes that the text has power to structure her experience" as a woman and so chooses to "take control of the reading experience" rather than to "submit to the power of the text."[6] Readers of Porter's "Old Mortality" are encouraged to see ideology in the narrative, whether that narrative be a product of the patriarchy or of the feminist movement. Porter structures the narrative so that from the beginning we question not only the facts of the Amy legend, and by extension the mystique of the Southern belle, but also the politics of its use.

Oddly enough, Porter uses naive, eight-year-old Miranda, who does not realize that the Amy legend has power to structure her experience, to reveal to readers the power of this myth in Miranda's life. In part I Miranda notices the discrepancies between the statements her father makes, such as "There were never any fat women in the family, thank God," and the great-aunts she knows, such as Great-Aunt Eliza, who "squeezed herself through doors," and Great-Aunt Keziah, whose husband would not allow her to ride his good horses after she reached 220 pounds.[7] Furthermore, Miranda cannot fit her father's descriptions of Aunt Amy's great beauty and mesmerizing charm to the photograph of Amy that she and her sister Maria have studied closely—a photograph that reflects, in their minds, clothes and a hairstyle that are "most terribly out of fashion" (p. 173). Porter does not suggest that Miranda and Maria's assessment of Amy is any closer to fact than their father's memory, which has been frozen in time by his own definition of female beauty and an intense loyalty to his sister—merely that their judgment is clouded by their own contemporary notions of beauty and fashion. Porter reveals the ideologies that shape both father's and daughters' perspectives and suggests, as cognitive psychologists Mary Crawford and Roger Chaffin have demonstrated, that "understanding is a product of both the text and the prior knowledge and viewpoint that the reader brings to it."[8]

And yet I cannot help but wonder if the omniscient point of view Porter uses in "Old Mortality," which gives the reader a sense of power *over* the text— the power that Schweickart champions—does not conflict with the ending of this story, where the narrator denounces as naive Miranda's belief that she will be a better reader of her own life than her father and Eva have been of Amy's. At the same time that readers of "Old Mortality" see the ideology that shapes each narrative of Amy, we also see the difficulty of controlling the "reading" experience through Miranda's captivation with the Amy story despite her awareness very early on of its contradictions. In part I the very young Miranda has difficulty separating life from representations of it. She is a literal reader, the type J. A. Appleyard calls a "player" in a fictional world.[9] When she sees a play about Mary, Queen of Scots, she thinks the actress in black velvet is the queen, and is "pained to learn that the real Queen had died long ago, and not at all on the night she, Miranda, had been present" (p. 179). Similarly she has trouble understanding the use of figurative language, because of her concrete way of thinking.[10] When her Uncle Bill tells her that Aunt Amy was as beautiful "as an angel," Miranda's mental image of "golden-haired angels with long blue pleated skirts dancing around the throne of the Blessed Virgin" (p. 176) does not match either the dark-haired, dark-eyed woman in the photograph or the spirited enchantress of family stories. Miranda spends a great deal of her childhood wondering, "Oh, what did grown-up people *mean* when they talked, anyway?" (p. 197). Paradoxically her father, who obviously understands the use of figurative language, counters the girls confusion and incredulity with lines like, "Now what has that to do with it? . . . It's a poem" (p. 181), but he seems as tricked by his own tropes[11] about Amy as his daughters. The constant equation between Amy and angel in his and his family's stories has resulted in their own literal reading—they have begun to think of Amy not simply as perfect, but as the perfect woman—a reading that has disastrous consequences for Miranda's definition of woman and thus for her view of herself.

This problem is compounded because as Miranda grows older and begins to focus on her own identity, she views the Amy story as a narrative of gender definition as well. Miranda persists "in believing, in spite of her smallness, thinness, her little snubby nose saddled with freckles, her speckled gray eyes and habitual tantrums, that by some miracle she would grow into a tall, cream-colored brunette" (p. 176). Even when Maria tells her that they will always have freckles and therefore will "never be beautiful," Miranda "still secretly believed that she would one day suddenly receive beauty. . . . She believed for quite a while that she would one day be like Aunt Amy, not as she appeared in the photograph, but as she was remembered by those who had seen her" (p. 177). In *Reconstructing Desire*, Jean Wyatt speculates that "Children, with their undiminished faith in the possibilities of life, their eagerness to try on new experience, and their proximity to the age of permeable ego boundaries may read novels with a passionate identification closed off to adult readers." Because Aunt Amy is the heroine of family stories, Miranda wants to be like her. In Appleyard's developmental study of reading, he argues that for the seven- to twelve-year-old child such larger-than-life characters are "the fantasized embodiments of the unambiguous virtue, skill, popularity, and adult approval that will resolve confusion about identity."[12]

While at twelve Maria is a better judge of life's possibilities than Miranda, she is still susceptible to the definitions of female beauty and the single goal of marriage for young women that their father and grandmother advance in the family stories. The adults' authority and the society's validation of the charming Southern belle, Aunt Amy, and castigation of the bitter "old maid," Cousin Eva, who lives alone and works for women's rights, make it difficult for the young girls to see the patriarchal ideology in their father's and grandmother's stories of either Amy or Eva. Another mitigating factor is that the girls know Eva and consider her a part of their "everyday world of dull lessons to be learned . . . and disappointed expectations," while Amy, dead but brought to life by family legend, belongs "to the world of poetry" (p. 178). They love to hear her story because, as Jean Wyatt suggests, we read to experience what life has not provided us.[13]

In the course of "Old Mortality," Porter emphasizes, however, that the girls hear not only a biased story but an incomplete one. When their grandmother tells them about Aunt Amy's life, she plots it with the romance and adventure of fancy balls, broken engagements, midnight rides, and family scandals, but ends it properly and appropriately with marriage. The story that the girls hear is a fantasy of romantic love, which defines a woman's power as the ability to attract a man and which makes a man the agent of a woman's destiny, the sole cause of her happiness or unhappiness.[14]

Porter, however, supplies the reader of "Old Mortality" with a different ending to the Amy story than the one the young girls hear. We read two letters, which significantly the narrator tells us the girls are not allowed to see until they are grown. Porter makes it clear that while the girls think Amy's story follows the conventional love plot, it may very well have been a quest for adventure, starring Amy as the active agent in her own destiny. Because Amy's family will not allow Amy, who is so beautiful, to remain unmarried like Cousin Eva, which she vehemently says she wants to do, Porter suggests that Amy uses marriage to Gabriel, a man she does not really love, as an escape from her family and a way to New Orleans for Mardi Gras and perhaps a meeting with her old beau Raymond. The ending that we construct from the letters is an unhappy one: vivacious Amy, constricted by a disappointing marriage, takes her own life just six weeks after her wedding. She dies, not from tuberculosis as even the eighteen-year-old Miranda thinks, but from an overdose of pills.

Perhaps Amy, even in her flight, was still in thrall to the fantasy of romantic love with the right man, but Porter early on gives her readers hints of Amy's desire for creative autonomy. Amy insists that she "could not imagine wanting to marry anybody" and would rather be "a nice old maid like Eva Parrington" (p. 183). While Amy's desire for "a good dancing partner" (p. 183) to guide her through life suggests that she is more interested in being a belle than in having a career, it is clear that she wishes to have some control over the predictable pattern of life that her family has determined for her—if only to remain a vivacious belle rather than to become "a staid old married woman" (p. 192). After a three-day ride to Mexico from which she returns with a fever, Amy refuses to allow her parents to scold her, declaring, "if I am to be the heroine of this novel, why shouldn't I make the most of it?" (p. 189). It is significant that Amy, much to her mother's dismay, rewrites the script of her wedding, choosing to wear grey rather than white: " 'I shall wear mourning if I like,' she said, 'it is my funeral, you know' " (p. 182). This detail, which Miranda's grandmother does convey to her, is one that the young girl must not have been able to make sense of given the endings of the conventional marriage plots she was used to.

In part 2 Miranda comes face to face with Gabriel, the hero of the stories she has heard so often as a young child. Porter portrays Miranda, who is now ten, as a different sort of reader than she was at eight—no longer reading novels with passionate identification, but able to distinguish fiction from reality: "They had long since learned to draw the lines between life, which was real and earnest, and the grave was not its goal; poetry, which was true but not real; and stories, or forbidden reading matter, in which things happened as nowhere else . . . because there was not a word of truth in them" (p. 194). Miranda's experience of dull convent life in a Catholic girls' boarding school teaches her that the "thrilling paperbacked version" (p. 194), in which she reads about "beautiful but unlucky maidens . . . trapped by nuns and priests . . . 'immured' in convents, where they were forced to take the veil" (p. 193), does not reflect her own experience. For this reason, Miranda and her sister dismiss the stories as untrue even though they adopt the word *immured* to refer to their condition, thinking that it gives "a romantic glint to what was otherwise a dull life" (p. 194). Porter's narrator, however, conveys a more subtle point about the way the girls have read this "forbidden reading matter" (p. 193). The narrator explains that the girls have adopted the word because it represents to some degree their feelings of confinement at the school, whose grounds they leave only occasionally when relatives take them to the horse races. The narrator also emphasizes the politics of reading, or certainly the politics of giving books as gifts, by humorously suggesting that a Protestant cousin "with missionary intent" (p. 193) had left the book behind at their grandmother's farm, hoping that the Catholic girls would be influenced by it.

The primary event in part 2 is the girls' first meeting with Uncle Gabriel, the "handsome romantic beau" (p. 197) they have envisioned from the family stories about Amy. Miranda's correct assessment of Gabriel as a drunkard, based on descriptions she has read of drunken people, shows that she continues to use fiction as a source of information about life, even though she recognizes that it is not always an exact representation. That Gabriel is "a shabby fat man with bloodshot blue eyes . . . and a big melancholy laugh" (p. 197) causes momentary confusion and disappointment and validates Miranda's new belief that stories are more romantic than life. However, her disillusionment about Gabriel does not cause her to question other parts of the Amy legend or to notice that Honey, Gabriel's second wife, has suffered from his continued preoccupation with the long-dead Amy. Most importantly, it fails to provoke Miranda to assess the role the legend has had in her own loss of self-esteem.

Part 3 centers on Miranda as a young adult. At age eighteen she is returning home for Gabriel's funeral. On the train she meets her Cousin Eva, whom the family has used in their stories as Amy's foil, the epitome of a woman who has not succeeded in becoming a Southern belle. Because of her "weak chin," she has failed to attract men with her looks; because of "strong character" and her preoccupation with intellectual subjects, she has failed to charm men with her conversation. Or so her family says, particularly Amy. As Eva and Miranda reminisce about the past, Miranda receives a very different interpretation of the Amy legend. Eva gives Miranda a feminist critique of the other aunt's story. She thinks Amy and girls like her were driven to chasing men because of their need for husbands to support them, and that their dreams of romantic love were a pretty cover-up for what could not be spoken—female sexual desire.[15] Eva suggests that women of Amy's generation would have been better off if they had used their minds, as she did, not just their bodies, and if they had dared to think for themselves and learned to take care of themselves, as she has. Eva attributes Amy's difficulty in choosing an independent life to the family's narrow definition of female beauty and worth, a definition that Eva says was pervasive, but one that she believes was more tenacious in the South than elsewhere in the United States.

For the first time, Miranda is forced to think about storytelling, not as an extension of reality or an attempt to represent reality, but as the production of reality. In talking about Gabriel's request to be buried next to Amy rather than Honey, Eva compels Miranda to consider how the legend of Amy may have affected Miss Honey's life. Eva says, "After listening to stories about Amy for twenty-five years, she [Honey] must lie alone in her grave in Lexington while Gabriel sneaks off to Texas to make his bed with Amy again. It was a kind of life-long infidelity, Miranda, and now an eternal infidelity on top of that" (pp. 210–11). Eva's remarks make Miranda wonder for the first time what Honey was like before she met Gabriel and had to live with his endless comparisons to Amy. Interestingly enough, Miranda still does not seem to see the effect that growing up in Amy's shadow has had on Eva. She keeps wondering why Eva is so bitter, why she hates Amy so much. Eva's version of the story allows Porter's readers, however, to see that although Eva's bitterness at being another victim of the Amy legend shapes the way she tells the story, her family's version of the Amy story has caused Eva's bitterness. Indeed, it has shaped her life.

Listening to Eva's storytelling, Miranda finds herself in the situation Diana Fuss describes. "In reading, for instance, we bring (old) subject positions to the text at the same time the actual process of reading constructs (new) subject-positions for us. Consequently, we are always engaged in a 'double reading' . . . in the sense that we are continually caught within and between *at least* two constantly shifting subject-positions" that may be "in complete contradiction."[16] Miranda must negotiate between her loyalty to an old family story and her fascination with Cousin Eva's new perspective. As Eva presents new interpretations of Amy's behavior, "She was a bad, wild girl" (p. 214), Miranda counters with the readings she has grown up with, "everybody said she was very beautiful" (p. 214). Eva stands her ground, "Not everybody" (p. 214). As Eva implicates Amy in the suffering Eva experienced as a child, Miranda responds with another interpretation:

> She [Amy] used to say to me [Eva], in that gay soft way she had, "Now, Eva, don't go talking votes for women, when the lads ask you to dance. Don't recite Latin poems to 'em," she would say, "they got sick of that in school. Dance and say nothing, Eva," she would say, her eyes perfectly devilish, "and hold your chin up, Eva. . . . You'll never catch a husband if you don't look out," she would say.
> "She was joking, Cousin Eva," said Miranda, innocently, "and everybody loved her."
> "Not everybody, by a long shot," said Cousin Eva in triumph. "She had enemies. If she knew, she pretended she didn't. If she cared, she never said. You couldn't make her quarrel. She was sweet as a honeycomb to everybody. *Everybody,*" she added, "that was the trouble. She went through life like a spoiled darling, doing as she pleased and letting other people suffer for it, and pick up the pieces after her." (p. 211)

But beneath Miranda's verbal protests, she finds that Eva's version of the story, in which Amy dies and Eva survives, confirms an old maxim, "Beauty goes, character stays" (p. 215). While drawn to this view, Miranda is deflected from it by the way her family has taught her to see "strong character" in a woman. She continues to view "a strong character" as "deforming" (p. 215), and therefore, sees Eva as unattractive. Eva's habit of frankness runs counter to Southern manners, which require a lady to be polite but evasive when faced with unpleasantness.

But the message of Eva's story—the tremendous effect family stories can have on a young girl's development and self-esteem—has parallels in Miranda's own experience, and these parallels are what create Miranda's "horrid fascination with the terrors and the darkness Cousin Eva has conjured up" (p. 214). In part 3 Miranda reads Eva's stories with a self-consciousness she did not have as a child. Typical of adolescents, she is aware of her own subjectivity, which is sometimes in conflict with the social roles she must play, and she uses reading to think about possibilities of expressing a truer self.[17] She sees similarities between herself and Cousin Eva: they both have had to wear hand-me-down dresses as children, and they both are interested in women's suffrage. As she listens to Eva's storytelling, Miranda's burning question is, "What was the end of this story?" (p. 214).

Miranda's desire to know another ending comes from her knowledge that the traditional ending for women, that marriage will produce happiness and fulfillment, has not worked for her. After her father told her she would never be tall and therefore would not become a great beauty like Aunt Amy, Miranda eventually developed other fantasies of self-fulfillment—at first, to be a jockey or to play the violin, and finally, to be an airplane pilot. However, she must have perceived her desires as transgressive for a female because she kept them secret, planning to train in private and to surprise her family with her career choice only when she had succeeded. Despite Miranda's conscious fantasies and her awareness of contradictions in the Amy stories, Miranda has unconsciously patterned her life after Amy's by eloping from her convent, a fact that Porter surprises her readers with in part 3. The romantic Amy legend and the forbidden reading material about the convent have mingled in Miranda's mind to produce a plot and an ending very close to the fictional ones she has been brought up with: spirited young woman, immured in convent, is rescued by dashing young man. But she has quickly grown dissatisfied with this ending to her own life.

In spite of Miranda's intense interest in Eva's ending to the Amy story, Miranda does not appreciate Eva's reduction of all romance to female rivalry for men and festering sexual desire. At this point she declares Eva's story as fantastic as her father's. Miranda simply refuses to consider her mother's courtship and marriage in such terms. However, Eva's conclusion that the family is "the root of all human wrongs" (p. 217) is substantiated for Miranda by the way her father snubs her when they get off the train, a sign of his continuing disapproval of her elopement. Miranda's subsequent decision to cut all family ties, even those to her husband and his family, is predicated on her listening to Eva's version of the Amy story, but Miranda remains unconscious of the effect Eva's story has had on her own thoughts. While Miranda now perceives that a story is not simply a representation of the world but of the storyteller's vision of the world, she does not realize that meaning comes from a reader's interpretation as well.[18] Miranda does not realize that Eva's story validates and clarifies what she has not been able to articulate about her marriage and her family, but what she is now beginning to realize: "She knew now why she had run away to marriage, and she knew that she was going to run away from marriage, and she was not going to stay in any place, with anyone, that threatened to forbid her making her own discoveries" (p. 220).

Such knowledge and the refusal of the heterosexual romance plot as sole key to a woman's happiness might provide the ending of a feminist bildungsroman, but Porter does not conclude at this point. Porter's bildungsroman ends with what Martin Swales has defined as the conventional ending of the traditional German and modern British bildungsroman—its questioning of the narrator's and ultimately the reader's capacity for self-reflection and its concern with the values and assumptions that shape human experience.[19] Miranda rightly sees that her father's, grandmother's, and Cousin Eva's stories of Amy are only versions of the truth, but she still persists in thinking she can know the truth about herself. The narrator states that she does so "in her hopefulness, her ignorance" (p. 221). If Katherine Anne Porter had followed her feminist inclinations, instead of the fictional models of her male modernist predecessors,[20] perhaps "Old Mortality" would have concluded with a less ambiguous ending, one more in keeping with Jane Tompkins's statement that "When discourse is responsible for reality and not merely a reflection of it, then whose discourse prevails makes all the difference."[21]

While it is clear from Miranda's father's and grandmother's versions of the Amy story that the romance plot certainly separates love and quest, as Rachel DuPlessis argues in *Writing beyond the Ending*,[22] Porter suggests that a feminist plot does the same, only reversing the emphasis, rewriting the resolution so that love is repressed instead of quest. The independent Eva, who has reduced love to hormones and marriage to economics, lives alone, but she is unhappy and bitter, and Miranda seems to be following in her footsteps—a direction the narrator judges as very problematic. When Miranda decides that in order to make "her own discoveries" she must give up relationships, Porter writes, "I hate love, she [Miranda] thought, as if this were the answer, I hate loving and being loved, I hate it. And her disturbed and seething mind received a shock of comfort from this sudden collapse of an old painful structure of distorted images and misconceptions. 'You don't know anything about it,' said Miranda to herself, with extraordinary clearness as if she were an elder admonishing some younger misguided creature. 'You have to find out about it'" (pp. 220–21). The narrator undercuts Miranda's decision to renounce love with the phrase, "as if this were the answer"—a phrase Porter added in revising the story.[23]

Although "Old Mortality" ends before Miranda discovers anything more about love, life, stories, or reading, Porter is not finished with Miranda. In a companion piece, "Pale Horse, Pale Rider," Miranda has a life after divorce, but her career is a rather dull job as a theater critic for a Denver newspaper (an assignment reserved for women), and she is looking for love. She finds the perfect Adam—tall, tanned, and blond—who, in a reversal of roles, nurses her when she becomes deathly ill with the flu. This story ends with his death and Miranda's return to life, but Porter describes it as a life that stretches out before her in "the dead cold light of tomorrow."[24] Porter is clearly frustrated with the available plots for women, but in neither her life nor her fiction is she able to imagine a love relationship that is mutually supportive of each individual's work.[25] As a result, Porter undoes the marriage plot in "Old Mortality" and the quest plot in "Pale Horse, Pale Rider," although in both she resists the conventional fictional closure for women's lives—marriage or death.

The dates that Porter uses in "Old Mortality" encourage comparisons to her own life, even though her narrative persona is uncharacterized. At the same time that Porter acknowledges in her notes a similarity between Miranda's experiences and her own, she emphasizes that "Old Mortality" is "not an autobiographical story" and that Miranda is "by no means intended to represent herself."[26] As if to suggest a link but not an exact comparison to her protagonist's experiences, Porter has Maria's birth date rather than Miranda's correspond with her own. However, 1912, the date of part 3, was a momentous year for Porter as it was for Miranda—a time when Porter was reassessing her marriage to John Koontz, her first husband. Because he was on the road that year as a traveling salesman, she experienced freedom for the first time (she had married at sixteen), and she wrote her first short story while he was away. When she left him later that year, her father disowned her. Katherine Anne Porter must have felt in 1912 as Miranda did in 1912, that the beautiful fantasies of romantic love that young girls grow up on can be dangerous. Eva's declaration that the family is a "hideous institution . . . the root of all human wrongs" (p. 217) must have been rather close to Porter's own assessment. In 1936 a few days after finishing "Old Mortality," Porter decided to end her third marriage. She described the last few months of 1936, a period of incredible productivity, as "the most wonderful" of her life. Cloistered in the Water Wheel Tavern in Doylestown, Pennsylvania, she attributed the disruption of her creativity to the arrival of her husband, Eugene Pressly. This realization led her to decide that she must have complete freedom and solitude if she were going to write. Six months later, however, she found she could not tear herself away from Albert Erskine, a handsome young man who looked like Adam in "Pale Horse, Pale Rider"[27] and who was as captivated by Porter as Gabriel was by Amy. Porter agreed to marry Erskine a year after her decision to break up with Pressly; the marriage to Erskine lasted two years.

Porter's biographer Joan Givner has detailed Porter's contradictory attitudes toward feminism, from her early support of women's rights as evidenced in correspondence with her brother in 1909[28] to her derogatory remarks in the 1960s and 1970s about Simone de Beauvoir and Betty Friedan. Porter's comments reveal that she was uncomfortable with strains of feminist thinking that set forth monolithic definitions of *woman* and that portrayed women as victims and passive sufferers. Of Beauvoir's *The Second Sex* Porter said in a 1962 interview, "Whenever I find a book that begins 'Women are . . .' or 'Women do . . .' or 'Women . . . ,' I say 'That's enough.' " To a March 1970 question asking if she was ready to join the Women's Liberation Movement, Porter replied, "I will not sit down with you and hear you tell me men have abused you. Any man who ever did wrong to me got back better than he gave."[29] Porter's dismissal of feminism reveals her fundamental dislike of women's passively occupying stories, not her lack of support for women's rights.[30] In "Old Mortality" the narrator undercuts both Eva's "woman as victim" stories and the rest of the family's "woman as Southern belle" stories.

Porter's ambivalence toward feminism is felt in "Old Mortality" in the tension between her narrative positioning of Eva as the character who dismantles the Amy myth and the stereotypical way in which the narrator describes her: "She had two immense front teeth and a receding chin, but she did not lack character" (p. 206). Givner believes that Porter "was torn between wishing to be an accomplished, independent woman, speaking out authoritatively on literature and world events and wishing to be a charmingly capricious belle, sought after for her beauty and arousing chivalrous thoughts in every male breast."[31] Porter's portrait of Eva suggests that although Porter believed in women's rights, she bought into the patriarchal ideology of her day, which depicted feminists as ugly, as alone, and as interested in careers and women's causes only because no men would have them. Porter's portrait of the ill-fated Amy suggests that although Porter saw the dangers for women in the Southern-belle role, that vision of female beauty and charm was deeply imbedded in her unconscious. So too was the fantasy of romantic love.

The narrator's ironic distance from the Amy story and from Miranda's predicament belies Porter's own deep entanglement in both, and supports the final irony of "Old Mortality." Miranda's assumption that she will have total control over her own life—both in living it and in understanding it—is undercut repeatedly by the narrator at the end of "Old Mortality":

> Oh, what is life, she asked herself in desperate seriousness, in those childish unanswerable words, and what shall I do with it? It is something of my own, she thought in a fury of jealous possessiveness, what shall I make of it? She did not know that she asked herself this because all her earliest training had argued that life was a substance, a material to be used, it took shape and direction and meaning only as the possessor guided and worked it; living was a progress of continued and varied acts of the will directed towards a definite end. (p. 220)

Miranda's attempt to be done with the stories of the past fails because the teachings embodied in these stories have become part of her unconscious— "she did not know that she asked herself this." Porter succeeds in discrediting the stories Miranda has grown up with, but she gives Miranda little control over their lingering effects. In "Old Mortality" Porter demonstrates the difficulty of reading or writing a story rather than being read or written by it— the problem of unconsciously playing out old plots, even after one has become a feminist reader aware of their dangers. Porter's ending undermines the reader's attempt to control her text.

Notes

My thanks to Alison Booth for her editorial suggestions.

1.   For a discussion of Porter's modernist themes, see Robert Penn Warren, "Irony with a Center," in *Katherine Anne Porter, a Collection of Critical Essays,* ed. Robert Penn Warren (Englewood Cliffs, N.J.: Prentice-Hall, Inc., 1979), pp. 93–108; M. M. Liberman, *Katherine Anne Porter's Fiction* (Detroit: Wayne State Univ. Press, 1971), pp. 37–51; Willene Hendrick and

George Hendrick, *Katherine Anne Porter* (Boston: G. K. Hall & Co., 1988), pp. 55–59; Janis P. Stout, "Miranda's Guarded Speech: Porter and the Problem of Truth-Telling," *Philological Quarterly* 66, no. 2 (1987): 259–78. For a discussion of Porter's Southern themes about the dangers of idealizing the past, see John Edward Hardy, *Katherine Anne Porter* (New York: Frederick Ungar Publishing Company, 1973), pp. 24–33; Darlene Harbour Unrue, *Truth and Vision in Katherine Anne Porter's Fiction* (Athens: Univ. of Georgia Press, 1985), pp. 124–31; and Ray B. West, Jr., "Katherine Anne Porter and 'Historic Memory,' " in *Southern Renascence: The Literature of the Modern South,* ed. Louis B. Rubin, Jr., and Robert D. Jacobs (Baltimore: Johns Hopkins Univ. Press, 1953), pp. 278–89. In *Katherine Anne Porter's Women* (Austin: Univ. of Texas Press, 1983), Jane Krause DeMouy provides a feminist critique of the social roles Porter's characters were expected to play (pp. 145–57).

2.   K. A. Porter papers, dated 24 June 1948, Special Collections, University of Maryland at College Park Libraries.

3.   Katherine Anne Porter, "The Necessary Enemy," in her *The Collected Essays and Occasional Writings of Katherine Anne Porter* (New York: Delta, 1973), p. 185. See also " 'Marriage Is Belonging' " (pp. 187–92).

4.   In *Becoming a Reader: The Experience of Fiction from Childhood to Adulthood* (Cambridge: Cambridge Univ. Press, 1990), J. A. Appleyard takes up the very developmental issues about reader response that interested Porter and that have eluded many reader-response critics.

5.   For example, in *Hypatia: or Women and Knowledge* (New York: E. P. Dutton & Co., 1925), Dora Russell is exasperated with people who force women to "choose": " 'Choose,' say the Bishops and the school-managers (often the same thing); 'choose,' say the public authorities who support the Church and rather wish women would get out of this indelicate profession of surgery and medicine, 'choose between love and duty to the male and service to the community.' This is not feminism—feminists have fought it persistently—it is medieval Christianity. It presents a choice between physical pleasure and service to the mind or soul" (p. 31).

6.   Patrocinio P. Schweickart, "Reading Ourselves: Toward a Feminist Theory of Reading," in *Gender and Reading: Essays on Readers, Texts, and Contexts,* ed. Elizabeth A. Flynn and Patrocinio P. Schweickart (Baltimore: Johns Hopkins Univ. Press, 1986), p. 49. An excellent review essay of some recent works on gender and reading is Pamela L. Caughie's "Women Reading/Reading Women," *Papers on Language and Literature* 24, no. 3 (Summer 1988): 317–35.

7.   Katherine Anne Porter, "Old Mortality," in *The Collected Stories of Katherine Anne Porter* (New York: Harcourt Brace Jovanovich, 1979), p. 174. Subsequent quotations from this edition will hereafter be cited parenthetically by page number.

8.   Mary Crawford and Roger Chaffin, "The Reader's Construction of Meaning: Cognitive Research on Gender and Comprehension," in *Gender and Reading,* ed. Flynn and Schweickart, p. 3.

9.   Appleyard, *Becoming a Reader,* p. 14.

10.   Appleyard's chapter "Early Childhood: The Reader as Player" (pp. 21–56) in his *Becoming a Reader* is a good description of the cognitive limitations of children's thinking and of the psychological studies of young children and reading.

11.   See Mary Jacobus's discussion of Breuer and Freud's being tricked by their own figures of speech about women in *Reading Woman: Essays in Feminist Criticism* (New York: Columbia Univ. Press, 1986), pp. 198–200.

12.   Jean Wyatt, *Reconstructing Desire: The Role of the Unconscious in Women's Reading and Writing* (Chapel Hill: Univ. of North Carolina Press, 1990), p. 219; Appleyard, *Becoming a Reader,* p. 77.

13.   Wyatt, *Reconstructing Desire,* p. 45.

14.   In *Becoming a Woman through Romance* (New York: Routledge, 1990), Linda K. Christian-Smith argues that "Although romance bestows recognition and importance on heroines, it constructs feminine subjectivity in terms of a significant other, the boyfriend" (p. 28).

15. In "Irony with a Center," Robert Penn Warren suggests that Eva's critique is Marxist and Freudian, which indeed it is, but he fails to see that it is feminist as well. (Warren, ed., *Katherine Anne Porter,* p. 105).

16. Diana Fuss, "Reading Like a Feminist," in her *Essentially Speaking: Feminism, Nature, and Difference* (New York: Routledge, 1989), p. 33.

17. See Appleyard, "Adolescence: The Reader as Thinker," in his *Becoming a Reader,* pp. 94–120.

18. In *Becoming a Reader* Appleyard argues that "The discovery of multiple levels of significance deriving from authorial intention is perhaps the limit of an adolescent's ability to deal with the idea of meaning in a story. . . . To go further would require taking the point of view that meaning results from an act of interpretation by the reader, which is the issue faced in the next stage of development. Adolescents interpret, but they do not have a theory of interpretation. They debate about interpretations, but the point at issue is which one is the right one" (p. 112). At the end of "Old Mortality" eighteen-year-old Amy continues to be preoccupied with truth.

19. See Martin Swales, *The German Bildungsroman from Wieland to Hesse* (Princeton, N.J.: Princeton Univ. Press, 1978), pp. 98–102, and "The German *Bildungsroman* and the Great Tradition" in *Comparative Criticism,* ed. Elinor Shaffer (Cambridge, Mass.: Cambridge Univ. Press, 1979), pp. 91–105. Also of interest is Carol Lassaro-Weis's "The Female *Bildungsroman:* Calling It into Question," *NWSA Journal* 2, no. 1 (Winter 1990): 16–34.

20. See Joan Givner's *Katherine Anne Porter, A Life,* rev. ed. (Athens: Univ. of Georgia Press, 1991); Joan Givner, ed. *Katherine Anne Porter: Conversations* (Jackson: Univ. Press of Mississippi, 1987); and Porter's *The Collected Essays and Occasional Writings of Katherine Anne Porter* (New York: Delta, 1973) for modernist influences on her fiction, especially the work of James Joyce.

21. Jane P. Tompkins, "An Introduction to Reader-Response Criticism," in *Reader-Response Criticism, from Formalism to Post-Structuralism,* ed. Jane P. Tompkins (Baltimore: Johns Hopkins Univ. Press, 1980), p. xxv.

22. See Rachel Blau DuPlessis's *Writing beyond the Ending: Narrative Strategies of Twentieth-Century Women Writers* (Bloomington: Indiana Univ. Press, 1985), pp. 1–19.

23. Liberman, *Katherine Anne Porter's Fiction,* p. 48.

24. Katherine Anne Porter, "Pale Horse, Pale Rider," in *The Collected Stories of Katherine Anne Porter* (New York: Harcourt Brace Jovanovich, 1979), p. 317.

25. Recently feminist critics have called for a reinventing of both marriage and work as well as a reimagining of both marriage plots and quest plots. In *Writing a Woman's Life* (New York: W. W. Norton & Company, 1988), Carolyn G. Heilbrun argues that "new definitions and a new reality about marriage must be not only lived but narrated" (p. 89). She defines as "revolutionary" a marriage in which "both partners have work at the center of their lives and must find a delicate balance that can support both together and each individually" (p. 81). In "Texts to Grow On: Reading Women's Romance Fiction" (*Tulsa Studies in Women's Literature* 7, no. 2 [Fall 1988]: 239–59), Suzanne Juhasz argues for a reexamination of both self-realization and the idea of quest. She believes that self-realization can include relationships, not just the "action, adventure, knowledge, vocation" linked to the quest motif (p. 248).

26. K. A. Porter Papers, Special Collections, University of Maryland at College Park Libraries.

27. Joan Givner, *Katherine Anne Porter, a Life,* pp. 97–98, 298–300, 305.

28. While Katherine Anne Porter's letter to her brother is not extant, its profeminist contents are implied in Paul's reply, dated 23 March 1909, in K. A. Porter Papers, Special Collections, University of Maryland at College Park Libraries.

Dear Callie: I haven't answered your welcome letter for I hardly knew what to make of it at first. You certainly took me by surprise with your vehemence. It must have been written on one of your off days. What was the trouble; had JK [John Koontz] asserted himself in contravention of the laws or rather, rights, of woman. Poor old JK. He is probably an h.p. suffragist at home any way if merly [*sic*] for the sake of peace. You will find that the average man does not activly [*sic*] oppose the ballot for women, but merly [*sic*] regards it with uneasy tolerance as liable to disturb the present relation between the sexes. Dear, why should you butt your head against hard facts; there is no practical reason for allowing you the ballot. I admit it would gratify their vanity, but aside from that it would be of no earthly use to women. It would not help the moral or economic conditions and would bring the millenium [*sic*] no nearer. False pride and ignorance account for a great many of the women who champion the cause, women whose views are inflated because of natures [*sic*] stinginess in brain and who blindly follow a lead with out the least conception of what it all means. They become bitter from a fanatical struggle for imaginary rights not knowing an effort not directed by common sense will invariably fail. They do not discriminate between bigness and fineness, unable to see that any influence that they could bring to bear along that line would not equal the influence of the feminine in maternal relations of the home. The worlds [*sic*] greatest need today is of good mothers, which is the master proffesion [*sic*] for women requiring every art and talent to perfect, of women who live close to their children, who will bear impressions of her training all through life. The farther away a woman gets from the thought that she was made to be the helpmate of man, and the mother of his children, the farther she will be from her usefulness. Competition between the sexes is unnatural, you should be mans [*sic*] inspiration, not his competitor. What effort you make for equality renders you unwomanly and consequently less deserving of the deference which is a womans [*sic*] portion. American women enjoy more liberty than any other nation on the earth and what are the results. Divorces, soul mates, and numerous other evils. If that is equality it would be far better to keep them fettered than to let them turn liberty into license. You say women are slaves; bound by routine and unappreciated labor. I should call them the White Mans [*sic*] Burden. . . . A man loves a woman on a pedestal, when she comes down he leaves her. It matters little whether women vote or not, as man is boss now will he be then; finis.

29. Joan Givner, ed., *Katherine Anne Porter: Conversations*, pp. xvii, 76, 155–56.

30. On 26 March 1958, Porter wrote to literary critic Edward Schwartz, because she did not like his Freudian analysis of Miranda's behavior in "Pale Horse, Pale Rider" as a wish "to assume the active male role": "What they [women] really want, I think, is not a change of sex, but a change of the limited conditions of their lives which have been imposed because of their sexual functions" (*Letters of Katherine Anne Porter,* ed. Isabel Bayley, p. 548). In Porter's letters, she often espouses feminist ideas at what she terms "the risk of being called a horrid name like Feminist" (pp. 503, 508). Porter is also refusing to read her life in anything but individualist terms (hence her repayment in kind to any one abusive man, but her dislike of a general women's movement).

31. Givner, ed., *Katherine Anne Porter: Conversations, p. xiv.* Givner also attributes the inconsistency in Porter's attitudes toward feminism to her "overriding desire to entertain and woo her audience," a desire that was surely fostered by her own early training as a Southern belle, whose "reflex is to make a conquest" (pp. xvii–xviii). Givner gives as an example the radically different ways in which she responds to a question about gender and writing depending on the sex of her interviewer. In a 1962 interview with Maurice Dolbier, Porter claims, "I've never felt that the fact of being a woman put me at a disadvantage, or that it's difficult being a woman in a 'man's world.' The only time men get a little tiresome is in love—oh, they're OK

at first but they do tend don't they, to get a little bossy and theological about the whole business?" (p. 77). And yet, a year later when Barbara Thompson asked her if being a woman presented a writer with any "special problems," Porter responded differently, "You're brought up with the notion of feminine chastity and inaccessibility, yet with the curious idea of feminine availability in all spiritual ways, and in giving service to anyone who demands it. And I suppose that's why it has taken me twenty years to write this novel [*Ship of Fools*]; it's been interrupted by just anyone who could jimmy his way into my life" (p. 95).

Structure and Imagery in Katherine Anne Porter's "Pale Horse, Pale Rider"

Sarah Youngblood

Katherine Anne Porter has long been regarded as one of the finest writers of contemporary fiction, and the justice of this respect is felt by most readers familiar with her work. A consideration of structure and imagery in one of her major works may, by explicating its richnesses, serve to show more specifically the reasons for Miss Porter's place in contemporary fiction. This is one of the functions which explicative criticism may perform, not only the unfolding of a work for our widest contemplation but also the establishing or affirming of canons of respect. An examination of *Pale Horse, Pale Rider* illuminates the dimensions of both her work and her reputation.

Structurally, this short novel can be viewed as three units or sections of action, each section presenting action of an increasingly psychological kind, in a setting generally different from the others. The first section introduces Miranda and extends to her collapse from illness; the second describes her night of delirium in the room of the boarding-house; the third presents her hospital experience. It will be noted that the first section opens with Miranda in the isolation of a dream, but this isolation is immediately intruded upon when she wakes to the reality of her room and the world she must enter for survival. Thereafter, the first section can be said to present Miranda-in-the-world, as, in the narrowing psychological focus of the story, the succeeding sections present Miranda-and-Adam, and Miranda alone. The last section would seem to be a reverse reflection of the first, since it concludes with Miranda's preparation to move back into the world.

In terms of spatial movement, the opening section is thus the largest and most inclusive. This spatial inclusiveness is appropriate to the initiation of themes in the novel, and all of the themes stated here in image or action figure in the later sections as motivation and explanation. The themes— political, social, psychological, and moral in their implications—require a certain largeness of stage for postulation, and this is available in the shifting

Reprinted with permission of the Johns Hopkins University Press from *Modern Fiction Studies* 5 (Winter 1959–60): 344–52.

scenes of the opening section: the room, the newspaper office, the theater, the dance-hall, the streets of the city. Also available is a necessarily large cast of characters, by which we follow Miranda's reaction to her world: the newspaper staff, the bond salesmen, the Junior League girls, the lovers in the dance-hall, the soldiers in the hospital, the has-been vaudeville actor. And over all this stage and its actors, and conditioning it all, is the state of war, which provides a prime mover for all of the issues, since war is examined not only in its political and social implications, but particularly in its psychological or moral implications: ". . . the worst of war is the fear and suspicion. . . . It's the skulking about and the lying. It's what war does to the mind and the heart. . . ." The presence of war is a conditioning factor in the action and themes of the novel. War is the "gong of warning" which wakes Miranda from sleep and beats the rhythm of the day for her. It focuses in the day-to-day world of Miranda the theme of death which haunts her dream, since war has unreined the "pale horse" of destruction. War posits, in the relationship of Adam and Miranda, the conflict of the individual's obligations to society, and to himself, since in a state of war, in the non-life that war creates (Miranda speaks of peacetime or pre-war time as "in life," making the distinction in time a distinction in being). Adam and Miranda are bound by obligations to society which prevent their unity, even though, ironically, the only dedications which could have value for them now in a war-world would be those based upon love for each other. They are compelled to fulfill obligations created by a society operating upon hatred, not love.

A corollary of this theme is the confusion of appearance and reality which so disturbs Miranda's equilibrium in the world. The war creates fear and suspicion, distrust and hypocrisy, which transforms daily reality into a disturbing set of distorting mirrors. "Towney" may, in the cloakroom, privately despair of the pressures placed upon her by flag-waving tyrants acting as patriots, but in the office later she can summon her "most complacent patriotic voice" to praise the idea of Hut Service. Miranda's wondering reaction to this is repeated in her later, rather terrified, reaction to the theater-crowd, which enthusiastically responds, in a kind of conditioned reflex, to the patriotic jargon of the bond salesman: "There must be a great many of them here who think as I do, and we dare not say a word to each other of our desperation, we are speechless animals letting ourselves be destroyed, and why? Does anybody here believe the things we say to each other?" These contradictions in apparent reality, "the disturbing oppositions in her day-to-day existence," find pervasive expression in the general pattern of hypocrisy which the cautious citizen in war must assume. It is noteworthy, therefore, that everything in Miranda's experience of the daily world that rightly should have been an act of love has degenerated to an act of duty done out of fear: the buying of bonds, the comforting of soldiers. This is a part of what she calls the "disturbing oppositions" in her existence, and one illustration of the appearance/reality theme. (Note, for example, the specific irony of the title of the bonds she is compelled to buy.) The theme is operative at the minor levels of the story, as in the reference to Chuck's father, who "beamed upon him with the bleared eye of paternal affection while he took his last nickel," as well as within the larger plot-development of the novel wherein the golden health of Adam and the sickliness of Miranda conceal the ultimate conclusion of Adam's death and Miranda's survival.

War conditions the action in other ways. It creates the necessity for a "code" or "system" among the younger generation, much like the code of Hemingway's characters, which makes possible for them a "proper view" of chaos, a proper existentialist formula of casualness and flippancy for maintaining cynical control: because the situation is absurd, behave as if it were amusing. When the bond-salesmen accuse Miranda of ignoring the war, she meets the absurdity of the accusation with her formal system:

> "Oh, the war," Miranda had echoed on a rising note and she almost smiled at him. It was habitual, automatic, to give that solemn, mystically uplifted grin when you spoke the words or heard them spoken, "C'est la guerre," whether you could pronounce it or not, was even better, and always, always, you shrugged.

Miranda's conversations with Adam in this section of the novel make use of "the kind of patter going the rounds" as a way of suppressing the sense of the chaotic which informs both characters. "Their smiles approved of each other, they felt they had got the right tone, they were taking the war properly." Above all, thought Miranda, "no tooth-gnashing, no hair-tearing, it's noisy and unbecoming and it doesn't get you anywhere." This is, finally, only another of the masks of reality war has forced them to assume. The system of attitudes is so rigidly adhered to that only delirium can finally compel Miranda to admit in speech to Adam the reality of her terror and her love.

The result of all these interacting implications of war is to assure the isolation of each individual. Since Miranda is the point-of-view character whose reactions are the strict concern of the reader, her isolation and her lucid awareness of it require some examination. Enough has been said of the effect of war in her world to indicate her response to that external condition; the war-theme is, besides, the most obvious nucleus of implication in the story, and other elements demand more explication.

At the psychological level *Pale Horse, Pale Rider* is the dramatization of Miranda's death-wish, a dramatization presented in the ironic form of a reversal, and taking the metaphorical form of a journey. The title of the novel indicates the primacy of the death-theme (of which the war is only, for Miranda, a kind of specific vehicle; one feels that in a situation devoid of war conditions, another vehicle would have been present for her). The title also presents the major symbol of the story, which appears in Miranda's first dream in a kind of double vision. Miranda is pursued by the pale rider, "that lank greenish stranger," but she is also herself the pale rider on Graylie, the pale horse, since she carries the seeds of death within her. This dream foreshadows the final outcome of the story, since "the stranger rode on." Almost all of the images of the dream suggest images in the later dreams: the journey is reiterated in varying forms later (the ship on the river; the journey toward and back from the seashore paradise). The "daylight" images are here, as later associated with vision, clarity, the ability to distinguish reality from illusion: "Early morning is best for me because trees are trees in one stroke . . . there are no false shapes or surmises. . . ." The memory-laden house is clearly a symbol of the past, and of stranglingly close human relationships which Miranda desires to escape from, and she both seeks death as an escape, and yet flees from it; it is this journey I do not mean to take," and her attitude toward death is here ambivalent. She desires isolation, and freedom from the past ("I'll take Graylie because he is not afraid of bridges"), but she also cries to the stranger, "I'm not going with you this time—ride on!" As the dream fades, and before Miranda is completely conscious, she draws herself "out of the pit of sleep, waited in a daze for life to begin again." This image also, by suggesting the bottomless pit described in Revelations, forms part of the pattern of religious imagery in the story.

The pale rider allusion of the title is the most obvious, but others can be remarked on in this first section of the novel. Adam's name is symbolic since he is "committed without any knowledge or act of his own to death," and since he is a vessel of innocence, golden "purity," as Miranda calls it: "Pure, she thought, all the way through, flawless, complete, as the sacrificial lamb must be." In this remark she views him simultaneously as Adam, Unfallen Man, and Isaac, the victim offered to propitiate the wrath of God. As the latter he shares with all the young soldiers the role of sacrificial victim. To increase the symbolic value of his character, his health is emphasized (in a symbolic pun he is compared to a "fine healthy apple"), and his golden, glowing appearance is repeatedly described, suggesting not only his health and handsomeness but also a certain "man of the Golden Age" quality which his physical perfection connotes and Miranda's idealism confirms. Adam himself, far from being a romantic, is a very stable and normal person, which Miranda senses, and she clings to a strength in him which she lacks. That she realizes the idealism of her view of him is made clear in the irony of the line immediately following her thought of him as a sacrificial lamb: "The sacrificial lamb strode along casually, accommodating his long pace to her, keeping her on the inside of the walk in the good American style. . . ."

Related to this religious imagery associated with Adam is Miranda's remark about the epidemic of influenza: "It seems to be a plague . . . something out of the Middle Ages," since this calls into focus two sets of religious associations: the plague as a sign of God's wrath, and the *danse macabre* (in which the "lank stranger" symbol of death is also operative). The influenza epidemic is also, of course, the physical counterpart of the illness of society at war.

II

The second section of the novel opens, as does the first, with Miranda in sleep, waking to discover that a day has passed. In her illness her memory "turned and roved after another place she had known first and loved best," a place clearly Southern, which merges into a dream in which death is represented as a tropical jungle of vivid colors, sulphur-colored light, and the "hoarse bellow of voices." As in the first dream, Miranda commits herself to the journey but does not complete it: she boards the ship, but does not arrive at the jungle, the "secret place of death," before she wakes. Nevertheless, in her talk with Adam afterwards, she speaks as if she were already dead: "Let's tell each other what we meant to do," and her review of her life and attitudes is carefully kept in the past tense, except for her impulsive outburst about the sensuous delights of being alive: her love of weather, colors, sounds. In this conversation the religious theme again occurs, here introduced in an explicit discussion of religion between the characters. Miranda is revealed to be a Catholic, and her preoccupation with religion, anticipated by her earlier allusions, is emphasized here and will recur in later crises. The Negro spiritual which she and Adam try to sing (there are "about forty verses" and they can't remember the third line) gives another element of meaning to the title of the novel since it combines the religious and the love themes.

The scene is followed by another dream, in which Adam figures, and which repeats many of the images of the second dream: the jungle is here an "angry dangerous wood," the voices of the second dream recur, their sound compared to arrows which pierce Adam and Miranda. This curious simile, although its phallic symbolism is apparent, seems also to be a subconscious extension of Miranda's earlier remark, "I even know a prayer beginning O Apollo," since Apollo is associated with pestilence and plagues, which in Greek drama are often referred to as the darts or arrows of an angry Apollo. This is a pagan analogy of the medieval Christian view of plagues; and within the dream, the arrows are also associated with the everydayness of valentines and arrows, a symbolism she is later able to explain rationally. The attitude of Miranda reflected in the dream is also significantly changed from that of her first dream. The ambivalence of her desire for death is absent. "Like a child cheated in a game," she demands her right to die, and "selfishly" attempts to die and save Adam's life. He dies only because of her intervened presence, having before undergone "a perpetual death and resurrection," and this also foreshadows the actual outcome of the plot.

III

The time of the third section extends over a month; yet Miranda's experience in the hospital telescopes this time into a series of dreams. Her illness is enough advanced that even in the passages of time in which she is relatively conscious, her surroundings impinge upon her mind in the dimensions of dream-experience. For example, the incident of the two interns, hidden by a screen, removing a dead body from the bed next to hers, is to Miranda a "dance of tall deliberate shadows" (an image suggesting again the *danse macabre* theme, like churchwall paintings) whose significance she does not fully comprehend—the shroud of the corpse she describes as "a large stiff bow like merry rabbit ears dangled at the crown of his head." Likewise the incident of the filthy old man being dragged down the hall between "two executioners" may be a dream but is more likely a half-conscious, half-dream interpretation of an actual sight in the hall where Miranda's bed is placed. The sight is distorted in her own half-conscious mind by her own sense of guilt, which had been the dominating emotion of her last dream, and by her idea of the plague as a punishment of the guilty, in which the persons society regards as saviours (the doctors) become the executioners. Here again, the earlier allusion to Apollo is relevant, in his dual function as saviour (god of healing) and destroyer (sender of plagues).

To Miranda the whiteness of her hospital environment is its most impressive feature. Beds, shadows, persons, walls, lights are white; even the fog which rises around everything, as her mind loses its rational grasp of experience, is "pallid white." This is to be contrasted with the lush colors of the earlier dream, particularly since the whiteness seems to her to represent not death but oblivion, the road to death, "the landscape of disaster." In the first section of the novel, Miranda had at one point "held her hands together palms up, gazing at them and trying to understand oblivion," which she there identified with her future loneliness without Adam. Later in this section she speaks of oblivion as a "whirlpool of gray water." The images of whiteness seem to be a general symbol of negation; the passage recalls Melville's chapter on the whiteness of the whale; here there is the same element of terror in response to the whiteness.

Miranda's dream of Dr. Hildesheim, who becomes, like the Hun torturer in her nightmare, a variant of the pale rider figure and almost a parody of it, indicates how deeply her mind has absorbed the jargon of the current propaganda which she hates. The dream, by verging on the ridiculous (he carries "a huge stone pot marked Poison in Gothic letters), is like a poetic-justice punishment vaguely threatened by the bond salesmen to those who don't buy bonds. Besides being a revealing comment on the insidious corruption wrought by propaganda, the brief nightmare contains two images which, in her later dream of paradise, reappear as transfigured symbols: the "pasture on her father's farm" and "a well once dry" with the "violated water" of the poison. The dream also reveals her present fear of death, a fear both conscious and subconscious:

> The road to death is a long march beset with all evils, and the heart fails little by little at each new terror, the bones rebel, at each step, the mind sets up its own bitter resistance and to what end? The barriers sink one by one, and no covering of the eyes shuts out the landscape of disaster. . . .

Her dreams in this period have the duality of her earlier daily experience: "Her mind, split in two, acknowledged and denied what she saw in the one instant," and this anticipates the final conflict between her rational will to die and her irrational instinct to live. It is ironic that the "angry point of light" symbolizing her will to live is the ultimate source of the radiance which spreads and curves into the rainbow of her paradise. This has a metaphorical logic also in that she has earlier desired death as escape but feared it as a dark jungle of evil things and of guilt. Here in her dream of paradise her mind postulates what death ideally should be (all that actual life is not), and its features are the opposite of those associated with death in the earlier nightmares. The jungle, the angry wood, becomes the meadow, the darkness becomes radiance, the incessant voices become silence and "no sound," the serpents and exotic evil animals become human beings transfigured in beauty who "cast no shadows"—that is, who no longer have any duality or ambivalence of being, but are "pure identities." In this paradise there is solitude for everyone (what Miranda desired in her dream-escape from her childhood home) but not loneliness or isolation: "each figure was alone but not solitary." The distinctive features of the paradise are silence, radiance, joy. In its features this paradise suggests the traditional mystical experience, and Miranda's later revulsion to the colorless sunlight and pain of the actual world suggests the disillusioned "state of experience" which a mystic undergoes after his return to the world of a tangible reality. This suggestion of the mystical experience is strengthened by the variety of religious imagery elsewhere in the story, and by the presence within the paradise of the rainbow-symbol. The paradise is Miranda's personal interpretation of the apocalyptical revelation alluded to in the title.

She is drawn back from this paradise by the awareness that "something, somebody was missing . . . she had left something valuable in another country," and her remark that "there are no trees here" seems to be the form her memory of Adam, by association, takes (as her earlier comparison of him to "a healthy apple"). The dead are absent, and she has consistently viewed Adam as committed to death, so that she is forced back through the wasteland of her march, "the strange stony place of bitter cold," to find him. There is also here the implication that all of the real world is the world of the "dead." The imagery of the world she returns to is dominantly that of violent noise, and gray colorless light, "where the sound of rejoicing was a clamor of pain" and "it is always twilight or just before morning, a promise of day that is never kept." To Miranda now "the body is a curious monster, no place to live in," as the flesh is alien to the returned mystic, and she is like "an alien who does not like the country in which he finds himself, does not understand the language." But the conspiracy must not be betrayed, the illusion that life is preferable must be maintained out of courtesy to the living. The irony of Miranda's situation is overwhelming: the "humane conviction and custom of society" insist that life is best, and will force her to pay twice for the gift of death, making her endure again at some future date the painful journey to the blue sea and tranquil meadow of her paradise. It is a part of this irony that Adam, for whom she returned, is already dead. The casual understatement with which she and the reader are informed of his death is consistent with her situation: since she has lost paradise, the other loss is inevitable and even unsurprising. It doesn't touch her because her heart is "hardened, indifferent. . . ."

She makes symbolic preparation for re-entrance into the world of "dead and withered beings that believed themselves alive," by requesting a number of significant things. They are her symbolic armor and mask, and they include cosmetics (". . . no one need pity this corpse if we look properly to the art of the thing" applies not only to her physical mask of cosmetics but to her mask of future behavior); a pair of gloves, which she calls *gauntlets;* and a walking stick. The last object is richly connotative. Its silvery wood and silver knob suggest Miranda's emphasis upon "the art of the thing," the appearance she must maintain. Its purpose is to help her, a kind of cripple, through her journey back again to death. When Towney warns against its expensiveness and comments that walking is hardly worth it, Miranda's "You're right" is an assured and cynical answer which arises out of her awareness of the symbolic act implied. Her mental image of herself as Lazarus come forth with "top hat and stick" is a dual vision of herself as he has been and as she will be in the world where appearances must be maintained; imagistically, we have come full circle again to the "disturbing oppositions" of that world of appearances. She is, with her walking stick, herself the pale rider, unhorsed and alone now, crippled by her first journey and preparing for her next: "Now there would be time for everything."

Katherine Anne Porter's "Holiday"

John Edward Hardy

In "Holiday," first published in 1960, Katherine Anne Porter treated in a complex comic mode the themes of bestiality and human recognition which are central to the satiric tragedy of *Ship of Fools*.

The long story is told, it would seem many years after it happened, by an unnamed woman whom it is probably most convenient to identify with Miss Porter herself. Seeking escape from certain unspecified troubles, the narrator asks the advice of a friend in choosing a place for an isolated and inexpensive spring holiday. The friend makes arrangements for her to go to the Texas farm home of an immigrant German family, "not far from the Louisiana line," where she herself has spent a summer vacation. In her description, it is all very charming:

> "I know the very place," said Louise, "a family of real old-fashioned German peasants, in the deep blackland Texas farm country, a household in real patriarchal style . . . Old father, God Almighty himself, with whiskers and all; Old mother, matriarch in men's shoes; endless daughters and sons and sons-in-law and fat babies falling about the place; and fat puppies . . . cows, calves, and sheep and lambs and goats and turkeys and guineas roaming up and down the shallow green hills, ducks and geese on the ponds."

When the narrator arrives, "tossed off like an express package from a dirty little crawling train onto the sodden platform of a country station," she is considerably disheartened. The March landscape of desolate, muddy fields, swept over by a bitter wind, gives little promise of the summer opulence her friend pictured.

The family are the simple, healthy, hardworking people she has been promised. They are not inhospitable. But eternally busy, and clannish, speaking German among themselves, they leave her alone most of the time. And she is actually grateful for this, since it leaves her free to think through her own problems—during long hours in her attic room, and, as spring approaches, on solitary walks through the orchard and along a path beside the river. She feels comfortingly surrounded, but not confined, by the life of the family.

Reprinted with permission of the author from the *Southern Literary Messenger* 1 (1975): 1–5.

I liked the thick warm voices, and it was good not to have to understand what they were saying. I loved that silence which means freedom from the constant pressure of other minds and other opinions and other feelings, that freedom to fold up in quiet and go back to my own center.

But there is more than a touch of the merely brutish in the Müllers' rude earthiness. The patriarchal rule of the old man over the three generations of his family who inhabit the farm is revealed more and more clearly as a ruthless tyranny. The women, who wait on the men hand and foot, are permitted to keep up only a tenuous attachment to their hereditary Lutheran faith, for the basic ritual purposes of weddings, christenings, and funerals. The patriarch himself, ironically the richest landowner in the county, is an inveterate student of Karl Marx, but in no way morally enlightened by his studies.

The weekly dances at the *Turnverein*, in a building located on land owned by old Müller himself, provide the family almost their only opportunity for social contact with the neighbors. They speak a low German dialect so corrupted by three generations of its isolated use in America that it would be unintelligible anywhere else in the world. With their intellects trained by the broken lights of a neglected religion and the old man's eccentric reading of Marx, the Müllers pursue an existence that only the most determined sentimentalist could see as anything but sadly benighted and brutalizing. The capacity for human cruelty that underlies their animal good spirits is most obviously revealed in their treatment of the dumb and deformed, crippled serving-girl, Ottilie.

That the poor creature is required to work very hard, preparing and serving the family's huge meals, is not in itself necessarily inhumane. For she seems, despite her afflictions, "tough and wiry." Perhaps, it is suggested, an enforced idleness, depriving her of the opportunity to contribute anything to the family's welfare, would be psychologically more damaging than the exhausting physical labor.

But no one speaks to her, or otherwise recognizes her existence, except to give her orders. She lives in a small, dingy ill-furnished room behind the kitchen. And the narrator has been at the farm some weeks before she discovers, to her peculiar horror, that the wretched Ottilie is not, as she had naturally supposed, a hired servant, but a member of the family.

Apparently recognizing a sympathetic spirit in the visitor, Ottilie shows her an old photograph of a healthy little girl about five years old, whom by sign language, touching the picture and then her own face, she identifies as herself. The child in the picture, the narrator sees, is unmistakably a Müller, with the same heavy blonde hair and round face, the same pale, slightly slanted eyes that characterize all the present generation of youngsters in the family. And at second glance she can dimly but surely make out the broken image of that face in the adult Ottilie's twisted features.

What occurs in the episode of the photograph—something on the order of a classic "recognition scene," with modern improvements—is symbolic of a deeper, mutual human recognition between the narrator and Ottilie. The long, slowly developing story reaches its climax with the account of a great storm that inundates and wrecks the farm. The crops are ruined. Many of the farm animals are lost. The family exhaust themselves trying to save what they can, wading out at the height of the storm to get some of the animals under shelter in the barn, and bringing a drowning lamb into the house to revive it.

The next day, with the rain diminishing, they have begun to take stock and rather calmly to prepare for the work of cleaning up and restoring that faces them. But old Mother Müller has at last overextended herself, and almost before the bewildered family can grasp what is happening, she contracts pneumonia and dies. On the afternoon of the second day thereafter, as soon as the subsiding flood makes the roads accessible, they bury her. And the departure of the family for the funeral provides occasion for the narrator's last encounter with Ottilie.

Awakened from a bad dream by what she first thinks is the howling of a dog, she goes downstairs to find Ottilie sitting alone in the kitchen in a frenzy of inarticulate grief. Clearly, she had wanted to be taken along to their mother's funeral; but the others, as usual, have forgotten her. With the thought of catching up to the procession before it reaches the cemetery, the narrator hitches up a pony to the wobbly, ramshackle spring wagon that is the only vehicle left, and pulls and hauls the helpless Ottilie out of the house and up into the absurd equipage.

It is the same pony and wagon with which one of the younger boys had met the narrator at the railroad station upon her arrival a month before. The harness is a mysterious makeshift of broken straps and bits of rope and twine and twisted wire; the bouncing, lurching wagon threatens to fall apart at any moment, its loose wheels "spinning elliptically in a truly broad comic swagger" as they move out into the rutted road. Glancing apprehensively now and again at the "jovial antics" of the wheels, and holding on to her howling charge to keep her from falling off the seat, the narrator is trying to calculate her chances of overtaking the funeral procession, when suddenly she realizes that the bestial sounds of sorrow that Ottilie was making have changed to something that is "unmistakably laughter." It is a beautiful, bright day, the land coming brilliantly alive after the flood has passed, and a strange joy has touched Ottilie's tortured consciousness.

> The feel of the hot sun on her back, the bright air, the jolly senseless staggering of the wheels, the peacock green of the heavens: something of these had reached her. She was happy and gay, and gurgled and rocked in her seat, leaning upon me and waving loosely about her as if to show me what wonder she saw.

The narrator decides that she will not, after all, try to catch the funeral procession, but makes the most of Ottilie's rare happiness and takes her for a ride down the lane by the orchard to the river. "There would be time . . . to get back to the house before the mourners returned. There would be plenty of time for Ottilie to have a fine supper ready for them. They need not even know she had been gone."

Thus the story ends, with the two strange friends joining in a kind of celebration of the rites of spring—turning their backs on the funeral, the celebration of death, and facing instead toward life. A major achievement of the story is its sensitive and brilliant treatment of the natural setting, the narrator's record of her responses to the phenomena of seasonal change. But the landscape painting is more than background, of course. It is coincident with the narrator's whole purpose in the vacation she spends with the Müllers. The reader is not explicitly told when she plans to leave the farm, but it is clearly to be assumed that her long holiday is ending with this day on which she decides to take "the little stolen holiday" with Ottilie. In her surrender to the ecstasy of the first day of full spring, after the storm, she has found what she came for in the first place. But it seems that it is only with and through Ottilie that the experience is possible. The human sharing is essential. But what justification is there for the narrator's feeling that she *is* sharing something?

In his Twayne series book on Katherine Anne Porter, George Hendrick points out, besides the echoes of Eliot, allusions to two Frost poems in the closing episodes of "Holiday." But Hendrick makes little of the essential differences between the situation in the story and that in either "Stopping By Woods" or "The Road Not Taken." Besides the fact that one of the poems is set in winter and the other in autumn, while "Holiday" is a story of spring, it is essential to observe that Frost's protagonists have no human companions. The speaker in "The Road Not Taken" is entirely alone; the one in "Stopping by Woods" is accompanied only by his horse, to whom he ironically attributes human sensibilities. Observing that in "Holiday" it is Ottilie rather than the pony who becomes restless when the cart is stopped in the road, Hendrick takes only passing notice of the crucial facts that Porter's narrator has both the beast and the human being for companions and that the roles of the two are distinguishable.

The elaborate pattern of animals and their relationships with human beings is of fundamental importance in the development of the moral theme. It is one of the more obvious ironies of the situation that Mother Müller dies as a result of her overexertions in trying to save the animals during the storm, while her daughter Ottilie's human feelings are so callously ignored by the family that they do not even think of taking her along to the funeral.

By the time the narrator turns back on the road to the cemetery, choosing to see the day of death as instead a "lovely, festive afternoon," she has long since come to terms with the Müllers' attitude toward Ottilie, and acquitted them of ultimate culpability in the matter. It is difficult at first for her to understand how even the gentle-hearted Annetje, who "was full of silent, tender solicitudes (for) the kittens, the puppies, the chicks, the lambs and calves . . . seemed to have forgotten that Ottilie was her sister." But she charitably reasons that Annetje as well as the others "forgot her in pure self-defense," ignoring both her obvious physical pain and the possibility of her mental suffering while at the same time expecting her to do her share of the household work.

> It was not a society or a class that pampered its invalids and the unfit. So long as one lived, one did one's share . . . Suffering went with life, suffering and labor.

But the narrator herself, of course, does not belong to that society and that class. And try as she will to imitate the family, she cannot put Ottilie out of mind. She can no more will her out of her consciousness than she can will her out of her life—hoping every day, as she does, that when mealtimes come the twisted body will not stagger through the doorway from the kitchen, that they will find her dead in her room. And, at first glance, her acceptance of Ottilie's sudden change of spirits during the wagon ride might seem to go beyond the terms of her acquittal of the Müllers, on the simple human grounds of "self-defense." It might seem that she now feels she had misinterpreted Ottilie's sorrowful howlings as an expression of truly human grief, in her mother's death and in being denied the right to attend the funeral. Perhaps we are to see Ottilie as having no really human emotions at all, as merely an animal, in short, responding by simplest instinct to the warmth and brightness of the day, whom the narrator sensibly decides she might as well indulge in her mindless merriment while it lasts.

But such an interpretation will not, I think, survive a second reading of the passage. The story's ending is not just grotesquely comical. It is comic, and the comedy is high human comedy.

In the first place, Ottilie's grief is not necessarily invalidated by the delight that so abruptly succeeds it. Such transitions, especially under great emotional stress, are not at all uncommon in normal human experience. It is only that people who lead normally regulated lives are trained by custom to suppress any emotions that are inappropriate to the social occasion. Ottilie, of course, had had no such training in the observance of convention. We may suppose her to be more than a little addled by her long years of exile within the family, and by the evident physical pain that she constantly endures. Perhaps the illness that crippled her and struck her dumb sometime in early childhood also affected her brain. The details of her medical history are not very clear. But there is no indication anywhere that she is totally or constantly mindless. And the emphasis throughout these closing pages of the story is precisely on her human aspects.

It is, when she takes hold on her to keep her from falling out of the wagon, just the narrator's sense of "her realness, her humanity, this shattered being that was a woman" which is so shocking that the narrator herself is on the point of emitting a "doglike howl." The fact that the narrator does *not* howl, does not yield to the hysterical impulse of bestiality, is of crucial importance. She summons her will to sustain her conviction that this "shattered being" is a human being.

To be sure, she reflects: "There was nothing I could do for Ottilie, selfishly as I wished to ease my heart of her; she was beyond my reach as well as any other human reach." But she goes on then to ask herself, "and yet, had I not come nearer to her than I had to anyone else in my attempt to deny and bridge the distance between us, or rather, her distance from me?"

If Ottilie is "beyond . . . human reach," it is essentially in the same way that all human beings are inaccessible to one another. That inaccessibility, indeed, defines the human. It is, paradoxically, the very intensity of her realization that Ottilie cannot be reached which brings the narrator "nearer to her than . . . to anyone else" in human recognition.

Mr. Hatch's Volubility
and Miss Porter's Reserve

Janis P. Stout

When Mr. Homer T. Hatch walks onto the Thompsons' farm and into the world of Katherine Anne Porter's "Noon Wine," we know him at once for the shabby character he is. Why? Simply, or almost simply, because he talks too much. Hatch's talk, at once loose and calculated, violates a set of unspecified but very clear standards Porter has already projected both in her own narrative style and in the contrasts she has drawn between Mr. Thompson, the farmer, and Olaf Helton, his Swedish hired man. These are drawn chiefly as contrasts in conversational patterns, verbal manner. Helton is silent, almost to the point of surliness, Thompson is garrulous, and Hatch voluble. For Porter, this is no small matter. Verbal style is for her an issue of the utmost seriousness, not only aesthetically and as a matter of decorum (very much in the Austenian sense), but morally as well. In "Noon Wine," speech is character, or at any rate, the primary index to character. Within the context of Porter's own concise narrative style, the dialogue of "Noon Wine" takes us to the heart of her elusive artistic and moral vision.

In its outlines, "Noon Wine" is a simple, direct story. Mr. Thompson, a farmer in Texas, hires a handyman, Mr. Helton, who proves to be oddly taciturn (perhaps because his English is limited) but capable and hardworking. Helton's only activity outside his work on the farm is playing a single repetitious tune on the harmonica. After nine years, during which Helton brings the farm from bare subsistence to prosperity, a stranger calling himself Homer T. Hatch comes looking for him and says that Helton is an escaped mental patient who once killed his own brother. When Hatch tells Mr. Thompson that he intends to take Helton back to North Dakota and collect a reward, Thompson kills Hatch with an ax. After this, although he is acquitted of murder, Mr. Thompson spends his time driving around the countryside explaining his innocence to his neighbors. At last, despairing of ever fully exonerating himself, he commits suicide.

Reprinted with permission of Western Illinois University from *Essays in Literature* 12.2 (Fall 1985): 285–93.

Almost deceptively simple, the story well illustrates that quality of limpidness and textual perfection that has both established Porter's reputation as a stylist, a "classical writer,"[1] and made her work so resistant to definition. It is as if the actual verbal structure of the story were simply a transparency laid over a set of real objects and scenes. The images of the story themselves shine through in what Robert Penn Warren has called "a kind of indicative poetry."[2] The author seems to step aside and let her rigorously selected details establish themselves autonomously. That is, the style of "Noon Wine" is not at all an external decoration draped over the skeleton of a story. Indeed, the difficulty of determining what the story is "about" is that its style and its substance are so inseparable. For Porter, manner is matter. As she put it herself, "the style is you."[3] It is this interrelatedness of manner and meaning that is the key to "Noon Wine" and the reason the story occupies such a central position in Porter's work.

The frequently noted economy of Porter's style is particularly evident here in the way she establishes an aura of mystery surrounding Mr. Helton. By avoiding omniscience, limiting herself instead to what Helton tells the Thompsons—very little—and what they can observe of him, Porter forces the reader to share the Thompsons' ignorance and their puzzlement, or what should be their puzzlement. For the Thompsons, the mystery is not pressing. Helton is so unobtrusive that they easily become accustomed to his presence, and so useful that they are glad to accept the benefits of his work without wondering about him as a person. Indeed, the ease with which the Thompsons dismiss the mystery of Helton's character is one of the story's judgments on them. For the reader, however, the mystery is very real, primarily because it is so sharply particularized in Helton's peculiar and slightly ominous fixation on his collection of harmonicas.

This peculiarlity is established in few words, chiefly in two main incidents. When Mrs. Thompson goes out to the hired man's shack on his first day to meet him, she notices his harmonicas and intimates that they may attract the attention of her two little boys. Her husband, she mentions, used to play an old accordion until the boys broke it. At this, Helton "stood up rather suddenly, the chair clattered under him, his knees straightened though his shoulders did not, and he looked at the floor as if he were listening carefully."[4] The reader is tantalized by the intensity of his reaction, but Mrs. Thompson goes imperturbably on, advising Helton to take protective measures. Whereupon, Helton, "in one wide gesture of his long arms, swept his harmonicas up against his chest, and from there transferred them in a row to the ledge where the roof joined the wall. He pushed them back almost out of sight" (p. 228). In the quickness and the absoluteness of the "one wide gesture," the protectiveness of his gathering them "against his chest," and his care to push them "back almost out of sight," Porter conveys how overwhelmingly concerned Helton is for the safekeeping of the harmonicas and creates a mystery as to why he feels so strongly.

Some two years later, a second incident jars the story with its unexpected intensity. Walking back from the garden one spring day, Mrs. Thompson catches sight of Helton wordlessly shaking the two boys, first one and then the other, by the shoulders. His face is "terribly fixed and pale" in a look of "hatred," and the action is performed "ferociously" (pp. 237–38). This brief glimpse of the man's silent fury, which has been evoked by the children's meddling with his harmonicas, fixes him in a dense aura of mystery that is never dissipated. As Thomas Walsh observes, "however he is atomized," the quiet Helton "remains, like Melville's Bartleby, a mystery."[5] He is last seen, at his moment of capture, trying to retrieve two harmonicas that have fallen out of his jumper pocket. The reader is left with the question of why the harmonicas were so important to him.

As the motif of Helton's mystery demonstrates, Porter's concise, disciplined style achieves not only spareness itself but also a clear focus on the telling detail. It achieves also a sense of unspoken depth. In this, perhaps more than in any other way, Porter resembles Jane Austen, to whom she has often been compared for the quality of her irony and her dryness.[6] For both writers, what is unsaid is as important as what is said. We are invited to speculate about the unsaid, and that act of speculation in itself lends weight to the said. This weightiness, this sense that something has been kept in reserve, makes Porter's style indeed, as it has been called, "compact with meaning."[7] Like Austen, she is able to achieve the great in the small.

The standards of conciseness and reserve demonstrated in Porter's narrative style are elaborated in the contrasting speech styles of the characters. As we have noted, Helton is a man of extreme reticence, who never says two words if one will do. On first approaching Mr. Thompson, he announces bluntly, " 'I need work . . . You need a man here?' " (p. 223). In response to Mr. Thompson's roundabout questioning, he gives only the barest facts: his origin (North Dakota), his name, and a terse summary of his qualifications: " 'I can do everything on farm . . . cheap. I need work' " (p. 223). Later, when Mrs. Thompson comes out to introduce herself, he says even less, a total of ten words to her two hundred and sixteen. His silence is emphasized by narrative comment: "Not a word from Mr. Helton" (p. 229). Mr. Thompson finds him " 'the closest mouthed fellow I ever met up with' " (p. 229).

Mr. Thompson himself is not close-mouthed at all. We see from the start that he is given to empty talk, filling conversational space just for the sake of filling it. When Helton approaches him asking for work, he replies with extraneous chat about his previous two hired hands. When Helton says where he is from, Thompson muses vacantly, " 'North Dakota . . . That's a right smart distance off, seems to me' " (p. 223). Sensing a bargain at hand, he warms to a forced geniality, saying "in his most carrying voice" that he guesses that they had better " 'talk turkey' " (p. 223). Porter adds that in business dealings Thompson "grew very hearty and jovial" to disguise his dislike of spending money (p. 224). It is more an amusing fault than a vicious one, but in this small way Mr. Thompson does use a friendly manner and a stream of talk to dissemble. It is a point worth noting, since it will contribute to the pattern of doubling developed later in the story. In sum, Mr. Thompson is a "hearty good fellow among men" (p. 234), or as Frederick Hoffman says,[8] a man of "broad, self-sustained" speech who cares greatly for "his dignity and his reputation" among his neighbors (p. 233). Each aspect of Mr. Thompson established here in such brief terms will come to bear on the ending of the story.

The contrast between Helton and Thompson is particularly evident in their different disciplinary approaches to the two Thompson boys. Mr. Thompson is all bluster, making dire threats and working himself up into rages (p. 240), with little effect. By contrast, the one time Helton is seen chastising the boys he does so without a word, and they remember it. Indeed, when we see them after Helton has been on the farm nine years, they are no longer disorderly but "good solid boys" (p. 242). Helton's effect on the boys is typical of his effectiveness in general. He gets things done. By contrast, Mr. Thompson is generally ineffectual, as much in his farming as in his child-rearing. He is harmless and well-intentioned, but full of false pride and excuses for not getting things done, and under his management the farm is generally run down. We cannot say that there is any cause and effect relationship, but the story firmly associates Mr. Thompson's kind of talkativeness with shiftlessness or shallowness and, positively, associates reserve with dignity and workmanlike performance. The person with a reserved demeanor is accorded more respect than the big talker. Still waters, Porter seems to indicate, do indeed run deep.

It is no wonder, then, that Mr. Hatch enters the story on so jarring a note, with his roar of false joviality and his unfunny joke. We see at once that his waters, which are far from still, do not run deep. Yet, in a sense, they do. Or more precisely, Mr. Hatch roils his waters to keep the bottom hidden. Almost as soon as we decide he is not deep, we decide that we do not trust him.

Mr. Hatch has, as Porter says, a "free manner" (p. 243). He introduces himself senselessly by saying he has come about buying a horse, then explains wordily that he didn't mean it, he only says that to draw people into conversation. This small ploy warns us, here is a man not entirely to be trusted. Hatch's boisterous laughter elicits an echoing laugh from Mr. Thompson but, significantly, a limited one ("haw haw" rather than "haw haw haw"). Mr. Thompson, too, is on the alert. He has noticed that the "expression in the man's eyes didn't match the sound he was making" (p. 243). Later, when Mr. Thompson laughs at his own witticism about youth breaking out like measles all over a person but leaving "no ill effects" (p. 245), Mr. Hatch's laugh is again the louder and longer, "a kind of fit." And once again Mr. Thompson notices that it doesn't ring true, that Hatch "was laughing for reasons of his own" (p. 245).

Hatch's talk is shot through with simple untruth. He claims to be from Georgia and to have family "up the country a ways" (p. 244), but later refers to things "back home in North Dakota" (p. 251). He claims he wants to have "a little talk" with Mr. Helton, but actually wants to capture him. Worse than that, though, his talk is purposely, deviously false; it is used for ulterior motives, false in a calculating sense. His opening gambit about the horse, which he calls "an old joke of mine" (p. 243), is admittedly a ploy, a calculated use of language to ingratiate himself so he can pursue other motives. When he later says that a reference to Mr. Helton's having been in an asylum "just slipped out" (p. 247), we know it was no slip, even though it is precisely the kind of careless mischief that might be worked by a voluble man. Indeed, he counts on Mr. Thompson's thinking so. He has played on his own volubility to set up his "slip." Hatch is more than a loose talker; he is a man practiced in devious talk.

Hatch's effect on Mr. Thompson is to evoke not only irritation and profound dis-ease, but, at the same time, echoing behavior, like the echoing "haw haw." Indeed, it is partly because he does evoke echoing behavior in Mr. Thompson that he evokes Mr. Thompson's dis-ease. Hatch sets off a series of false conversational leads that take Mr. Thompson down branching by-ways of empty talk. Hatch's explanation of why he uses the ploy about the horse leads Thompson to explain needlessly that he always trusts a person until he has reason not to, an explanation that clouds the conversational air by raising the possibility of untrustworthiness. Hatch's reference to family origins leads to Mr. Thompson's defensive claim to a long family history in this part of Texas, provoking Hatch to ask if they first came from Ireland, provoking Mr. Thompson to ask why he thinks so. And so it goes. The simple cutting of tobacco plugs leads to a page-long exchange on types and prices of chewing tobacco, with mounting overtones of mutual disparagement and hostility. Hatch's volubility evokes even more needless talk than Thompson would usually indulge in. In this respect, Hatch is Thompson writ large, the enlarged mirror image of Thompson's back-slapping "public" self.[9]

Hatch becomes Mr. Thompson's double, a "grotesque parody of Thompson's own nature,"[10] reflecting and magnifying his accustomed patterns of behavior and his latent feelings. Hatch has the same glad-handed volubility, but raised to a pitch that provokes Thompson's, and the reader's, distrust. When Mr. Thompson defends Helton for his steady, sober behavior, mentioning in passing that he " 'never got married' " and concluding that " 'if he's crazy . . . I think I'll go crazy myself for a change,' " Hatch laughs uproariously and picks up on that wish in a surprising way: " 'Yeah, that's right! Let's all go crazy and get rid of our wives and save our money, hey?' " Dismayed at the twist of his conversational line, Thompson feels he is "being misunderstood" (p. 247). Again, when Mr. Thompson remarks on his wife's poor health and their high medical bills, Hatch takes him up vigorously: " 'I never had much use for a woman always complainin'. I'd get rid of her mighty quick' " (p. 248). Poor Mr. Thompson has not meant to wish himself rid of his wife, or at any rate he has not thought he meant that. But his situation does make it plausible that he might harbor the repressed urges that Hatch expressed so baldly. Mr. Thompson thinks to himself that Hatch "certainly did remind" him of "somebody" (p. 244) but, stifling the realization that it is himself he is reminded of, decides he must be mistaken.

More surprisingly, Helton, too, becomes Mr. Thompson's double. As we have seen, Mr. Thompson is given to empty talk, while Helton is taciturn. The two are opposites. Yet Hatch takes Mr. Thompson for an Irishman, just as Mr. Thompson earlier took Helton for an Irishman. Helton kills his brother abruptly and apparently without warning on a hot day; Mr. Thompson suddenly and without thought kills Hatch on a day of "almost unbearable" heat (pp. 242 and 252). Helton is a stranger in the land; Mr. Thompson, for all his family roots and his familiarity, becomes a stranger after his act of murder.[11] Helton is never able to express himself in words to anyone; Mr. Thompson is never able, either during his trial or afterward, to convey to anyone his sense of what has happened.

Indeed, in the last section of the story, when Mr. Thompson drives from one neighbor's farm to another trying to justify himself to them, he acts out his relation of doubling both to Helton and to Hatch. We have seen that Mr. Thompson is very anxious about the esteem of his neighbors, his good name among them. He cannot live with the suspicion that they no longer consider him respectable, particularly since he himself can no longer feel absolutely certain of his own rectitude. Compulsively, he goes over and over it in his own mind, and over and over it to his neighbors. Like Helton he is isolated by his inability to explain himself, but like Hatch he is voluble in the attempt. It is a painful sequence; we share Mrs. Thompson's embarrassment, sitting "with her hands knotted together" and listening to her husband repeat his story, and we share Mr. Thompson's chagrin as he sees "something in all their faces that disheartened him" (p. 262). At the end of the story, writing his suicide note, Mr. Thompson makes one more attempt to explain his motives and his view of what happened. But when he writes the words "my wife" he stops, thinks a while, and obliterates the two words before finishing with a concise summary statement: "It was Mr. Homer T. Hatch who came to do wrong to a harmless man. He caused all this trouble and he deserved to die but I am sorry it was me who had to kill him" (p. 268). He has recognized both the futility and the indignity of continuing with lengthy pleas that would throw into public view more and more of his private life and feelings. That he recognizes this, that he chooses instead to cut off his plea with the most direct, unembellished statement he can make, is a measure of his increased stature. Both in its conciseness, its avoidance of wordy grovelling before an unsympathetic, but very curious, public, and in its honesty, his suicide note is also a measure of his distance from Mr. Hatch.

The kind of lesson Mr. Thompson learns in "Noon Wine" is for Porter the key to real dignity. Her characters are measured personally by the adequacy, the honesty, and the economy of their language. Not that she holds Mr. Helton up as a standard of measurement. Though he is at the opposite extreme from the voluble and disagreeable Hatch, his limited, halting speech is clearly shown to be a deficiency and an impediment. To be sure, it is clear that in the ambiguous world of "Noon Wine," Helton occupies a much higher position in the reader's and the author's esteem than does Hatch. If we must choose, we take honest deficiency over devious excess. Indeed, for most of the story Helton occupies a higher position, despite his limitation and his oddity, than Mr. Thompson, who is simply an ineffectual babbler until he learns to maintain the dignity of reserve. Characters in other stories who are similarly shown as being both talkative and weak include Mrs. Whipple, of "He," and Uncle Gabriel, of "Old Mortality." The child Miranda sees through Uncle Gabriel at once. In "Pale Horse, Pale Rider," the young women "wallowing in good works" (p. 275) and the War Bond solicitors mouthing jingoistic slogans about "the Huns overrunning martyred Belgium" (p. 273) also define themselves as unworthy in contrast to Miranda's tight-lipped resistance to all the "perfect nonsense" around her (p. 283).

For Porter, indulgence in loose talk betrays lack of discipline, lack of personal integrity. She chooses as the elect of her fictional world characters who view life with dry detachment and resist spreading out their private griefs before the muddying feet of the multitude. We hear the same note in her approving comment on Eudora Welty: "She considers her personal history as hardly worth mentioning."[12] By contrast, Porter turns her devastating mockery on Gertrude Stein largely because of the latter's apparent conviction that anything was "important because it happened to her and she was writing about it."[13] The standard she invokes in these judgments of others is the same standard by which she governed her own stance before the public and her own fictional presence. It was a standard, or "code," of "decorum, grace, toughmindedness, and control."[14] The most biographical of Porter's commentators has complained that she was "extremely reticent in revealing biographical information."[15] One thinks, by way of contrast, of F. Scott Fitzgerald or Hart Crane, writers very much engaged in playing up their own personalities. But the reserve that is an inconvenience for the biographer is the source of Porter's distinctive voice and, perhaps, her strength. She was able at once to utilize her personal experience and to efface the pecularities of self and self-concern in order to focus her attention and her language fully on the work at hand, the object of contemplation. Observing this quality of self-effacement, or reserve, her friend Glenway Wescott said that "in fiction she has been free from herself" and has "maintained a maximum impersonality, a disengagement from any sort of autobiographical point of view."[16]

Other critics, noting this quality of personal and narrative reserve, have not been so positive in their response. William L. Nance, for instance, admits a wish that Porter "would paint with bolder, broader strokes" and "wouldn't be so cautious."[17] John W. Aldridge speaks sneeringly of the "paucity" of her production as "the mark of a talent so fine that it can scarcely bring itself to function" and finds the "purity of her English" to be a "testimony to . . . psychic and artistic limitations."[18] More often, critics have praised her as a stylist, extolling the clarity and spareness of her language and its aptness to her concise forms. But references to limitation or preciousness recur as frequently with regard to Porter as they do with regard to Austen. Both have made critics uncomfortable. Since the early comments of the 1930s, even when critics have lauded Porter's work, they have often confessed themselves unable to say exactly why they esteemed her so highly or to define the unifying character or themes of her work. Nance, in the study that has become widely accepted as the standard account of Porter's work, has identified her dominant theme as "rejection," while more recently Jane De Mouy argues that it is the divided nature, or "fragmentation and vulnerability," of women.[19] In short, although Porter's conciseness and restraint have been recognized and generally praised, anything like a definitive assessment of her work or her place in the literary hierarchy has eluded the critical establishment.

The key, I believe, is to see the unity of Porter's work. Critics who have spoken of her concise style as her most notable characteristic have been essentially correct, but have not accorded their perception its full weight. It has been said of "Noon Wine" that its " 'logic' . . . is the same as its character."[20] Much the same can be said of Porter's work as a whole. Its logic—that is, its formal arrangement and the texture of its rhetoric, the argument its language makes—is at one with its fullest meaning. Porter's fiction both affirms and enacts the positive value of reserve as a defense against falling into bathetic excess and falsity. The same standard that informs her judgment of character and her own artistic presence informs her dry, quiet style. It is all of a piece. In characters, a bent toward idle patter implies, as we have seen, a tendency toward self-indulgence, self-importance, and distortion, even deviousness. Porter equates restraint with honesty and authenticity as she judges, and as she practices, verbal style. Grandstanding is not tolerated.

In this way, as in others, Porter is closely akin to Jane Austen, whose work is equally governed by the standard of decorum and characterized by restraint and the weight of the unsaid. Porter stated in an interview that Austen's work did not "really engage" her until she was "quite mature."[21] Her statement may imply a limited influence, but surely points to an affinity of real substance, the mature discovery of a congenial mind. For Porter, as for Austen, manner is not just surface, but a revelation of essence. Manner, or style, is an indicator of character, serious and to be taken seriously. Their fiction is very much "about" the connection between substance and manner. Mr. Hatch and the lesser villains and clowns of Porter's fiction define themselves by their garrulous, unreliable way of speaking, just as her tight-lipped

Miranda and Porter herself, with her spare incisiveness, define themselves by their reserve.

Notes

1.   M. M. Liberman, *Katherine Anne Porter's Fiction* (Detroit: Wayne State Univ. Press, 1971), p. 52.

2.   Robert Penn Warren, "Irony with a Center, Katherine Anne Porter (1941–52)," in *Selected Essays* (New York: Random House, 1958), p. 144.

3.   Barbara Thompson, "Katherine Anne Porter: An Interview," *Paris Review*, 8, No. 29 (1963), 107.

4.   Katherine Anne Porter, *The Collected Stories of Katherine Anne Porter* (New York: Harcourt, Brace and World, 1965), p. 228. Further references will be noted within the text.

5.   Thomas F. Walsh, "Deep Similarities in 'Noon Wine,' " *Mosaic*, 9 (1975), 87.

6.   Robert B. Heilman, "*Ship of Fools;* Notes on Style," *Four Quarters,* 1962; rpt. Lodwick Hartley and George Core, ed., *Katherine Anne Porter: A Critical Symposium* (Athens: Univ. of Georgia Press, 1969), p. 203.

7.   M. Wynn Thomas, "Strangers in a Strange Land: A Reading of 'Noon Wine,' " *American Literature,* 47 (1975), p. 245.

8.   Frederick J. Hoffman, *The Art of Southern Fiction: A Study of Some Modern Novelists* (Carbondale: Southern Illinois Univ. Press, 1967), p. 45.

9.   Walsh, p. 90.

10.   Hoffman, p. 46.

11.   Thomas, p. 246.

12.   Katherine Anne Porter, *The Days Before* (New York: Harcourt, Brace and Co., 1952), p. 101.

13.   Porter, *The Days Before,* p. 47.

14.   Lodwick Hartley and George Core, "Introduction," in *Katherine Anne Porter: A Critical Symposium,* p. xvii.

15.   George Hendrick, *Katherine Anne Porter* (New York: Twayne, 1965), p. 15.

16.   Glenway Wescott, "Katherine Anne Porter Personally," in *Images of Truth: Remembrances and Criticism* (New York: Harper and Row, 1962), p. 35.

17.   William L. Nance, S. M., *Katherine Anne Porter and the Art of Rejection* (Chapel Hill: Univ. of North Carolina Press, 1963), p. 312.

18.   John W. Aldridge, "Art and Passion in Katherine Anne Porter," in *Time to Murder and Create: The Contemporary Novel in Crisis* (New York: David McKay, 1966), pp. 179–81.

19.   Jane Krause De Mouy, *Katherine Anne Porter's Women: The Eye of Her Fiction* (Austin: Univ. of Texas Press, 1983), p. 9.

20.   Thomas, p. 245.

21.   Thompson, p. 5.

[Art and Malignity in Porter's "The Leaning Tower"]

WILLENE HENDRICK AND GEORGE HENDRICK

"The Leaning Tower" (1941) is set in Berlin at the time Porter lived there in 1931–32, and in the story she used many people she knew and events she witnessed or experienced.[1] For instance when she and [Eugene] Pressly were looking over a pension, Pressly touched a fragile replica of the Leaning Tower of Pisa and it crumbled. As [Joan Givner] notes, Porter then lashed out at him: "Why must you touch things? Why must you always touch and destroy things?"[2] Porter herself appears as the central character Charles Upton, and his friend Kuno is based on her childhood friend Erna Schlemmer. One can properly ask why Porter assumed the persona of a male. Givner thinks it "possibly reflects her identification with Eugene Pressly during the Berlin period."[3]

Many of the characters in the story are named for people Porter met in Berlin, but with their characteristics sometimes changed. For instance, she rather liked her own landlady, but Rosa Reichl in the story becomes a disagreeable tyrant. In other instances, Porter seems to have used characteristics of other people she had known, as in the character of Tadeusz Mey who takes on fragments from the life of Joseph Retinger, one of Porter's lovers in Mexico during the early 1920s.[4]

Some journal notes Porter made in December 1931 are also useful for understanding the background of her story. A young poet she knew in Berlin objected that she should not bother reading Rilke's *Elegies:* "He belongs to the old romantic softheaded Germany that has been our ruin. The new Germany is hard, strong, we will have a new race of poets, tough and quick, like your prize fighters." The poet gave Porter some of his poems, and she found that the "words were tough and the rhythms harsh, the ideas all the most grossly brutal; and yet, it was vague weak stuff in the end."[5]

In another note she describes a conversation with L. [unidentified] and von G. [Göring] about Nietzsche: "Nietzsche is dangerous because his mind

Reprinted with permission of the authors and Twayne from Willene Hendrick and George Hendrick, *Katherine Anne Porter* (Boston: Twayne, 1988), 90–96.

has power without intelligence; he is all will without enlightenment. His phrases are inflated, full of violence, a gross kind of cruel poetry—like Wagner's music. They both throw a hypnotic influence over their hearers. But I could always resist hypnotists. When I think of Nietzsche and Wagner . . . I find charlatans. . . . And madness. In Nietzsche's case . . . his diseased brain gave his style the brilliance of a rotting fish. L. and von G. worship them both with a religious awe."6 In 1941 she captured, in her short novel, much of the spirit of that impression and rumination of 1931.

In 1932, still in Berlin Porter wrote that R. [not otherwise identified] was a man filled with maliciousness, one who spoke evil of everyone, and he told her that she could know nothing of the higher levels of religious experience because "religious experience belongs exclusively to the masculine principle." Without seeing the irony of his words, he assured her that "only ample, generous natures are capable of the love of God."7 Porter reflected some of these philosophical, religious, and aesthetic statements in "The Leaning Tower," and she also incorporates the malignity she saw in German society that she was writing about in her journal in 1931 and 1932.

The story may be divided into five major parts: the café as a place of memory, of Charles's childhood illusions of Germany and the reality he now sees; the search for a new room and the exit from the hotel; the new room and the inhabitants of the pension; the night club; and the final revelation in the room. Charles Upton, from whose point of view we see the events, is given a background similar to Porter's. Sensitive but, like Miranda, naive, he came from a central Texas farming family with Kentucky ties; and he had, against the initial wishes of his family, been interested in art—just as Porter, against the wishes of her family, had determined to be a writer. He had come to Berlin largely because of his boyhood friendship with Kuno Hillentafel, who had died on a trip to his homeland and whose mother was alleged to have been a countess. Through a romantic projection of Kuno's descriptions, Charles had imagined Berlin to be a great city of castles towering in the mists.

Alone in the strange city that Christmas season, left with his memories of Kuno, Charles finds Berlin depressing as he sits in the café. Among the heavy buildings are heavy, piglike people or slim young students all dressed alike; he had seen in his few days in the city the desperate poverty of the country, the streetwalkers, the beggars. His impressions had been harsh and poignant. The shock of being in a strange city and culture have robbed him even of sexual desire, and he has been unable to show interest in the streetwalkers. His impressions are not ordered; his is not a reflective mind, and he cannot generalize about the German society he finds so disturbing. He is storing his impressions for his drawings, which can be brutally accurate, as when he sketches the hotel owners: the woman as a sick fox and the man as half-pig, half-tiger. Charles's isolation is total, and the larger the crowd he finds himself in, the more isolated he becomes.

The rush of impressions subsides as Charles sets out to search for a room, for the rooms fall into an easily distinguished pattern of stuffy, faded elegance or expensive modernity. At the apartment of Frau Rosa Reichl—she had once been rich, had employed many servants, but now lived in reduced but not poverty-stricken circumstances—he accidentally breaks a plaster souvenir of the Leaning Tower of Pisa, a tottering structure in actuality and, in replica, a fitting symbol of a society soon itself to fall. Frau Reichl is aware of the significance of Charles's blunder. Outwardly she sees the fragile souvenir as a memento of her honeymoon, but it had also come to be a symbol of her cherished past. Charles can see that she regrets having left it out for crude foreigners to touch.

When Charles announces his intentions of leaving the hotel where he has been staying, the hotel owners lost all civility. He is outrageously overcharged, threatened with police action if he protests the bill, and intimidated by passport inspection—he had been told he would feel like a criminal in Germany.

The outward bestiality disappears once he moves into Rosa's room. On the day of his move, he learns, in a quiet scene in a barber shop, that a shouting politician (obviously Hitler) had made one particular hair style popular. This third section of the story presents Rosa's apartment, and the inhabitants as a microcosm of German society in 1931, but since Porter includes only three Germans, one American, and one Pole, her cast is limited. Charles says of Rosa and the guests: "They were all good people, they were in terrible trouble, jammed up together in this little flat with not enough air or space or money, not enough of anything, no place to go, nothing to do but gnaw each other." Charles has the best room and pays the most rent because Americans are thought to be rich. This mythic wealth also protects him from Rosa's sharp tongue, but her favorite in the house is Hans von Gehring (Porter's name for Hermann Goering), an aristocratic-looking young man, a student at Heidelberg, where he had fought a duel and is now receiving treatment for his infected wound. Charles wants to like the young man, but he is unable to comprehend a society that admires such barbaric acts. He rejects the wound and everything that allows such behavior, even though he had seen the antique dueling pistols of his own great-grandfather. Hans is proud of his scar, often fingers it, and Charles sees in the young man's face his true nature: "amazing arrogance, pleasure, inexpressible vanity and self-satisfaction."

Rosa's scapegoat is Herr Otto Bussen, a Platt Deutsch, whose inferior social station and poverty give Rosa license to intimidate and demean him at every opportunity. That he is a brilliant student at the university makes no difference to Frau Reichl. When Herr Bussen poisons himself, accidentally or otherwise, she is as concerned about her rugs as about his health.

The other lodger, Tadeusz Mey, a Polish-Austrian pianist and a cosmopolitan at home in London and Paris, is living in Berlin because there is a good teacher there. Mey is aware of the evils in society and opposes them, but he is cynical enough to study and live in a corrupt German society.

In a dream Charles's premonitions about the society, as personified by the house and its inhabitants, surface vividly. The house is burning, pulsing with fire. Charles walks from the building with all the paintings he would ever do in his life. When he turns to look back, he thinks at first that they have all escaped, but he hears a ghostly groan and sees no one. Symbolically Charles knows that he could and would walk away from a society that was destroying itself and its members. His artistic creations are more important to him than any attempt to save the unsavable, to save those who, we must assume, would misunderstand his act and turn on him ferociously. Charles does not reflect on his dream when he wakens, stifling in the feather coverlets, and he does not think of it when he considers giving an extra coat to Herr Bussen, an act that Mey says would be a great mistake.

The story then moves from the rooming house to a newly opened, middle-class bar where the young men go to celebrate the New Year. In many ways, this section confirms Tadeusz's view that losing the war damaged the "nation's personality," but it goes beyond that to search for personality traits that were established long before the war. At the night club, Charles sees a variety of Germans in a social setting: Lutte, a thin, blonde model, to Hans a perfect German type; a large barmaid, attractive to Herr Bussen; two movie stars; and a large crowd of noisy, sentimental revelers.

As the conversation swirls on into a long discussion of races and cultures, fat Otto, an aspiring intellectual, insists that "the true great old Germanic type is lean and tall and fair as gods." Charles, who like Miranda has rejected the mythic view of a "splendid past" that his parents had taught him, cannot compete in the conversation since he knows almost no history. Drawn into the gaiety of the night, he dances with Lutte, but finds that she is interested in him only if he can get her to Hollywood. She soon turns her attention to the more aristocratic Hans. Tadeusz speaks of his family, which has lived in the same house for eight centuries, of the stifling society of his childhood, of the anti-Semitic attitudes implicit in religious dogma; his memories of the past are mixed, "something between a cemetery and a Lost Paradise." Otto, who grew up in a Lutheran family, speaks of his dismal childhood, of building his life on a romantic view of Luther, and of his apparent willingness to follow anyone he sees as great.

At midnight, nobody notices the irony when a wooden cuckoo announces the New Year. A toast is drunk, a "disordered circle formed," and there is much sinning and drunken revelry until "the circle broke up, ran together, whirled, loosened, fell apart." This tourists' Germany of light-hearted gaiety cannot last, and the young men have to get the drunken Otto home, his befuddled moribund state symbolic of the German intellectual. As he is carried past Rosa, she looks at her young men fondly. In his drunken state Charles sees (or thinks he sees) the Leaning Tower, now repaired, behind the glass door of the cabinet, and he knows he can crush again the frail, useless thing—it is "a whimsical pain in the neck . . . yet [it] had some kind of meaning" that tries to break into his consciousness but cannot. He feels a "desolation of the spirit" because he is beginning to see that the society is going to fall, that it will involve him, and that there is nothing he will do. "He didn't feel sorry for himself," but he does know that "no crying jag or any other kind of jag would ever, in this world, do anything at all for him."

The story has many brilliantly conceived scenes; it is not the failure that many critics have found it to be. Charles has vague portents of the meaning of what he sees; in his dream, he realizes the society is facing destruction, and he has learned that his initial reaction to the Germans is true: "They were the very kind of people that Holbein, Dürer and Urs Graf had drawn . . . their late-medieval faces full of hallucinated malice and a kind of sluggish but intense cruelty that worked its way up from their depths slowly through the layers of helpless gluttonous fat."

"The Germans," Porter said in an interview in the 31 March 1962 *Saturday Review*, "are against anybody and everybody, and they haven't changed a bit." She never believed reconciliation with the German people was possible. In "The Leaning Tower" she was engaged in an early literary probing of the German problem, of the nature and meaning of evil; she was to continue that study in *Ship of Fools*.

Notes

1.   Charles Allen, "The Nouvelles of Katherine Anne Porter," *University of Kansas City Review* 29 (December 1962), 92–93; Jane DeMouy, *Katherine Anne Porter's Women: The Eye of Her Fiction* (Austin: University of Texas Press, 1983), 6–7, 177; Joan Givner, *Katherine Anne Porter: A Life* (New York: Simon & Schuster, 1982), 47, 61, 152, 254, 268, 319–22, 329, 340, 603–4, 607, 611; John Edward Hardy, *Katherine Anne Porter* (New York: Frederick Ungar, 1973), 8, 113, 115; James William Johnson, "Another Look at Katherine Anne Porter," *Virginia Quarterly Review* 36 (Autumn 1960), 603–4, 607, 611; M. M. Liberman, *Katherine Anne Porter's Fiction* (Detroit: Wayne State University Press, 1971), 95–103; Enrique Hank Lopez, *Conversations with Katherine Anne Porter: Refugee from Indian Creek* (Boston: Little, Brown & Co., 1981), 173–74, 178–79, 242–44; Harry John Mooney, Jr., *The Fiction and Criticism of Katherine Anne Porter* (Pittsburgh: University of Pittsburgh Press, 1957), 34–38; William L. Nance, S. M., *Katherine Anne Porter & the Art of Rejection* (Chapel Hill: University of North Carolina Press, 1964), 69–79; Marjorie Ryan, "*Dubliners* and the Stories of Katherine Anne Porter," *American Literature* 31 (January 1960), 472–73; Darlene Harbour Unrue, *Truth and Vision in Katherine Anne Porter's Fiction* (Athens: University of Georgia Press, 1985), 139–45; Ray B. West, Jr., *Katherine Anne Porter* (Minneapolis: University of Minnesota Press, 1963), 30–32; Edmund Wilson, "Katherine Anne Porter," in *Classics and Commercials* (New York: Farrar, Straus, & Co., 1950), 220–21; Vernon A. Young, "The Art of Katherine Anne Porter," in *American Thought— 1947* (New York: Gresham Press, 1947), 234–37.

2.   Givner, 254.

3. *Ibid.,* 319. Kuno Hillendahl was the name of Porter's sister Baby's first husband. Porter also named the Mullers' dog [in "Holiday"] "Kuno."

4. *Ibid.,* 320.

5. Katherine Anne Porter, "Notes on Writing," *The Collected Essays and Occasional Writings of Katherine Anne Porter* (New York: Delacorte Press, 1970), 443.

6. *Ibid.*

7. *Ibid.*

Ship of Fools: Notes on Style

ROBERT B. HEILMAN

I

Katherine Anne Porter is sometimes thought of as a stylist. "Stylist" is likely to call up unclear images of coloratura, acrobatics, elaborateness of gesture, a mingling of formalism probably euphuistic with conspicuous private variations, like fingerprints. It might call to mind Edward Dahlberg's peremptory dense texture of crusty archaism and thorny image, a laboriously constructed thicket so well guarding the estate of his mind that it often becomes that estate. It is not so with Miss Porter. There is nothing of arresting facade in her style, nothing of showmanship. Though on the lecture platform she can be all showman, and slip into the prima donna, in her proper medium both the public personality and the private being vanish from the stage. At least they are not easily detectable presences. In *Ship of Fools*[1] the style is a window of things and people, not a symbolic aggression of ego upon them. It seems compelled by the objects in the fiction; it is their visible surface, the necessary verbal form that makes their identity perceivable. It seems never the construction of an artist imposing, from her own nature, an arbitrary identity upon inert materials, but rather an emanation of the materials themselves, finding through the artist as uninterfering medium the stylistic mold proper to their own nature. Miss Porter is ruling all, of course, but she seems not to be ruling at all: hence of her style we use such terms as "distance," "elegance," and of course the very word for what she seems to have ceded, "control." She is an absentee presence: in one sense her style is no-style. Nostyle is what it will seem if style means some notable habit of rhythm or vocabulary, some uninterchangeable (though not unborrowable) advice that firmly announces "Faulkner" or "Hemingway." Miss Porter has no "signal" or call letters that identify a single station of wave length. She does not introduce herself or pre-

Reprinted with permission of La Salle University from *Four Quarters* 12 (November 1962): 46–55. Copyright La Salle University.

sent herself. Much less does she gesticulate. She does not pray on street corners; wrestle with her subject in public as if she were barely managing to
throw a troublesome devil; or lash her tail and arch her back like a cat
demonstrating expertise with a mouse. She does not cry "Look, ma, no
hands"; she just leaves hands out of it. Her style has neither birthmarks nor
those plaintive rebirth-marks, tattoos. Not that she disdains embellishment;
in her there is nothing of unwashed Kate in burlap ("I am life"). Nor, on the
other hand, is there anything of frilly femininity tendering little dainties from
a fragile sensibility ("I am beauty," "I am feeling").

II

No-style means a general style, if we may risk such a term, a fusion of proved
styles. She can do ordinary documentary whenever it is called for: the ship's
passengers "advertised on little thumbtacked slips of paper that they had lost
or found jeweled combs, down pillows, tobacco pouches, small cameras,
pocket mirrors, rosaries." Here she sticks to nouns; yet she has no fear of the
adjectives somewhat in disrepute now: "In the white heat of an early August
morning a few placid citizens of the white-linen class strolled across the hard-
baked surface of the public square under the dusty shade of the sweet-by-
night trees . . ." She relies without embarrassment on the plain, direct, ordinary, explicit. Veracruz "is a little purgatory"; Amparo decided "prematurely"
that trouble was over. "Herr Lowenthal, who had been put at a small table by
himself, studied the dinner card, with its list of unclean foods, and asked for a
soft omelette with fresh green peas. He drank half a bottle of good wine to
comfort himself . . ."

On such sturdy foundations of style she can build in several ways. Without altering the everyday, matter-of-fact manner, she gets below the surface.
Glocken, the hunchback, "scared people off; his plight was so obviously desperate they were afraid some of it would rub off on them." "Rub off": imaging casually a world of prophylactic finickiness. Captain Thiele paces the deck
"alone, returning the respectful salutations of the passengers with reluctant
little jerks of his head, upon which sat a monumental ornate cap, white as
plaster." The commonplace comparison, dropped in without commotion at
the end, unobtrusively deflates the large official figure. Of a shipboard Communion service: "The priest went through the ceremony severely and hastily,
placing the wafers on the outstretched tongues expertly and snatching back
his hand." The plain adverbs suggest a minor public official in a distasteful
routine: "snatching," the fear of contamination. Mrs. Treadwell leaves a self-
pitying young man: "If she stayed to listen, she knew she would weaken little
by little, she would warm up in spite of herself, perhaps in the end identify
herself with the other, take on his griefs and wrongs, and if it came to that,

feel finally guilty as if she herself had caused them; yes, and he would believe it too, and blame her freely." The easy lucidity never shirks depths or darks, which to some writers seem approachable only by the involute, the cryptic, or the tortuous.

Using the kind of elements that she does, she can organize them, elaborately if need be, with control and grace. The local papers "cannot praise too much the skill with which the members of good society maintain in their deportment the delicate balance between high courtesy and easy merriment, a secret of the Veracruz world bitterly envied and unsuccessfully imitated by the provincial inland society of the Capital." Under the gentle irony and the rhythm that serves it, lie in easy and well articulated orders a remarkable number of modifiers—such as Hardy would have fouled into knotty confusion, and James, pursuing precision, would have pried apart with preciosity in placement. She manages with equal skill the erection of ordinary terms, both concrete and analytical, into a periodic structure in which all elements converge unspectacularly on a climax of sudden insight: "The passengers, investigating the cramped airless quarters with their old-fashioned double tiers of bunks and a narrow hard couch along the opposite wall for the unlucky third comer, read the names on the doorplates—most of them German—eyed with suspicion and quick distaste luggage piled beside their own in their cabins, and each discovered again what he had believed lost for a while though he could not name it—his identity." A compact sketch of outer world and inner meaning, it is never crowded or awkward or rambling.

Language as guarantor of identity: it is the kind of true perception regularly conveyed in terms modest and unstraining, but fresh and competent. Of the troubles of boarding ship: "This common predicament did not by any means make of them fellow sufferers." Each kept "his pride and separateness within himself"; "there crept into eyes meeting unwillingly . . . a look of unacknowledged, hostile recognition. 'So there you are again, I never saw you before in my life,' the eyes said." Of David Scott's special capacity for triumph as a lover: "Feeling within him his coldness of heart as a real power in reserve, he . . . laid his hand over hers warmly"—with just a shadow of oxymoron to accent the reality without calling attention to itself. Jenny Brown, his girl, had a "fondness for nearness, for stroking, touching, nestling, with a kind of sensuality so diffused it almost amounted to coldness after all": the plain tactile words preparing for the shrewd analysis in which the paradox is not thrust triumphantly at one but offered almost experimentally. There is a good deal of this relaxed movement between the physical and the psychic or moral, each grasped directly and surely. The Spanish dancers "would look straight at you and laugh as if you were an object too comic to believe, yet their eyes were cold and they were not enjoying themselves, even at your expense." The vocabulary is hardly more than elementary, and the words are arranged in a classic compound structure, almost as in an exercise book, yet they communicate a disturbing hardness. The next sentence is of the same stamp but is trimmed back sharply to an almost skeletal simplicity: "Frau Hutten had observed them from the first and she was afraid of them." The fear is ours, but not through a tensed-up stylistic staging of fear.

Miss Porter can combine words unexpectedly without becoming ostentatious: for instance, an adjective denoting mood or value with a neutral noun—"serious, well-shaped head," "weak dark whiskers," or, more urgently "strong white rage of vengeful sunlight"; or sex words with gastric facts—"They fell upon their splendid full-bodied German food with hot appetites." She pairs partly clashing words: "softened and dispirited" (of a woman affected by childbirth), "with patience and a touch of severity" (of people waiting for the boat to leave), "oafish and devilish at once" (of a nagging inner voice), "at once crazed and stupefied" (of the air of a bad eating place): and gets inner contradictions in sharp phrases: "this pugnacious assertion of high breeding," "classic erotic-frowning smile" (of a dancer), "shameless pathos" (of an angry face). She can surprise, and convince, with a preposition: a newly married couple's "first lessons in each other."

She has strong, accurate, but not conspicuous, metaphors: "soggy little waiter," "pink-iced tea-cake of sympathy," "hand-decorated hates," "making conversation to scatter silence," a "laugh was a long cascade of falling tinware." But metaphors are less numerous than similes, that now less fashionable figure to which Miss Porter turns with instinctive ease, rarely without amplifying the sense or shading the tone, and always with the added thrust of imagistic vitality. She may fix the object visually: Elsa Lutz had a "crease of fat like a goiter at the base of the throat"; on her canvases Jenny Brown painted cubistic designs "in primary colors like fractured rainbows." She has a sense of how the inanimate may creep up on or take over the human: the steerage passengers "slept piled upon each other like dirty rags thrown out on a garbage heap"; or how a human attribute may be dehumanized: the Spanish dancers' voices "crashed like breaking crockery." When a woman, confident of her worldly knowingness, is publicly snubbed by the Captain, she first turns red; then her blush "vanished and left her pale as unborn veal"—colorless, unknowing, pre-innocent, pre-calf. When his wife bursts forth with a public expression of views contrary to his own, Professor Hutten "sat like something molded in sand, his expression that of a strong innocent man gazing into a pit of cobras." It is a complete picture of mood and man. Miss Porter confers her own incisive perception of character upon Jenny Brown when she has Jenny thinking about David Scott, ". . . I'll be carrying David like a petrified fetus for the rest of my life." Jenny's sense of rigidity and immaturity in her lover is really an echo of her creator's sense of many of her human subjects: she sees them with easy clarity and goes right to the point. Her images for them come solidly out of life; they are not stylistic gestures, literary exercises, but unlabored responses to need, responses from experience against which the door of feeling and knowing have never been closed.

The difficulty of describing a style without mannerisms, crotchets, or even characteristic brilliances or unique excellences leads one constantly to use such terms as *plain, direct, ordinary, unpretentious, lucid, candid*. These are neither derogatory nor limiting words, nor words that one is altogether content with. The qualities that they name are not inimical to the subtle or the profound, to the penetrating glance or the inclusive sweep. Whether Miss Porter's basic words are a multitude of documentary nouns or adjectives, are literally descriptive or pointedly or amplifyingly imagistic, are terms that report or present or comment or analyze, she composes them, without evident struggle, in a great variety of ways—in combinations of revelatory unexpectedness; tersely or compactly or with unencumbered elaboration, either in a succession of ordered dependencies or in structured periods where everything builds to a final emphasis; with an apparently automatic interplay of force and fluency; meticulously but not pickily or gracelessly; with a kind of graceful adjustment to situation that we call urbanity, yet by no means an urbanity that implies charm or agreeableness at the expense of firmness or conviction.

III

Certain of Miss Porter's arrangements disclose characteristic ways of perceiving and shaping her materials. She describes Veracruz as a "typical port town, cynical by nature, shameless by experience, hardened to showing its seamiest side to strangers: ten to one this stranger passing through is a sheep bleating for their shears, and one in ten is a scoundrel it would be a pity not to outwit." The traditional rhetoric—the triad series; the first half balanced against the second, which is balanced internally; the antithesis and chiasmus—is the instrument of clarity, analytical orderliness, and detachment. Miss Porter has a notable talent for the succinct summarizing sequence; she often employs the series, which combines specification with despatch; through it a packing together of near synonyms may master by saturation, or a quick-fingered catalogue may grasp a rush of simultaneous or consecutive events. A dancer's "pantomime at high speed" to an infatuated pursuer communicates "pity for him or perhaps his stupidity, contempt for the Lutzes, warning, insult, false commiseration, and finally, just plain ridicule." A series may define by a concise anatomy: William Denny's "mind seemed to run monotonously on women, or rather, sex; money, or rather his determination not to be gypped by anybody; and his health." Such series remind one of Jane Austen, who can often look at people and things as logically placeable, sometimes dismissible by a quick list of traits, or naturally amenable to a 1-2-3 kind of classification. Miss Porter has a marked Jane Austen side, which appears, for instance, in the dry summation of a girl and her parents: their "three faces were calm, grave, and much alike," with the anticlimax offhand instead of sharpened up into a shattering deflation. Miss Porter's comic sense is like Austen's both in the use of pithy geometrical arrangements and in the presentment of observed ironies, sometimes suffusing a whole scene, sometimes clipped down as in neoclassical verse: Elsa Lutz spoke "with a surprising lapse into everyday common sense" (cf. "But Shadwell seldom deviates into sense"); Herr Lowenthal felt "he was living in a world so dangerous he wondered how he dared go to sleep at night. But he was sleepy at that very moment." (Cf. "And sleepless lovers, just at twelve, awake.") The irony is Austen-like when, though piercing, it is less censorious than tolerantly amused: "With relief he seized upon this common sympathy between them, and they spent a profitable few minutes putting the Catholic Church in its place." It may catch a social group, gently replacing the group's sense of itself by another: at the Captain's table Frau Rittersdorf "turned her most charming smile upon the Captain, who rewarded her with a glimpse of his two front teeth and slightly upturned mouthcorners. The others ranged round him, faces bent towards him like sunflowers to the sun, waiting for him to begin conversation." It may go beneath the surface to capture habits of mind, setting them up in a neat balance that comments on their insufficiency: Jenny Brown thinks wryly of " 'the family attitude'—suspicion of the worst based on insufficient knowledge of her life, and moral disapproval based firmly on their general knowledge of the weakness of human nature."

Yet to a passage with a strong Austen cast Miss Porter may make an inconspicuous addition that will elusively but substantially alter it. When Lizzi Spockenkieker runs carelessly into pompous Captain Thiele, he "threw an arm about her stiffly," and she, "blushing, whinnying, cackling, scrambling, embraced him about the neck wildly as if she were drowning." There is the Austen series crisply hitting off the ludicrous behavior, but there is more visual imagery than Austen uses, more of the physically excessive, and "whinnying" and "cackling," dehumanizing words, carry the joke beyond the usual limit of the Austen mode. It is more like Charlotte Brontë, who could often plunge into the comic, but was likely to do it more fiercely and scornfully. With Brontë, the absurd more quickly edged into the grotesque and even the sinister; she had an awareness of potential damage not easily contained within a pure comic convention. Miss Porter is much closer to Brontë than to Austen in her description of Dr. Schumann when he catches the evil Spanish twins in another destructive practical joke: he "examined the depths of their eyes for a moment with dismay at their blind, unwinking malignance, their cold slyness—not beasts, though, but human souls."

Or consider this comment on a group of first-class passengers looking down on a steerage meal and feeling that the poor people there were being treated decently: "Murmuring among themselves like pigeons . . . (they) seemed to be vaguely agreed that to mistreat the poor is not right, and they would be the first to say so, at any time. Therefore they were happy to be spared this unpleasant duty, to have their anxieties allayed, their charitable feelings soothed." With the subdued ironic contemplation of the group, and with the series that dexterously encompasses their mood, this could be Austen's; and yet behind the smile-provoking self-deceit there is a kind of moral frailty, a trouble-breeding irresponsibility, and in the steerage sights a degree of wretchedness, that extends beyond the borders of the comic perspective. Here, as elsewhere, Miss Porter's manner is reminiscent of George Eliot's—of a carefully, accurately analytical style that is the agent of a mature psychic and moral understanding. David Scott observes the non-dancers: "the born outsiders; the perpetual uninvited; the unwanted; and those who, like himself, for whatever sad reason, refused to join in." The series serves no comic end, speaks for no rationally organizing mind; it makes nice distinctions among the members of a class, somberly, with a mere touch of restrained sympathy to soften the categorical lines. Freytag mentally accuses boat travelers, who "can't seem to find any middle ground between stiffness, distrust, total rejection, or a kind of invasive, gnawing curiosity." The general precision is especially notable in the fresh, climactic joining of the learned "invasive" with the common "gnawing," the latter used uncharacteristically of an external trouble. There is an Eliot-like perceptiveness in Freytag's discovery "about most persons—that their abstractions and generalizations, their Rage for Justice or Hatred of Tyranny or whatever, too often disguised a bitter personal grudge of some sort far removed from the topic apparently under discussion" and in the matter-of-fact postscript that Freytag applied this only to others, never to himself. Miss Porter has repeated need for a vocabulary of emotional urgency, of tensions beyond comedy, as in Jenny Brown's concluding observation on the split with her family: "But that didn't keep you from loving them, nor them from loving you, with that strange longing, demanding, hopeless tenderness and bitterness, wound into each other in a net of living nerves." Here the terms for human contradictions are different in kind from those which present simply laughable incongruities. There is an Eliot note both in this and in another passage on the same page in which we are given a saddened sense of necessities which might, but does not, drift into bitterness: "She did not turn to them at last for help, or consolation, or praise, or understanding, or even love; but merely at last because she was incapable of turning away."

The language and syntax reveal Miss Porter's eye for precision, specification, and distinctions. There is the same precision in the definition of Freytag's "hardened expression of self-absorbed, accusing, utter righteousness" and of a stewardess's "unpleasant mixture of furtive insolence and false abasement, the all too familiar look of resentful servility." Freytag himself distinguishes the phases of another personality: "overfamiliar if you made the mistake of being pleasant to him; loud and insolent if he suspected timidity in you; sly and cringing if you knew how to put him in his place." David prefers, he thinks, "Mrs. Treadwell's unpretentious rather graceful lack of moral sense to Jenny's restless seeking outlaw nature trying so hard to attach itself at any or all points to the human beings nearest her: no matter who." Miss Porter confers her own flair for distinctions upon certain characters. Thus Dr. Schumann, planning to go to confession: ". . . he felt not the right contrition, that good habit of the spirit, but a personal shame, a crushing humiliation at the disgraceful nature of what he had to confess." And it is near the end of the book that Jenny, the most sentient and spontaneous character, reflects upon her griefs over love that did not fulfill expectations: "—and what had it been but the childish refusal to admit and accept on some term or other the difference between what one hoped was true and what one discovers to be the mere laws of the human condition?" The clarity in words comes here from the character's clarity of thought, and this in turn from the writer's clarity of mind. Thus an examination of style in the narrower sense of verbal deportment leads, as it repeatedly does, to the style in conceiving—to the "styling" of, we might say—episode and character, and from this on to the ultimate style of creative mind: the grasp of fact and the moral sense.

We have been following Miss Porter's range: from wit to wisdom, from the sense of the laughable slip or flaw to the awareness of graver self-deception and self-seeking, and to the feeling for reality that at once cuts through illusion and accepts, among the inevitable facts of life, the emotional pressures that lead to, and entangle, fulfillment and discord. Now beside this central sober work of reflective intelligence and alert conscience put the gay play of the Captain's being driven, by a "lethal cloud of synthetic rose scent" at dinner, to sneeze: "He sneezed three times inwardly, on forefinger pressed firmly to his upper lip as he had been taught to do in childhood, to avoid sneezing in church. Silently he was convulsed with internal explosions, feeling as if his eyeballs would fly out, or his eardrums burst. At last he gave up and felt for his handkerchief, sat up stiffly, head averted from the room, and sneezed steadily in luxurious agony a dozen times with muted sounds and streaming eyes, until the miasma was sneezed out, and he was rewarded with a good nose-blow." This is farce, the comedy of the physical in which mind and feelings are engaged either not at all, or only mechanically: of the perversity of things and circumstances that render one absurd or grotesque with merely formal suffering, not the authentic kind that by stirring sympathy cuts off outrageous laughter. To say that it is in the vein of Smollett is to emphasize both its present rareness outside the work of committed funnymen and the extraordinariness of having it juxtaposed with writing of sensitiveness and thoughtfulness. Farce may have a satirical note, as in this note on Lizzi Spockenkieker's disappointment with Herr Rieber, her would-be lover: "Every other man she had known had unfailingly pronounced the magic word *marriage* before ever he got into bed with her, no matter what came of it in fact." A little earlier, Herr Rieber, a short fat man, having gone through suitable amatory preliminaries, decided that his hour had come and, "with the silent intentness of a man bent on crime," maneuvered Lizzi, a tall thin woman, "to the dark side of the ship's funnel. He gave his prey no warning . . . It was like embracing a windmill. Lizzi uttered a curious tight squeal, and her long arms gathered him in around his heaving middle . . . She gave him a good push and they fell backward clutched together, her long active legs overwhelmed him, she rolled him over flat on his back, . . . Lizzi was spread upon him like a fallen tent full of poles, . . ." Herr Rieber's passion for flesh and conquest is defeated, turned into grief, by the vigorous surrender that has swept him into unorthodox subordination, and he can get rid of his victorious victim, who is in a "carnivorous trance," only by gasping to her in agony that they are watched by Bebe, the fat and generally seasick dog of Professor Hutten. Bebe, only three feet away, "the folds of his nose twitching, regarded them with an expression of animal cunning that most embarrassingly resembled human knowledge of the seamy side of life." After all the modern solemnities about sex, this sheer farce—with the farcical morality of the dog as grave censor—is reassuring evidence that a fuller, more flexible, less doleful sense of sexual conduct can be recovered.

For a final note on Miss Porter's great range, we can contrast this hilarious Smollettian jest with two quite dissimilar passages. One is the vivd imaging, in her visible gestures, of the inner unwellness of a Spanish countess: "Thumbs turned in lightly to the palm, the hands moved aimlessly from the edge of the table to her lap, they clasped and unclasped themselves, spread themselves flat in the air, closed, shook slightly, went to her hair, to the bosom of her gown, as if by a life of their own separate from the will of the woman herself, who sat quite still otherwise, features a little rigid, bending over to read the dinner card beside her plate." Though here there is a more detailed visualization of the symbolizing object, the feeling for the troubled personality is like Charlotte Brontë's. To this Countess, Dr. Schumann feels attracted, guiltily. After seeing her, "He lay down with his rosary in his fingers, and began to invite sleep, darkness, silence, that little truce of God between living and dying; he put out of his mind, with deliberate intention to forget forever, the last words of that abandoned lost creature; nettles, poisoned barbs, fish hooks, her words clawed at his mind with the terrible malignance of the devil-possessed, the soul estranged from its kind." In the meditative element, in the imaging of a remembered frenzy, and most of all in the particular moral sense that leads to the words "soul estranged from its kind," the account is reminiscent of Conrad.

Range means contrasts such as these. Often, too, there is direct juxtaposition of different styles. Miss Porter can write page after page of sonorous periods—plausible, not overplayed—for Professor Hutten's dinner disquisitions to a captive audience, and then shift bluntly to Frau Hutten's perspective: "He was boring them to death again, she could feel it like vinegar in her veins"— another trenchant simile. Here are two ways of commenting on intelligence: the cultivated irony of "[Elsa's] surprising lapse into everyday common sense," and, on the next page, Jenny's breezy colloquial hyperbole for the Cuban students, "The trouble . . . is simply that they haven't been born yet." David Scott solemnly claims a high disgust for sexual binges: "He had felt superior to his acts and to his partners in them, and altogether redeemed and separated from their vileness by that purifying contempt"; Jenny retorts, with pungent plainness, "Men love to eat themselves sick and then call their upchuck by high-sounding names." Or there is the innocent, flat-voiced irony of Miss Porter's comment on the "lyric prose" of newspapers reporting parties "lavish and aristocratic—the terms are synonymous, they believe" and on newly boarded passengers wandering "about in confusion with the air of persons who have abandoned something of great importance on shore, though they cannot think what it is"; and beside this the vulgar force appropriate to a tactical thought of Herr Rieber's: "A man couldn't be too cautious with that proper, constipated type, no matter how gamey she looked."

IV

In their slangy vigor or insouciance, their blunt and easy immediacy, their spurning of the genteel, their casual clinicality, their nervous grip on strain and tension, some of these passages have an air that, whether in self-under-standing or self-love, we call "modern." The novel has many such, and they evidence in another way the range of Miss Porter's style. However, the modernity need be stressed only enough to acknowledge that the style, like any well-wrought individual style, cannot be wholly placed by comparison with well-known styles. My principal points, nevertheless, have been that Miss Porter's style has strong affiliations with the Austen and Eliot styles, that its main lines are traditional rather than innovating, and that it is markedly devoid of namable singularities, mannerisms, private idioms, self-indulgent or striven-for uniquenesses that give a special coloration. These points are interrelated; to some extent, they are different emphases of a central truth.

To claim for a writer affinities with Austen and Eliot (and to note, as evidence of her variety, occasional reminiscences of other writers) may seem faint praise in an age quick to think, in many areas, We have left all that behind us. The procedure does have its risks, and a disavowal or two may be in order. To note a resemblance in styles is not to make premature judgments of over-all merit, which involves other problems not dealt with here, and which in the end must be left to history. It is not to suggest influences, imitation, idle repetition, failure of originality, or limitedness. On the contrary, it is a way of suggesting superiority in the individual achievement: here is a writer working independently, composing out of her own genius, and yet in her use of the language exhibiting admirable qualities that seem akin to those of distinguished predecessors. It is a way of proposing, perhaps, that she has got hold of some central virtues of the language, virtues whether of strength or grace, that tend to recur and that, whatever the modification of them from writer to writer, may in essence be inseparable from good writing. To say this is to imply a traditional style, or core of elements of style. To hypothesize a tradition is precarious, since the word seems likely to make critics either a bit solemn, seven-candled, and hieratic on the one hand, or, on the other, self-righteous, flambeaux-lighted, and rebellious with an anticlerical fervor. I venture the word, not to beg a theoretical issue or invoke a charm or scorn a curse, but to suggest figuratively a group of long-enduring ways of using the language, apparent norms of utility, representative workings-out of possibility. These would constitute a discipline of eccentricity but not a constraint on originality; to call a writer a traditionalist in style would involve the old paradox of unique personality seizing on the universal thing or mode.

It is in such terms that one must approach Miss Porter's style. Though it looks easy rather than hard, it has a certain elusiveness that makes it not quite easy to account for. It would be difficult to imitate or parody, for what is most open to copying or travestying is the novelty, the idiosyncrasy, the raw ego in words that betokens a flight from or an inability to get hold of some persisting "nature" in the art forms of one's own tongue. Miss Porter has a very wide vocabulary, but no pet vocabulary; she has considerable skill in compositional patterns but no agonized specializations of order. She is exact and explicit; she eschews mystery in the medium without losing the mystery in the matter. The solidity of her writing, of the *how* that implies the *what* we signify by naming her peers. Her variety appears in an obviously wide spectrum of tones and attitudes, rarely with the pen as pardoner of all, or the stylus as stiletto, but within these extremes modulating easily among the contemptible, the laughable, the pitiable, the evasive laudable, and, most of all, the ever-present contradictory—of face and heart, belief and deed, illusion and fact—that regularly compels one to look anew at all familiar surfaces.

Note

1. I am arbitrarily limiting this essay to the latest work. One cannot talk about style without using many examples; to bring in the stories and novellas would expand the study to inordinate length.

Ship of Fools

SMITH KIRKPATRICK

When you read Katherine Anne Porter's novel, you will find yourself already aboard her *Ship of Fools,* not overtly, not through the usual identification with one of the characters, but through a more subtle involvement with a familiar action.

Miss Porter's ship is a real, not purely symbolic, ship traveling from Vera Cruz to Bremerhaven during the early thirties and is peopled with passengers talking and traveling in that troubled time, but as the journey aboard the *Vera,* truth, continues the passengers tend to develop more towards caricature than characterization. And this is very close to Miss Porter's point. She has no clearly identifiable protagonist or antagonist. Her subject is too large to be shown through a central character; for as the ship progresses from the "true cross" to the "broken haven" she shows us how each passenger journeys not only to Bremerhaven but through life. In so doing she shows us the common manner in which we make the voyage, and she shows us the necessarily concomitant subject of what she views life to be.

Since the reader cannot identify himself with one of Miss Porter's characters, just how does she involve his heart? She has chosen to locate the novel aboard a ship, to limit her action within the confines of a sea voyage where the characters for the most part are strangers to one another. With the ship-board opportunity for new friendships and fresh self-appraisals it is important to look at what the passengers bring with them on their journey. As the title says, the voyagers are all fools. The nature of their foolery is what the passengers bring aboard with them, and Miss Porter reduces the foolery to the oldest mark of the fool, the one thing that all fools in all time have had in common: the mask. She shows how intricately contrived are the masks. Each man wears not one but many. He peers at his existence from behind the various masks of nationality, age, sex, creeds, social rank, race, wealth, politics, and all other existential distinctions made by both the elemental and civilized man.

At times the masks are as pathetically simple as that of Frau Baumgartner, who in the tropic heat is momentarily too angry with her small son to

Reprinted with permission of the editor and the author from the *Sewanee Review* 71.1 (Winter 1963): 94–98. Copyright 1963 by the University of the South.

heed his pleas to remove the buckskin suit in which she has wrongly encased him. She taunts him over his inability to endure the riding costume meant for mountain coldness and even begins to enjoy her cruelty and the pleasant feeling of hurting the pride of the boy sitting on the divan ". . . yearning for kindness, hoping his beautiful good mother would come back soon. She vanished in the frowning scolding stranger, who blazed out at him when he least expected it, struck him on the hand, threatened him, seemed to hate him." But in the next moment she "sees him clearly" and is filled with pity and remorse and tenderness.

At other times the intricacy of the masks is nearly as confusing as it is to Denny the Texan, whose bible is *Recreational Aspects of Sex as Mental Prophylaxis—A True Guide to Happiness* and whose consuming passion on the voyage is to buy, at *his* price, the wares of Amparo, a dancer in the zarzuela company. Sitting in the ship's bar Denny has an atheist on one side speaking like a bolshevik and over here a Jew, criticizing Christians and meaning Catholics. He didn't like Jews *or* Catholics and knew if he said, "I think Jews are heathens," he would be accused of persecuting Jews. He wished himself home in Brownsville ". . . where a man knew who was who and what was what, and niggers, crazy Swedes, Jews, greasers, bone-headed micks, polacks, wops, Guineas and damn Yankees knew their place and stayed in it."

Denny wants the mask simple and set and Miss Porter shows the results of a mask settling into reality through Mrs. Treadwell, an American divorcee, to whom the past is so bad, as compared to a future full of love she had expected as a child, it seems something she has read in newspapers. Denny in his final determination to conquer Amparo confuses the door and drunkenly mistakes for the face Amparo the face of "unsurpassed savagery and sensuality" which Mrs. Treadwell in drunken idleness painted on herself following the failure of the young ship's officer to arouse any feeling in her. She shoves Denny to the deck, and using her metal capped high heel beats in the face of the fallen and stuporous man with "furious pleasure" and is afterwards delighted at the sight of her "hideous wicked face" in her mirror. When worn as a reality, the mask comes close to covering insanity, which becomes a terrifying comment on all the Brownsvilles in the world.

Usually, though, the masks shift and change like the postures of a dance. Jenny and David, the American painters who have been living together but are now traveling in separate cabins, approach each other with feelings of love only to have their feelings turn suddenly into hatred and the hatred as it shows itself on their faces evokes the love again. They can no more decide their emotional destiny than they can decide their physical destination. One wants to visit Spain; the other, France. In the course of their constant argument they even swap positions but always the change is in reaction to an action or reaction in the other. And here Miss Porter takes the breath away with her absolute genius. Never, not once in the seemingly unending continuum of emotional and rational action and reaction, whether between total strangers operating behind the complicated masks of their civilized pasts or whether between selves almost submerged in old marriages, never, no matter how abrupt may be the reversal of a position or of a thought pattern, is there anything but complete belief that, yes, this is the way it would really be.

This constant change is the reason the passengers tend towards caricature. Exactly when is the passenger undergoing the final unveiling to his ultimate truth? Amparo and her pimp, Pepe, steal, swindle, and blackmail behind a flurry of costumery and poses and when at last they are left together, away from their victims, Amparo still full of the strange smells and heats of the recently departed liberal Swede, Arne Hanson, the final truth of these two seems about to be revealed. And the truth is beautifully revealed of them as pimp, whore, and lovers; but the scene ends with the revelation that both parties have long before planned, and even now are working towards, their mutual betrayals.

Perhaps the truth of the characters lies not in revealing the total man facing an action as large as life itself (perhaps no man can) but in the manner or the method with which the characters face life. If in this or that situation they wear this or that ready-made mask and in the next situation wear yet another of the thousand faces molded by the forms of civilization and elemental men, then perhaps we really are caricatures with our true selves forever unrealized. Certainly the passengers behind their masks hide from each other their love. Mrs. Treadwell says the passengers are all saying to each other, *"Love me, love me in spite of all! Whether or not I love you, whether I am fit to love, whether you are able to love, even if there is no such thing as love, love me!"*

The Germanic mask of discipline and family is so stolid on the face of Dr. Schumann, the ship's doctor, that even though he loves the beautiful Cuban Condesa, who has forsaken herself to ether and self-caresses, he degrades her and wants rid of her. In horror of himself he renounces all human kinship and in his own drugged sleep the Condesa's death-like, bodiless head danced before him still smiling but shedding tears. "Oh, Why, Why?" the head asked him not in complaint but wonder. Tenderly he kissed it silent. This was probably the last opportunity for love in his life.

The one unmasked act of love aboard the ship, an act nearly performed earlier by Dr. Schumann when he risked overtaxing a weak heart by stepping forward to save a cat, was performed by a man in steerage, a wood carver who cries like a child when his knife is taken from him and who, when the white dog is thrown overboard into the night sea, leaps after the white object without hesitation or knowledge of whether it is a man or a dog and is drowned saving it. In the lean raggedness of this "worn but perhaps young" wood carver, who cannot but bring to mind another worker in wood, and in his unselfish act, is an opportunity for the passengers to see behind man's facade. But even the parent-like owners of the dog want only to forget the wood carver's name, and they lose themselves in the carnal interest the act has rediscovered for them.

The wood carver's burial ends with the priests turning their backs while their Catholic flock in steerage nearly kills a taunting atheist. The final results of the wood carver's act are that the dog is saved and fun is had by Ric and Rac, the twin children who threw the dog overboard in the first place.

If La Condesa can say of the Cuban students, "They are just their parents' bad dreams," then certainly this can be said of Ric and Rac even though their parents are in the zarzuela company and are almost bad dreams themselves. Ric and Rac have named themselves for two comic cartoon terriers who "made life a raging curse for everyone near them, got their own way invariably by a wicked trick, and always escaped without a blow." And this is Ric and Rac. They steal, kill, destroy, and hurt not for gain but from some profound capacity for hatred which with the capacity and need for love lurks always behind the mask. It is almost as though this capacity for hatred is the reason of being for the masks of civilization, and Miss Porter is writing of civilized men. She is writing of the passengers living in the upper decks, and they are terrified of the masses of humans traveling in animal misery in steerage. All weapons are taken from the masses, even the wood carver's knife. The elemental man is too apparent. Jenny is haunted by the memory of two Mexican Indians, a man and woman locked in a swaying embrace, both covered with blood and killing each other with cutting weapons. "They were silent, and their faces had taken on a saintlike patience in suffering, abstract, purified of rage and hatred in their one holy dedicated purpose to kill each other." In her dreams she is horrified to see that this is she and David.

And no matter how tightly the passengers may be enclosed in their formalized attitudes the zarzuela company reveals how thinly surfaced they are. By subverting the masks the whores and pimps make the passengers pay them to usurp the Captain's table, toast confusion, send the pompous Captain fleeing, and in their hatred mock the passengers by parodying them on the dance floor. The dance itself being a formalization, the parody by the whores and pimps becomes not only a parody of the individual passenger but of everything he considers civilized.

And the parody is meaningful because the passengers themselves are parodies, fools. Fools because behind all the masks and the love and the hatred is a selfishness, and the most selfish of all is the old religious zealot. His final prayer is that he be remembered for one merciful moment and be let go, given eternal darkness, let die forever—be the one man in all time released from the human condition, which must be lived to whatever its ends may be.

The novel comes to no conclusions, answers no questions; its ending is the end of the journey. But these masks are our masks; this is the way we cover our naked selves for the swift passage; this life is our lives moving steadily into eternity, the familiar action in which we are all involved. And the novel is a lament for us all, a song artistically resolved, sung by a great artist of the insoluble condition of man.

Looking-Glass Reflections:
Satirical Elements in *Ship of Fools*

JON SPENCE

Katherine Anne Porter's *Ship of Fools* has been the subject of an adverse body of criticism which finds the author's philosophic view of man pessimistic and misanthropic. By reading the novel as a satire, however, one perceives that Miss Porter's philosophic and artistic purpose is neither misanthropic nor pessimistic. *Ship of Fools* is a criticism of mankind by a woman who cares deeply about humanity. She derides human folly that arises from man's delusions about the evil within himself and from his failure to love. She aims to induce man to admit his own failings and then to strive to overcome them. But Swift in his preface to *The Battle of the Books* points out one of the principal problems of such satire: "Satyr is a sort of Glass, wherein Beholders do generally discover everybody's Face except their Own." The adverse critics of *Ship of Fools* affirm the continued validity of Swift's perception of the nature of satire and its audience.

In the traditional satirical manner Katherine Anne Porter isolates her characters' most repugnant traits by identifying those traits with animals. She reflects through her use of animal imagery her almost medieval hierarchical view of world order, in which man's fall from grace manifests itself in his exhibiting qualities of lower forms of life. Miss Porter provides the perfect image of man's dehumanization in the description of the beggar who "had been in early life so intricately maimed and deformed by a master of the art, in preparation for his calling, he had little resemblance to any human being." She examines men whose souls have been as maimed as the beggar's body. The zarzuela company are described as beautiful and brightly plumed birds, but their actions reveal them to be a "thieving flock of crows"; the cold and ridiculous Huttens look like two frogs in their lovemaking; and David Scott looks like a "willful cold-blooded horse." Many such descriptions provide not only a key to the personalities and human failures of the characters, but also a perfect comic barb, as when Rieber, who has been lusting after Lizzi, gets into a fight with Hansen: "He bleated like a goat, 'Baaah, meeeeh!' and charged

Reprinted with permission of the editor from the *Sewanee Review* 82.2 (Spring 1974): 316–30. Copyright 1974 by the University of the South.

Herr Hansen, butting him accurately in the sensitive midriff just where the ribs divide." The animal imagery thus reflects the perversions of human nature which lower men to the level of animals.

Descriptions such as Rieber's fight with Hansen and Denny's pursuit of the water girl in Santa Cruz provide a comic matrix for the satire. Glenway Wescott says that Miss Porter once told him: "I promised myself solemnly: in this book I will not load the dice. . . . I would not take sides." But she observes her characters from an ironic point of view and emphasizes through comedy and irony the grotesque and absurd aspects of their actions. Although one is supposed to laugh at the ridiculous characters and their situations, Miss Porter makes clear, by negative example, *how* one must laugh. The Spanish dancers are a banal but menacing force of evil, and their perversity is unrelieved by comedy. The dancers parody the other passengers with an invective that has no purpose except self-amusement and malevolence. Their laughter is filled with malice and cold ridicule. But Miss Porter's satire does not end with deflation of character or with sheer amusement. She seeks to evoke laughter of recognition, laughter of compassionate understanding of the absurdities that man himself creates.

In contrast the satiric comedy employed in the treatment of the condesa and the doctor is gentle, the elements of the absurd and the grotesque being subdued. Katherine Anne Porter attributes to these two characters qualities which she believes are necessary if man is to make a stand against evil and rise from the animalistic level to his true place as a human being. She has said that "awareness is the great thing for us really—to find out what we're doing and then if we are doing evil, make a fight against it." She continues, saying that good in man comes more from "the struggle, the will to be good," than from what man achieves by doing good. Both the doctor and the condesa possess traits which Miss Porter admires in man. Because the condesa is a lost soul by her own choice, she cannot stand as the moral norm of the satire. But from her unflinching refusal to have delusions about herself and other men, the doctor learns to acknowledge the evil in himself, emerging as a man with understanding of human failures and human suffering.

The doctor has appointed himself to a position of moral perfection from which he views the condesa—and practically everyone else aboard ship— "with a good deal of moral disapproval." While the other characters lose their humanity by acting like animals, the doctor loses his by performing like a machine. Each is an intolerable deviation from humanity. The condesa says of the doctor's cold morality: "Oh, my friend, have you gone mad with virtue and piety, have you lost your human feelings, how can you have forgotten what suffering is?" The doctor's terrible failure is implicit in his physical defect: he has a serious heart ailment. His concern for his own moral superiority has left him without any capacity for human love. Dr. Schumann's religious beliefs have so undermined his human feelings that he can only conceive of his love for the condesa as springing from lust.

The doctor recoils from the two aspects of the condesa's decadence: her sexual perversity and her drug addiction. He dissociates himself personally from her by ministering to her needs as a physician instead of as a lover. For the human love he could have given her, he substitutes the narcotic-filled hypodermic. In the last moments before she leaves the ship, the doctor "brought out the needle and the ampule and prepared deliberately to give her another *piqûre*." The doctor's guilt is underlined by the use of the word *deliberately* and by the use of *piqûre*, which is used figuratively in French to mean *une petite blessure morale*. The small moral wound is his own as well as the condesa's. He fulfills her unnatural need for drugs, rather than her natural need for love, marking his complicity in her decadence as impersonal and inhuman. Dr. Schumann's inability to acknowledge human needs and frailties is the crux of his failure. But he finally realizes his own culpability, his own failings: "He had refused to acknowledge the wrong he had done La Condesa his patient, he had taken advantage of her situation as a prisoner, he had tormented her with his guilty love and yet refused her—and himself—any human joy in it."

Miss Porter is as critical of the doctor's selfish and egotistical piety as she is of the condesa's physical depravity: she rejects the doctor's superhuman morality as well as the condesa's subhuman immorality. But Dr. Schumann eventually recognizes evil in himself and learns the value of human love. When the other characters are faced with their own failures and the failures of others, they turn their backs, as shown quite literally in Mrs. Treadwell who sits with her back to the *Vera* as she is being rowed ashore to France, and in the Huttens who turn away from the dancers who are robbing shops in Santa Cruz. Dr. Schumann does not turn his back: he recognizes evil, he suffers, and he regains his humanity. His triumph lies in the struggle itself, from beginning to end.

We last see the doctor when he tells Denny who his attacker was on the evening of the fiesta. Schumann is now neither "the voice of rebuke itself lifted in the wilderness" nor is he in a "wallow of compassion for every suffering thing." He is a human being who rightfully feels "a real glow of some kind of malicious satisfaction mixed with moral unction." To know that justice is operative in the world does "Dr. Schumann's heart good." Because he has suffered and has faced his own failures, he is privileged to see even this comic vision of justice. The other characters are denied the comfort, because in spite of their suffering they turn their backs on both truth and evil. With the exception of Dr. Schumann and the condesa, the passengers on the ship simply move from one illusion to another, from the failed hopes of Mexico to the new illusions of their various harbors. Their fruitless searches are pointed out in Miss Porter's working title for the novel: *No Safe Harbor*. Only the doctor moves from foggy self-delusion to an acceptance of truth. He has by no means achieved moral perfection, but he has reached the point where he can be called a human being, in the noblest sense of those words.

Within the episodic structure of the satire the relationship of Dr. Schumann and the condesa is isolated from the convoluted interactions of the other characters. The reactions of the other characters to their own plights and those of the people about them compose small plot movements, which themselves comprise larger movements. Each smaller episode shows the gathering forces of evil which build up to the three main sequences: the Freytag episode, the Bébé episode, and the climactic fiesta episode, which involves virtually every character except the doctor and the condesa. These three episodes move from the most impersonal evil and hatred to the most personal, and all arise from the chaotic feelings and attitudes of the passengers on the *Vera*.

From the beginning of the novel Miss Porter sets the various nationalities one against the other in encounters which are thinly veiled expressions of hatred. Within the groups of each nationality there is conflict between people of different social and economic strata, different regions, different ethnic and religious backgrounds. The chaotic world in which they live exists because of their insistence on stressing differences in themselves and other people and in making those differences the basis for hatred. The smug superiority of the Germans emerges as the dominant influence and sets the tone for the Freytag episode. Character after character reveals his prejudices, his personal little snobberies, and the tension arising from these feelings is first released in the Germans' demand that Freytag be removed from the captain's table.

Nearly all Freytag's thoughts center around his feelings of guilt for having married a Jewess. Even though he loves his wife and has seen the insults she has had to endure, he is infected by strong feelings of German nationalism. At times he cannot quite believe what he has done: "He, a German of a good solid Lutheran family, Christian as they come . . . against his own better judgment, against all common sense and reason, had married a Jewish girl." He cannot reconcile his shame and pride, his desire to keep his secret and his wish to tell everyone. His obsession with his knowledge degenerates into self-pity. Freytag arouses the suspicions of the other Germans at the captain's table by observing Jewish dietary laws, refusing to eat pork and forbidden seafood. He tacitly goes along with the anti-Jewish jokes they make about his not eating pork, because he is too weak to denounce their prejudice until they have discovered the truth and have made it impossible for him to show any real moral strength. Freytag's concern is for himself, not for his wife. He seeks sympathy by confiding in Mrs. Treadwell, who accepts his confession nonchalantly, offering no sympathy or even any real interest. She casually tells Lizzi that Freytag's wife is Jewish. This disclosure leads to the climactic scene in which the other passengers at the captain's table insult Freytag and expel him from their group.

Miss Porter does not leave the situation at this point. Freytag moves to Löwenthal's table and discovers that the Jew hates him as much as the others do. Miss Porter satirizes all prejudice, all hatred, all bigotry by showing that

Löwenthal and Rieber are essentially the same. They both hate Freytag, but each for a reason dictated by his own perverted view of the world. Had Löwenthal lived in a country where gentiles were persecuted, he would have been like Rieber, grinning with glee at the thought of genocide. Miss Porter's satire, by showing prejudice from two opposite angles, transcends the topical, shopworn outrage against anti-Semitism and becomes an attack on human beings who forget the humanity of their fellow men.

The irony of the episode lies not only in the similarities of Rieber and Löwenthal, but in the historical perspective: the voyage takes place in 1931. The historical irony is emphasized by Professor Hutten's praise of the captain's removal of Freytag from their table: "Any hesitation on your part . . . would have resulted in a state of affairs false to our true spirit, and weakening to the whole fabric of our society. It might seem quite an unimportant incident . . . but it is these apparently minor decisions that help to remind us most clearly of our principles, and to see whether or not we are in harmony with the great pattern of our tradition." Much of Hutten's speech is unconsciously ironic. The incident is *not* unimportant, but its importance lies in its indicating a cancerous hatred in the human heart, not a strength of character and a righteousness in which the Germans can take pride. With Hutten's words Miss Porter reminds the reader that these minor incidents should make him examine his own principles and "the great pattern of our tradition." Her constant concern is that the reader understand the importance of individual responsibility for the great evils of the world. Nazi Germany was not created by one man, and it did not come into being on the day Hitler took power. It grew out of a terrible climate of hatred and out of a belief in a harmony and great pattern of tradition that was grounded in the most ignominious sort of evil and the most erroneous sense of reason. Professor Hutten speaks for himself and for most of the other Germans on the *Vera,* not only heightening the irony of the episode but directly establishing himself as a man who sanctioned those things for which Nazi Germany stood. His speech thus prepares for Miss Porter's satiric attack on him in the Bébé episode.

The satiric import of the Freytag episode is by no means self-contained. Much of its thrust results from its juxtaposition with the Bébé episode. The Huttens, who have been among Freytag's persecutors, now themselves become the persecuted. Just as their hatred for Freytag is impersonal, so the mischief of Ric and Rac is impersonal. By putting the Spanish children in the position of persecutors, Miss Porter shows the prejudice of the Germans and the Jew to be as infantile and as irrational as the mischief of the twins. This parallelism is reinforced by Ric and Rac's incestuous relationship—their imitation of the adult world. The use of parallel episodes stresses not only the absurdity of mindless hatred, but also the serious consequences—namely death—that can result from such foolish and destructive hatred. The death of the woodcarver in his attempt to save Bébé provides the tragic element for the episode and for the entire novel. The satiric power of the Bébé episode lies primarily in the irony, which Miss Porter achieves by blending comic, absurd, and tragic elements into one satiric sequence.

The Huttens' treatment of Bébé at the beginning of the novel foreshadows the comic absurdity of the episode. The Huttens elevate their dog to human status, providing a comic inversion of Miss Porter's use of animal imagery. They treat the dog as if he were a child: holding his head when he is seasick, pampering him, reminiscing about his "childhood," and identifying themselves as his parents. Continuing the use of analogy and inversion, Miss Porter associates the twins who throw Bébé overboard with animals:

> They were christened Armando and Dolores, but they had renamed themselves for the heroes of their favorite comic cartoon in a Mexican newspaper: Ric and Rac, two lawless wire-haired terriers whose adventures they followed day by day passionately and with envy. The terriers—not real dogs of course, but to their idolaters real devils such as they wished to be—made fools of even the cleverest human beings in every situation, made life a raging curse for everyone near them, got their own way invariably by a wicked trick, and always escaped without a blow.

In this world of fools, humans name a dog "Baby," and treat the animal as if he were their son; and children who are treated like dogs name themselves after dogs in their own private jest against their collective enemy—the adult world. The explicit humanization of Bébé by the Huttens carries with it, through the parallelism, an implicit statement of the responsibility for the dehumanization of the twins. The irony in the animal-human motif is twofold: the Huttens show more humanity toward their dog than they do toward other human beings, and the dog is made human while the humans are made animals.

On the evening that the twins throw Bébé overboard the passengers at the captain's table become involved in a philosophic discussion of the nature of good and evil. Professor Hutten says that he believes "unshakably in the fundamental goodness of human nature as a principle." His wife, who disagrees with him, believes that men are generally evil by nature and by choice: "We encourage these monsters by being charitable to them, by making excuses for them, or just by being slack. . . . Too indifferent to be bothered so long as they do not harm *us*. And sometimes even if they *do* harm us." The professor's inability to conceive that the woodcarver died in an unselfish attempt to save Bébé shows his philosophical belief to be no more than empty rhetoric. Frau Hutten ironically proves the validity of her point when she and her husband see the dancers robbing the shops in Santa Cruz and turn their backs. Frau Hutten says: "It is not our affair, not in the least." Miss Porter criticizes the Huttens, not only because of their stupid prejudices but also because evil *is* "our affair." The Huttens ignore the evil they see around them, and they cannot recognize good, as in their attempt to turn the good and selfless act of the woodcarver into a selfish, egotistical act arising from ignoble motives.

The woodcarver's motivation to save Bébé is never explained. Although Hutten suggests that the man was suicidal and several critics have thought this theory possibly valid, it seems quite unlikely. Certainly little textual evidence supports such a claim. The woodcarver's being deprived of his knife during the month's voyage is hardly the sort of catastrophic event that drives a man to suicide. Dr. Schumann provides the only real hint as to why the woodcarver would jump overboard to save a drowning dog. Earlier in the novel the doctor rescues the ship's cat, which the twins were about to throw overboard. Reconsidering this event, the doctor wonders about his own motivation: "Given a moment of reflection, would he have leaped so and risked the stopping of his own heart to save—even his wife?" Each rescue involves an animal and the twins, each could have easily ended in death, and by implication each rescuer acted instinctively. Miss Porter invites comparison of the two events, not only by the similarities of circumstances, but also by having Dr. Schumann remember his rescue of the cat just after he has examined the drowned woodcarver and has discussed with a priest the man's possible motives.

An added complexity in the human-animal motif comes with Miss Porter's making Bébé's rescuer a carver of small wooden animals. Although she has shown that animalistic traits in man, as well as man's humanization of animals, reveal man's loss of humanity, she does not imply that animals are in themselves evil. At the woodcarver's funeral the passengers see three whales, and the sight of the three animals has a cathartic effect: ". . . Not too far away for a good view, three enormous whales, seeming to swim almost out of the water, flashing white silver in the sunlight, spouting tall white fountains, traveling with the power and drive of speedboats, going south—not one person could take his eyes from the beautiful spectacle until it was over, and their minds were cleansed of death and violence." The woodcarver conveys through his carvings whatever he sees in animals that is beautiful. The whales testify to the natural beauty of animals, a beauty which exists only in their physical existence, as in the grace and majesty of the whales. The woodcarver, lover of animals, acts to preserve their beauty by preserving life, just as he has tried to capture something of their beauty in his carvings. Miss Porter implies here parallels between the physical beauty of animals and the spiritual beauty of man, between the artist as carver of animals and the artist as satirist. The woodcarver's purpose is to save the dog, poor specimen of animal beauty though Bébé is, from physical death; the satirist's purpose is to save man, in spite of his spiritual defects, from spiritual death.

The characters in *Ship of Fools* are threatened with spiritual death not only from their inability to love on an impersonal level, but also from their human failure in personal relationships, as Miss Porter describes in the fiesta episode. At the fiesta the powers of chaos rule, and the passengers respond automatically to the amoral and permissive atmosphere, revealing themselves to be unequivocal fools. The objects of the satire are those passengers who are perverted in various ways from their understanding of love, of which sex is a real and important part. Rieber fails in his long-planned seduction of Lizzi because of his hatred for Hansen; Jenny is saved from adultery with Freytag only because she passes out as they begin to make love; the Baumgartners use sex as a brief respite from their hellish marriage; Elsa has her chance to dance with the Cuban student to whom she is attracted but rejects him for fear of his discovering her ineptness in even the most casual and innocent romantic relationship; Herr Graf at last gives money to Johann, who sleeps with Concha and experiences some of the tenderness of which he has been robbed by his uncle's cold and harsh religiosity; Mrs. Treadwell and Denny encounter each other in a grotesque and absurd situation in which Denny suffers his own animalistic sexuality in the violence of Mrs. Treadwell's suppressed eroticism. The selfish ends the characters all seek either are denied to them or are in turn perverted by the selfishness of others into grotesque parodies of their original foolish desires.

Of these relationships none provides a better example of Miss Porter's satirical skill than that of Mary Treadwell and William Denny. The very presence of Denny the gross lustful boor and Mrs. Treadwell the frigid, sexually frustrated lady in the lawless world of *Ship of Fools* generates those qualities which mark the work as satire. Although the outward appearances of Mrs. Treadwell and William Denny make their eventual encounter seem unlikely, Miss Porter builds up to their confrontation very carefully. The most outrageous sense of chance, which functions so effectively in satire, is combined with a terrible and just inevitability to bring about the encounter.

Denny's human failure arises from stupidity, not evil. Amoral as an animal, he harms no one except himself. His prejudices, the closest he comes to evil, are so diffuse that their potential evil is lost. Denny's cabinmate, David Scott, judges him accurately: "Denny did not exist at all; at least, as nothing more than a bundle of commonplace appetites and cranky local prejudices." Everything about Denny is a joke, and the satire, tempered with low comedy, shows the inane folly of his daily existence. Denny is the comic sex maniac at the beginning of the novel, and nothing new appears in his personality: he rushes through the novel seeking his own just deserts, which are not at all what he imagines them to be. On the night of the fiesta Denny says of Pastora, who has earlier duped him into buying her a bottle of champagne: "I'm collecting off that gal tonight or I'll damn well know why not." Denny's sexual appetite, devoid of the human elements of love and tenderness, is the object of Miss Porter's satire. In his encounter with Mrs. Treadwell, the harm Denny has done himself is reflected in the physical injury Mrs. Treadwell inflicts on him.

Mrs. Treadwell is a far more complex character than Denny. She divides her life into two parts, the pleasant and the unpleasant, and refuses to acknowledge the reality of the unpleasant. In the same way she creates two faces for herself: the sophisticated, slightly cynical woman of experience and the naive girl who still wears her hair brushed "back from her forehead and bound with a white ribbon, in the Alice in Wonderland style she had worn in bed since she was four or five." Mrs. Treadwell does realize that perhaps, as her bedtime hair style indicates, she has never grown up: "Had she simply gone without knowing it from childhood to age, without ever becoming . . . 'mature?' " She has not become mature because she has refused to admit the reality of either the unpleasant events in her life or her being in any way responsible for their occurrence: "This is just an accident, like being hit by a truck, or trapped in a burning house . . . not the common fate of persons like me." It was Mrs. Treadwell's first love that "cut her life in two." She was married to a man who beat her until she "bled at the nose," an experience which led her to associate sex with brutality and to reject not only the unpleasant experience itself but sex as well. In her romantic scheme sex exists only in a Platonic context. She imagines herself and a faceless escort in Paris stopping at a café for coffee: "We will kiss each other because we've had such a good time together . . . and are such good friends." A passionate kiss as a prelude to sex is something else completely. On the night of the fiesta when the young German officer tries to kiss her, she is passive, frigid. Miss Porter satirizes Mrs. Treadwell because of her refusal to admit her own needs, which she suppresses by cultivating her romantic vision of what life *should* be. Mrs. Treadwell's whole view of life denies the importance of any kind of close personal relationship, shown clearly in her rejection of Freytag when he attempts to move their friendship from an impersonal to a personal plane. Mrs. Treadwell's sexual frigidity, like the doctor's weak heart, is a physical manifestation of a spiritual failure, her inability to be warm, tender, loving. On the evening of the fiesta her artificial life—the precariously poised duality of her worldly charm and her ingenuous romanticism—is momentarily shattered by her encounter with William Denny.

Mrs. Treadwell, quite drunk, returns to her cabin and amuses herself by making up her face to look like one of the zarzuela company. She unconsciously attempts to put on the youth of the girls whom she has envied earlier in the evening. She feels that her age is a "mask painted on her face that she could by some simple magic wash away at any moment in her bath." Rather than washing off her age, she ironically paints on the whorish youth of the dancers: "She covered her eyelids with bluish silver paint, weighted her lashes with beads of melted black wax, powdered her face a thick clown white, and at last drew over her rather thin lips a large, deep scarlet, glistening mouth, with square corners, a shape of unsurpassed savagery and sensuality." The mask represents a very real aspect of her personality, an aspect she has repressed. But Mrs. Treadwell does recognize the mask as something frighteningly real and true, "a revelation of something sinister in the depths of her character." In this guise she takes on all the aggressive viciousness of one of the Spanish prostitutes and yet retains the ingenuousness of her Alice-in-Wonderland self.

When Denny comes to Mrs. Treadwell's cabin by mistake, he grabs her at the door and says, "Come out here, you whore." The innocent Mrs. Treadwell, whose personality is not yet in harmony with her new face, says, "You are terribly mistaken. You'd better look again!" Denny leans over and examines her face, concluding, "Oh, come on, come on, you can't fool me." Denny knows a whore when he sees one. But he does not bargain for what he gets. The roles of Denny and Mrs. Treadwell, whose actions begin to suit her face, are reversed, with great effect in creating the irony as well as in heightening the grotesque aspects of the situation. Denny, the constant pursuer, becomes the pursued, and Mrs. Treadwell, heretofore the image of passive frigidity, becomes the savage aggressor. She vents her rage on Denny, releasing her sexual frustrations in a bacchanal of physical violence. The phallic high-heel of her golden evening sandal (later identified by Denny as an ice pick) is her weapon, and she uses it with all the animalistic cruelty that she identifies with masculine lust. This total reversal of roles reveals the follies that Mrs. Treadwell and Denny commit by perverting in quite different ways the love and tenderness of their own sexuality. Denny does not even realize who has attacked him, and Mrs. Treadwell reemerges as a slightly naughty little girl, smiling "delightedly at her hideous wicked face in the looking glass. . . . Mrs. Treadwell washed her disfigured face lavishly, slapping on warm water, anointing, patting, restoring herself to a semblance she recognized. Blissfully she sang a tuneless song under her breath as she tied her Alice in Wonderland hair ribbon and slipped into her white satin gown with the bishop sleeves." Both Denny and Mrs. Treadwell ignore the truths about themselves inherent in their encounter, marking themselves as stupid and self-deluding, those qualities which characterize them as fools.

The newlyweds in *Ship of Fools,* isolated in their new and still perfect love, are seen only in their strolls about ship, oblivious of the fools about them. The failure of love, the only refuge in a world gone mad with hatred, Miss Porter shows, arises from a deadly selfishness which allows men to seek only the fulfillment of their own egotistical desires, be they the fanatical religiosity of Herr Graf, the sterile lust of Rieber and Denny, the romanticism of Mrs. Treadwell, or the superhuman moral perfection of Dr. Schumann. The characters rob themselves as well as others, creating a life which is at best a limbo, at worst a hell, from which there is no escape without love. The result is a spiritual suicide of which the characters themselves are never quite aware. Miss Porter satirizes the follies of man by describing the absurd and ironic aspects of human relationships. She holds up to the reader an image of the fool reflected in her mirror of satire. But Katherine Anne Porter's ultimate hope is that he will recognize his own face as well as those of other men and will strive to correct those failures which deprive him of his own humanity.

REVIEWS OF THE NONFICTION

◆

THE DAYS BEFORE

They Wrote with Differing Purpose

RUTH CHAPIN

It is this reviewer's opinion that when George Eliot wrote that the purpose of her novels was to "gladden and chasten human hearts," she placed herself, at least by intent, in a line of fiction writing that may be said, without disrespect, to go back to the parables of Jesus. Such writing is not didactic; when it slips in that direction, as George Eliot's sometimes does, it has failed. Nor is it necessarily allegorical. It is rather the direct posing of a human situation for the illumination—and ultimate remedying—that is to come therefrom. To the extent that a novelist genuinely achieves this he completely justifies his art.

With Katherine Anne Porter it is quite another matter.

A volume of collected criticism and other short pieces puts its author at an appalling disadvantage. Torn from their context in time, their subjects a book or person already washed over with subsequent layers of events, the disparate essays are presented, huddled together, to what may be a whole new generation of readers.

Katherine Anne Porter comes off well from this ordeal. Having made a distinguished reputation in the short story, she announces here in the Foreword that she writes her stories in one draft and if possible at one sitting; by contrast these pieces, written on order and for deadline, have been worked and reworked, subject to her own second thoughts and outside advice. One would not know the difference: her usual high standards of workmanship are everywhere apparent. But her statement stands as a comment on different levels—both valid in their way—of integrity and achievement.

Indeed the unifying factor in all these critiques is Miss Porter's single-minded devotion to her art. Her eye for excellence is unerring in the range plotted out for her by her self-acknowledged masters: Jane Austen, Laurence Sterne, Emily Brontë, Henry James, Virginia Woolf. In her title essay she

Reprinted with permission of the publisher from the *Christian Science Monitor,* 4 December 1952, 18.

goes easily to the heart of James: "the main concern of nearly all his chief characters is that life shall be, one way or another, and by whatever means, a paying affair"; and again, in speaking of his early contact with Italian Primitives—"all frauds"—she says in a sentence that might refer as well to Proust, "Such events were sinking into him as pure sensation, to emerge from a thousand points in his memory of knowledge."

She admits the paradoxes in Ezra Pound, "one of the most opinionated and unselfish men who ever lived," and his predilection, in the Mediterranean tradition, for anti-monotheism. Whenever Pound ventured outside his province of pure art, he made appalling blunders, Miss Porter points out; but as "a lover of the sublime, and a seeker after perfection, a true poet," he filled the role of master for many a modern poet, notably Eliot.

It remains for Edith Sitwell to call out her fulsome praise, apropos of "The Canticle of the Rose." Her maturity, "an organic growth of the whole being," is likened to that of Yeats and James.

"In art and in religion," Miss Porter has written, agreeing with E. M. Forster, "are the only possibilities for any real order." Religion, except for basic morality, she leaves to others; her art, like Adam, asks no help from the Divine: but orders as best it can, out of its own materials, one corner of what seems an enigmatic universe.

THE COLLECTED ESSAYS
AND OCCASIONAL WRITINGS
OF KATHERINE ANNE PORTER

[A Mixed Blessing]

Anonymous

Katherine Anne Porter's essays and occasional pieces, unlike her fiction, are not models of ingenuity and craft, nor do they have the beautiful solidity of her best writing. The memorable cadences of *Flowering Judas* and *Noon Wine* disappear when she leaves her imaginary and near-perfect world and enters the arena of criticism or biographical sketches or records her impressions of passing events. Although she speaks always with directness and sometimes with desolating accuracy, only a quarter of the contents of this hefty collection covering four decades of marginal activity has the mastery of style associated with her name. The showpieces are "Gertrude Stein: Three Views," a lethal bit of deadly mimicry which caused a furor when it was published shortly after Miss Stein's death, and "A Wreath for the Gamekeeper," another bloody exhibit introduced during the recent obscenity trial concerning *Lady Chatterley's Lover,* Miss Porter appearing as star witness for the prosecution: Lawrence "wished to be the godhead in his dreary rigmarole of primitive religion . . . but must be the passive female too. Until he tires of it, and comes up with a fresh set of rules for everybody." Miss Porter is tart, chatty, descriptive (see the passages on Mexico), very much her own woman throughout. A mixed blessing.

Reprinted with permission of the publisher from *Kirkus Reviews* 37, 15 December 1969, 1360. Copyright Kirkus Associates, L. P.

THE NEVER-ENDING WRONG

Post Mortem

Eudora Welty

As this tale is being written, the Governor of Massachusetts has issued a proclamation calling for a memorial day on Aug. 23, the anniversary of the electrocution of Sacco and Vanzetti in the Charlestown Prison for a holdup and murder, and his legal counsel has cited "the very real possibility that a grievous miscarriage of justice occurred with their deaths." It has taken the law exactly 50 years to acknowledge publicly that it might have made a mistake. But after that same 50 years, the renowned short-story writer and novelist Katherine Anne Porter has written a book, "The Never-Ending Wrong," also to be published on Aug. 23, and it seems to her that she still believes and feels today the same as she believed and felt at that time, on that scene.

This book of 63 pages, a "plain, full record of a crime that belongs to history," as she states in a foreword, was not intended to establish the guilt or innocence of Nicola Sacco and Bartolomeo Vanzetti, but rather to examine the guilt or innocence of those on the outside, all those gathered there, like herself, to see the final scene played out.

"I did not know then and I still do not know whether they were guilty ... but I had my reasons for being there to protest the terrible penalty they were being condemned to suffer; these reasons were of the heart, which I believe appears in these pages with emphasis."

Her own participation was outwardly of little substance—a matter of typing letters Sacco and Vanzetti wrote to their friends on the outside, of showing up in the picket line and going through the motions of being arrested, jailed and bailed out. She knew herself to be largely in the dark about what was really going on. Questions rose out of personal feeling—deeply serious questions. She made some notes. This book, their eventual result, is a searching of a personal experience, whose troubling of the heart has never abated and whose meaning has kept on asking to be understood.

Reprinted with permission of the *New York Times* from the *New York Times Book Review*, 21 August 1977, pp. 9, 19.

The notes of that time have been added to, she says, "in the hope of a clearer statement," but the account is "unchanged in feeling and point of view."

The picket line in which she marched included the poets and novelists Edna St. Vincent Millay, John Dos Passos, Michael Gold, Grace Lumpkin, Lola Ridge. "I wouldn't have expected to see them on the same street, much less the same picket line in the same jail."

By today's standards, the conduct of these exercises was almost demure. "I never saw a lady—or a gentleman—being rude to a policeman in that picket line, nor any act of rudeness from a single policeman. That sort of thing was to come later, from officers on different duty. The first time I was arrested, my policeman and I walked along stealing perplexed, questioning glances at each other, . . . neither of us wished to deny that the other was a human being; there was no natural hostility between us."

She made notes:

"*Second day:*"

"He (taking my elbow and drawing me out of the line; I go like a lamb): 'Well, what have you been doing since yesterday?'

"I: 'Mostly copying Sacco and Vanzetti's letters. I wish you could read them. You'd believe in them if you could read the letters.'

"He: 'Well, I don't have much time for reading.' "

On the day they were all aware that the battle was lost, she said to him, "I expect this will be the last time you'll have to arrest me. You've been very kind and patient and I thank you." "Thank you," he replied.

They were bailed out by the same kind soul every time they were put in jail. Edward James, Henry James's nephew, invariably appeared and put up the money for all of them, even those who did not wish to be bailed out, "getting us set free for the next round."

But, it appeared, Sacco and Vanzetti did not trust their would-be rescuers. "Many of the anxious friends from another class of society found [it] very hard to deal with, not to be met on their own bright, generous terms in this crisis of life and death; to be saying, in effect, we are all brothers and equal citizens; to receive, in effect, the reserved answer: No, not yet. It is clear now that the condemned men understood and realized their predicament much better than any individual working with any organization devoted to their rescue." They "knew well from the beginning that they had every reason to despair, they did not really trust these strangers from the upper world who furnished the judges and lawyers to the courts, the politicians to the offices, the faculties to the universities, who had all the money and the influence. . . ."

What they may not have known, says Miss Porter, was that "some of the groups apparently working for them, people of their own class in many cases, were using the occasion for Communist propaganda, and hoping only for their deaths as a political argument. I know this because I heard and I saw."

It was a certain Rosa Baron who made this clear through her own words to Katherine Anne Porter, who had expressed the hope that even yet the men might be saved. This "grim little person" headed Miss Porter's particular group during the Boston demonstrations, and what Miss Porter remembers most vividly through the 50 years of time are Rosa Baron's "little pinpoints of eyes glittering through her spectacles at me and her shrill, accusing voice: 'Saved? Who wants them saved? What earthly good would they do us alive?' "

"In the reckless phrase of the confirmed joiner in the fight for whatever relief oppressed humanity was fighting for, I had volunteered to be useful wherever and however I could best serve, and was drafted into a Communist outfit all unknowing."

The account of her experience is clear and has the strength of an essence, not simply by virtue of its long distillation. It is clear through candor, as well. Miss Porter says of herself at this time:

"I was not an inexperienced girl, I was thirty-seven years old; I knew a good deal about the evils and abuses and cruelties of the world; I had known victims of injustice, of crime. I was not ignorant of history, nor of literature; I had witnessed a revolution in Mexico, had in a way taken part in it, and had seen it follow the classic trail of all revolutions. Besides all the moral force and irreproachable motives of so many, I knew the deviousness and wickedness of both sides, on all sides, and the mixed motives—plain love of making mischief, love of irresponsible power, unscrupulous ambition of many men who never stopped short of murder, if murder would advance their careers an inch. But this was something very different, unfamiliar."

There were many such groups, for this demonstration had been agitated for and prepared for many years by the Communists. They had not originated the protest, I believe, but had joined in and tried to take over, as their policy was, and is. . . ."

Being used! The outrage she had found unbearable for the men on trial in court she realized was also the outrage being inflicted on those who had tried to help them, and on others more vulnerable than picketers in their line.

Through Miss Porter's eyes we see their wives, Rosa Sacco and Luigia Vanzetti, being marched through the streets at the head of a crowd massing at a rally, on the night before the scheduled execution.

". . . and the two timid women faced the raging crowd, mostly Italians, who rose at them in savage sympathy, shouting, tears pouring down their faces, shaking their fists and calling . . . 'Never you mind, Rosina! You wait. Luigia! They'll pay, they'll pay!' It was the most awesome, the most bitter scene I had ever witnessed."

But the crowd assembled to await the execution itself was in contrast "a silent, intent assembly of citizens—of anxious people come to bear witness and to protest against the terrible wrong about to be committed, not only against the two men about to die, but against all of us, against our common humanity. . . ." The mounted police galloped about, bearing down on anybody who ventured beyond the edge of the crowd and rearing up over their heads.

"One tall, thin figure of a woman stepped out alone, a good distance into the empty square, and when the police came down at her and the horse's hoofs beat over her head, she did not move, but stood with her shoulders slightly bowed, entirely still. The charge was repeated again and again, but she was not to be driven away." Then she was recognized as Lola Ridge, and dragged to safety by one of her own; the strange, poignant, almost archetypical figure Miss Porter describes must remain indelible.

After that night was all over, the picketers themselves were given a trial; that is, "simply our representatives" (Edna St. Vincent Millay was one) "were tried in a group in about five minutes." The judge "portentously, as if pronouncing another death sentence, found us guilty of loitering and obstructing traffic, fined us five dollars each, and the tragic farce took its place in history."

The aftermath was numbness, silence; disbanding and going home. Miss Porter writes: "In all this I should speak only for myself, for never in my life have I felt so isolated as I did in that host of people, all presumably moved in the same impulse, with the same or at least sympathetic motive; when one might think hearts would have opened, minds would respond with kindness, we did not find it so, but precisely the contrary."

Katherine Anne Porter's fine, grave honesty has required of her, and she has given it to this account, a clarity of statement, a respect for proportion, an avoidance of exaggeration, a watchfulness against any self-indulgence, and a regard for uncompromising accuracy.

But the essence of the book's strength lies in its insight into human motivations, and the unique gifts she has brought to her fiction have been of value to her here as well—even in the specific matter of her subject. The theme of betrayal has always run in a strong current through her work. The worst villains of her stories are the liars, and those most evil are the users of others. Elements of guilt, the abandonment of responsibilities in human relationships, the betrayal of good faith and the taking away of trust and love are what her tragic stories are made of. Betrayal of justice is not very different from the betrayal of love.

And a nation is a living human organism. Like a person, a nation sometimes needs years to comprehend the full scope and seriousness of some wound that has happened to it or some act it has brought itself to perform. Though an experience in its history may have hurt it deeply, left a scar and caused it recurring discomfort and bad dreams, yet only slowly may its meaning grow clear to the sufferer.

"The never-ending wrong," says Miss Porter, "is the anguish that human beings inflict on each other," which she pronounces at the end "forever incurable." And she finds that "The evils prophesied by that crisis have all come true."

As no concerned citizen can argue, this book she has written out of her own life is of profound contemporary significance.

ESSAY ON THE NONFICTION
◆

The Way of Dissent: Katherine Anne Porter's Critical Position

EDWARD SCHWARTZ

The way of dissent and the way of orthodoxy are apt to be one and the same. Although Katherine Anne Porter consistently attacks "the military police of orthodoxy" in her essays, she does so not out of lack of faith but by "compulsion of belief," because she, like Thomas Hardy, is committed to the faith of "the Inquirers."[1] The articles of this faith, which, I suppose, is what Miss Porter means when she speaks of the "continuous, central interest and preoccupation of {my} lifetime,"[2] include insistence that the artist be concerned with the fate of individual human beings, with the individual's need for recognizing, understanding, and accepting his human opportunities, responsibilities, and limitations as an animal in nature; emphasis upon the use of reason, tempered by a suspicion that mysterious, irrational forces working in man's unconscious mind may invalidate reason and cause him to rationalize, to delude himself; awareness of the seething internal realities which often are obscured by external appearances; rejection of dogmas that provide easy answers to problems that may, after all, have no solutions; tolerance of the inquisitive spirit in man which enables him to participate with joy in everyday life and which causes him to attempt to see through his illusions, to discover what is "true" for him. Concomitants of Miss Porter's creed are her devotion to truth-telling (i.e., the art of fiction), her skepticism of abstract theories, and her exalted view of the devout artist, who, though he is only human, endued with the responsibilities of other men, is as worthy as the saint. Because Miss Porter's preoccupation is essentially religious, it is appropriate that such expressions as "saints and artists," the "vocation" of the artist, and the poet's songs to the "greater glory of life" recur in her essays.[3]

Reprinted with permission of the journal from *Western Humanities Review* 8 (Spring 1954): 119–30. Copyright the University of Utah.

259

II

Katherine Anne Porter's acceptance of her literary calling—"the basic and absorbing occupation, the line intact of my life, which directs my actions, determines my point of view, profoundly affects my character and personality, my social beliefs and economic status, and the kind of friendships I form"[4]— led to her early rejection of the orthodox religious and social beliefs accepted for generations by her family. Born in Indian Creek, Texas, on May 15, 1894 [1890, Ed.], Miss Porter belongs to "the lost generation" that reached maturity in the twenties, the jazz age. The world she knew as a child was governed by a fixed code administered by her Kentucky grandmother, her father, her uncles and aunts. This old order, nurtured during the Victorian age, knew what to expect from a young girl of good family and proper upbringing. But Miss Porter, a proud great-great-great granddaughter of Daniel Boone, confounded the family's expectations: when she was sixteen, she ran away from a Catholic convent school and was married.[5] The following year she left Texas, as she later commented, to escape "the South because I didn't want to be regarded as a freak. That was how they regarded a woman who tried to write. I had to make a rebellion. . . . When I left, they are all certain I was going to live an immoral life. It was a confining society in those days."[6]

But Miss Porter's rebellion was not complete; she did not intend it to be. Wherever she lived, whether in New Orleans, Chicago, Denver, New York, Hollywood, Bermuda, Mexico City, France, Spain, Germany, or Switzerland, she discovered within herself a past which somehow seemed to shape her present life, to determine her character and her fate. She desired to understand that past, to rediscover that childhood world and the familiar, though enigmatic, human beings who peopled it. In a far-off country where she could be fascinated by a new landscape with its mysterious inhabitants, Miss Porter found the "constant exercise of memory . . . to be the chief occupation of my mind, and all my experience seems to be simply memory with continuity, marginal notes, constant revision and comparison of one thing with another."[7] Neither abstract speculation nor rationalization about the meaning of life, but exact memory of past events concerned her. She set about to resist "one of the most disturbing habits of the human mind . . . its willful and destructive forgetting of whatever in its past does not confirm or flatter its present point of view."[8] Like Henry James, Miss Porter was determined to obtain "knowledge at the price of finally, utterly 'seeing through' everything"[9]—everything, even a sheltered childhood, which by most standards was fortunate and happy.

Critical as Miss Porter is of the inadequacies of the old order, she does not completely reject it or despise it. She understands what it can mean to live in a world in which people do not share ideas, intuitions, habits, and customs; so she values the stable society in which "there is no groping for motives, no divided faith; [the Mexican peons] love their past with that uncritical, unquestioning devotion which is beyond logic and above reason. Order and precision they know by heart. Instinctive obedience to the change-less laws of nature, strait fidelity to their inner sense mark all they do."[10] And she admired Henry James partly because

> nothing came to supplant or dislocate in any way [his] early affections and attachments and admirations. This is not to say he never grew beyond them, nor that he did not live to question them, for he did both; but surely no one ever projected more lovingly and exactly the climate of youth, of budding imagination, the growth of the tender, perceptive mind, the particular fresh-ness and keenness of feeling, the unconscious generosity and warmth of heart of the young brought up in the dangerous illusion of safety; and though no writer ever "grew up" with more sobriety and pure intelligence, still there lay at the back of his mind the memory of a lost paradise; it was in the long run the standard by which he measured the world he learned so thoroughly. . . .[11]

For Miss Porter, too, the old stable order provided the standard by which the failures (and the occasional successes) of modern man in a chaotic, mecha-nized world are measured. But for her the old order shares the responsibility for some of the failures of the new. And Miss Porter's memories of the matri-archal world of her childhood did not permit her to describe it as a lost par-adise, because the old order had its serious failures, too, its abnegation of important human needs and desires.

Victorian morality, the bulwark of the old, settled Southern society of Miss Porter's childhood, was based on such orthodox dogmas as original sin, the existence of a personal God, the purposiveness of all human life, the need for regarding man's life on earth as preparation for a refined spiritual life after death. When Miss Porter left the care of her family and moved out of the South, she revolted against not only the customs of the old order but also its fundamental convictions. The traditional dogmas of orthodox Christianity, Miss Porter came to believe, could only hinder the artist, who must find his own answers, his own truths. In a violent attack upon T. S. Eliot for his criti-cism of Thomas Hardy, Miss Porter renounces the tradition of orthodoxy and moves, with Hardy, "into another tradition of equal antiquity, equal impor-tance, equal seriousness, a body of opinion running parallel throughout his-tory to the body of law in church and state: the tradition of dissent."[12]

Recognizing "the unbridgable abyss" between the questions posed by Hardy and the answers offered by the orthodox Mr. Eliot, Miss Porter asserts that "the yawning abyss between question and answer remains the same, and until this abyss is closed the dissent will remain, persistent, obdurate, a kind of church in itself, with its leaders, teachers, saints, martyrs, heroes; a thorn in the flesh of Orthodoxy, but I think not necessarily of the devil on that account."[13] Intent upon probing her own world for the meaning of what she sees, hears, feels, thinks, Miss Porter is unwilling to relinquish her calling, the art of fiction, by accepting the catechism she was taught at the convent school; but she concedes that "there is at the heart of the universe a riddle no man can solve, and in the end God may be the answer."[14]

Perhaps what Miss Porter most deplores about organized religion is its misdirection of men, its cynicism and false otherworldly orientation. Man's mysticism, Miss Porter complains, "has been harnessed rudely to machinery of the most mundane sort, and has been made to serve the ends of an organization which ruling under divine guidance, has rules very little better, and in some respects, worse, than certain frankly man-made systems of government."[15] Organized religion, she continues, has justified "the most cynical expedients of worldly government by a high morality" and committed "the most savage crimes against human life for the love of God."[16] Furthermore, the leaders of the church, often "God-intoxicated mystics and untidy saints with only a white blaze of divine love where their minds should have been," are "perpetually creating as much disorder within the law as outside it."[17] Miss Porter, aware of man's self-deception, distrusts mystics because "the most dangerous people in the world are the illuminated ones through whom forces act when they themselves are unconscious of their own motives."[18]

The proper concern of man, according to Miss Porter, is the visible world. She rejects the theological notion that "the world [is] a testing ground for the soul of man in preparation for eternity, and that his sufferings [are] part of a 'divine' plan, or indeed, so far as the personal fate of mankind [is] concerned, of any plan at all."[19] Instead, she insists upon a humanistic, this-worldly orientation, for "both malevolence and benevolence originated in the mind of man, and the warring forces [are] within him alone; such plan as [exists] in regard to him he [has] created for himself, his Good and his Evil [are] alike the mysterious inventions of his own mind."[20] The tangible world was the one Miss Porter would have, so she, like Henry James, "strained and struggled outward to meet it, to absorb it, to understand it, to be part of it."[21]

Since Miss Porter believes that men bring evil upon themselves by attributing human ills to divine providence and by preparing for a spiritual after-life instead of concerning themselves with the everyday world, she insists upon the efficacy of social reform: "man could make the earth a more endurable place for himself if he would."[22] She believes, with Hardy, in the use of "reasonableness: the use of intelligence directed towards the best human solution of human ills."[23] But, while Miss Porter expects men to use reason to ameliorate human suffering, she qualifies whatever optimism might be implicit in her faith in reasonableness by her conviction that "the refusal to acknowledge the evils in ourselves which therefore are implicit in any human situation is as unworkable a proposition as the doctrine of total depravity."[24] These evils are inherent in man's unconscious life; they belong to that part of human nature which is "not grounded in commonsense, [that] deep place . . .

where the mind does not go, where the blind monsters sleep and wake, war among themselves and feed upon death."[25] This irrational element in human nature is "not subject to mathematical equation or the water-tight theories of dogma, and this intransigent, measureless force [is] divided against itself, in conflict with its own system of laws and the unknown laws of the universe."[26]

Respect for the dignity of the individual, whose complicated life, both conscious and unconscious, cannot be explained away by ingenious theories or impressive abstract words, enables Miss Porter to reject the dogmatic line of political parties as well as religious sects. The artist, Miss Porter believes, cannot restrict his view by adhering to a party line because "all working practical political systems . . . are based upon and operate in contempt of human life and the individual fate; in accepting any one of them and shaping his mind and work to that mold, the artist dehumanizes himself, unfits himself for the practice of an art."[27] Commending Eudora Welty for escaping "a militant social consciousness," Miss Porter observes that Miss Welty is supported by "an ancient system of ethics, an unanswerable, indispensable moral law," which has "never been the particular property of any party or creed or nation," but which relates to "that true and human world of which the artist is a living part; and when he dissociates himself from it in favor of political, which is to say, inhuman, rules, he cuts himself away from his proper society—living men."[28]

The artist's job or work is to deal with the "true and human world" he himself knows. He does this not as that "parochial visitor," Mr. Eliot, legislates, for the edification of his audience; "in the regions of art, as religion, edification is not the highest form of intellectual or spiritual existence."[29] The artist's creations, Miss Porter believes, "are considerably richer, invoked out of deeper sources in the human consciousness, more substantially nourishing than this lukewarm word can express."[30] Thus, her own work has been an attempt "to discover and understand human motives, human feelings, to make a distillation of what human relations and experiences my mind has been able to absorb."[31] And her admiration is for the writer who, like Katherine Mansfield, with "fine objectivity" bares "a moment of experience, real experience, in the life of some human being; [Miss Mansfield] states no belief, gives no motives, airs no theories, but simply presents to the reader a situation, a place, and a character, and there it is; and the emotional content is present implicitly as the germ is in the wheat."[32] This comes very close to being a description of Miss Porter's own method of composition, which is to record objectively her exact memory of life as she knows it, to avoid rationalizations, to trust her reader to find within the story or short novel the unifying and informing theme or symbol. Miss Porter begins with an image, an incident, a character: "a section here and a section there has been written—little general scenes explored and developed. Or scenes or sketches of characters which were never intended to be incorporated in the finished work have been developed in the process of trying to understand the full potentiality of the material."[33] At the critical moment, "thousands of memories converge, harmonize, arrange themselves around a central idea in a coherent form, and I write a story."[34]

Since Miss Porter's "aesthetic bias, [her] one aim is to tell a straight story and to give true testimony,"[35] she is convinced that the artist must retain a close, vital connection with society. She agrees with Diego Rivera's objection to early Mexican artists who "were still thrall to the idea that the artist is an entity distinct from the human world about him, mysteriously set apart from the community; . . . they still regarded painting as a priestly function. This is an old superstition, and though the artist did not invent it, he became ultimately its victim."[36] While Miss Porter looks upon her work as a "vocation," a "calling,"[37] and sometimes feels that "only the work of saints and artists gives us any reason to believe the human race is worth belonging to,"[38] she distrusts the romantic, illuminated artist: "I think the influence of Whitman on certain American writers has been disastrous, for he encourages them in the vices of self-love (often disguised as love of humanity, or the working classes, or God), the assumption of prophetic powers, of romantic superiority to the limitations of craftsmanship, inflated feeling, and slovenly expression."[39] Like Rivera, she feels that "when art becomes a cult of individual eccentricity, a meager precious and neurasthenic body struggling for breath; when it becomes modish and exclusive, the aristocratic pleasure of the few, it is a dead thing."[40] Miss Porter considers the artist's obligations to society to be "the plain and simple responsibility of any other human being, for I refuse to separate the artist from the human race."[41] The artist should expect no special privileges from society, no "guarantee of economic security"; for he "cannot be a hostile critic of society and expect society to feed [him] regularly. The artist of the present is demanding (I think childishly) that he be given, free, a great many irreconcilable rights and privileges."[42]

Preferring the kind of art that aims at "a perfect realism, a complete statement of the thing [the artist] sees," Miss Porter expects the artist to write about his own familiar country, the world and people he knows best.[43] She early took issue with critics who complained that the guild art of Mexico was provincial and lacked sophistication: "a peasant art," she wrote, "is what it is, what it should be."[44] Miss Porter also disagreed with the editors of *Partisan Review* who (when it was fashionable) were critical of the renewed emphasis in American literature on the specifically native elements in contemporary culture; she thought "the 'specifically American' things might not be the worst things for us to cultivate, since this is America and we are Americans, and our history is not altogether disgraceful."[45] Thus her enthusiasm could be aroused by such a writer as Willa Cather, who was

a provincial, and I hope not the last. She was a good artist, and all true art is provincial in the most realistic sense; of the very time and place of its making, out of human beings who are so particularly limited by their situation, whose faces and names are real and whose lives begin each one at an individual unique center. Indeed, Willa Cather was as provincial as Hawthorne, or Flaubert, or Turgenev, or Jane Austen.[46]

Besides reflecting Miss Porter's special interest in her own particular region, her strong defense of provincialism is an extension of her skepticism of modern industrial progress, which, she fears, destroys individuality and results in an empty uniformitarianism. Miss Porter further suspects that should the artist be removed from his "fructifying contact with his mother earth, condemned daily to touch instead the mechanics and artifices of modern progress, he might succumb as do the aristocratic arts, . . . to the overwhelming forces of a world turned dizzingly by a machine."[47] While Miss Porter directs her irony at the "myth creativeness which has always marked the ideas of men pitiably eager to explain himself to himself, to open the door to eternity with the key of his human imagination," she values the "symbols of the racial mind" that the artist can discover by concerning himself with individuals of a particular time and place.[48]

Related to Miss Porter's taste for provincial literature is her conviction that really good art, like the early twentieth-century peasant art of Mexico, must be natural, organic—"a living thing that grows as a tree grows, thrusting up from its roots and saps, knots and fruits and tormented branches, without an uneasy feeling that it should be refined for art's sake."[49] The writer, too, must come by his art organically; artistic technique "is an internal matter."[50] A writer is "dyed in his own color; it is useless to ask him to change his faults or his virtues; he must . . . work out his own salvation."[51] The art of fiction "cannot be taught, but only learned by the individual in his own way, at his own pace and his own time."[52] Or, as Miss Porter once advised young writers, "if you have any personality of your own, you will have a style of your own; it grows, as your ideas grow, and as your knowledge of your craft increases."[53]

Although Miss Porter seems to accept an organic theory of art, she prefers Henry James to such an "organic" writer as Whitman, because she holds with "the conscious disciplined artist, the serious expert against the expansive, indiscriminately 'cosmic' sort."[54] Her skepticism moves in two directions—against the academic teacher and the literary cult that obstructs the artist from following his calling in his own individual way, and against the egotistical artist who wants to express himself, to become (as Emerson wanted to) the mystical eyeball of the universe. Miss Porter considers the artist's job to be the creation of order, of form, but she does not value technical virtuosity for its own sake; "unless my material, my feelings, my problems on each new . . . work are not well ahead of my technical skill at the moment, I should distrust the whole thing. When virtuosity gets the upper hand of your theme, or is better than your idea, it is time to quit."[55] Miss Porter's concern with problems of style, then, stems from her desire to curb the artist's emotional tendencies and to make his ideas more precise.

Miss Porter's interest in the technical problems of her craft also results from her affinity for "the new way of writing."[56] But the new movement in literature involved much more than a change of style; it included a view of reality that (its adherents thought) was radically different from that of Arnold Bennett or H. G. Wells or other Edwardian writers. The Edwardians described the fabric of things, the externals, but the new writers were to be concerned with the internal reality, the truth of the human heart. Miss Porter found in Virginia Woolf's first novel, *The Voyage Out,* "the same sense of truth I had got in early youth from Laurence Sterne . . . , from Jane Austen, from Emily Brontë, from Henry James."[57] These and W. B. Yeats, James, Joyce, T. S. Eliot, and Ezra Pound seemed "in the most personal way . . . to be my contemporaries; their various visions of reality merged for me into one vision, one world view."[58]

To express this vision of reality adequately a writer needed new techniques, new forms; he needed to develop an exact, nondiscursive fiction which could simultaneously contain detailed, objective description and intricate patterns of symbols. In his own way, each writer Miss Porter admires had developed the necessary tools. Miss Porter values James' "extreme sense of the appearance of things, manners, dress, social customs, [through which] he could convey mysterious but deep impressions of individual character."[59] She also could admire in Katherine Mansfield's stories "the sense of human beings living on many planes at once with all the elements justly ordered and in right proportion."[60] Miss Porter's acceptance of the new world view and her desire to find a proper vehicle to contain it result in her "deeply personal interest" in the kind of story "where external act and the internal voiceless life of the imagination almost meet and mingle on the mysterious threshold between dream and waking, one reality refusing to admit or confirm the existence of the other, yet both conspiring toward the same end."[61]

Like Willa Cather, Katherine Anne Porter never has been primarily concerned with literary theory. And so Miss Porter's critical position may sometimes seem ambiguous, at times even contradictory. Her preference for the conscious artist who is alert to the technical problems of his craft, for instance, may seem to contradict her advocacy of an organic theory apparently akin to that of Whitman, whose "expansive, indiscriminate 'cosmic'" impulse the skeptical, rational Miss Porter distrusts. And her concept of the poet as a "seer" set apart and to be trusted more than other men may not be entirely compatible with her notion of the poet as being like other men, with the usual social responsibilities and privileges.[62]

But the most striking paradox in Miss Porter's position emerges from her consistent definition of the nature of her devotion to her "basic and absorbing occupation," for Miss Porter's language suggests religious devotion and faith: she speaks of art as a "calling," of "saints and artists," of giving "true testimony," of the indispensable moral law," of the necessity for "order and precision," of the "only two possibilities for any real order: art and religion." The paradox of Miss Porter's negation of the orthodoxy of her Catholic family, of her denial of social and political authoritarianism, is that its end is affirmation: extremes meet; "the way up and the way down is one and the same," as Heraclitus was wont to say and as the orthodox T. S. Eliot seems to agree (in "Burnt Norton"). For Miss Porter—ironically, in view of her skepticism—declares her faith in the continuity of human life through art. The arts, Miss Porter declares,

> do live continuously, and they live literally by faith; their names and their shapes and their uses and their basic meanings survive unchanged in all that matters through times of interruption, diminishment, neglect; they outlive governments and creeds and the societies, even the very civilizations that produced them. They cannot be destroyed altogether because they represent the substance of faith and the only reality. They are what we find again when the ruins are cleared away. And even the smallest and most incomplete offering at this time can be a proud act of faith in defense of that faith.[63]

Like Henry James, Miss Porter's quest for moral definition led not to philosophy or religion but to art. She thus became the inheritor of a great tradition—the tradition of dissent and inquiry, of selfless devotion of the search for meaning and order to the world of fiction.

Notes

1. "Notes on a Criticism of Thomas Hardy," *Southern Review*, VI (1940), 150–161.
2. *The Days Before* (New York: Harcourt, Brace and Co., 1952), p. vii.
3. *The Days Before, passim.*
4. "Autobiographical Sketch," *Authors Yesterday and Today*, ed. S. J. Kunitz (New York: H. W. Wilson Co., 1933), p. 538.
5. Three years later, she was divorced. She was subsequently married (in 1933) to Eugene Pressly, an American career diplomat, and (in 1938) to Albert R. Erskine, Jr., an English teacher at Louisiana State University. These marriages also ended in divorces. [This history of Porter's marriages is inaccurate. Ed.]
6. Archer Winsten, "The Portrait of an Artist," *New York Post*, May 6, 1937, p. 17.
7. "Notes on Writing," *New Directions*, 1940, ed. James Laughlin (Norfolk, Conn.: New Directions, 1940), p. 203.
8. *Ibid.*, p. 203.
9. "The Days Before," *Kenyon Review*, V (Autumn, 1943), 492.
10. *Outline of Mexican Popular Arts and Crafts* (Los Angeles: Young & M'Callister, Inc., 1922), p. 39.
11. "The Days Before," p. 494.

12. "Notes on a Criticism of Thomas Hardy," p. 153.

13. *Ibid.,* pp. 153–54.

14. *Ibid.,* p. 155.

15. *Ibid.,* p. 155.

16. *Ibid.,* p. 155.

17. *Ibid.,* p. 154.

18. "James' *The Turn of the Screw,*" *New Invitation to Learning,* ed. Mark Van Doren (New York: Random House, 1942), p. 230. Cf. "A Bright Particular Faith," *Hound and Horn,* VII (January, 1934), 246–257; and "A Goat for Azazel," *Partisan Review,* VII (May, 1940), 188–199. In these chapters from an unfinished biography of Cotton Mather, Miss Porter seems most impressed with the egotism, pride, and self-deception of the early American "saint."

19. "Notes on a Criticism of Thomas Hardy," p. 157.

20. *Ibid.,* p. 157.

21. "The Days Before," p. 492.

22. "Notes on a Criticism of Thomas Hardy," p. 156.

23. *Ibid.,* p. 156.

24. "Love and Hate," *Mademoiselle,* October, 1948, p. 204.

25. "Notes on a Criticism of Thomas Hardy," p. 157.

26. *Ibid.,* p. 157.

27. Introduction, *A Curtain of Green,* by Eudora Welty (New York: Doubleday, Doran and Co., 1941), pp. xii–xiv.

28. *Ibid.,* p. xiii, Cf. "Corridos," *Survey,* LII (May, 1924), 158. "Such things [as revolution] are ephemerae to the maker of ballads. He is concerned with the eternal verities."

29. "Notes on a Criticism of Thomas Hardy," p. 154.

30. *Ibid.,* p. 154.

31. "The Situation in American Writing," *Partisan Review,* VI (Summer, 1939), 38.

32. "The Art of Katherine Mansfield," *Nation,* CXLV (October 23, 1937), 436.

33. "Notes on Writing," p. 203.

34. *Ibid.,* p. 203.

35. "Autobiographical Sketch," p. 539.

36. "The Guild Spirit in Mexican Art" (as told to Katherine Anne Porter by Diego Rivera), *Survey,* LII (May 1924), 175.

37. Cf. "Homage to Ford Madox Ford," *New Directions, Number 7,* ed. James Laughlin (Norfolk, Conn.: New Directions, 1942), p. 175.

38. "Transplanted Writers," *Books Abroad,* XVI (July, 1942), 274.

39. "The Situation in American Writing," p. 36.

40. "The Guild Spirit in Mexican Art," p. 175. Cf. "Gertrude Stein: A Self-Portrait," *Harper's,* CXCV (December, 1947), 519–528.

41. "The Situation in American Writing," p. 39. Cf. "Transplanted Writers," p. 274.

42. *Ibid.,* p. 38.

43. *Outline of Mexican Popular Arts and Crafts,* p. 42. Cf. "Defoe's *Moll Flanders,*" *New Invitations to Learning,* p. 143. "I like the introspective novel very much, . . . but I do think that the weakness of it is that when a novelist gets inside a character, he finds only himself, and the great art really is to be able to look at the world and individuals and present characters that readers will recognize and will know and feel they know." Cf. "The Days Before," p. 491.

44. *Ibid.,* p. 33.

45. "The Situation in American Writing," p. 38.

46. "The Calm, Pure Art of Willa Cather," *New York Times Book Review,* Sept. 25, 1949, p. 1.

47. *Outline of Mexican Popular Arts and Crafts,* p. 38.

48. *Ibid.,* pp. 5, 9.

49. *Ibid.,* p. 33.

50.   "Notes on Writing," p. 195.
51.   "The Situation in American Writing," p. 35.
52.   Introduction, *A Curtain of Green,* p. xii.
53.   "No Plot, My Dear, No Story," *Writer,* LV (1942), 168.
54.   "The Situation in American Writing," p. 34.
55.   "Notes on Writing," p. 196.
56.   "Example to the Young," *New Republic,* LXVI (April 22, 1931), 279.
57.   "Virginia Woolf's Essays," *New York Times Book Review,* May 7, 1950), p. 3.
58.   *Ibid.,* p. 3.
59.   "The Days Before," p. 491.
60.   "The Art of Katherine Mansfield," p. 436.
61.   Introduction, *A Curtain of Green,* p. xviii.
62.   Cf. "Quetzalcoatl," *New York Herald Tribune Books,* March 7, 1926, p. 1; and "The Situation in American Writing," p. 39.
63.   Introduction, *Flowering Judas and Other Stories* (New York: Modern Library, 1940), p. ii.

Index

◆